A Research Agenda for Law, Finance and the Environment

Elgar Research Agendas outline the future of research in a given area. Leading scholars are given the space to explore their subject in provocative ways, and map out the potential directions of travel. They are relevant but also visionary.

Forward-looking and innovative, Elgar Research Agendas are an essential resource for PhD students, scholars and anybody who wants to be at the forefront of research.

For a full list of Edward Elgar published titles, including the titles in this series, visit our website at www.e-elgar.com.

A Research Agenda for Law, Finance and the Environment

Edited by

MEGAN BOWMAN

The Dickson Poon School of Law, King's College London, UK

LAURA MAI

Faculty of Law, University of Amsterdam, the Netherlands

Elgar Research Agendas

Edward Elgar
PUBLISHING

Cheltenham, UK · Northampton, MA, USA

Published by

Edward Elgar Publishing Limited
The Lypiatts
15 Lansdown Road
Cheltenham
Glos GL50 2JA
UK

Edward Elgar Publishing, Inc.
William Pratt House
9 Dewey Court
Northampton
Massachusetts 01060
USA

Authorised representative in the EU for GPSR queries only: Easy Access System Europe – Mustamäe tee 50, 10621 Tallinn, Estonia, gpsr.requests@easproject.com

A catalogue record for this book is available from the British Library

Library of Congress Control Number: 2025950545

This book is available electronically in the **Elgar**online
Law subject collection
https://doi.org/10.4337/9781035313877

MIX
Paper | Supporting responsible forestry
FSC® C014540
www.fsc.org

ISBN 978 1 0353 1386 0 (cased)
ISBN 978 1 0353 1387 7 (eBook)
ISBN 978 1 0353 9409 8 (ePub)

Printed and bound in the UK by Short Run Press Ltd, Exeter EX2 7LW

We dedicate this book to those who are yet to come.

Contents

List of contributors

Phoebe A. Bower is a PhD candidate at King's College London, UK and a member of King's College London's Centre for Climate Law and Governance.

Megan Bowman is Professor of Law and Founding Director of the Centre for Climate Law & Governance, King's College London.

Anita Foerster is Associate Professor in climate change and environmental law at the Monash Business School, Monash University, Melbourne, Australia.

Hannah Getachew is an Ethiopian-British climate justice advocate based in the UK.

Laura Knöpfel is Lecturer in Environmental Law at the University of Bern (Switzerland) and Head of Research and Consulting at the Swiss Human Rights Institution.

Naga Aditya Koneru is an Australian Actuary (AIAA) and an admitted Lawyer at the Supreme Court of NSW, working in Capital Management at the London-based general insurer, DLG.

Lyla Latif is Lecturer at the University of Nairobi and Chief Executive of Lai'Latif & Co Advocates.

Feja Lesniewska is Senior Lecturer in Sustainable Transitions and Environmental Law and Co-Director of the Surrey Centre for International and Environmental Law at Surrey Law School, the University of Surrey, UK.

Felicia H M Liu is Lecturer in Sustainability at the University of York, UK.

Jukka Mähönen is Professor of Cooperative Law at the Faculty of Law, University of Helsinki, Finland, and Professor of Law at the Faculty of Law, University of Oslo, Norway.

Laura Mai is a Senior Researcher at the Faculty of Law, University of Amsterdam, the Netherlands.

Stephen Minas is Professor at Peking University School of Transnational Law, Beijing, China.

Bronwen Morgan is Professor of Law in the Faculty of Law and Justice at UNSW Sydney, Australia, and co-founder of the New Economy Network of Australia Cooperative Ltd.

Jose Raisey-Skeats is a public servant working for an Australian state government (Victoria) and is studying for a PhD in Economics at the University of Reading, UK.

Beate Sjåfjell is Professor of Law at the Faculty of Law, University of Oslo, Norway, Visiting Professor at College of Europe, Belgium, Academic Chair in the European University Alliance Circle U, and Coordinator of Daughters of Themis: International Network of Women Business Scholars.

Tom Tayler is Director of Policy and Finance at Earth Capital Nexus at the London School of Economics and at the time of writing was Head of International Sustainability Policy Advocacy at Aviva plc, former member of the UN High-Level Climate Champions finance team, and a co-author of the UNFCCC Climate Action Pathway for Finance.

1

Introduction to *A Research Agenda for Law, Finance and the Environment*

Megan Bowman and Laura Mai

1. (Re)Framing a research agenda for law, finance, and the environment in a time of planetary crisis

Traditionally, the worlds of 'finance' and 'the environment' have been regarded as two key pillars of sustainability strategy: important in their own right, but siloed and sometimes incompatible (Richardson, 2009; Bowman, 2015). Yet over the past decade it has become very clear that the worlds of finance and the environment are not pillars at all but rather threads that are inextricably intertwined for better and for worse, like a braided marriage knot. Finance is required to help accomplish sustainability goals (UNFCCC, 2023) as exemplified by the trillions of dollars required to facilitate a global low-carbon transition, increase climate resilience, and alleviate poverty (UNFCCC, 2016; McKinsey, 2022). Conversely, however, business-as-usual behaviours perpetuate an inequitable and unsustainable status quo (Intergovernmental Platform on Biodiversity and Ecosystem Services, 2024). Concomitantly, sustainability issues impact upon finance actors and the functioning of markets that depend on healthy ecosystem services, including fresh water, clean air, and arable soil for economic productivity. Yet those ecosystem services or 'natural capital' are compromised by planetary crises such as global warming, biodiversity depletion, and water scarcity, which in turn threaten the existence of financial stability and price stability in global economies (Bolton et al., 2020; Kedward et al., 2023).

For these reasons, finance actors such as central banks and insurers have publicly acknowledged the intertwining of financial stability and environmental sustainability. In the words of Günther Thallinger, former CEO of Allianz Investment Management, 'Heat and water destroy capital. Flooded homes lose value. Overheated cities become uninhabitable. Entire asset classes are degrading in real time' (Carrington, 2025). Nonetheless, there is still a long way to go in a very tight timeframe to bring these two fields into true alignment. Prior claims that sustainability issues have become mainstreamed in the financial system (Thimann, 2021) are sadly incorrect, as so starkly illustrated by the disparaging concept of 'woke ESG' and the ready abandonment of corporate climate disclosure rules in Europe and the USA (Uvarova, 2025; Sidley, 2025). Moreover, whilst Article 2.1(c) of the Paris Agreement envisages the alignment of finance flows with low carbon and climate resilient development, alarmingly, the Intergovernmental Panel on Climate Change (IPCC) has found that 'finance flows for fossil fuels are still greater than those for climate adaptation and mitigation' (IPCC, 2022, p. 14).

Yet sustainability crises do not magically disappear if we stop looking at them. Despite political changeability, there has been no corresponding change to the physical and transition risks arising from the climate crisis (Actuaries Climate Risk Index, 2024). And each year that governments and businesses postpone necessary action, it becomes more expensive and chaotic to transition (Stern, 2007; Carrington, 2025). For these reasons, regulators and legislators have started asserting their role as market shapers not only in relation to traditional financial risks but also with respect to environmental concerns. The seminal speech titled the 'Tragedy of the Horizon' by then-Governor of the Bank of England, Mark Carney (2015), instigated a fundamental reframing of climate change as a strategic and financial risk rather than a peripheral ethical issue for corporate and financial actors. This in turn stimulated the creation of new regulatory and governance institutions such as the Network of Central Banks and Supervisors for Greening the Financial System (NGFS) in 2017, which is publicly committed to 'strengthening the global response required to meet the goals of the Paris agreement and to enhance the role of the financial system to manage risks and to mobilize mainstream finance in the context of environmentally sustainable development' (NGFS, n.d.), and the Coalition of Finance Ministers for Climate Action in 2019, which 'brings together fiscal and economic policymakers from over 90 countries in leading the global climate response and in securing a just transition towards low-carbon resilient development' (The Coalition of Finance Ministers for Climate Action, 2021). Other stakeholders also wield power in financial and regulatory spaces that range from shareholder activism to climate litigation in a growing momentum for catalytic change that defies political vicissitude and institutional recalcitrance.

These opportunities and tensions provide the motivation for this book at this moment in time. In essence, this volume posits that law and regulation provide a necessary bridge or third thread between the domains of finance and sustainability. In the years since Carney's speech, much has been written about sustainable finance from the view of economics, business, and geopolitics (e.g., Pickering et al., 2015; Bracking, 2015; Robins et al., 2023), yet these analyses often overlook the legal dimensions of finance in the context of sustainability. We the editors contend that the legal voice is critical for effective and equitable sustainable finance scholarship and practice for three key reasons: it helps to explicate the status quo and highlight where change could best occur from transactional to systemic levels; it can inform better decision-making to benefit myriad constituents; and it enhances institutional linkages, transparency, accountability, and trust-building for the longer term.

Equally, we acknowledge that law and regulation can entrench the status quo and obfuscate change. Hence also the need for robust critical analysis of institutional phenomena that include: taken-for-granted practices ranging from breathing clean air to decision-making based on business case logic; emerging contestations around whose perspectives and which voices should inform climate finance discourses; nuanced engagement with key terms and concepts such as 'climate', 'green', 'brown', 'transition', and 'transformation'; normative preferences that underpin the status quo or conversely motivate radical change; and optimal places and spaces for accountability, whether internally in corporate boardrooms and annual general meetings or externally through litigation and third sector activism.

Responding to these tensions, this volume explicates and problematizes foundational concepts that underpin a critical mass of legal thinking and praxis at the intersection of finance and sustainability, whilst offering innovative ways forward for reframing narratives and repurposing agendas and architectures. Key concepts such as 'finance', 'law', 'regulation', 'the environment', and 'public/private' are thus conceived broadly within its pages. Chapter contributions include notions of finance as money but also cover international investment and trade, tax initiatives, and alternative currencies, as well as corporate law and supply chain regulation given that companies are the economic vehicles of society to which finance is allocated and through which it can be transformed. Similarly, this volume exemplifies how law and regulation are made in many rooms, including courtrooms and boardrooms, at international, transnational, national, and sub-state levels.

Critical to fulfilling its stated aims, this book showcases diverse voices and perspectives to offer a comprehensive volume on environment and finance from across geographic regions and areas of expertise and, in so doing, to make a novel contribution to existing literature. Comprising practice-oriented and theoretical contributions from multiple jurisdictions and perspectives, the chapters have been contributed by the brightest emerging scholars as well as leading experts and practitioners from around the world to provide a diverse array of legal and regulatory perspectives. Contributions to this edited volume cover: financial instruments and institutions that directly mobilize green capital at scale; facilitative modalities to enable systemic change and mainstream sustainable finance; and unconventional ideas and interventions that seek to unsettle established ways of approaching law, regulation, and finance.

Finally, embracing the ethos of the Elgar Research Agendas series, this tome is forward-looking and motivational. We consider it an important part of our academic job to facilitate change for the better by providing intellectual firepower, exploratory research, and clear communication to help illuminate solutions and challenges for moving forward. Therefore, this compendium does not just restate what the law *is* but also embodies a legal grimoire containing prompts about what the law *could be* and *should be*. In these ways, this volume seeks to 'trail' rather than 'trap' current concepts and new frontiers, to use the language of British mythologist Dr Martin Shaw (2020). The intent is to inspire readers to undertake generative research and decision-making that is thoughtful, well-evidenced, and beneficial to people and planet. Accordingly, we charged our contributing authors to be relevant and also visionary by concluding each chapter with provocations and potential future research topics. In so doing, we have positioned this volume as an essential resource for scholars (especially postgraduates and PhD students), practitioners, policymakers, and anybody who wants to be at the forefront of the law, regulation, finance, and sustainability nexus.

2. Conceptual framing of this edited volume

We draw on aquatic imagery to frame and structure this volume. We feel that water, as a metaphor, can help readers to conceptually grasp the relationship between finance and the environment. For example, contrast the glacial nature of taken-for-granted thinking and practices with the whitewater fluidity and dynamism of shifting regulatory initiatives in this space. Similarly, the lexicon of money itself is often infused with aquatic imagery. Think of 'floating' and 'frozen' assets, 'pools' of resources, cash 'flows', 'sunk' costs, 'liquid' reserves, revenues that 'dry up', companies that 'drown' in debt, and money which is 'poured into' businesses to help them 'stay afloat'. These examples illustrate how watery images are used to conceptually grasp the versatility, mobility, and elusiveness of finance.

Moreover, this shared language of water conveys relational symbiosis – or at least conceptual commonality – between finance and the environment. Water has its own sentience and links us all. As so poignantly articulated by British-Turkish novelist, Elif Shafak, even 'miniature orbs' of water droplets hold the secrets of infinity and memory such that 'the story of humanity cannot be written without the story of water' (2024, p. 230). Water provides the perfect prism through which to see shared spaces of understanding in a time of crisis. Importantly, by approaching the book in this way, we seek not only to complement but also adjust well-rehearsed categories and vocabularies to explicate the urgency, complexity, and importance of the issues that are explored and debated within the chapters.

In addition to this conceptual framing, three cross-cutting themes interweave throughout the volume:

- *Power and responsibilities in a justice context*: across global regions (spatial dimension) and inter- and intra-generational equity (temporal dimension).
- *Purpose and meaning*: what finance seeks and needs to achieve and for whom, including dominant narratives (such as business case logic) versus normative imperatives (such as equitable and/or existential), and taken-for-granted legal heuristics.
- *Pluralism and diversity*: including pluralisation of actors and regulatory and financial arrangements (such as decentralisation versus hierarchical) as well as diversity of voices, knowledge, value systems, and world views.

3. Structure and contributions

This book is structured in three parts. Part I comprises chapters that explore a range of legal and financial instruments, actors, and regimes directly involved in mobilizing financial resources at scale. As the title of this Part indicates, the quantity of finance required is not a mere 'flow' but a 'surge' in order to provide the means to implement changes on the ground and replace existing unsustainable structures, practices, and processes with sustainable, low-carbon, resilient, and equitable alternatives.

Part II acknowledges that finance will not magically find its way to the spaces and places that need it most. Rather, as chapters in this Part make clear, a groundswell of enabling regulatory modalities is required to ensure equitable and efficacious capital allocation through capacity building, knowledge transfer, corporate transparency and accountability, and by facilitating the required cultural, structural, and behavioural changes that can support and mainstream sustainable finance.

Contributions in Part III explore ideas and interventions that unsettle established ways of approaching finance, including alternative business models and ways of doing commerce, emerging finance platforms and products, and unconventional market paradigms. Chapters in this Part acknowledge that creativity and courage are required from legal, regulatory, and financial experts as much as attention to compliance.

Part I – From flows to surge: mobilizing finance at scale

This book opens with **Felicia H M Liu's** chapter on finance and sustainability governance in Asia. Liu explores the rise of instruments in Asia, such as green *sukuk*, and green and sustainability-linked bonds and loans, before analysing the policy and regulatory developments underpinning sustainable finance growth in three Asian financial centres, namely Hong Kong, Kuala Lumpur, and Singapore. Her findings reveal how different environmental, economic, and political priorities shape market outcomes, and why an instrumental or technocratic approach to sustainable finance can lead to superficial commitments by market players. Her chapter recommends that future research focus on contextual, procedural, and motivational questions behind (in)effective sustainable finance governance approaches and policy design.

Laura Mai examines the temporality of voluntary governance initiatives in the climate finance context. Drawing on interviews and field observations, she develops an empirical case study of the 'Mainstreaming Climate in Financial Institutions' alliance – a transnational coalition of 54 banks that have developed a voluntary framework for integrating climate considerations into financial decision-making. Her analysis shows how voluntarism risks creating the illusion of immediate action while, in fact, focusing primarily on the future, thus delaying the fundamental transformations needed to align the financial system with global climate goals. Looking forward, Mai emphasises the importance of paying attention to how voluntary governance arrangements and multiple forms of soft law intersect with legal and regulatory frameworks at national and international levels.

The chapter by **Stephen Minas** focuses on multilateral finance for environmentally sound technology development and transfer. It explores the development and functioning of international legal frameworks for technology financing by examining several regimes at different stages of development, namely the United Nations

Framework Convention on Climate Change (UNFCCC), the management of greenhouse gas emissions from international transport under the International Civil Aviation Organization and the International Maritime Organization, and the new treaty on conservation and sustainable use of biological diversity in areas of the sea beyond national jurisdiction. The chapter demonstrates that legal design features in multilateral financing can unlock broader flows of finance by incorporating tech transfer and facilitating enabling environments. He recommends a range of topics for future research, including precedents for stocktaking and institutional learning across regimes, and potential bases for privileging certain existential issues such as the preservation of planetary boundaries in the face of geopolitical upheavals.

The co-authored chapter by **Megan Bowman and Tom Tayler** concludes the first part of the book. Their contribution provides a legal examination of the 'finance imperative' in Article 2.1(c) of the Paris Agreement, and its structural importance in relation to Article 9 and the New Collective Quantified Goal on climate finance. It posits two macro approaches to actioning the finance imperative, being a re-examination of the International Financial Architecture and thoughtful national law and regulation that not only aligns economic activity but also mainstreams accountability and transparency for the net zero transition. Looking forward, it highlights some ideas for studies that can underpin the delivery of Paris objectives through what they call a 'trust transition' by, for example, developing qualitative metrics to incorporate a 'duty of care and dignity' into climate finance decision-making.

Part II – Building a groundswell: enabling modalities

In her chapter on gender equality and climate finance, **Phoebe A. Bower** argues that public climate finance must explicitly and systematically recognize the gender-climate nexus to ensure a fairer allocation of resources and reflect the pivotal roles of women in climate mitigation and adaptation efforts. Focusing specifically on state commitments contained in the Convention on the Elimination of Discrimination Against Women, the 2030 Agenda for Sustainable Development, the UNFCCC, and the Paris Agreement, she shows how climate finance and gender equality are closely intertwined and provides practical examples to guide policymakers. She encourages future researchers to investigate more inclusionary approaches to climate finance that attend to socio-economic status, race, and disability, and hold states accountable for progress on equity.

The chapter by **Anita Foerster** uses the concept of 'ecologically rational regulation' to analyse the evolving landscape of financial regulation in Australia. It shows how the recognition of climate change as a financial risk has prompted regulatory developments within existing financial frameworks and spurred new strategies by civil society groups, investor coalitions, and industry bodies that include advocacy, investor engagement, and strategic litigation. While these efforts increasingly reflect ecological concerns and challenge conventional market practices, the chapter questions whether a risk-based regulatory response is sufficient. Foerster shows how early signs of an ecological approach to financial regulation are emerging, but further research is essential to assess the impact and effectiveness of these developments.

Laura Knöpfel analyses how climate change litigation has become a legal and financial risk for corporations. Using the case study of *Asmania et al. v. Holcim Ltd,* a lawsuit awaiting a decision in Switzerland, she reveals connections between global financial flows and local climate impacts, and shows how this necessitates translations of different understandings of 'climate' across financial, political, scientific, and legal systems. By tracing the production and contestation of these translations, the chapter offers a novel theoretical perspective on corporate climate litigation and poses further questions for developing a more comprehensive understanding of the role of law and legal institutions in the unfolding climate crisis.

Also focusing on businesses as central actors in the environment and finance space, **Beate Sjåfjell and Jukka Mähönen** draw on comparative theories of corporate law to present an expanded view of corporate purpose that goes well beyond shareholder primacy and resolving agency conflicts to provide a whole-of-society benefit. They contest existing legal doctrine to show how the introduction of an overarching corporate purpose to create 'sustainable value' and mitigate pressures on planetary boundaries, alongside revised board duties, could align unsustainable business activity with the imperatives for a safe and just world. They encourage readers to imagine how these reforms might be encoded in legislation around the world.

Part III – Chasing the rapids: turbulent actions and experiments

Lyla Latif explores the potential of *zakat*, an Islamic wealth redistribution system, as part of modern tax policy and sustainable finance in Africa. She argues for integrating zakat into formal tax structures to support domestic revenue mobilization for climate mitigation. In so doing, she shows how plural fiscal systems could be leveraged to address sustainable development challenges while enhancing tax policy effectiveness, cultural relevance, and the decolonization of African fiscal systems. Latif envisages future research questions at the interface between Islamic law and the diverse legal systems prevalent in Africa to enrich both socio-legal scholarship and the broader discourse of fiscal sociology.

Hannah Getachew's contribution stays with the African continent and examines how the African Continental Free Trade Area Agreement (AfCFTA) could serve as an institution to channel financial reparations that would address legacies of the climate crisis, slavery, colonialism, and neo-colonialism. Using Pan-African and Afrocentric perspectives, she argues that the AfCFTA would be well-positioned to distribute reparations in a manner that marries anticipated economic growth with the imperative of a net-zero transition that supports climate justice concerns. Getachew urges future scholars and decision-makers to investigate how to integrate these dimensions to realise the African Union's Agenda 2063, supporting the vision of an economically prosperous, socially inclusive, and environmentally sustainable African continent.

In their co-authored chapter, **Jose Raisey-Skeats, Bronwen Morgan, and Naga Aditya Koneru** explore the disruptive concept of the fictional 'carbon coin' from Kim Stanley Robinson's novel *The Ministry for the Future* (2020). Their contribution provides a valuable framework for reconceptualizing the relationship between finance and the environment by comparing the fictional carbon coin with real-world alternative financial proposals. In so doing, they show how institutional imagination can help to unlock the flow of finance whilst encouraging the reader to perceive ways to move more seamlessly from fiction to real life.

The final chapter of this volume by **Feja Lesniewska** shows how public procurement could stimulate demand for circular design, innovative business models, and the use of secondary materials at scale. Developing a case study of the Dutch construction sector, she shows that harnessing the potential of public procurement to support the transition to a circular economy requires not only changes in procurement processes but also broader reform of relevant legal, financial, and economic systems across the European Union. Lesniewska highlights how reforms are often difficult to implement due to limited capacity and knowledge within governments and businesses up and down the supply chain. She encourages decision-makers and researchers to investigate ways to improve knowledge sharing and capacity to help drive a global circular economy transformation.

4. Concluding thoughts

Providing a state-of-the-art overview of the legal and regulatory pluralism at the intersection of finance and the environment, this edited volume does not seek to offer definitive answers to ongoing institutional, conceptual, and normative debates. Instead, it aims to explicate and also (re)frame these debates, shedding light on tensions, opportunities, and obstacles while identifying critical avenues for future research and policy development. As our distinguished contributors make clear, key questions going forward concern normative assumptions, taken-for-granted values, and power dynamics that have shaped – and continue to shape – sustainable finance. There is, for instance, a pressing need to examine how legal, institutional, and cultural pluralism can support more inclusive, equitable, and transformative approaches to climate finance. Further, the chapters highlight the importance of interrogating the intersections between formal and informal legal and regulatory regimes, the role of imaginative thinking, creativity, and alternative paradigms, and advancing capacity-building and structural change across and within scales. Equally, scholars and practitioners must remain attuned to the rapidly shifting political, economic, and technological conditions that shape the law-finance-environment nexus. This is a fast-moving field that requires continuous critical engagement with political disruptions, emergent business models and imperatives, and technological innovation. Our contributors have exemplified how such engagement can take multiple forms, offering diverse methodologies and theoretical inroads for future work.

Beyond its substantive contribution to contemporary debates on law, finance, and the environment, this edited volume also underscores the importance of sustained collaboration and interdisciplinary literacy within academia, between researchers and practitioners, and across regions and cultural contexts. With contributions from law and socio-legal scholars, governance experts, geographers, economists, and practitioners from public, private, and third-sector organizations, the diversity of perspectives represented in this book is not a 'nice-to-have'. It is essential. Crucially, this imperative extends beyond research and knowledge exchange to education itself, calling for reflexivity and innovation in undergraduate and postgraduate curriculum development and design, and the delivery of professional training. In this sense, this book not only advances scholarly and policy debates but also calls for a rethinking of how we train, collaborate, and engage across disciplines, sectors, and regions to respond to the challenges at the nexus of finance, law, and the environment.

References

Actuaries Climate Risk Index (2024) *Actuaries Climate Risk Index Data*. Available at: https://actuariesclimateindex.org/data/ (Accessed: 20 June 2025).

Bolton, P., Despres, M., Pereira Da Silva, L.A., Samama, F. and Svartzman, R. (2020) *The Green Swan: Central banking and financial stability in the age of climate change*. Basel: Bank for International Settlements.

Bowman, M. (2015) *Banking on climate change: How finance actors and regulatory regimes are responding*. Alphen aan den Rijn: Wolters Kluwer.

Bracking, S. (2015) 'The anti-politics of climate finance: the creation and performativity of the Green Climate Fund', *Antipode*, 47(2), pp. 281–302.

Carney, M. (2015) *Breaking the tragedy of the horizon – climate change and financial stability*. Speech delivered at Lloyd's of London, 29 September. Bank of England.

Carrington, D. (2025) 'Climate crisis on track to destroy capitalism, warns top insurer', *The Guardian*, 3 April. Available at: https://www.theguardian.com/environment/2025/apr/03/climate-crisis-on-track-to-destroy-capitalism-warns-allianz-insurer (Accessed: 20 June 2025).

Intergovernmental Panel on Climate Change (IPCC) (2022) *Climate change 2022: Mitigation of climate change. Contribution of Working Group III to the Sixth Assessment Report of the Intergovernmental Panel on Climate Change*. Cambridge University Press.

Intergovernmental Science-Policy Platform on Biodiversity and Ecosystem Services (IPBES) (2024) *Thematic assessment report on the interlinkages among biodiversity, water, food and health of the Intergovernmental Science-Policy Platform on Biodiversity and Ecosystem Services*. Edited by P.A. Harrison, P.D. McElwee and T.L. van Huysen. Bonn: IPBES Secretariat. Available at: https://www.ipbes.net/nexus-assessment (Accessed: 20 June 2025).

Kedward, K., Ryan-Collins, J. and Chenet, H. (2023) 'Biodiversity loss and climate change interactions: financial stability implications for central banks and financial supervisors', *Climate Policy*, 23(6), pp. 763–781.

McKinsey & Company (2022) *The net-zero transition: what it would cost, what it could bring*. Available at: https://www.mckinsey.com/capabilities/sustainability/our-insights/the-net-zero-transition-what-it-would-cost-what-it-could-bring (Accessed: 30 April 2025).

NGFS (Network of Central Banks and Supervisors for Greening the Financial System) (n.d.) *Origin and purpose*. Available at: https://www.ngfs.net/en/about-us/origin-and-purpose (Accessed: 20 June 2025).

Pickering, J., Skovgaard, J., Roberts, J.T., Roassti, D., Stadelmann, M. and Reich, H. (2015) 'Acting on climate finance pledges: inter-agency dynamics and relationships with aid in contributor states', *World Development*, 68, pp. 149–162.

Richardson, B.J. (2009) 'Can socially responsible investment provide a means of environmental regulation?', *Monash University Law Review*, 35(2), pp. 262–295.

Robins, N., Curran, B., Plyska, O., Burge, L. and Van Coppenolle, M. (2023) *Mobilising global debt markets for a just transition*. Available at: https://www.lse.ac.uk/granthaminstitute/wp-content/uploads/2023/12/Mobilising-global-debt-markets-for-a-just-transition-policy-insight.pdf (Accessed: 11 December 2025).

Robinson, K.S. (2020) *The ministry for the future*. Orbit Books.

Shafak, E. (2024) *There are rivers in the sky*. Penguin.

Shaw, M. (2020) *Courting the wild twin*. Chelsea Green.

Sidley LLP (2025) 'SEC ends defense of climate-related disclosure rules', *Sidley Insights*. Available at: https://www.sidley.com/en/insights/newsupdates/2025/04/sec-ends-defense-of-climate-related-disclosure-rules (Accessed: 20 June 2025).

Stern, N. (2007) *The economics of climate change: The Stern review*. Cambridge University Press.

The Coalition of Finance Ministers for Climate Action (2021) 'Who we are'. Available at: https://www.financeministersforclimate.org/ (Accessed: 20 June 2025).

Thimann, C. (2021) 'Foreword: Sustainable finance and the need for a "new and sustainable globalisation"', in Fisher, P. (ed.) *Making the finance system sustainable*. Cambridge: Cambridge University Press, pp. xx–xxvii.

United Nations Framework Convention on Climate Change (UNFCCC) (2016) *Paris Agreement, FCCC/CP/2015/L.9/Rev.1*. Adopted on 12 December 2015, entered into force on 4 November 2016.

United Nations Framework Convention on Climate Change (UNFCCC) (2023) *Key findings from the technical dialogue of the first global stocktake*. Available at: https://unfccc.int/documents/631857 (Accessed: 30 April 2025).

Uvarova, O. (2025) 'The simplification omnibus and the rule of law: undermining corporate sustainability in the EU and beyond?', *Business and Human Rights Journal Blog*. Available at: https://bhrj.blog/2025/03/12/the-simplification-omnibus-and-the-rule-of-law-undermining-corporate-sustainability-in-the-eu-and-beyond/ (Accessed: 20 June 2025).

PART I

From flows to surge: mobilizing finance at scale

2

Governing finance and sustainability in Asia: actors, processes, and politics

Felicia H M Liu

1. Introduction

Ambitious commitment and urgent action from Asian economies are crucial to achieving global climate goals. This region contributes over a third of global carbon emissions, primarily due to its heavy reliance on fossil fuels like coal, oil, and gas for energy, constituting 50%, 25%, and 10% of their energy supplies respectively (IEA, 2018). Economic growth in the past thirty years has substantially raised carbon emissions and other environmental destruction in the region (Nasir et al., 2019), with only COVID-19 putting a disruptive but short halt to carbon emissions (Carbon Brief, 2020). To meet climate targets, rapid decarbonisation is imperative. However, Asian economies have traditionally been sluggish to make substantial commitments, citing their low historic contribution to global carbon emissions and the priority given to economic development (Hamilton-Hart, 2006).

In recent years, there has been a noticeable shift in this trend as individual nations are obligated to declare and implement nationally determined contributions under Article 4.2 of the Paris Agreement (UNFCCC, 2015). Governments and regulators in Asia have begun to take a leadership role in introducing and promoting sustainable finance as part of their climate strategies. This top-down approach to constructing and fostering the sustainable finance market is a stark contrast to how sustainable finance developed in Europe and North America, where heightened awareness of climate- and other sustainability-related financial risks amongst asset owners drove market-led demand for more responsible approaches to investing (Monk and Perkins, 2020).

Sustainable finance is a rapidly evolving field, with ongoing debates regarding its purpose and anticipated impact continuously influencing how it is practised and governed (Busch et al., 2021; Kölbel et al., 2020). Notwithstanding these contestations, it represents an umbrella concept calling for a transformation of the current, unsustainable relationships between capital, nature, and society. It advocates a fundamental shift in objectives, incentives, and practices in the financial sector to ensure that investment flows are aligned with and contribute to global sustainability goals, including climate and other environmental targets. Finance must extend its focus beyond immediate economic profits to consider broader, long-term environmental and social risks and dependencies. Achieving these goals entails adopting new philosophies of responsible investment and stewardship, innovating investment tools to (re)allocate capital, and adopting novel methodologies for evaluating risk and return. Information like environmental, social, governance (ESG) strategy and performance becomes essential in assessing whether an investment aligns with broader sustainability objectives. While sustainability priorities and objectives may differ, sustainable finance demands the establishment of accountability mechanisms across complex investment chains to trace the material impact of investment.

Instigating such a fundamental shift in financial attitudes and practices poses challenges. As yet, there remains a vast investment gap in funding the timely achievement of climate, biodiversity, and other sustainable development goals (Barua, 2020). Similarly, aggregate financial flows are barely aligning with sustainability goals, with vast sums continuing to flow towards carbon-intensive and environmentally degrading assets and enterprises (Polzin and Sanders, 2020). Attempts to improve financial market accountability and transparency through various disclosure mechanisms are met with the challenge of greenwashing – where investors overstate the positive environmental and social impact of their investment – which in turn compromises market integrity and undermines efforts to stocktake both positive and negative environmental and social impacts of investments (de Freitas Netto et al., 2020).

Amidst these contestations, commitment to sustainable finance began to waver in Western liberal democracies as the result of the politicisation of climate change and 'ESG' policies (Hilson, 2024). As such, some scholars have called for attention to be paid to alternative state models for pathways to effective climate and environmental governance, typically found in Asian economies (Beeson, 2010; Engels, 2018). Existing literature has focused on the 'environmental authoritarianism' model, exploring whether authoritarian states, despite their apparent conflict with liberal democratic values, have a greater capacity to address complex environmental problems, such as curbing pollution and emissions, as they are not bound by short-term constituent demands, election cycles, and regular leadership changes (van der Kamp, 2021; Zinda, 2023). However, little has yet been said on how state-led capitalism models approach sustainable finance to effectively leverage market mechanisms as a catalyst for driving climate and environmental action. State-led development of sustainable finance in various Asian economies presents a timely opportunity to reflect on alternative environmental governance approaches. First, the state-led development of sustainable finance in Asian markets stands in stark contrast to the way sustainable finance emerged in Western markets in Europe and North America, which may present a more effective and efficient model in scaling and governing sustainable finance. Second, for Asian states, the active promotion of sustainable finance marks a departure from the previously ambivalent attitude towards climate and environmental action. It is therefore worthwhile investigating the underpinning motivation that drove this change to deploy interventionist developmental statist strategies to promote sustainable finance.

This can bear broader lessons for other emerging economies seeking to achieve economic development whilst balancing environmental concerns.

It is within this context that this chapter argues for the importance of exploring diverse models for sustainable finance governance. Presently, most sustainable finance governance literature places its empirical focus on Western economies, often overlooking the nuanced dynamics of emerging economies like those in Asia. Moreover, the bulk of the academic literature on sustainable finance has adopted quantitative methodologies that sought to find evidence for the quantifiable financial and environmental benefits of adopting various sustainable finance strategies (e.g., Atz et al., 2023; Friede et al., 2015; MacAskill et al., 2021). While such studies are valuable in testing various theories of sustainable finance, such as value creation of disclosure and materiality of ESG performance, they fall short of providing an in-depth explanation (or refutation) of why sustainable finance (fails to) deliver the intended outcomes. Subsequently, they also face limitations in capturing the geographical nuances of market behaviour, cultural factors, and governance styles in explaining divergence in market practices and development trajectories.

The analysis of this chapter will concentrate on the development of sustainable finance in three major East Asian financial centres: Hong Kong, Kuala Lumpur, and Singapore. These case studies are chosen due to their distinctive connectivity with the regional economy and political-economic developmental trajectories, which bear broader implications and lessons for the sustainable economic transition for the rest of the region. All three financial centres aspire to become sustainable finance hubs, and subsequently introduced similar sustainability disclosure regulations and green debt products between 2017 and 2018 to stimulate sustainable finance growth.

Methodologically, this chapter's analysis involves a multi-site, triangulated qualitative approach that combines document analysis, conference observation, and semi-structured elite interviews (n=61) conducted between September 2018 and March 2020 in the three financial centres. Based on policy documents, corporate disclosure, civil society reports, and media coverage, I analysed 120 sustainable finance deals transacting in the three markets between 2015 and 2020. Ongoing engagement with policy and industry stakeholders further informed the research.

The remainder of this chapter is structured as follows: Section 2 reviews the literature on the Asian economic development model and its relation to environmentalism. Section 3 provides a policy context to how the three case study markets approached sustainable finance development, which is detailed in Section 4. Section 5 critically evaluates the early market development and sustainability outcomes. Section 6 discusses its implications for sustainability progress in Asia. The final section concludes by discussing the implications of these findings and proposes a future research agenda.

2. Asian environmentalism and finance

Strong state involvement in sustainable finance in Asian economies can be traced back to a long history of state-led developmentalism. The term 'Asian developmental state' was initially coined by Chalmers Johnson (1982) to elucidate the rapid growth of the Japanese economy driven by the influential Ministry of International Trade and Industry. Initially theorised based on a single empirical study of Japan, the 'Asian development state' later found applicability to the four 'Asian Tiger' economies that share defining characteristics of bureaucratic state intervention that guides and propels economic growth. This economic model gained international recognition when the World Bank labelled these economies as 'Asian economic miracles' (World Bank, 1993), acknowledging an alternative model to the Washington Consensus (a model of economic development buttressed by free-market principles of liberalisation and privatisation) to effectively facilitate growth and development (Stubbs, 2009). Over time, these Asian development states took divergent pathways to grow and sustain their economic growth, especially after recovering from the 1997 Asian Financial Crisis (Gainsborough, 2009; Thurbon, 2014).

Notwithstanding, Asian developmental states continue to represent a 'developmentalist philosophy' distinctive to Western economies. This philosophy views economic development as integral to national security and stability, and this doctrine forms the foundation that informs subsequent policy strategies undertaken by the state (Kim and Thurbon, 2015). This in turn shapes the relationship between the state, market, and society, creating typical developmental state features such as heavy state intervention in the market economy, blurred distinctions between the public and private sectors, weak and muted civil society, and a shared belief in developmentalism between political and business elites that drives a coherent trajectory of economic development (Stubbs, 2009).

In the contemporary context, climate change and environmental degradation are increasingly acknowledged as threats to national survival and economic system stability (c.f., Miller, 2017; TCFD, 2017). Effective deployment of sustainable finance therefore bears greater significance than merely capturing a new opportunity for financial market growth and diversification, but rather becomes an integral part of safeguarding critical national interest. It thus leads me to ask whether and how Asian developmental states leverage their command of policymaking, regulatory muscle, and close relationship with the private sector to implement market-based solutions to climate and environmental challenges.

Developmentalist philosophy has evolved in different political economies in Asia which materialises into divergent approaches to financial policies. In Malaysia, a distinctive feature of economic development is its world-leading Islamic banking and finance sector. The development of Islamic finance aligns with its neoliberal ethnic-religious policy (bumiputra policy), which aims to expand the financial sector for the majority ethnic-Malays (Lai, J 2015; Lai and Samers, 2017). Since the 1980s, the government has adopted classic 'industrial policies', such as standard setting, tax incentives, and the adoption of new products by government agencies to boost the development of Islamic banking and finance (Lai, J 2015). Additionally, the Malaysian state has directed resources specifically to train Islamic financial professionals and set up Islamic banking and finance research institutes to support market development and innovation, which in turn lends legitimacy to Malaysia's Islamic financial practices amongst international practitioners (Lai and Samers, 2017; Poon et al., 2017).

Across the causeway, Singapore's market-driven and efficient bureaucracy has earned the island state the labels of 'Singapore Inc' and 'adaptive state', which highlight the city state's pragmatic, government-interventionist approach to economic growth (Holden and Demeritt, 2008; Low, 2001; Woo, 2018). In the 1970s, Singapore recognised the impending challenges posed by labour and land shortages for its low-skilled light manufacturing sector's continued growth, especially in competition with neighbouring countries (Haley and Low, 1998; Woo, 2016). In response, the government shifted its focus to financial services development, positioning Singapore as the 'Asian Dollar Market' through tax incentives for knowledge-intensive and service-oriented firms (Woo, 2016). Additionally, it established regulatory and trading institutions such as the Monetary Authority of Singapore (which acts as a central bank) and the Singapore International Monetary Exchange (which acts as a stock exchange, the predecessor to the current Singapore Exchange) to support financial centre development (Hamilton-Hart, 2018). As Singapore transitioned into a 'knowledge economy', close but informal relations arose amongst the business and political elites, who rotate between the public and private sectors, facilitating smooth and efficient implementation of economic policies.

Finally, Hong Kong's reputation as the world's 'freest economy' seemingly contradicts the interventionist developmental state model. However, in practice, the government has not hesitated to intervene in safeguarding market interests. An illustrative example is the recovery from the 1997 Asian financial crisis, during which the newly formed Hong Kong Special Administrative Region government took unprecedented measures to protect the Hong Kong Dollar's value from speculative attacks (Petersen and Roberts, 2003). Namely, the government established the Track Fund by acquiring a substantial portfolio of Hong Kong's stock market to sustain its value. In doing so, the government entrenched its presence within Hong Kong's financial markets (Petersen and Roberts, 2003). Furthermore, Hong Kong's business-government nexus has a longstanding history that evolved from the personal appointments of prominent businesspeople to the Executive Council, to the establishment of 'functional constituencies' in the Legislative Council, Hong Kong's legislative body, where the various industrial elites occupy seats in the Council without universal suffrage (Cheng, 2016; Ngok, 2016). The government has historically guided the general direction of macroeconomic development (Woo, 2015), and this has continued since the handover to align Hong Kong's financial development with China's national economic strategy (Lai, 2012).

Despite their history of economic interventionism, these governments' responses to climate and environmental issues had historically been ambiguous until recently.

Famously, though not uncontroversially, Beeson (2010) argues that authoritarian regimes are better equipped to navigate the challenges of the climate crisis and environmental degradation, as they do not face pressures of short electoral cycles, long lead times to implement environmental policies, and hurdles of social resistance. Existing empirical studies on Asian authoritarian environmentalism often draw examples from China, notably to explain the country's rapid response to curbing the air pollution crises in its cities (Ahlers and Shen, 2018; Lee and Zhang, 2013; Nie et al., 2020). In another example, Han (2017) argues that Singapore's top-down, non-participatory approach to greening the city's landscape and managing water pollution has successfully earned it an international reputation as a 'garden city'. Its thriving urban green spaces are now widely celebrated amongst Singaporeans and are deemed attractive to tourists and expatriates alike. Interestingly, Zinda (2023) argues that contemporary environmental authoritarianism thrives on controlled negotiation, constrained flexibility, and cultivated compliance, which is a departure from the common perceptions of rigid, coercive authoritarianism. Often, consensus settles on the common good between the economy and the environment (Anwar and Sam, 2012; Gouldson et al., 2008; Hills and Welford, 2002).

However, it remains uncertain how these Asian markets would navigate the trade-offs of a timely, low-carbon economic transition. Sustainable economic transitions come at unavoidable costs, for example, when certain carbon-intensive productions have to be retired prematurely (Ohlendorf et al., 2022), or generally when environmental taxes and regulations incur costs for businesses (Li and Su, 2017). To this end, to focus only on the 'win-win' scenarios constitutes a 'shallow' approach to sustainability that sees the environment as a means to economic ends, and avoids any fundamental but necessary changes in the economic system to reconcile existing unsustainable human-nature relationships (Tulloch and Neilson, 2014). In light of these challenges, it is essential to examine how the Asian developmental states navigate the complexities of achieving a sustainable economic transition.

3. Origins and motivations to develop sustainable finance

Across the three case studies, conversations about sustainable finance began with reporting. Shortly following the 2015 Paris Agreement which underscored the pivotal role of finance in contributing to individual nations' climate targets and collectively achieving global climate objectives (UNFCCC, 2015), the stock exchanges of Hong Kong, Malaysia, and Singapore mandated sustainability reporting as a listing requirement for new and existing firms. This practice aligns with the long-established tradition of financial accounting and reporting, where accounting, auditing, and disclosure serve as corporate governance mechanisms by providing stakeholders with information on financial performance, operations, and compliance (Power, 1997). As concerns about climate and other sustainability matters intensify, both investors and broader societal stakeholders demand that corporations disclose their environmental and social policies and performance (Sweeney and Coughlan, 2008). Advocates of sustainability reporting assert that such transparency encourages public accountability, investor scrutiny, and competitive peer pressure to 'race to the top' (Martin and Hadley, 2008). This strategy constitutes a 'soft' approach that nudges the financial industry to transition towards sustainability through setting norms and self-regulation (Bowman, 2010), thus avoiding the imposition of strict command and control regulations.

Nevertheless, similar to how corporate reporting and auditing can sometimes yield unintended and counterproductive outcomes for the audited entity (Power, 1997), critics of sustainability reporting question the environmental and social benefits it brings. Often, disconnections exist between corporate disclosure and improvements in corporate environmental performance (Higgins et al., 2020; Tang and Demeritt, 2018). With diverse and evolving global reporting standards, some companies exploit loopholes to engage in 'greenwashing', selectively disclosing favourable information while omitting unfavourable details (Uyar et al., 2020; Wang et al., 2018). Additionally, the mechanism of public accountability and reputational risk has its limitations, evident in cases of 'green hushing', referring to a phenomenon when a company refuses to publish ESG information, even if they are performing well to evade public scrutiny (Falchi et al., 2022; Strickler, 2023). Empirical evidence suggests that voluntary market-based mechanisms, like sustainability reporting, result in a long tail of poor compliance, rendering the disclosed information unusable for investors and stakeholders (Liu et al., 2019; Tang and Demeritt, 2018). Consequently, critics question the effectiveness of this neoliberal governance mechanism in expediting the necessary shift towards a low-carbon economy (Christophers, 2017).

Moreover, the efficacy of reporting in driving corporate behavioural change, which originated in the West, within the regulatory and corporate cultural frameworks of Asia, remains uncertain. In Asian developmental states, both corporations and governments are accustomed to regulatory command-and-control strategies. Implementing regulations to reduce corporate carbon emissions and mitigate environmental impact could potentially be more effective than relying on the indirect pressure of market peer influence to achieve similar results. Additionally, Asian firms often have high percentages of insider or state ownership (Chung, 2017), diminishing the impact of public disclosure, accountability, and pressure mechanisms.

Nevertheless, market regulators in Hong Kong, Malaysia, and Singapore adopted international sustainability reporting as part of their listing rules, almost simultaneously between 2015 and 2016, in response to the growing global trend to maintain legitimacy and competitiveness (Liu et al., 2019). Aligned with developmental logic, stock exchanges justified these new regulations by highlighting the potential for sustainable investment opportunities that the information availability enabled by mandatory reporting could unlock. The perception among Asian regulators that embracing sustainability reporting enhances their markets' competitiveness evidences the successful establishment of a global norm of reporting (Bowman, 2010; Brown et al., 2009). Recognising that listed companies might face challenges in adopting sustainability reporting, such as the shortage of reporting expertise and the cost of setting up informational infrastructure, all three exchanges have introduced a flexible 'comply or explain' policy in the initial years before gradually mandating reporting and enhancing the stringency of reporting requirements. This demonstrates a pragmatic compromise between elevating international competitiveness and avoiding overly strict domestic regulations to maintain a business-friendly atmosphere. This approach sets the tone for subsequent sustainable finance development, which is characterised by striking a fine balance between adhering to global norms to preserve reputation and competitiveness on the one hand, and managing the reception and capacity within domestic markets on the other.

4. Divergent policy approaches to sustainability

Buttressed by this common, overarching objective of preparing the market for sustainable finance and signalling to international investors market readiness, regulators of Hong Kong, Malaysia, and Singapore embraced different policy strategies for developing sustainable finance. These policies in turn reflect the specific political and economic contexts of these markets as they seek to construct sustainable finance to finance a low-carbon transition.

4.1 Hong Kong

In 2018, the Hong Kong Monetary Authority introduced a grant scheme to subsidise the costs of green bond issuance by way of boosting engagement with this sustainable finance instrument. This may appear unexpected, considering Hong Kong's image as a 'positive non-interventionist' market and the prevalence of small to medium enterprises in the city, which often lack the necessary capital demand and credit rating for viable bond issuance.

Upon closer examination, however, this policy is underpinned by a strategic motive. It mirrors Singapore's steps, a competing financial hub, which launched a similar grant scheme in June 2017 to attract green bond issuers and address cost concerns. More importantly, this focus on green bonds primarily targets Chinese issuers. Given China's substantial green capital demand due to meeting national climate commitments and supporting continuous economic development both domestically and in the Belt and Road partner countries, it is becoming the world's largest green bond market. This scheme positions Hong Kong as a platform for Chinese corporations seeking international recognition and a diversified investor base.

The Hong Kong Monetary Authority's emphasis on the Chinese green finance market is evident through the establishment of the Hong Kong Green Finance Association in 2018. This association's goal is to develop Hong Kong as a green finance hub, directing global investment into green infrastructure development in mainland China and the Belt and Road Initiative. Notably, Ma Jun chairs the association. He was also the Chief Economist of the People's Bank of China from 2014 to 2017 and currently serves as the Chairman of the China Green Finance Committee. Ma also represents China on the international stage on various matters related to green finance and the green economy, such as the G20 Green Finance Study Group. Thus, his leadership would ensure the alignment of Hong Kong's sustainable finance development with national climate and (green) finance strategies. Moreover, half of the association's membership is made up of mainland Chinese firms. The inclusion of mainland Chinese firms fosters networking and knowledge exchange. In 2018, Hong Kong's government issued a government green bond. This boosted liquidity in the Hong Kong green bond market and enhanced the visibility of this sustainable finance instrument, which contributed to boosting market confidence and engagement in this market by issuers and investors alike.

Despite being an early mover in government green bond issuance, informants who have observed sustainable finance development globally criticised the government green bond for being too cautious and lacking in environmental ambition, as the proceeds are used primarily for constructing and retrofitting green government offices. Instead, critics suggested that the proceeds could have been deployed to incubate local, smaller-scale green businesses and start-ups to create more scalable impacts.

In parallel to government-led green bond development, international banks based in Hong Kong began to introduce 'green loans' to the market. They have done so in response to growing interest from small- and medium-sized enterprises to go green, and subsequent demand for green financing. At the time, international discourse about other sustainable debt instruments beyond green bonds was nascent. Informants recalled that Hong Kong-based expatriate bankers identified a gap in the market in providing more flexible and affordable green financing, and subsequently designed and piloted the 'Green Loan Principles' by drawing from the sustainable finance expertise of their European colleagues and adding onto their knowledge of the loan market in Asia. Modelled against the 'Green Bond Principles', Green Loan Principles provide a voluntary set of recommendations for the selection, management, and reporting of how the proceeds of the green loan will be used, as a means of governing the environmental credentials of the debt instrument. This agile, resourceful approach yielded the world's first green loan issued in 2018, worth HKD 3.6 billion (equivalent to approximately USD 470 million), showcasing Hong Kong's adept financial sector.

Hong Kong's sustainable finance development encapsulates two transformative forces: catching up with the global trends of aligning financial flows with climate targets and redefining its political economic position post-handover (Yee, 2022). Despite some limitations due to the government's and regulator's unfamiliarity with sustainable finance, strategic interventions like jumpstarting the green bond market and fostering Hong Kong-mainland green finance collaboration position the city as a gateway for investment flow into the mainland and the Belt and Road region.

4.2 Malaysia

While Hong Kong positioned itself as the green financing hub for the mainland and the Belt and Road initiative, Malaysia drew upon its strength in Islamic finance in defining its green finance development trajectory. Among Islamic finance practitioners and scholars globally, an emerging discourse highlights the alignment between

Islamic values and climate action (Ahmed et al., 2015; Bennett and Iqbal, 2013). Guided by principles of societal welfare and justice, Islamic finance avoids practices that undermine fair and orderly societies (Obaidullah, 2018; Visser, 2013). This view asserts that Islamic finance naturally supports sustainable finance by directing investments towards environmentally and socially sustainable initiatives (see also Latif's contribution in Chapter 10 of this volume on *zatak* as a tax for sustainability).

In 2017, Kuala Lumpur introduced the world's first ever green *sukuk* – an Islamic-compliant green bond-like instrument – financing a solar energy farm. To promote green *sukuk*, Malaysia deployed a strategic, multi-pronged approach involving standardisation, multi-agency promotion, and global outreach. Collaborating with the World Bank, Malaysia aligned the Sustainable and Responsible Investment Sukuk Standard with the internationally recognised Green Bond Principles. By being the first mover in standard setting, Malaysia has effectively created a new green *sukuk* market and set expectations as to how sustainability and Islamic values can be integrated and reflected in the Islamic financial instrument (see also Latif's contribution in Chapter 10 of this volume on *zatak* as a tax for sustainability).

Despite Malaysia's leadership in innovating the new green *sukuk* instrument, initial adoption of green *sukuk* was modest. To address this, Malaysia launched a promotional campaign in partnership with statutory agencies. Drawing inspiration from Hong Kong and Singapore, the Commission introduced an incentive scheme, reimbursing external verification costs and offering a tax deduction for green *sukuk* issuance fees. To further promote green *sukuk*, they collaborated with Bank Negara Malaysia and the Ministry of Energy, Science, Technology, Environment, and Climate Change to provide sustainable finance training for banks, companies, and professional service providers. Leveraging its role as the capital markets regulator, the Commission proactively engaged potential *sukuk* issuers aligned with the Sustainable and Responsible Investment standard, creating capital market opportunities for them.

Furthermore, the Securities Commission Malaysia took proactive steps to promote green *sukuk* globally. Co-chairing the Association of Southeast Asian Nations (ASEAN) Capital Markets Forum in 2017, the Commission led the introduction of the ASEAN Green Bond Standards. This new standard mirrors the domestic Sustainable and Responsible Investment *sukuk* framework, legitimising the *sukuk* asset class across the capital markets within the regional trade bloc. Internationalisation efforts bore fruit in 2019 when Indonesia issued the first sovereign green *sukuk* that adhered to the framework, indicating wider acceptance of green *sukuk* as an appropriate asset class for Islamic finance and environmental sustainability goals. Beyond ASEAN, the Securities Commission Malaysia partnered with the United Nations Development Programme and the Islamic Development Bank in Saudi Arabia in September 2018 to promote Islamic sustainable finance in other Islamic markets. The involvement of the Islamic Development Bank lends theological credibility to green *sukuk*, given Saudi Arabia's stringent interpretation of Islamic laws.

Malaysia's innovation and promotion of green *sukuk* unlocked a new avenue for Islamic financial participants in the burgeoning global sustainable finance market. The development process echoes Malaysia's established developmental strategy of coordinated, multi-faceted market construction via standardisation, financial incentives, and market awareness and capacity-building (Poon et al., 2017; Rethel, 2018). Uniquely, to bridge the sustainable finance knowledge gap, Malaysian regulators partnered with the World Bank in designing this novel instrument. This resulted in an identical green *sukuk* standard that mirrored the Green Bond Principles, which was a trade-off between innovation and enhancement within the international green bond regime. Nonetheless, this partnership secured the legitimacy of Malaysia's green *sukuk* innovation and solidified its reputation as a pioneering Islamic finance hub among its Southeast Asian and Islamic market counterparts.

4.3 Singapore

In Singapore, sustainable finance discourse gained traction following severe transboundary haze episodes – an air pollution phenomenon caused by biomass burning in Indonesia and Malaysia, primarily caused by irresponsible agroforestry practices – between 2013 and 2015. Investigations by international civil society and think tanks revealed that some responsible agroforestry firms were listed on the Singapore Exchange and had received financing from Singaporean banks (Stampe and McCorran, 2015). This revelation negatively impacted the reputation of Singapore's financial sector. To restore the legitimacy of its financial sector and to keep up with growing international interest in sustainable finance, the Monetary Authority of Singapore, the central bank and capital markets regulator of Singapore, adopted measures to promote sustainable finance.

In 2017, Singapore pioneered the world's first grant scheme designed to subsidise the costs associated with a green bond issuance. However, during the initial years, green bond issuance was limited, as many firms faced challenges similar to those of small to medium enterprises in Hong Kong. These challenges included the perceived scarcity of viable projects in Singapore's land-constrained environment, resulting in insufficient capital demand for green bonds as an effective fundraising tool.

Responding to this market feedback, the Monetary Authority of Singapore collaborated with Enterprise Singapore, a statutory body tasked with promoting the interests of small to medium enterprises. They addressed the lack of capital demand for green bonds by extending the green bond grant scheme to include green loans and sustainability-linked loans. The former is a corporate loan equivalent to a green bond, which allows for greater flexibility in size and lower cost of issuance due to a simpler, bilateral relationship between lender and borrower. The latter is also a form of sustainability-labelled corporate bond, uniquely designed to link corporate sustainability performance with interest rates to create a financial incentive to go green. Corporates that meet their sustainability performance targets can get an interest rate discount, while corporates that fail to do so could get a penalty of a higher interest rate. The move to promote these loan instruments was particularly significant as it enabled small and medium businesses, which form a substantial portion of Singapore's economic landscape, to access sustainable borrowing options.

Concurrently, the Monetary Authority of Singapore took the lead in fostering confidence and injecting liquidity into the sustainable debt market. In 2019, the Monetary Authority of Singapore unveiled the Green Investment Programme, showcasing its commitment to investing in green bonds to enhance their prominence and instil confidence in this asset class. In subsequent years, various statutory bodies like the Housing Development Board (HDB) and the Public Utilities Board (PUB) embraced green bonds to support their operations related to public housing construction, maintenance, water, and sewage services. Building on these advancements, Singapore solidified its commitment to sustainable development in 2021 by passing the Singapore Infrastructure Government Loan Act, granting the government the authority to raise loans for green infrastructure. This pivotal legislation laid the foundation for Singapore's inaugural sovereign green bond, successfully launched in 2022, issued by the Ministry of Finance.

Beyond promoting sustainable debt instruments, the Monetary Authority of Singapore embraced a broader approach to sustainable finance. Building upon its initiatives to position Singapore as a leading fintech and digital hub, the Monetary Authority of Singapore also placed considerable emphasis on nurturing 'green fintech'. A notable example of this commitment is the launch of Project Greenprint in 2022 – a pioneering collection of fintech initiatives designed to harness digital technology to enhance data availability and facilitate investment opportunities. An integral element of Project Greenprint is the utilisation of blockchain technology to securely store sustainability certification information. This ensures the credibility and integrity of disclosed ESG data, creating a single point of access to trusted, certified ESG data flows. Advancing standardisation and enhancing reporting transparency, this initiative represents the world's first government-led effort to leverage digital tools in streamlining the collection, assessment, and utilisation of ESG information to address concerns about low-quality ESG disclosure and greenwashing.

Although the 'focussing event' – periods of intense transboundary haze – that sparked widespread interest in sustainable finance in Singapore remains unresolved, the Monetary Authority of Singapore's proactive promotion of sustainable finance has successfully reshaped Singapore into Asia's leading sustainable finance hub. The promotion of sustainable finance in Singapore was driven by the Monetary Authority of Singapore's leadership and coordinated collaboration across various government agencies, engaging diverse sectors of the economy. Singapore's approach capitalises on the synergies of its key economic strengths, especially in finance and digital technology. By leveraging these advantages, Singapore positions itself as a pioneer of innovative and relevant approaches for promoting, scaling, and effectively governing sustainable finance within the Asian context.

***

In sum, despite following divergent path-dependent strategies and policy focuses, the three case studies exhibited proactive governmental interventions to establish a sustainable finance market and promote the adoption of various sustainable finance instruments in line with broader green economic development goals. The divergent product promotion foci and coalitions of actors participating in sustainable finance reflect the unique composition of these economies. In Hong Kong and Singapore, the majority of borrowers for various types of sustainable debt were green buildings and financial institutions, while in Malaysia, renewable energy farms accounted for the largest share of green *sukuk* issuers. Additionally, in alignment with HKMA's core objective of promoting sustainable finance, mainland Chinese firms constituted the majority of issuers or borrowers in Hong Kong. Judging by the rapid market response, the government-led initiatives have been a success in kick-starting sustainable finance markets.

5. Sustainability outcomes

Government-led promotion may have effectively increased awareness and initiated market activity, but the existing measures have fallen short of fully integrating sustainability into financial practices and decision making. While markets have grown to varying degrees, proportionate to the size of the financial markets in Hong Kong, Malaysia, and Singapore (cf., CBI, 2022), sustainable finance still constitutes only a fraction of the overall financial market across the three case studies. In other words, government-led efforts to promote sustainable finance have yet to redirect capital flow away from 'business-as-usual' and towards sustainable assets at scale.

Of the 120 deals assessed in this study, over half lacked disclosure of the allocation of proceeds and did not provide external verification of the sustainability credentials of the deals. Informants noted that while opaque disclosure is a global concern (Sangiorgi and Schopohl, 2021), it is particularly pronounced in Asia due to limited scrutiny from investors. According to informants, asset managers and banks in Asia are primarily motivated by reputational gains from investing in labelled sustainable finance instruments and often fail to recognise the business case for addressing material sustainability issues. For investors, the substance behind the label's sustainability credentials is of less interest than the label itself (Liu and Lai, 2021). Focusing specifically on the loan market, informants highlighted that Asia's banking sector is fiercely competitive. As a result, banks offering green or sustainability-linked loans are hesitant to press borrowers for more information or more ambitious sustainability commitments, fearing the loss of a client. Informants also mentioned that due to a history of strong developmentalism, firms typically rely on explicit policy and regulatory guidance, especially in the unfamiliar realm of sustainable finance.

Consequently, rather than embracing materiality to systematically manage risks and impact, issuers tend to focus on superficial issues that fall short of committing to more substantive sustainability improvements. As a result, the sustainability credentials of sustainable finance instruments vary widely. Various sustainable finance instruments issued across these case study markets have been criticised by NGOs and the media for greenwashing. For instance, the Hong Kong Airport Authority issued a green bond in 2021 to fund a third runway's construction. The issuer justified the bond's 'greenness' by allocating proceeds to carbon-reduction retrofitting of terminal buildings and incorporating 'green design elements' into the runway's construction (HKAA, 2021). However, media and NGOs quickly highlighted additional carbon emissions from increased flight traffic due to the new runway, as well as the destruction of the indigenous habitat of the Chinese White dolphins during construction of the new runway (Reclaim Finance, 2021). Similarly, Singapore saw its share of environmentally controversial debt instruments. For example, Singapore-based agroforestry firm Halcyon Agri sought a sustainability-linked loan from Deutsche Bank to achieve various corporate sustainability goals, including net zero carbon emissions, responsible sourcing, and equitable livelihoods (Deutsche Bank, 2020). Nevertheless, international environmental NGO Greenpeace Africa (2020) uncovered that Halcyon Agri continued to displace indigenous communities and commit deforestation to expand plantations in Cameroon and Malaysia.

These examples reveal significant governance and scrutiny loopholes in voluntary disclosure and verification practices. Advocates of reporting argue that 'green' or 'sustainable' labelled deals would undergo rigorous scrutiny from external verifiers and investors, compelling issuers to enhance their environmental credentials or risk rejection. However, the fact that deals with questionable environmental credentials still enter the market and receive investment suggests that the market's self-governance mechanism is not as effective as claimed. While civil society organisations criticise some of these deals, indicating a degree of accountability, many more environmentally questionable deals have escaped public criticism. For instance, a green *sukuk* issued in Malaysia has been deployed to construct a new retail terminal at Kuala Lumpur International Airport (RAM Consultancy, 2017), and a green loan borrowed in Singapore was used to purchase an aircraft (ATR, 2019). These instances underscore the need for more consistent, robust, and transparent governance measures to ensure the integrity of sustainable finance instruments.

Instances of greenwashing that escape scrutiny point to key limitations of relying on civil society to govern sustainable finance. An inherent imbalanced power dynamic exists between civil society and the financial sector: civil society often faces resource shortages, which limit the scale of research and advocacy to comprehensively and consistently hold sustainable finance deals accountable. Moreover, as the financial sector is significantly better resourced than civil society organisations, it is uncommon for environmental NGOs to seek funding from the philanthropic arms of financial institutions. Thus, open criticisms of greenwashing may antagonise potential funders (Cerrato and Ferrando, 2020). Specifically within the contexts of the Asian developmental state, state-led economic growth came at the expense of a vibrant, active civil society. Consequently, civil society's ability to hold sustainable finance accountable, especially when issued by government-linked corporations, may be further muted.

Interestingly, governments, despite their proactive promotion of sustainable finance, are hesitant to regulate disclosure requirements and define what counts as 'green' or 'sustainable' beyond 'international best practice'. This is due partially to the lack of confidence to effectively regulate sustainable finance with their limited knowledge and experience. But more importantly, regulators feared that imposing overly stringent regulations might discourage participation, due partially to a lack of clarity. As a result, opportunistic corporates and financial institutions took advantage of the lenient disclosure regulatory requirements and provided minimal information, which falls short of a core objective of sustainable finance of creating a more transparent financial market that is accountable for its financial, environmental, and social impacts. This thus highlights the fundamental limitation of the economically driven developmental state.

6. Discussion

Does the Asian developmental state offer a more effective model for scaling and governing sustainable finance within the constrained timeline the world faces to address the climate crisis?

Hong Kong, Malaysia, and Singapore have successfully kick-started their sustainable finance markets, even in the face of scepticism or unfamiliarity from market actors regarding sustainability concepts (Liu et al., 2019). This 'success' can be attributed to two key factors. Firstly, these governments adeptly identified their market's key strengths and devised unique sustainable finance development strategies. This is evident in Malaysia's creation of the world's first 'Islamic green bond', Hong Kong's utilisation of its connectivity with mainland China, and Singapore's advancements in green fintech. Secondly, these governments employed traditional developmental strategies, implementing coordinated efforts to promote sustainable finance across finance ministries and industrial development bodies.

Nonetheless, the disparate sustainability credentials of sustainable finance instruments issued in these three markets highlight limitations in the developmentalist model for governing sustainable finance markets. What accounts for the apparent governance failure in effectively regulating the sustainable finance market despite a track record of successful economic growth through government intervention? I identify three contradictions between sustainability and the developmental state model that elucidate this phenomenon.

First, as newcomers to the international sustainable finance discourse, Asian markets encounter isomorphic pressure to conform to 'international' sustainability standards and practices originating from the West. This occurred even when these mechanisms were flawed and may not be the most suitable for Asian market governance (DiMaggio and Powell, 1983). Limited prior experience and knowledge in Asian governments and regulators regarding sustainable finance constrain their ability to tailor standards and guidelines to the Asian markets' specific needs. Moreover, Asian issuers and regulators seek legitimacy from the West due to its 'first mover' status in shaping existing sustainable finance norms and expectations. Furthermore, the majority of 'sustainable' investors remain Western-based. For Asian markets to attract new sources of 'sustainable' capital, they must behave according to the recognised norms (GSIA, 2020). Consequently, Asian governments and regulators, despite their history of intervention and command-and-control approaches, have hesitated to implement sustainable finance rules that deviate from so-called 'international best practice'.

Second, the three markets examined primarily justified sustainable finance promotion and development based on the economic opportunities it promises. As the developmental state transitions from rigid authoritarian regimes to more adaptable consensus-driven governance structures (Stubbs, 2009; Zinda, 2023), economic growth becomes a common ground for political and business elites to unite behind policy initiatives. This transition, however, necessitates more flexible governance frameworks to avoid discouraging market participants. In the case of sustainable finance, this entails voluntary compliance to 'soft' guidelines and standards rather than 'hard' rules. This approach aligns with previous empirical findings that highlight contradictions within the 'green growth' agenda advocated by Asian developmental states, where states focus on environmental measures that could concurrently bring new business opportunities, such as clean tech and carbon trading. In contrast, when there is a clear trade-off between the economy and the environment – for instance, if sustainability measures impose costs on corporations – governments may hesitate to take decisive action (Hamilton-Hart, 2006; Kim and Thurbon, 2015). This raises concerns about the developmental state's ability to deliver sustainable environmental outcomes. More importantly, it reflects a fundamental contradiction between the developmental states' legitimacy based on economic growth and environmental sustainability. It limits the developmental state to taking a 'shallow' approach to sustainability which focuses solely on capturing shorter-term economic opportunities within environmentalism, thus avoiding systemic, transformative shifts in how businesses interact with the environment, which could bring longer-lasting and substantive environmental benefits.

Third, and closely related to the point above, the fundamental question arises about the alignment of developmentalism with broader sustainability objectives. As I have alluded to in the introductory section, sustainable finance requires more than directing capital towards climate, environmental, and social goals; it entails a paradigm shift that demands capital's accountability to a wider array of stakeholders beyond shareholders. Sustainable finance's principles of transparency and accountability (Mason, 2020) clash with the developmental state's strengths in decisive action and delivery, fuelled by closed-door policymaking and insulation from public pressures (Mittiga, 2022). Critics contend that this lack of accountability can undermine policy effectiveness due to a dearth of feedback mechanisms (Li and Shapiro, 2020). The case studies discussed in this chapter underscore civil society's limited capacity to hold sustainable finance policy outcomes accountable, contributing to disparities in environmental quality and instances of greenwashing.

Nonetheless, this chapter observed an increasing emphasis on policy engagement and consensus-building in sustainable finance development, such as public consultations. This aligns with the transition of the developmental state's governance style toward flexibility and accommodation (Stubbs, 2009; Zinda, 2023). Asian states are moving away from the rigid intervention and control tools that underpinned their economic successes, opting for a more responsive and open governance approach. As sustainable finance development introduces transparency and accountability principles and practices, it triggers a growing demand for information over time. Rather than counting on authoritarian developmental states to drive effective and inefficient sustainability progress, sustainability may instead emerge as a new challenge for the evolving authoritarian state model (Zinda, 2023).

7. Conclusion and future research agenda

My examination of sustainable finance development in three prominent Asian financial centres – Hong Kong, Malaysia, and Singapore – highlights the unique strengths of the Asian developmental state in launching and growing novel sustainable finance markets. However, I also shed light upon inherent contradictions between developmentalism and sustainability principles, which explains why Asian developmental states are unlikely to pioneer any fundamental reforms of capital-nature-society relationships as required by principles of sustainability. My analysis of the drivers and processes of sustainable finance development not only explains the early outcomes of market development but also provides projections for future market trajectories. These projections can identify areas where further intervention may be needed to achieve more substantive sustainability improvements. I argue that such insights can only be obtained through interpretative, qualitative research approaches to studying sustainable finance, whereas prevalent quantitative approaches that focus on sustainable finance growth metrics or financial returns often fall short.

Thus, the findings of this chapter underscore the need for two key future research directions. First, I propose that global research on sustainable finance should adopt mixed methodologies to map sustainable finance capital flows, unearth divergent underlying market practices, and critically evaluate the uneven material environmental impact of sustainable finance. This involves using semi-structured interviews, ethnographic observations, and archival research to trace the evolution of market behaviour and critically evaluate the determinants of the uneven distribution of financial benefits and environmental outcomes.

Second, this chapter underscores the importance of conducting sustainable finance research in non-Western empirical contexts, not least because policy momentum and market interest in sustainability are growing rapidly internationally. For instance, ASEAN introduced the Sustainable Finance Taxonomy in 2021, and attention is rising regarding channelling private finance to sub-Saharan Africa (Michaelowa et al., 2021). As my chapter has elucidated, policy approaches and market processes towards sustainability are likely to take distinctive directions. The flow of sustainable finance to emerging and least-developed economies is pivotal for facilitating a just low-carbon and climate-resilient transition (Colenbrander et al., 2018). Therefore, to support a more equitable climate-changed future, research has an important role to play in scrutinising the processes, practices, and underlying power dynamics of global sustainable finance development.

References

Ahlers, A.L. and Shen, Y. (2018) 'Breathe easy? Local nuances of authoritarian environmentalism in China's battle against air pollution', *The China Quarterly*, 234, pp. 299–319.

Ahmed, H., Mohieldin, M., Verbeek, J. *et al.* (2015) *On the Sustainable Development Goals and the role of Islamic finance*. The World Bank Policy Research Working Paper 7266. Available at: https://openknowledge.worldbank.org/handle/10986/22000. (Accessed: 13 August 2023).

Anwar, S. and Sam, C.Y. (2012) 'Is economic nationalism good for the environment? A case study of Singapore', *Asian Studies Review*, 36(1), pp. 39–58.

ATR (2019) *ATR delivers first ever green finance aircraft*. Available at: https://www.atr-aircraft.com/presspost/atr-delivers-first-ever-green-financed-aircraft/

Atz, U., Van Holt, T., Liu, Z.Z. and Bruno, C.C. (2023) 'Does sustainability generate better financial performance? Review, meta-analysis, and propositions', *Journal of Sustainable Finance & Investment*, 13(1), pp. 802–825.

Barua, S. (2020) 'Financing sustainable development goals: a review of challenges and mitigation strategies', *Business Strategy & Development*, 3(3), pp. 277–293.

Beeson, M. (2010) 'The coming of environmental authoritarianism', *Environmental Politics*, 19(2), pp. 276–294.

Bennett, M.S. and Iqbal, Z. (2013) 'How socially responsible investing can help bridge the gap between Islamic and conventional financial markets', *International Journal of Islamic and Middle Eastern Finance and Management*, 6(3), pp. 211–225.

Bowman, M. (2010) 'The role of the banking industry in facilitating climate change mitigation and the transition to a low-carbon global economy', *Environment and Planning Law Journal*, 27, pp. 448–468.

Brown, H.S., De Jong, M. and Lessidrenska, T. (2009) 'The rise of the Global Reporting Initiative: a case of institutional entrepreneurship', *Environmental Politics*, 18(2), pp. 182–200.

Busch, T., Bruce-Clark, P., Derwall, J., Eccles, R., Hebb, T., Hoepner, A. *et al.* (2021) 'Impact investments: a call for (re) orientation', *SN Business & Economics*, 1, pp. 1–13.

Carbon Brief (2020) *Analysis: Coronavirus temporarily reduced China's CO2 emissions by a quarter*. Available at: https://www.carbonbrief.org/analysis-coronavirus-has-temporarily-reduced-chinas-co2-emissions-by-a-quarter/ (Accessed: 13 August 2023).

Cerrato, D. and Ferrando, T. (2020) 'The financialization of civil society activism: sustainable finance, non-financial disclosure and the shrinking space for engagement', *Accounting, Economics, and Law: A Convivium*, 10(2), 20190006.

Cheng, J. (2016) 'Business-government nexus: the special case of Hong Kong', *Asian Education and Development Studies*, 5(4), pp. 454–467.

Christophers, B. (2017) 'Climate change and financial instability: risk disclosure and the problematics of neoliberal governance', *Annals of the American Association of Geographers*, 107(5), pp. 1108–1127.

Chung, C.N. (2017) 'Myths about family businesses and their role in Asia's economies', *Forbes*, 19 December. Available at: https://www.forbes.com/sites/nusbusinessschool/2017/12/19/3-myths-about-family-businesses-and-their-role-in-asias-economies/?sh=439625491b8a/ (Accessed: 13 August 2023).

Climate Bonds Initiative (2022) *Sustainable debt: global state of the market*. Available at: https://www.climatebonds.net/files/documents/publications/Global-State-of-the-Market-Report-2022.pdf. (Accessed: 11 December 2025).

Colenbrander, S., Dodman, D. and Mitlin, D. (2018) 'Using climate finance to advance climate justice: the politics and practice of channelling resources to the local level', *Climate Policy*, 18(7), pp. 902–915.

de Freitas Netto, S.V., Sobral, M.F.F., Ribeiro, A.R.B. and Soares, G.R.D.L. (2020) 'Concepts and forms of greenwashing: a systematic review', *Environmental Sciences Europe*, 32(1), pp. 1–12.

Deutsche Bank (2020) *Deutsche Bank and Halcyon Agri Corporation partner on sustainability through innovative new loan*. Available at: https://www.db.com/news/detail/20200702-deutsche-bank-and-halcyon-agri-corporation-partner-on-sustainability-through-innovative-new-loan?language_id=1. (Accessed: 11 December 2025).

DiMaggio, P.J. and Powell, W.W. (1983) 'The iron cage revisited: institutional isomorphism and collective rationality in organizational fields', *American Sociological Review*, 48(2), pp. 147–160.

Engels, A. (2018) 'Understanding how China is championing climate change mitigation', *Palgrave Communications*, 4(1), pp. 1–6.

Falchi, A., Grolleau, G. and Mzoughi, N. (2022) 'Why companies might under-communicate their efforts for sustainable development and what can be done?', *Business Strategy and the Environment*, 31(5), pp. 1938–1946.

Friede, G., Busch, T. and Bassen, A. (2015) 'ESG and financial performance: aggregated evidence from more than 2000 empirical studies', *Journal of Sustainable Finance & Investment*, 5(4), pp. 210–233.

Gainsborough, M. (2009) 'The (neglected) statist bias and the developmental state: the case of Singapore and Vietnam', *Third World Quarterly*, 30(7), pp. 1317–1328.

Gouldson, A., Hills, P. and Welford, R. (2008) 'Ecological modernisation and policy learning in Hong Kong', *Geoforum*, 39(1), pp. 319–330.

Greenpeace Africa (2020) *Deutsche Bank's loan to Halcyon Agri: a new low in due diligence*. Available at: https://www.greenpeace.org/africa/en/press/11569/deutsche-banks-loan-to-halcyon-agri-a-new-low-in-due-diligence/. (Accessed: 13 August 2023).

GSIA (2020) *Global sustainable investment review 2020*. Available at: https://www.gsi-alliance.org/wp-content/uploads/2021/08/GSIR-20201.pdf. (Accessed: 13 August 2023).

Haley, U.C. and Low, L. (1998) 'Crafted culture: governmental sculpting of modern Singapore and effects on business environments', *Journal of Organizational Change Management*, 11(6), pp. 530–553.

Hamilton-Hart, N. (2006) 'Singapore's climate change policy: the limits of learning', *Contemporary Southeast Asia*, 28(3), pp. 363–384.

Hamilton-Hart, N. (2018) *Asian states, Asian bankers: central banking in Southeast Asia*. Cornell University Press.

Han, H. (2017) 'Singapore, a garden city: authoritarian environmentalism in a developmental state', *The Journal of Environment & Development*, 26(1), pp. 3–24.

Higgins, C., Tang, S. and Stubbs, W. (2020) 'On managing hypocrisy: the transparency of sustainability reports', *Journal of Business Research*, 114, pp. 395–407.

Hills, P. and Welford, R. (2002) 'Ecological modernisation as a weak form of sustainable development in Hong Kong', *The International Journal of Sustainable Development & World Ecology*, 9(4), pp. 315–331.

Hilson, C. (2024) 'Climate change and the politicization of ESG in the US', *Frontiers in Political Science*, 6, 1332399.

Holden, K. and Demeritt, D. (2008) 'Democratising science? The politics of promoting biomedicine in Singapore's developmental state', *Environment and Planning D: Society and Space*, 26(1), pp. 68–86.

Hong Kong Airport Authority (2021) *Sustainable finance framework*. Available at: https://www.hongkongairport.com/iwov-resources/file/sustainability/environment/sustainable-finance/AA_Sustainable_Finance_Framework_Final.pdf. (Accessed: 13 August 2023).

International Energy Agency (IEA) (2018) *Asia Pacific total energy supplies*. Available at: https://www.iea.org/regions/asia-pacific. (Accessed: 20 July 2021).

Johnson, C. (1982) *MITI and the Japanese miracle: the growth of industrial policy, 1925–1975*. Stanford University Press.

Kim, S.Y. and Thurbon, E. (2015) 'Developmental environmentalism: explaining South Korea's ambitious pursuit of green growth', *Politics & Society*, 43(2), pp. 213–240.

Kölbel, J.F., Heeb, F., Paetzold, F. and Busch, T. (2020) 'Can sustainable investing save the world? Reviewing the mechanisms of investor impact', *Organization & Environment*, 33(4), pp. 554–574.

Lai, J. (2015) 'Industrial policy and Islamic finance', *New Political Economy*, 20(2), pp. 178–198.

Lai, K.P.Y. (2012) 'Differentiated markets: Shanghai, Beijing and Hong Kong in China's financial centre network', *Urban Studies*, 49(6), pp. 1275–1296.

Lai, K.P.Y. and Samers, M. (2017) 'Conceptualizing Islamic banking and finance: a comparison of its development and governance in Malaysia and Singapore', *The Pacific Review*, 30(3), pp. 405–424.

Lee, C.K. and Zhang, Y. (2013) 'The power of instability: unraveling the microfoundations of bargained authoritarianism in China', *American Journal of Sociology*, 118(6), pp. 1475–1508.

Li, Y. and Shapiro, J. (2020) *China goes green: coercive environmentalism for a troubled planet*. John Wiley & Sons.

Li, Y. and Su, B. (2017) 'The impacts of carbon pricing on coastal megacities: a CGE analysis of Singapore', *Journal of Cleaner Production*, 165, pp. 1239–1248.

Liu, F.H.M. and Lai, K.P.Y. (2021) 'Ecologies of green finance: green sukuk and development of green Islamic finance in Malaysia', *Environment and Planning A: Economy and Space*, 53(8), pp. 1896–1914.

Liu, F.H.M., Demeritt, D. and Tang, S. (2019) 'Accounting for sustainability in Asia: stock market regulation and reporting in Hong Kong and Singapore', *Economic Geography*, 95(4), pp. 362–384.

Low, L. (2001) 'The Singapore developmental state in the new economy and polity', *The Pacific Review*, 14(3), pp. 411–441.

MacAskill, S., Roca, E., Liu, B., Stewart, R.A. and Sahin, O. (2021) 'Is there a green premium in the green bond market? Systematic literature review revealing premium determinants', *Journal of Cleaner Production*, 280, 124491.

Martin, A.D. and Hadley, D.J. (2008) 'Corporate environmental non-reporting – a UK FTSE 350 perspective', *Business Strategy and the Environment*, 17(4), pp. 245–259.

Mason, M. (2020) 'Transparency, accountability and empowerment in sustainability governance: a conceptual review', *Journal of Environmental Policy & Planning*, 22(1), pp. 98–111.

Michaelowa, A., Hoch, S., Weber, A.K., Kassaye, R. and Hailu, T. (2021) 'Mobilising private climate finance for sustainable energy access and climate change mitigation in Sub-Saharan Africa', *Climate Policy*, 21(1), pp. 47–62.

Miller, T. (2017) *Storming the wall: climate change, migration, and homeland security*. City Lights Books.

Mittiga, R. (2022) 'Political legitimacy, authoritarianism, and climate change', *American Political Science Review*, 116(3), pp. 998–1011.

Monk, A. and Perkins, R. (2020) 'What explains the emergence and diffusion of green bonds?', *Energy Policy*, 145, 111641.
Nasir, M.A., Huynh, T.L.D. and Tram, H.T.X. (2019) 'Role of financial development, economic growth & foreign direct investment in driving climate change: a case of emerging ASEAN', *Journal of Environmental Management*, 242, pp. 131–141.
Ngok, M. (2016) 'The making of a corporatist state in Hong Kong: the road to sectoral intervention', *Journal of Contemporary Asia*, 46(2), pp. 247–266.
Nie, Y., Cheng, D. and Liu, K. (2020) 'The effectiveness of environmental authoritarianism: evidence from China's administrative inquiry for environmental protection', *Energy Economics*, 88, 104777.
Obaidullah, M. (2018) 'Managing climate change: the role of Islamic finance', *Islamic Economic Studies*, 26(1), pp. 31–62.
Ohlendorf, N., Jakob, M. and Steckel, J.C. (2022) 'The political economy of coal phase-out: exploring the actors, objectives, and contextual factors shaping policies in eight major coal countries', *Energy Research & Social Science*, 90, 102590.
Petersen, D. and Roberts, E.V. (2003) 'The Hong Kong business environment since 1997', in R. Ash, P. Ferdinand, B. Hook and R. Porter (Eds), *Hong Kong in transition: one country, two systems*. Routledge, pp. 11, 13.
Polzin, F. and Sanders, M. (2020) 'How to finance the transition to low-carbon energy in Europe?', *Energy Policy*, 147, 111863.
Poon, J.P., Pollard, J., Chow, Y.W. *et al.* (2017) 'The rise of Kuala Lumpur as an Islamic financial frontier', *Regional Studies*, 51(10), pp. 1443–1453.
Power, M. (1997) *The audit society: rituals of verification*. Oxford University Press.
RAM Consultancy (2017) *Segi Astana Sdn Bhd. Second opinion report*. Available at: https://gatewayklia2.com.my/pdf/171122_Second%20Opinion%20Report_Segi%20Astana_Final.pdf. (Accessed: 13 August 2023).
Reclaim Finance (2021) *High-flying greenwashing around a new green bond for Hong Kong Airport*. Available at: https://reclaimfinance.org/site/en/2022/01/04/high-flying-greenwashing-around-a-new-green-bond/. (Accessed: 13 August 2023).
Rethel, L. (2018) 'Economic governance beyond state and market: Islamic capital markets in Southeast Asia', *Journal of Contemporary Asia*, 48(2), pp. 301–321.
Sangiorgi, I. and Schopohl, L. (2021) 'Why do institutional investors buy green bonds: evidence from a survey of European asset managers', *International Review of Financial Analysis*, 75, 101738.
Stampe, J. and McCorran, B. (2015) *Sustainable finance in Singapore, Indonesia and Malaysia*. Available at: http://www.climateaction.org/images/uploads/documents/WWF_Sustaianable_Finanace_Report.pdf?. (Accessed: 13 August 2023).
Strickler, E. (2023) *Green hushing & the anti-ESG movement: why is it important for companies to still talk about ESG?* Available at: https://www.keteres.com/resource/green-hushing-the-anti-esg-movement
Stubbs, R. (2009) 'What ever happened to the East Asian Developmental State? The unfolding debate', *The Pacific Review*, 22(1), pp. 1–22.
Sweeney, L. and Coughlan, J. (2008) 'Do different industries report corporate social responsibility differently? An investigation through the lens of stakeholder theory', *Journal of Marketing Communications*, 14(2), pp. 113–124.
Tang, S. and Demeritt, D. (2018) 'Climate change and mandatory carbon reporting: impacts on business process and performance', *Business Strategy and the Environment*, 27(4), pp. 437–455.
TCFD. (2017). *Final report: recommendations ofthe task force on climate-related financial disclosures*. Available at: https://assets.bbhub.io/company/sites/60/2021/10/FINAL-2017-TCFD-Report.pdf

Thurbon, E. (2014) 'The resurgence of the developmental state: a conceptual defence', *Critique internationale*, 63(2), pp. 59–75.

Tulloch, L. and Neilson, D. (2014) 'The neoliberalisation of sustainability', *Citizenship, Social and Economics Education*, 13(1), pp. 26–38.

United Nations Framework Convention on Climate Change (2015) *The Paris Agreement*.

Uyar, A., Karaman, A.S. and Kilic, M. (2020) 'Is corporate social responsibility reporting a tool of signaling or greenwashing? Evidence from the worldwide logistics sector', *Journal of Cleaner Production*, 253, 119997.

Van der Kamp, D.S. (2021) 'Blunt force regulation and bureaucratic control: understanding China's war on pollution', *Governance*, 34(1), pp. 191–209.

Visser, H. (2013) *Islamic finance: principles and practice*. Edward Elgar Publishing.

Wang, Z., Hsieh, T.S. and Sarkis, J. (2018) 'CSR performance and the readability of CSR reports: too good to be true?', *Corporate Social Responsibility and Environmental Management*, 25(1), pp. 66–79.

Woo, J.J. (2015) *Business and politics in Asia's key financial centres: Hong Kong, Singapore and Shanghai*. Springer.

Woo, J.J. (2016) *Singapore as an international financial centre: history, policy and politics*. Springer.

Woo, J.J. (2018) *The evolution of the Asian developmental state: Hong Kong and Singapore*. Routledge.

World Bank (1993) *The East Asian miracle: economic growth and public policy. Policy research report*. World Bank. Available at: https://documents1.worldbank.org/curated/en/975081468244550798/pdf/multi-page.pdf. (Accessed: 13 August 2023).

Yee, W.L. (2022) 'Denaturalizing natural tropes: thinking through ecocritical discourse in post-handover Hong Kong', *Cultural Studies*, 36(2), pp. 185–207.

Zinda, J.A. (2023) 'Unpacking authoritarian environmental governance: gauging authoritarian elaboration in China and beyond', *Sociology of Development*, 9(2), pp. 195–216.

3

Out of time: voluntarism, climate change, and finance

Laura Mai

1. Introduction

Implementing the Paris Agreement requires finance at scale. Prevailing financial, legal, and regulatory practice, however, perpetuates insufficient finance for this purpose. In its 2022 assessment report, the Intergovernmental Panel on Climate Change (IPCC) found that '[t]racked financial flows fall short of the levels needed to achieve mitigation goals across all sectors and regions', with investment requirements up to six times greater than current levels (IPCC, 2022, p. 51). In light of this dramatic gap between how much finance is needed and how much is provided (see Bowman and Tayler, 2026), this chapter focuses on a lesser-discussed aspect of climate finance – its temporality. Exploring how climate finance is bound up with time, it shows how the speed, temporal orientations, and time frames involved in (not) providing finance for climate mitigation and adaptation matter.

To engage with the temporalities of climate finance, this chapter takes article 2(1)(c) of the Paris Agreement as its starting point. This provision envisions the 'alignment' of 'finance flows' with the mitigation and adaptation goals of the treaty. Commentators (Bodle and Noens, 2018) have noted that this objective goes beyond the traditional notion of 'climate finance', which refers primarily to inter-governmental financial transfers from developed to developing countries (see e.g., Zahar, 2017).[1] Instead, article 2(1)(c) takes a systemic approach, aiming to 'transform the global economy through deep reform of incentives and disincentives' (Thorgeirsson, 2018, p. 128). The new Collective Quantified Goal on Climate Finance, agreed at COP29 in November 2024, confirmed that finance required to reach globally agreed mitigation and adaptation goals will need to come from both public and private sources (UNFCCC, 2025., para 7).[2]

Given that financial flows required to reach the goals of the Paris Agreement involve both public and private actors, this chapter focuses on transnational climate governance initiatives. These are cross-border alliances of sub-national and non-state actors that voluntarily pledge to support global mitigation and adaptation efforts (Pattberg and Stripple, 2008; Andonova, Betsill, and Bulkeley, 2009). As of March 2025, the *Global Climate Action Portal*, the online database of non-state climate action maintained by the UN Climate Secretariat, listed 176 officially registered initiatives, with 38 active initiatives tagged as relevant to climate finance.[3] Since the adoption of the Paris Agreement in 2015, transnational alliances and non-state actor implementation efforts have been officially acknowledged and progressively integrated into processes under the international climate regime (Hale, 2016; Mai, 2018; Bulkeley et al., 2018; Mai and Elsässer, 2022).

Building on existing literature, this chapter is based on a case study of a transnational climate governance initiative: the Mainstreaming Climate in Financial Institutions alliance.[4] This coalition comprises more than 50 public and private sector banks that have developed a voluntary framework for integrating climate considerations into financial decision-making practices. Case study materials comprise ten in-depth interviews with staff of the Mainstreaming Initiative and technical experts employed by member banks.[5] The case study also draws on participant observations of workshops held by the Initiative, including at the New York Climate Action Week 2019 and at the 2019 and 2020 UN climate conferences in Katowice and Madrid. Further, it considers relevant documents, such as public declarations, reports, and press releases. To reveal the temporalities at work in the Mainstreaming Initiative, qualitative content analysis of interview transcripts, fieldnotes, and documents was complemented with in-depth analysis of the legal technicalities which are employed by the Mainstreaming Initiative. In this context, 'legal technicalities' comprise the material, aesthetic, and epistemic dimensions of legal practice (Riles, 2005; Michaels and Riles, 2021), such as document types and formats, and rules of legal interpretation, argumentation, and systematisation (Valverde, 2015; Riles, 2011; Latorre, 2012).

The next section describes the emergence of transnational governance initiatives and their role in the international climate regime and the climate finance context following the adoption of the Paris Agreement. Having provided context, section 3 fully introduces the Mainstreaming Climate in Financial Institutions initiative as the case study of this chapter, describing its history, aims, and institutional structure. Section 4 contains the core of the chapter's empirical analysis. It compares the temporalities at work within the Mainstreaming Initiative with those that characterise the unfolding climate crisis, showing how and why voluntary governance arrangements struggle to adequately respond to climatic temporalities. Synthesising interdisciplinary literature on transnational governance, climate finance, and the international climate regime, section 5 considers how recent international developments could help to synchronise financial and climatic temporalities. Section 6 concludes.

2. Transnational climate governance, finance flows, and the international climate regime

The international climate regime comprises a diverse set of institutional arrangements, including intergovernmental treaties, such as the Paris Agreement; official decisions of the Conference of the Parties (COP), the climate regime's central decision-making body that formally convenes all signatory governments;[6] the UN Climate

Secretariat, the permanent international agency mandated to facilitate the multilateral process; and informal documents and arrangements, such as declarations of the presidencies that chair annual meetings and reports released by working groups, officially appointed representatives, and other regime participants. While the climate regime traditionally facilitated intergovernmental negotiations on international climate targets and programmes (Bodansky, Brunnée, and Rajamani, 2017, pp. 96–117), the adoption of the Paris Agreement at COP21 in December 2015 marked a 'turning point' in the development of the regime (Kinley, 2016). With a durable and long-term legal framework in place (Bodansky, 2016, p. 290), the logic of the climate regime shifted from negotiation to implementation. Whereas formerly the imperative was to forge consensus between governments, post-COP21 'action', as it is framed in international climate policy speak, has taken centre stage. Simply put, now that global climate mitigation, adaptation, and finance targets have been agreed, the primary task is to operationalise programmes that work towards these goals (Rajamani and Bodansky, 2019, p. 1025).

With the shift in logic from negotiation to implementation, transnational climate governance initiatives have received increasing attention. The Paris Decision, the COP21 decision accompanying the Paris Agreement, for instance, expressly 'welcomed' voluntary implementation efforts and encouraged governments to collaborate with subnational and non-state actors, including civil society organisations, the private sector, financial institutions, and local authorities (UNFCCC, 2016). Research has documented how members of these initiatives engage in a diverse set of activities, including capacity building, information sharing, monitoring, certification, funding, rule generation, and target setting (Bulkeley et al., 2014). In the climate finance context, transnational initiatives do not primarily aim to mobilise or leverage capital. Rather, they tend to support financial flows with 'facilitative modalities' (Bowman, 2022b), including by enhancing technical capacities, developing and sharing best practices, and providing platforms for knowledge exchange.

While article 2(1)(c) of the Paris Agreement articulated the objective to align finance flows with global mitigation and adaptation targets, there has, until recently, been no institutional platform within the climate regime to discuss how such alignment might be achieved in practice (Bodle and Noens, 2018).[7] In the absence of formal intergovernmental institutions, expert groups and pioneering 'coalitions of the willing' took the lead. Prominent examples include the *Task Force on Climate-related Financial Disclosures*, a global working group of technical experts that published a climate risk reporting standard for the financial sector in 2017;[8] the *Network for Greening the Financial System*, a transnational coalition of central banks and financial regulators that collaboratively seek to develop best practices for managing systemic climate risks;[9] and the *Glasgow Finance Alliance for Net Zero*, a coalition of private finance actors who commit to mobilising capital for decarbonising the economy.[10]

3. The Mainstreaming Climate in Financial Institutions Initiative

The Mainstreaming Initiative is one example of a voluntary governance arrangement that, in the absence of formal institutional mechanisms within the climate regime, began to explore and formulate what article 2(1)(c) of the Paris Agreement might mean in practice. Initially launched under the name 'Climate Action in Financial Institutions' at COP21 in December 2015, it aims to develop practices for 'mainstreaming' climate change in the banking industry. This implies making 'climate change considerations a core component of how financial institutions conduct business' (Climate Action in Financial Institutions, n.d.). A respondent, working for the secretariat of the Initiative, explained this objective as follows:

> The finance sector has looked at climate change in terms of projects, products, and sectors. The concept of 'mainstreaming' requires actors to take a different approach. It requires institutions to look at all operations and all activities, rethinking investments, strategies, operations, institutional set-up and so on ... mainstreaming climate change means that finance actors develop and implement new ways of doing business.

Purportedly, thus, from its very beginning, the Initiative took up the logic of article 2(1)(c) of the Paris Agreement. Aiming to move climate finance from being framed as a peripheral issue serviced by niche products and specialised experts to a systemic concern, it published the *Five Voluntary Principles for Mainstreaming Climate Change* – a list of five loosely formulated propositions intended to guide Initiative members. Substantively, the Principles suggest that mainstreaming climate change will require financial organisations to 'commit to climate strategies' (Principle 1), 'manage climate risks' (Principle 2), 'promote climate smart objectives' (Principle 3), 'improve climate performance' (Principle 4), and 'account for climate action' (Principle 5) (Climate Action in Financial Institutions, n.d.).

Case study materials show that Initiative members are expected to use best efforts to voluntarily implement the Five Voluntary Principles. A respondent, working at a founding member of the Initiative, for instance, explained that 'there is a level of expectation that, when an institution joins [the Initiative], climate action in accordance with the Principles will be undertaken'. Another respondent, working at a bank that joined the Mainstreaming Initiative at a later stage, confirmed this perception:

> The idea is that all the institutions who are part of this initiative are working towards operationalising the Principles ... So, while there is no follow-up in terms of each individual Principle, it is pre-supposed that all supporting institutions respect these Principles and explore ways of how to move them forward.

Given that the Mainstreaming Initiative depends entirely on voluntary commitment and buy-in at the institutional level, it is subtle dynamics that maintain the status of the Principles as the normative core of the alliance. These include a formalised joining procedure – future members have to sign and submit a 'Statement of Support' to become part of the Initiative, explicitly 'acknowledging' the 'guidance' provided by the Principles (Mainstreaming Climate in Financial Institutions, n.d.), and regular meetings and other forms of engagement, including, amongst other things, thematic workshops, consultations, surveys, and the 'Supporting Institutions Assembly', a forum that convenes all initiative members on an annual basis.

4. Climatic temporalities and voluntary governance

While the Five Voluntary Principles articulate a collective vision for making climate change a core consideration of financial decision-making in the banking sector, they do not exist in a time vacuum. On the contrary, in the context of climate change, time is of the essence. The IPCC's most recent climate models project that without speculative reliance on negative emission technologies (see Anderson and Peters, 2016), reaching the most ambitious mitigation goal of the Paris Agreement would require global greenhouse gas emissions to have peaked by 2025, with 'rapid', 'deep', and 'sustained' emission reductions in the following decades (IPCC, 2022, p. 30). What is needed, thus, is immediate action and continued engagement in the medium- and long-term.

Crucially, the extent of (in)action in the coming months and years will determine what will be necessary, and what remains possible, in the following decades (IPCC, 2022, p. 27). Accordingly, instead of singular, linear, and forward-looking conceptions of time, in the context of climate change, multiple temporal dimensions slide into each other and become mutually constitutive: climate futures are already existing (or 'antecedent') in what is and what has been; and pasts and presents are spilling into times to come (Mai, 2024). What matters – simultaneously – are 'the emissions from yesterday, today, and those released in the next few years' (Anderson and Bows, 2012, p. 639). In this sense, climate change fundamentally challenges conceptions of the past as that which is done and complete (the 'there and then'), and understandings of the future as a potpourri of opportunities that emerge on the temporal horizon. Rather, in the context of the unfolding climate crisis, pasts, presents, and futures interact and are mutually constitutive.

Deliberately constructed ambiguity

Analysing which legal technicalities the Principles rely upon, and which ones they deliberately avoid, reveals how they seek to produce a carefully calibrated degree of ambiguity in relation to what is expected, of whom, and at which points in time. Looking at the format of the Principles, for instance, it is notable that they have maintained a specific layout and structure since their publication at COP21. Set out as a list of five propositions, each Principle comprises a concise headline statement which is supplemented by an explanatory paragraph. For example, Principle 2 is headed by the phrase 'MANAGE Climate Risks', before explaining:

> Be active in managing climate risk. Assess your portfolio, pipeline and new investments. Work with clients to determine appropriate measures for building resilience to climate

> impacts and improving the long-term sustainability of investments. (Mainstreaming Climate in Financial Institutions, n.d.)

This format allows the Principles to provide maximum leeway for interpretation. It avoids exact specification of what is expected of whom by when. Steering clear of modal auxiliary verbs commonly found in legal documents, such as 'shall', 'should', 'will', and 'may' (see Rajamani, 2016), the Principles use the bare infinitive form of the verb, which, in English, is the same as the imperative mood. While the imperative is used to convey instructions, permissions or advice, the infinitive mood simply references an action or state of affairs. Further, the syntax of a sentence in the imperative mood does not necessarily include a subject, and the bare infinitive cannot be used to reference a subject. As such, it is left to addressees to decide who might be best placed to take action. Finally, the Principles make clear that there are several options as to how they may be implemented. This becomes apparent on close reading of the explanatory paragraphs which supplement each headline statement. For example, Principle 3 ('PROMOTE Climate Smart Objectives') contains the following enumeration of options:

> ... mobilizing and catalysing additional financing and developing specialized financing vehicles/products, such as green bonds, risk sharing mechanisms or blended finance. Engage clients and other stakeholders (e.g. rating agencies, accounting firms) on climate change risks and resilience, and share lessons of experience to help further mainstream climate considerations into activities and investments. (Mainstreaming Climate in Financial Institutions, n.d.)

The Principles' reliance on document formats and drafting techniques that produce ambiguity helps to account for the priorities, concerns, and capacities of their diverse membership base, which includes both public and private sector banks as well as early-moving pioneers and latecomers. Finding the right balance between articulating normative expectations and providing members with options on how to operationalise the Principles is key. After all, given the voluntary character of the Principles, uptake depends entirely on the extent to which the Principles find resonance within the banking sector. Clearly though, while ambiguity can help to attract and retain membership, it leads to the Principles failing to clearly articulate and insist on the urgency of aligning finance flows with global mitigation and adaptation goals. Ultimately, by remaining vague about who is expected to do what within which time frame, the Principles risk lending support to strategies of deferral and obfuscation.

Aspirational logic and future orientation

In addition to deliberately produced ambiguity, it is the aspirational logic of the Mainstreaming Initiative that inadequately takes account of climatic temporalities. Given their voluntary character, the Principles cannot commit to a logic of compliance. Instead, they articulate the expectation that members will work towards operationalising them over time. For instance, the document that launched the Principles at COP21 explained that the purpose of the Principles is to 'guide financial institutions *moving forward* in the process of adapting to and promoting climate smart development' (Climate Action in Financial Institutions, n.d., emphasis added). In a similar vein, a respondent working for a founding member of the Initiative described the Principles as follows:

> They [the Principles] are what we aim to achieve, really as an end-point … If you look at them, they are really quite comprehensive in terms of objectives. They set out, more or less, what banks' climate teams would say: 'Once we have implemented all these Principles, we have fully integrated climate change.'

Reminiscent of notions of 'progression' and 'ambition' which are enshrined in the Paris Agreement itself (Rajamani and Guérin, 2017, pp. 77–78; Heyvaert, 2019, pp. 128, 248–249; Duvic-Paoli, 2023), the Principles envision a future trajectory of gradually intensifying action. In its most recent strategic plan, the Mainstreaming Initiative describes itself as driven by a 'commitment to increase[e] ambition over time' (Mainstreaming Climate in Financial Institutions, 2021, p. 7).

From a member's perspective, the aspirational logic and future orientation of the Principles allow banks to start acting, even in light of imperfect information, knowledge, and resources. For instance, during one of the Initiative's workshops on the sidelines of the UN Climate Action Summit in New York, a participant representing a regional development bank explained that 'the banking community really needs to get going … It is better to be factually incorrect and act now, rather than being slow or inactive'. Highlighting the importance of timing, the participant went on to note: 'Things can always be corrected later, but we have to move now.' Similarly, a respondent working at a pioneer supporting institution that was involved in formulating the Principles ahead of COP21 explained their logic as follows:

> I don't see the Principles as something like, you know, you can only join the initiative if you already comply with all these requirements. I think it is, and it should be, a looser concept … so that institutions which are not there yet, or which might just have formulated their climate strategy, but who are not doing the whole thing yet … I don't think that should prevent them from joining the initiative. On the contrary, I think they should join the initiative.

Accordingly, instead of aiming for compliance, the Principles allow for a pragmatic approach to implementation which enables Initiative members to get work under way in the short term and learn and optimise over time. In theory, such pragmatism could help to respond to the need for immediate action, acknowledging that medium- and long-term climate responses fundamentally depend on what happens (or not) in the short term. Interview materials and field observations, however, reveal that the aspirational logic of the Principles leads banks to adopt a 'wait and see' approach, ultimately deferring the deep and systemic changes needed to mainstream climate change within financial institutions' operations. A respondent working for a private sector bank, for instance, explained that they were 'holding off until governments create a level-playing field'. In a similar register, another respondent explained how their bank was 'one of the few domestic lenders' which 'asked clients for information about positive and negative climate impacts before making investment decisions'. They continued:

'It would be great if that practice could become a legal requirement, so that the client does not have to resist.' They made clear that the bank was aware of the fact that clients may 'get frustrated' and seek funding from competitors: 'It is very difficult to be the bank that asks questions.' In a similar register, staff at development finance institutions pointed to operational frames of reference set out in their mandates.

Given their need to generate buy-in (including by remaining deliberately ambiguous about what is expected of members) and their inability to enforce compliance (instead having to rely on an aspirational logic), voluntary governance arrangements go some but not all of the way to align finance flows with global climate goals. While voluntary governance arrangements create experimental spaces for learning, collaboration, and testing, uncomfortable and immediate changes that contradict the current logic and operational imperatives of how finance institutions do business will require mandatory regulation. A respondent working for a private sector bank put it bluntly: 'We need to make money.' The bottom line, then, is that, in the absence of adequate legal and regulatory frameworks, most banks will opt to defer urgently needed change as long as current ways of allocating finance remain lucrative (Bowman, 2015).

5. Shifting gear? International developments

As of March 2025, recent developments have seen shifts in international climate law and policy. For one, COP27 acknowledged the need to clarify the meaning and practical implications of article 2(1)(c) of the Paris Agreement, launching the so-called 'Sharm el-Sheikh Dialogue' as a platform for discussion among governments and non-state actors (UNFCCC, 2023, para 68). The Dialogue is mandated to hold two workshops per year and report back to the COP. Past topics include technical deliberation about how the concept of 'finance flow' relates to the notion of 'climate finance', as well as practical discussions about adaptation finance, finance for sustainable development, and modalities for tracking how much funding is being provided.[11] With this, the Dialogue provides the first dedicated institutional forum within the official inter-governmental climate process for building a common understanding of what alignment of finance flows with global mitigation and adaptation goals might mean in concrete terms. The outcome of the Dialogue could, for instance, include practical guidance on globally applicable taxonomies for measuring and assessing climate finance flows (Rajamani et al., 2023, p. 13).

Further, COP27 expressly acknowledged the need to transform the structures and processes of the global financial system – a process which is envisioned to involve 'governments, central banks, commercial banks, institutional investors and other financial actors' (UNFCCC, 2023, para 55). The COP specifically highlighted the role of Multilateral Development Banks and international financial institutions, articulating not only quantitative expectations (calling for more climate finance), but explicitly highlighting the need to 'reform' their 'practices and priorities' and define a 'new vision' and 'operational models' (UNFCCC, 2023, pp. 61–62). With this call for reform, COP27 is seen to have broken 'new ground' (Rajamani et al., 2023, p. 20).

The background to this shift in official narrative is what has become known as the 'Bridgetown Initiative' – a strategically placed and carefully orchestrated diplomatic initiative advanced by Barbados' Prime Minister Mia Mottley (see World Economic Forum, 2023; Farand, 2022). In light of debt and cost of living crises brought about by intensifying climate impacts, the Covid-19 pandemic, and the Russian invasion of Ukraine, the Bridgetown Initiative aims to reform the global financial system.[12] Marrying the climate and development agendas, it rehearses well-established demands, such as lightening debt burdens on developing countries. In so doing, however, it makes three innovative strategic moves that illustrate how climate finance is bound up with time. First, the Bridgetown Initiative calls for emergency liquidity and the rapid scaling up of investments for low-carbon development across all relevant sectors. Quoting from the initial version of the declaration, the imperative is to 'act now'.[13] This sense of urgency is reiterated in the most recent version of the Initiative, which concludes with the following statement: 'Progress on this agenda is critical. Failure to tangibly advance … by the end of 2025, will yield unthinkable costs to lives, livelihoods and our planet.'[14] Clearly, thus, in contrast to transnational governance arrangements like the Mainstreaming Initiative, the Bridgetown Initiative makes explicit the urgency of climate finance.

Second, in addition to insisting on the need for immediate action, the initial version of the Bridgetown Initiative called for 'reconstruction grants for any country just imperilled by a climate disaster'.[15] The most recent version released in 2024 further concretises this proposal, listing a range of measures to help 'shock proof' economies, such as making available immediate liquidity support facilities, the introduction of natural disaster clauses in lending instruments, and expanding insurance markets and regional risk pools.[16] To some extent, these proposals dovetail with the emerging discourse on loss and damage which has been gaining traction in the international climate regime. For instance, new fora, including the Santiago Network and Glasgow Dialogue, have been set up to address issues relating to loss and damage (UNFCCC, 2020, para 43; UNFCCC, 2021, para 73); and, most recently, a dedicated financial mechanism for loss and damage materialised (UNFCCC, 2024). These developments within official intergovernmental discourse begin to acknowledge, albeit in an insufficient way, that climate pasts, presents, and futures are co-constitutive: At this point in time, certain losses have already been baked into emission levels that have accumulated in the atmosphere over the centuries.

Third, and finally, to achieve its aims within an arguably vexed geopolitical climate, the Bridgetown Initiative presents climate change as a global problem. Accordingly, instead of reinscribing discourse that pitches the interests of developing countries against those of developed countries, it seeks to bridge historical divides and construct a new collective 'we' that is responsible for taking care of the climate as a common good. Framed as a 'call for collective action' that 'moves beyond country-by-country responses that have become bogged down by issues of who should do more', the initial draft of the Bridgetown Initiative appealed to a shared sense of vulnerability that was palpable in the aftermath of the global pandemic.[17] This attempt to forge a sense of global collectivity and responsibility is strategically ambiguous in its temporal commitments. On the one hand, it could be read as an ahistorical discourse that glosses over historical responsibilities of developed countries for colonial injustices (Gosh, Shawoo, and Nazareth, 2025). On the other hand, however, the Bridgetown Initiative can also be interpreted as making this diplomatic move to strategically open up space for addressing exactly these historical responsibilities in terms of both immediate action in the form of emergency funding, as well as long-term systemic changes within the structures of the global financial system (Zylinski, 2024). What remains to be seen is whether in contrast to the Mainstreaming Initiative, where ambiguity leads to obfuscation and delay, the Bridgetown Agenda can harness the play with its temporal commitments to, in fact, align financial with climatic temporalities.

6. Conclusion

A staff member of a founding institution of the Mainstreaming Initiative explained that including the term 'voluntary' in the title of the Principles was a deliberate decision that was taken when setting up the Initiative:

> I think the word 'voluntary' is important, because if it was like a certification scheme … that would prevent many people from joining. … In this sense, it is important to stress this voluntary adjective there.

They went on to explain that when asking top-level management for approval to join climate finance initiatives, the key consideration revolves around what exactly is required and expected of the institutions: 'When we go to get the approval, they [management] ask: "So what are we signing up to?". And then they say "Ah yes, it is voluntary". So, they really want to see this word there.' Given that, by their very nature, voluntary governance arrangements can neither induce compliance nor push members to commit to things that run contrary to their own interests, such arrangements are strategically dispositioned to appear non-threatening to accommodate and appeal to the broadest possible range of member institutions.

This chapter discussed how the logic of voluntary climate governance is out of sync with the temporalities of the unfolding climate crisis. While voluntary commitments and initiatives can support agenda-setting, learning, collaboration, and testing, they fundamentally depend on the discretionary support and goodwill of their members. As such, voluntary governance arrangements are highly unlikely to bring about uncomfortable changes that are needed in the short term, especially when such changes sit at odds with the interests and operational logics of their constituencies. In this sense, voluntary arrangements may be regarded as an advance guard that can test the waters within existing frames of reference. In order to shift gear, however, decisive and strategic government interventions are needed (Bowman, 2015; 2022a; 2022b).

In domestic contexts, mandatory regulation is required to create market conditions within which climate-damaging financial practices and products become unprofitable or are outright banned. At the international level, diplomatic initiatives, like the

Bridgetown Agenda, can help to articulate the urgency of climate finance and bring hitherto disregarded temporal aspects into focus, specifically those that articulate demands for reparative justice (see already Burkett, 2009). Given the limits of voluntarism identified in this chapter, paying close attention to how state-backed mandatory and industry-led voluntary initiatives interact with each other will be key going forward.

Notes

1. For a detailed account of the complexities involved in defining what counts as 'climate finance', see UNFCCC Standing Committee on Climate Finance (2023).
2. A consultation process on how to achieve the new climate finance goal with the support of both public and private actors has been launched (UNFCCC, n.d., para 27). See also 'Message from the Presidencies of the Sixth and Seventh Conference of the Parties serving as the Meeting of the Parties to the Paris Agreement on the "Baku to Belém Roadmap to 1.3T"' (21 February 2025) https://unfccc.int/sites/default/files/resource/message_to_parties_and_observers_baku_to_belem_roadmap.pdf.
3. Accessible via https://climateaction.unfccc.int/Initiatives.
4. See 'Mainstreaming Climate in Financial Institutions' https://www.mainstreamingclimate.org.
5. Specifically, interviews comprise two interviews with the secretariat of the Mainstreaming Initiative, five interviews with public banks, and three interviews with private banks.
6. Throughout this chapter, the acronym 'COP' is used to refer to both the Conference of the Parties to the UN Framework Convention on Climate Change and the Conference of the Parties to the Framework Convention serving as the Meeting of the Parties to the Paris Agreement.
7. See further section 5.
8. See 'Task Force on Climate-related Financial Disclosures' (legacy site) www.fsb-tcfd.org.
9. See 'Welcome to the NGFS Website' www.ngfs.net/en.
10. See 'Glasgow Financial Alliance for Net Zero' www.gfanzero.com.
11. The website of the UN Climate Secretariat is regularly updated to reflect calls for input, information about planned sessions, and outcomes. See https://unfccc.int/topics/climate-finance/workstreams/sharm-el-sheikh-dialogue/sharm-el-sheikh-dialogue.
12. Since its launch, the Bridgetown Initiative has undergone several iterations. Initially proposed by Prime Minister Mia Mottley during her address to the UN General Assembly on 22 September 2022 (see https://www.youtube.com/watch?v=y4lUZ-K1YJNo) and her Opening Statement at the World Leaders' Summit at COP27 (see https://www.youtube.com/watch?v=5JoegwAfOow), the second version of the Initiative was presented in June 2023, and the most recent version was published in 2024. All versions are available at https://www.bridgetown-initiative.org/history/.
13. 'The 2022 Bridgetown Initiative for the Reform of the Global Financial Architecture' https://www.bridgetown-initiative.org/wp-content/uploads/2024/05/The-2022-Bridgetown-Initiative.pdf.
14. 'Bridgetown Initiative on the Reform of the International Development and Climate Finance Architecture Version 3.0', p. 7 https://www.bridgetown-initiative.org/bridgetown-initiative-3-0/.

15. n 12.
16. n 13, p. 5.
17. n 12.

References

Anderson, K, and Bows, A. (2012) 'A new paradigm for climate change', *Nature Climate Change*, 2(9), pp. 639–640.

Anderson, K. and Peters, G. (2016) 'The trouble with negative emission technologies', *Science*, 354(6309), pp. 182–183.

Andonova, L.B., Betsill, M.M. and Bulkeley, H. (2009) 'Transnational climate governance', *Global Environmental Politics*, 2(9), pp. 52–73.

Bodansky, D. (2016) 'The Paris Climate Change Agreement: a new hope?' *American Journal of International Law*, 110(2), pp. 288–319.

Bodansky, D., Brunnée, J. and Rajamani, L. (2017) *International climate change law*. Oxford University Press.

Bodle, R. and Noens, V. (2018) 'Climate finance: too much on detail, too little on the big picture', *Carbon and Climate Law Review*, 12(3), pp. 248–257.

Bowman, M. (2015) *Banking on climate change: how finance actors and transnational regulatory regimes are responding*. Wolters Kluwer.

Bowman, M. (2022a) *Regulatory leadership for a net zero transition: central banks and financial regulators: levers and limits*. King's College London. Available at: https://www.kcl.ac.uk/climate-law/assets/regulatory-leadership-for-a-net-zero-transition-dr-megan-bowman.pdf (Accessed: 8 July 2024).

Bowman, M. (2022b) 'Turning promises into action: "legal readiness for climate finance" and implementing the Paris Agreement', *Carbon and Climate Law Review*, 16(1), pp. 41–55.

Bowman, M. and Tayler, T. (2026) 'Law and the international financial architecture: pathways and pivot points for achieving Paris objectives', in Bowman, M. and Mai, L. (eds) *A research agenda for law, finance and the environment*. Edward Elgar Publishing, pp. 69–96.

Bulkeley, H., Andonova, L.B., Betsill, M.M., Compagnon, D., Hale, T., Hoffmann, M.J., Newell, P., Paterson, M., Roger, C. and VanDeveer, S.D. (2014) *Transnational climate change governance*. Cambridge University Press.

Bulkeley, H., Betsill, M., Compagnon, D., Hale, T., Hoffmann, M., Newell, P. and Paterson, M. (2018) 'Transnational governance: charting new directions post-Paris', in Jordan, A. *et al.* (eds), *Governing climate change: polycentricity in action?* Cambridge University Press, pp. 63–80.

Burkett, M. (2009) 'Climate reparations', *Melbourne Journal of International Law*, 10(2), pp. 509–543.

Climate Action in Financial Institutions (n.d.) *Principles for mainstreaming climate action*. Available at: www.un.org/pga/71/wp-content/uploads/sites/40/2017/06/IDFC-Climate-Action-in-Financial-Institutions-Initiative-Flyer.pdf (Accessed: 8 July 2024).

Duvic-Paoli, L-A. (2023) 'International law: a discipline of ambition' *Leiden Journal of International Law*, 36(2), pp. 233–249.

Farand, C. (2022) 'Mia Mottley builds global coalition to make financial system fit for climate action', *Climate Home News*, 23 September. Available at:https://www.climatechangenews.com/2022/09/23/mia-mottley-builds-global-coalition-to-make-financial-system-fit-for-climate-action/ (Accessed: 8 July 2024).

Gosh, E., Shawoo, Z. and Nazareth, A. (2025) *Decolonial climate finance in practice: assessing proposed reforms*. Stockholm Environment Institute working paper 2025. Available at:https://www.sei.org/publications/decolonial-climate-finance-assessing-proposed-reforms/ (Accessed: 5 March 2025).

Hale, T. (2016) '"All hands on deck": The Paris Agreement and nonstate climate action', *Global Environmental Politics*, 16(3), pp. 12–22.

Heyvaert, V. (2019) *Transnational environmental regulation and governance: purpose, strategies and principles.* Cambridge University Press.

Intergovernmental Panel on Climate Change (IPCC) (2022) *Climate Change 2022: Mitigation of climate change. Summary for policymakers.* Available at: www.ipcc.ch/report/ar6/wg3 (Accessed: 8 July 2024).

Kinley, R. (2016) 'Climate change after Paris: from turning point to transformation' *Climate Policy*, 17(1), pp. 9–15.

Latorre, S. (2012) *Legal technicalities in conditions of political conflict: the case of land tenure disputes in Colombia.* PhD dissertation. Cornell University.

Mai, L. (2018) 'The growing recognition and importance of transnational climate governance initiatives in the UN climate regime: implications for legal scholarship', *Climate Law*, 8(3–4), pp. 184–193.

Mai, L. (2024) 'Navigating transformations: climate change and international law', *Leiden Journal of International Law*, 37(3), pp. 535–556.

Mai, L. and Elsässer, J.P. (2022) 'Orchestrating global climate governance through data: the UNFCCC Secretariat and the global climate action platform' *Global Environmental Politics*, 22(4), pp. 151–172.

Mainstreaming Climate in Financial Institution (n.d.) *Join us.* Available at:www.mainstreamingclimate.org/join-us/ (Accessed: 8 July 2024).

Mainstreaming Climate in Financial Institutions (2021) *2021–2025 strategy.* Available at: https://mainstreamingclimate.org/wp-content/uploads/2021/10/Mainstreaming-Initiative-5-year-Strategic-Plan_final-version.pdf (Accessed: 8 July 2024).

Michaels, R. and Riles, A. (2021) 'Law as technique', in Foblets, M.C. *et al.* (eds) *The Oxford handbook of law and anthropology.* Oxford University Press, pp. 860–878.

Pattberg, P. and Stripple, J. (2008) 'Beyond the public and private divide: remapping transnational climate governance in the 21st century', *International Environmental Agreements*, 8(4), pp. 367–388.

Rajamani, L. (2016) 'The 2015 Paris Agreement: interplay between hard, soft and non-obligations', *Journal of Environmental Law*, 28(2), pp. 337–358.

Rajamani, L. and Bodansky, D. (2019) 'The Paris rulebook: balancing international prescriptiveness with national discretion', *International and Comparative Law Quarterly*, 68(4), pp. 1023–1040.

Rajamani, L. *et al.* (2023) *Re-invigorating the UN Climate Regime in the wider landscape of climate action.* Centre for Climate and Energy Solutions (C2ES). Available at: https://www.c2es.org/wp-content/uploads/2023/11/reinvigorating-the-un-climate-regime-in-the-wider-landscape-of-climate-action.pdf. (Accessed: 8 July 2024).

Rajamani, L. and Guérin, E. (2017) 'Central concepts in the Paris Agreement and how they evolved', in Klein, D. *et al.* (eds) *The Paris Agreement on Climate Change: analysis and commentary.* Oxford University Press, pp. 74–90.

Riles, A. (2005) 'A new agenda for the cultural study of law: taking on the technicalities', *Buffalo Law Review*, 53(3), pp. 973–1034.

Riles, A. (2011) *Collateral knowledge: legal reasoning in the global financial markets.* University of Chicago Press.

Thorgeirsson, H. (2018) 'Objective (Article 2.1)', in Klein, D. *et al.* (eds) *The Paris Agreement on Climate Change: analysis and commentary.* Oxford University Press, pp. 123–130.

UNFCCC (2025) *Decision 1/CMA.6: New collective quantified goal on climate finance.* FCCC/PA/CMA/2024/17/Add.1.

UNFCCC (2016) *Decision 1/CP.21: Adoption of the Paris Agreement*. FCCC/CP/2015/10/ Add.1.

UNFCCC (2020) *Decision 2/CMA.2: Warsaw International Mechanism for Loss and Damage associated with Climate Change Impacts and its 2019 review*. FCCC/PA/CMA/2019/Add.1.

UNFCCC (2021) *Decision 1/CMA.3: Glasgow Climate Pact*. FCCC/PA/CMA/2021/10/Add 1.

UNFCCC (2023) *Decision 1/CMA.4: Sharm el-Sheikh Implementation Plan*. FCCC/PA/CMA/2022/10/Add.1.

UNFCCC (2024) *Operationalization of the new funding arrangements, including a fund, for responding to loss and damage referred to in paragraphs 2–3 of Decisions 2/CP.27 and 2/CMA.4*. FCCC/PA/CMA 2023/16/Add.1.

UNFCCC Standing Committee on Climate Finance (2023) *Report on clustering types of climate finance definitions in use*. Available at:https://unfccc.int/sites/default/files/resource/Definitions_final_231117%20BLS23393%20UCC%20Climate%20Finance.pdf.

Valverde, M. (2015) *Chronotopes of law: jurisdiction, scale and governance*. Routledge.

World Economic Forum (2023) *The Bridgetown Initiative: here's everything you need to know*. Available at: https://www.weforum.org/stories/2023/01/barbados-bridgetown-initiative-climate-change/ (Accessed: 5 March 2025).

Zahar, A. (2017) *International climate finance law*. Routledge.

Zylinski, S. (2024) 'Coloniality dressed in green: in its current form, climate finance risks becoming a new tool for colonial rule', *Global Political Economy*, 3(2), pp. 315–322.

4

A drop in the ocean? Multilateral finance for environmentally sound technology development and transfer

Stephen Minas

1. Introduction

This chapter aims to demonstrate the development and functioning of international legal frameworks for technology financing. It foregrounds the competing interests perceived by groups of states which set the parameters for such frameworks, synthesised through processes of multilateral negotiation. It does so with references to four international legal frameworks. These frameworks have been selected for two reasons. First, because of their centrality to international responses to climate change. Second, because, among a larger set of international frameworks concerned with climate change, the selected frameworks enable comparison of regimes at different stages of development, produced in different contexts regarding scientific knowledge, technological capabilities, international priorities, and the world correlation of forces.

The chapter goes on to identify key challenges in multilateral financing for environmentally sound technology and proposes approaches to address these challenges. As most states are, to varying degrees, reliant on external support to implement their responses to global environmental challenges, addressing these challenges is of critical importance to the collective response to climate change and related problems. The discussion of key challenges will be of particular salience to international negotiators and national officials responsible for domestic implementation of international frameworks.

The current international system, based as it is on the formal equality of sovereign states, accounts in many ways for the different circumstances and capabilities of states. It recognises in particular that poorer states will often need practical assistance or other concessions in order to fully enjoy rights recognised in international law or to fully implement the commitments that they have made under international agreements. It is therefore common for multilateral agreements, including multilateral environmental agreements (MEAs), to provide for practical assistance to be channelled to certain categories of poorer or otherwise disadvantaged states. This assistance, or 'means of implementation', is often divided into finance, technology development and transfer (TDT), and capacity-building. In reality, these categories are not hermetically sealed from each other. Rather, they often overlap and can be mutually reinforcing. One particularly important overlap is the mobilisation of finance for TDT.

In addition to bilateral finance flows which are outside the scope of this chapter, donors have channelled finance for TDT through an array of multilateral institutions, mechanisms, and initiatives which have varied in mandate, size, governance, and legal formality. Regarding such finance for *environmentally sound* technologies in particular, the period since the early 1990s has seen much institutional experimentation and an increasingly crowded domain of actors with overlapping missions. These phenomena are most obvious in the domain of climate change but can also be observed with respect to other global environmental challenges. This period has also surfaced a range of key issues bearing on multilateral finance for TDT which will be examined below. These issues can be seen in multilateral regimes which, regarding TDT, are at varying stages of development and coherence.

The remainder of the chapter is structured as follows. Section 2 places multilateral technology finance in historical and legal context. It highlights the central place technology occupied in ideological and legal contests concerning the redistribution of resources to developing states and how these enduring contests informed the framing of TDT and associated financing provisions in MEAs. This history provides the backdrop for the three TDT regimes introduced in section 3: the United Nations Framework Convention on Climate Change (UNFCCC); the management of greenhouse gas emissions from international transport under the International Civil Aviation Organization (ICAO) and the International Maritime Organization (IMO); and the new treaty – yet to enter force at the time of writing – on conservation and sustainable use of biological diversity in areas of the sea beyond national jurisdiction (BBNJ). Section 4 discusses key issues for multilateral financing of TDT which can be distilled from these regimes, including design features of multilateral mechanisms, the incorporation of technology into general programming, the creation of enabling environments in recipient states, and the place of such mechanisms in broader finance flows. The conclusion offers some generalised observations for strengthening multilateral finance for environmental TDT, including on responding to the overarching concern of recipient states that the amount of multilateral finance for TDT is insufficient.

2. Multilateral technology finance in historical and legal context

The provisions for TDT in multilateral agreements did not fall from the sky. They are the results of decades of contestation in the UN system and other fora concerning the terms of economic relations between developed and developing countries. This background is not just of historical interest but continues to condition reactions to questions such as the financing of TDT.

In summary, the retrenchment of empires following the Second World War resulted in waves of decolonisation. The newly independent states, sovereign but poor, soon constituted a majority in the recently established UN and its General Assembly. These states began to pursue a redistribution of wealth and economic capacity from their former colonial masters and other wealthier states. The call for more or less compulsory technology transfer featured prominently in this agenda, as reflected in UN Conference on Trade and Development documents following its establishment in 1964 (UNCTAD, 1964).

The General Assembly's 1974 'Programme of Action on the Establishment of a New International Economic Order' (NIEO) called for the formulation of 'an international code of conduct for the transfer of technology corresponding to needs and conditions prevalent in developing countries' (UNGA, 1974). Negotiations began within UNCTAD on an 'International Code of Conduct on Technology Transfer'. This document aimed to be 'universally applicable in scope' and would have placed significant obligations on states, including with respect to binding dispute resolution (UNCTAD, 1985). Developed countries opposed a code of conduct with regulatory implications, and the process was continued after the final draft in 1985.

Calls for technology transfer were also made through what became the 'sustainable development' agenda, with the first milestone being the 1972 UN Conference on the Human Environment in Stockholm. The resulting declaration included among other references, at Principle 20, the statement that 'environmental technologies should be made available to developing countries on terms which would encourage their wide dissemination without constituting an economic burden on the developing countries'. The Rio Declaration twenty years later expanded upon this call for technology transfer by inviting states to enhance 'the development, adaptation, diffusion and transfer of technologies, including new and innovative technologies' (Principle 9).

The 'Agenda 21' action plan that accompanied the Rio Declaration included a chapter on 'Transfer of Environmentally Sound Technology, Cooperation and Capacity-Building'. Agenda 21 defined ESTs as technologies that 'protect the environment, are less polluting, use all resources in a more sustainable manner, recycle more of their wastes and products, and handle residual wastes in a more acceptable manner than the technologies for which they were substitutes' (UNCED, 1992, para. 34.1). It also noted that ESTs 'are not just individual technologies, but total systems which include know-how, procedures, goods and services, and equipment as well as organizational and managerial procedures' (UNCED, 1992, para. 34.3). ESTs, then, are defined by their outcomes and their better environmental impacts (relative to competing technologies) and include systemic as well as individual technologies.

While not legally binding on states, the outcomes of the Stockholm and Rio conferences were influential in setting expectations for the subsequent or concurrent development of international environmental law, including that concerning technology (Sand, 1992). The broad, purposive Rio definition of TDT has been reflected in the multilateral technology support provided under MEAs. To take one example from the UNFCCC: The Climate Technology Centre and Network (CTCN), which provides technical assistance for developing countries, drafted a national electric vehicle (EV) policy for Papua New Guinea as well as a concept note for Green Climate Fund financing. Following this, the PNG government initiated projects to implement the policy, including to create a sustainable urban mobility plan with funding from the Asian Development Bank (CTCN, 2024, p. 10). The UNFCCC technology support is an intervention directed at systemic change – concerning transport in this case – and unlocking larger-scale financing for the multiple technologies needed to roll out EVs in a small island developing state.

In line with the Stockholm and Rio outcomes, TDT provisions have become a common feature of multilateral environmental agreements, as well as agreements on other topics. By 2007, over eighty regional and international agreements included technology transfer provisions (Anderson, Sarma, and Taddonio, 2007, p. 5), with the number continuing to grow since then. The technology transfer provisions of MEAs follow the approach of the Stockholm and Rio principles in encouraging, or requiring, transfers to developing countries but without mandating terms or abrogating intellectual property rights. Quite representative is the 1994 Desertification Convention, which provides at Article 18.1 that the 'Parties shall … facilitate access, in particular by affected developing country Parties, on favourable terms, including on concessional and preferential terms, as mutually agreed, taking into account the need to protect intellectual property rights, to technologies most suitable to practical application…'.

It can therefore be seen that the NIEO did not entirely fail on the question of TDT. While the high-water mark claim for mandatory technology transfer was never realised, the principle that TDT in favour of developing countries (however categorised) is a necessary element of environmental agreements is broadly if not universally accepted. However, the precise terms of TDT, including how it is to be financed, are under regular negotiation as treaties are developed, conferences of parties make decisions, and international financial bodies adapt their funding criteria. The precise terms of financing for TDT therefore differ both over time and between substantive regimes.

3. Technology transfer in the climate, high seas, and international transport regimes

3.1 The UNFCCC

Finance for TDT has been an enduring element of the UNFCCC regime since the adoption of the UN Climate Convention in 1992. The Convention provides both for technology support to be provided via the UNFCCC Financial Mechanism and for developed Parties to finance technology transfer more generally.

Regarding the Financial Mechanism, Article 4.3 provides that Annex II Parties (i.e., all developed Parties except for the post-communist 'economies in transition') 'shall … provide such financial resources, including for the transfer of technology, needed by the developing country Parties to meet the agreed full incremental costs of implementing measures that are covered by paragraph 1 of this Article and that are agreed between a developing country Party and the international entity or entities referred to in Article 11 [i.e., operating entities of the Financial Mechanism], in accordance with that Article'. This commits the Annex II Parties to provide finance through the Financial Mechanism operating entities for the implementation of developing countries' climate policies and measures. The operating entities are the Global Environment Facility (GEF), the Green Climate Fund (GCF) established in 2010, and the fund for responding to loss and damage, which the COP and CMA designated as an operating entity in 2023 (COP/CMA, 2023, para. 5).

Article 4.5 provides that the Annex II Parties 'shall take all practicable steps to promote, facilitate and finance, as appropriate, the transfer of, or access to, environmentally sound technologies and know-how to other Parties, particularly developing country Parties, to enable them to implement the provisions of the Convention'. It also notes that '[o]ther Parties and organizations in a position to do so may also assist in facilitating the transfer of such technologies'. Unlike under Article 4.3, the support to be provided under Article 4.5 includes but is not limited to finance and need not flow through the Financial Mechanism. These and other 'support' provisions of the Convention reflect the reality that effective developing Party implementation of Convention commitments depended on support received from developed Parties, as explicitly acknowledged in Article 4.7.

Initially, the main instrument for multilateral TDT financing under the UNFCCC was the GEF, as the sole operating entity of the Financial Mechanism until the establishment of the GCF in 2010. The role was solidified through the initiation, by the Conference of Parties (COP) in 2007, of what became the Poznan Strategic Programme on Technology Transfer (PSP). The COP requested the GEF to 'elaborate a strategic programme to scale up the level of investment for technology transfer to help developing countries address their needs for environmentally sound technologies' (Decision 4/CP.13, para. 3). The GEF approved the PSP in 2008 and in 2010 it was broadened to encompass five elements: support for regional climate technology centres, which have been hosted by regional development banks; piloting priority projects; public-private partnerships; support for technology needs assessments (TNAs); and catalytic GEF support for technology transfer.

As this range of activities under the PSP indicates, financial support for TDT includes support for the development of national policies to direct and enable climate technology uptake in-country. Supported policy processes include TNAs, the related production of technology action plans and various other instruments. The need for appropriate policy frameworks for climate technology is generally recognised as self-evident. However, developing Parties have regularly complained that while they can access support for policy development, support for the transfer of 'hardware' – physical technologies – has been insufficient.

In the wake of the infamous 2009 Copenhagen conference, the COP in 2010 reset the provision of multilateral TDT support by creating a new structure, the Technology Mechanism (Minas, 2021a). This mechanism includes two bodies: the Technology Executive Committee (TEC), which as the 'policy arm' provides recommendations to the COP, publishes papers, and engages with other climate institutions; and the CTCN, the 'implementation arm' which provides technical assistance to developing Parties, among other services.

The TEC does not itself provide financial support. Rather, it influences the financial support provided by others through activities such as recommendations to COP, inputs to draft guidance to the Financial Mechanism entities, collaboration with financial bodies on the development of technology financing programmes, publications and documents such as its evaluation of the PSP, and events such as the workshop on linkages between the Financial Mechanism and Technology Mechanism mandated for 2024. TEC activities are funded from the UNFCCC Secretariat budget.

The CTCN also is not a financial body *per se*. It is best seen as a service provider that can enable Parties to access finance for TDT. This can be achieved, for example, by Parties using the outputs of CTCN technical assistance to develop funding proposals to international financial institutions. The CTCN has collaborated with the UNFCCC financial bodies to varying degrees and has more recently explored partnerships with multilateral development banks. The COP decided that the CTCN itself 'should be funded from various sources, including the financial mechanism of the Convention, bilateral, multilateral and private-sector channels, philanthropic sources as well as financial and in-kind contributions from the host organization [UNEP] and participants in the Network' (Decision 2/CP.17, para. 139). In practice, funding from the CTCN has overwhelmingly come from several developed Parties. A resource mobilisation strategy adopted in 2023 aims to tap the private sector and the booming climate philanthropy landscape in order to increase and diversify funding for TDT under the UNFCCC.

Alongside the Technology Mechanism, the COP in 2010 created the GCF as the second operating entity of the Financial Mechanism (Bowman and Minas, 2019). As the largest dedicated climate fund, the GCF is a major disburser of finance for TDT. This support is far from limited to the GCF's direct collaborations with the TEC and CTCN. Figures based on the GCF's internal project taxonomy indicate that 75 per cent of GCF projects support technology. Like the GEF, the GCF has its own decision-making structure and internal legal order determining access to finance.

The 2015 Paris Agreement provided an updated legal framework for TDT support in its Article 10, which is dedicated to technology. Article 10.6 provides that '[s]upport, including financial support, shall be provided to developing country Parties for the implementation of this Article, including for strengthening cooperative action on technology development and transfer at different stages of the technology cycle, with a view to achieving a balance between support for mitigation and adaptation'. This passage can be distinguished from the Climate Convention's text on TDT in several respects: the requirement to provide support is not limited to Annex II or developed Parties – indeed, the addressee of this 'shall' is not specified; support must be channelled to the different stages of the technology cycle; and balancing support between mitigation and adaptation has become an objective. This passage is complemented by Article 10.5, which identifies the criticality of 'innovation' and provides that '[s]uch effort shall be, as appropriate, supported, including by the Technology Mechanism and, through financial means, by the Financial Mechanism of the Convention'. Following the Paris Agreement, Parties determined that the Adaptation Fund created under the Kyoto Protocol (and which is not an operating entity of the Financial Mechanism) would also serve the Paris Agreement. One consequence of this is that the Adaptation Fund is enabled to collaborate with the Technology Mechanism, in addition to the GEF and GCF.

The amount of money dedicated to multilateral climate finance is relatively low. The UNFCCC Standing Committee on Finance has reported that 79 per cent of 'climate-specific finance' in 2019–2020 was provided through bilateral, regional, and other channels, rather than multilateral channels (SCF, 2022, p. 7). In 2020, UNFCCC and other multilateral climate funds approved $3.5 billion in financing, while multilateral development banks provided $45 billion in climate finance (SCF, 2022, p. 8).

A significant proportion of multilateral climate finance supports technology development and transfer. For example, the GCF has reported that 75 per cent of its approved projects 'had at least one technology component' (GCF, 2023, para. 117). Donor countries have reported that technology transfer is 'integrated into climate finance projects in recognition of the cross-cutting, multisectoral needs of developing countries' (UNFCCC, 2023, para. 36). The biennial transparency reports (BTRs) required under the Paris Agreement can be expected to shed new light on the sources of climate finance and its use for technology development and transfer. The first BTRs were due to be submitted by Parties by the end of 2024 (Decision 18/CMA.1, para. 3).

3.2 International transport emissions regulation under the ICAO and IMO

GHG emissions from international transport (aviation and shipping) are significant and growing contributors to climate change. Shipping alone accounted for an estimated 2.89 per cent of global anthropogenic emissions in 2018, with an increase in shipping emissions from 2012 to 2018 (IMO, 2020, p. 1). While there are different estimations, the EU recently suggested that in a business-as-usual scenario, international shipping emissions would increase by 34 per cent from 2015 to 2050 (Council of the European Union, 2023, preambular recital 14). It will therefore be impossible to achieve the goals of the Paris Agreement without addressing international transport emissions.

The international governance of GHG emissions from international transport (aviation and shipping) is structured in a fundamentally different way to MEAs such as the Paris Agreement and the UNCLOS and its implementing agreements including the

BBNJ agreement. This different approach, introduced below, has major implications for the provision of multilateral finance for technology development and transfer.

International transport emissions have been dealt with differently to national emissions since the early years of the UNFCCC regime. In 1995, the UNFCCC COP decided that it would 'address the issue of the allocation and control of emissions from international bunker fuels' 'taking fully into account ongoing work' in the ICAO and IMO (Decision 4/CP.1). The 1997 Kyoto Protocol added that Annex I Parties which had joined the protocol 'shall' control aviation and shipping emissions 'working through' the ICAO and IMO respectively (Article 2.2). (This binding reference to work through the two transport bodies, of course, applies only to a minority of states who are responsible for a steadily diminishing proportion of annual emissions.)

Since these early decisions, the ICAO and IMO have been left to respond (or not) to the challenge of international transport emissions without much input from the UNFCCC COP and its subsidiary bodies, which are regularly deadlocked and unable to produce substantive outcomes on these matters. In sum, the deadlock results from the fact that developing parties in the UNFCCC want to apply the principle of common but differentiated responsibilities and respective capabilities (CBDR-RC) to the shipping and aviation processes, while developed parties object that this principle is not part of the ICAO and IMO legal orders and that treating emissions differently based on vessel nationality would be unworkable and self-defeating (Ringbom, 2021, pp. 132–135).

The ICAO is addressing international aviation emissions through a 'basket of measures' that include aircraft technologies, operational improvements, sustainable aviation fuels (SAFs), and the Carbon Offsetting and Reduction Scheme for International Aviation (CORSIA), which is the first global market-based mechanism for a particular industry. CORSIA is currently in a voluntary first phase with, however, the participation of 127 states. In 2022, ICAO parties adopted a 'collective long-term global aspirational goal for international aviation (LTAG) of net-zero carbon emissions by 2050' (ICAO, 2022, p. 6).

Mobilisation of financial support for technology transfer would be a new challenge for the ICAO and its legal order. The 2022 resolution adopting the 2050 target also affirmed that 'specific measures to assist developing States as well as to facilitate access to financial support, technology transfer and capacity building should be initiated as soon as possible'. It called on the ICAO Council (the governing body that takes decisions while the plenary Assembly is not in session) to take several actions to assist developing states. These include to 'initiate specific measures or mechanisms' to facilitate access to private investment and funding from financial institutions, 'further consider the establishment of a climate finance initiative or funding mechanism under ICAO', and 'promote the voluntary transfer of technology, in particular for developing countries and States having particular needs, to enable them to adapt to cutting-edge technology and to enhance their contribution to achieve the LTAG'. The same resolution, however, simultaneously acknowledged the Paris Agreement principle of 'common but differentiated responsibilities and respective capabilities, in light of different national circumstances' and the 'principles of non-discrimination and equal and fair opportunities to develop international aviation' of the ICAO's founding charter, the Chicago Convention. The design of measures consistent with both international climate law and international aviation law represents a difficult circle to square.

For its part, the IMO through its Marine Environment Protection Committee (MEPC) has developed regulations for shipping emissions. In 2011, the MEPC amended the 1973 Convention for the Prevention of Pollution from Ships (MARPOL) to create requirements concerning the energy efficiency of ships (both existing and new builds). The amendments entered into force in 2013. These regulations apply to internationally trading ships of 400 gross tonnage or above. All such ships are required to have a Ship Energy Efficiency Management Plan (SEEMP) in place, while new ships are rated against a technology-neutral Energy Efficiency Design Index (EEDI). In 2016, the MEPC adopted a further requirement for ships of 5,000 gross tonnage or above (accounting for around 85 per cent of CO_2 emissions from international shipping) to report their fuel oil consumption. The data is reported to the relevant flag state, which shares the data with the IMO and issues a Statement of Compliance. The IMO has however decided that this data is confidential.

The MEPC went further in 2018 by adopting an Initial IMO Strategy on Reduction of GHG Emissions from Ships, which targeted a reduction of international shipping emissions by at least 50 per cent by 2050 and introduced new mandatory measures. The strategy aims for consistency with the Paris Agreement temperature goals and sets the targets of reducing international shipping emissions by at least 40 per cent by 2030 and 50 per cent by 2050, compared to 2008. Many stakeholders criticised these targets as insufficiently ambitious. The strategy includes as 'short-term measures' the Energy Efficiency Existing Ship Index (EEXI), which measures the energy efficiency of ships against a strengthened EEDI and requires ships to meet minimum energy efficiency standards, and the Carbon Intensity Indicator (CII), an annual measure of the carbon intensity of ships of 5,000 gross tonnage or above which provides for 'corrective action plans' to be introduced in the case of poor performance. Both measures became mandatory at the beginning of 2023.

The growth of IMO policy and measures targeting shipping emissions, which apply also to ships from developing countries, has led to demands for technology transfer. Following the amendment to MARPOL, the MEPC adopted in 2013 a resolution on 'promotion of technical co-operation and transfer of technology relating to the improvement of energy efficiency of ships'. Noting the IMO principles of 'non-discrimination' and 'no more favourable treatment' as well as the UNFCCC principle of CBDR-RC, the resolution called on the IMO to provide technical assistance and assist in 'sourcing of funding' for states, particularly developing states, requesting technology transfer (IMO, 2013, para. 1). The same document recorded that technology transfer 'needs to respect property rights, including intellectual property rights, and to be on mutually agreed terms and conditions'. Further steps in providing assistance for developing parties included the creation of an Integrated Technical Cooperation Programme and a Multi-donor GHG Trust Fund. By the time of writing, the IMO had developed several small-scale initiatives with technology transfer components (summarised at IMO, 2023, p. 15ff).

In July 2023, the MEPC adopted a new 'strategy on reduction of GHG emissions from ships' that aligns with the ICAO target and the broader agenda for net-zero by 2050. The new IMO strategy sets an ambition to 'peak GHG emissions from international shipping as soon as possible and to reach net-zero GHG emissions by or around, i.e. close to, 2050, taking into account different national circumstances', and nominates 'indicative' emission reduction targets for 2030 and 2040 (IMO, 2023, p. 6). In 2025, the IMO adopted draft regulations for a 'net-zero framework', including a carbon pricing mechanism. The framework, subject to final approval by parties, includes the creation of an IMO Net-Zero Fund which would disburse revenue from carbon transactions, *inter alia*, for zero emissions technology R&D and technology transfer (IMO, 2025, Regulation 41).

3.3 High seas

The provision for development and transfer of marine technology (TMT) in the 2023 BBNJ agreement can be seen as a reaction to the very limited implementation of the technology transfer clauses of the UN Convention on the Law of the Sea (UNCLOS) (for an overview, see Minas, 2021b). The BBNJ agreement under the UNCLOS has created the potential for increased technology support including financing, at least concerning the roughly two-thirds of the ocean that are beyond national jurisdiction.

The BBNJ agreement, formally the agreement under the United Nations Convention on the Law of the Sea on the conservation and sustainable use of marine biological diversity of areas beyond national jurisdiction, is the result of two decades of negotiation in various formats. These negotiations addressed the particular challenge of crafting a multilateral regime for the protection of an environment that cannot be subjected to national jurisdiction and where one group of states cannot impose regulations on another group. The resulting agreement, adopted at an intergovernmental conference in June 2023, is 'under' the UNCLOS. As an implementing agreement of the UNCLOS, it is designed to give practical effect to aspects of the Convention's general rules on the protection of the high seas, including with respect to technology transfer. Indeed, the UN General Assembly's mandate for negotiation specified that capacity-building and transfer of marine technology would be one of the four pillars of the eventual agreement, together with marine genetic resources, area-based management tools including marine protected areas, and environmental impact assessments.

It is noteworthy that the agreement includes an expansive definition of 'marine technology', which:

> includes, inter alia, information and data, provided in a user-friendly format, on marine sciences and related marine operations and services; manuals, guidelines, criteria, standards and reference materials; sampling and methodology equipment; observation facilities

> and equipment for in situ and laboratory observations, analysis and experimentation; computer and computer software, including models and modelling techniques; related biotechnology; and expertise, knowledge, skills, technical, scientific and legal know-how and analytical methods related to the conservation and sustainable use of marine biological diversity. (Article 1.10)

This text is drawn from the 2003 IOC-UNESCO 'Criteria and Guidelines on the Transfer of Marine Technology', with some modifications and additions. The absence of practical follow-up in the years following the adoption of the IOC document contributed to developing states' calls for robust technology provisions in the BBNJ agreement (Long, 2022, p. 80). The IOC document's previously unimplemented definition of marine technology has now gained a second life by incorporation into the new treaty. The definition is complemented by details on '[t]ypes of capacity-building and of the transfer of marine technology' in Article 44 and Annex II of the agreement. The definition and open-ended list of activities create the potential for a wide programme of work to assist developing states. The agreed definition of marine technology and indicative list of technology transfer activities constitutes an advance on the UNFCCC regime, in which parties have never reached a consensus on what 'climate technology' is or on what technology development and transfer entail.

The objectives of the capacity-building and TMT part of the agreement relevantly include to '[d]evelop the marine scientific and technological capacity, including with respect to research, of Parties, in particular developing States Parties, with regard to the conservation and sustainable use of [BBNJ], including through access to marine technology by, and the transfer of marine technology to, developing States Parties' and to support developing parties of various categories through capacity-building and TMT to achieving the objectives regarding the other three pillars of the agreement (Article 40). These objectives are to be achieved through cooperation among parties and with 'all relevant stakeholders' (Article 41). Reflecting prior experiences of capacity-building and technology transfer, the agreement states that parties 'shall ensure' that provision of this assistance is 'not conditional on onerous reporting requirements' (Article 41.3).

The agreement sets out modalities of capacity-building and TMT, taken together, and additional modalities for TMT specifically. These modalities reflect the lived experience of the UNFCCC regime and other multilateral environmental agreements in which technology transfer has been operationalised. These elements include the need to take into account the 'special circumstances' of small island developing states and least developed countries, the preference for 'country-driven' (as opposed to top-down or standardised) capacity-building and TMT and the role of 'needs assessments' in shaping assistance (Article 42). Moreover, the requirement that 'Parties shall provide, within their capabilities, resources to support such capacity-building and the development and transfer of marine technology and to facilitate access to other sources of support' (Article 42.2) reflects a trend towards broadening donor bases by not limiting obligations to developed countries (which in practice will nevertheless provide the majority of public finance for the foreseeable future).

The modalities specific to TMT likewise incorporate precedents from earlier MEAs. The provision of TMT modalities copies almost word-for-word the opening paragraph of the Paris Agreement's provision on technology, which provides: 'Parties share a long-term vision on the importance of fully realizing technology development and transfer in order to improve resilience to climate change and to reduce greenhouse gas emissions' (Article 10.1). The equivalent provision in the BBNJ agreement records that: 'Parties share a long-term vision of the importance of fully realizing technology development and transfer for inclusive, equitable and effective cooperation and participation in the activities undertaken under this Agreement and in order to fully achieve its objectives' (Article 43.1). This language was introduced during the final intergovernmental negotiating session and the 'long-term vision' concept helps to bridge the divide between developed and developing states. In the case of the Paris Agreement, the 'long-term vision' was given substance by the detailed technology framework providing overarching guidance to the UNFCCC technology bodies, agreed by the Conference of Parties serving as the meeting of parties to the Paris Agreement (CMA) in 2018 (Minas, 2021a). It is implicit in the BBNJ agreement that its COP will play a similar role, as detailed below.

Consistent with the history reviewed in section 2 above, specific instances of technology transfer are by agreement rather than compulsory. Article 43.2 provides that TMT 'shall take place on fair and most favourable terms, including on concessional and preferential terms, and in accordance with mutually agreed terms and conditions as well as the objectives of this Agreement'. This language draws heavily on the Convention on Biological Diversity (Article 16.2), its Nagoya Protocol (Annex 2), and the International Treaty on Plant Genetic Resources for Food and Agriculture (Article 13.2).

In addition to drawing on textual precedents from earlier MEAs, the BBNJ agreement provides that capacity-building and TMT 'shall build upon, as appropriate, and not duplicate existing programmes and be guided by lessons learned, including those from capacity-building and transfer of marine technology activities under relevant legal instruments and frameworks and relevant global, regional, subregional and sectoral bodies' (Article 42.3). This will require the agreement's parties to have regard to existing technology transfer processes when putting the agreement into practice.

In addition to the provisions adapted from earlier MEAs, what distinguishes the BBNJ agreement from the TMT provisions of the UNCLOS is the institutional architecture established by the 2023 document, which creates the prospect of actual implementation. The key institutions, similarly if not identically to the UNFCCC regime, are a COP, a capacity-building and transfer of marine technology committee ('the committee'), a clearing-house mechanism, and a financial mechanism.

The COP established at Article 47 includes all parties and performs the supreme decision-making function under the treaty, replicating the familiar model of MEA governance (Brunnée, 2002). Concerning TMT, the COP has several functions, including electing the committee and considering and acting on its reports and recommendations (Article 46) and to 'periodically, as necessary, review, assess and further develop and provide guidance on the indicative and non-exhaustive list of types of capacity-building and of transfer of marine technology elaborated in Annex II, to reflect technological progress and innovation and to respond and adapt to the evolving needs of States, subregions and regions' (Article 44). The COP is also to determine the modalities of, and assign functions to, the Clearing-House Mechanism (Article 51) and provide guidance on 'overall strategies, policies, programme priorities and eligibility for access to and utilization of financial resources' (Article 52.9).

The committee, whose members are to possess 'appropriate qualifications and expertise' and 'serve objectively in the best interest of the Agreement', is to 'submit reports and recommendations that the Conference of the Parties shall consider and take action on as appropriate' (Article 46). These attributes and functions closely track those of the TEC in the UNFCCC regime, as does the requirement for equitable geographical representation and dedicated seats for small island developing states and least developed countries (with the addition, in the BBNJ context, of 'landlocked developing states'). The committee 'under the authority' of the COP will periodically monitor and review capacity-building and TMT, aiming at the assessment of developing party needs, reviewing support provided and identifying and mobilising funds, *inter alia* (Article 45). Again, this competence mirrors the TEC's role in technology needs assessments and its linkages with the UNFCCC Financial Mechanism. The committee will also receive reports from Parties concerning 'monitoring and review' of capacity-building and TMT (Article 45.3).

The Clearing-House Mechanism established in Article 51 has functions including to '[f]acilitate the matching of capacity-building needs with the support available and with providers for the transfer of marine technology' and to serve as a 'centralized platform' of information on TMT. To be managed by the agreement's secretariat and consisting 'primarily of an open-access platform' (Article 51.2), the mechanism does not match the structure of the CTCN but has a similar purpose regarding technology transfer (as well as other purposes which are not technology-specific).

The agreement establishes a financial mechanism which is to 'assist developing States Parties in implementing this Agreement, including through funding in support of capacity-building and the transfer of marine technology' (Article 52.3). The mechanism includes several components. Of these, the GEF and a 'special fund' (to be funded from various sources) are to fund 'capacity-building projects under this Agreement, including effective projects on the conservation and sustainable use of marine biological diversity and activities and programmes, including training related to the transfer of marine technology', as well as more broadly to assist developing parties in implementing the agreement (Article 52.6). The GEF had signalled its willingness to operate as a funding body under the agreement and welcomed the agreement's finalisation (GEF, 2023). In February 2024, the GEF Council approved guidelines for GEF support to countries to prepare for and to ratify the agreement (GEF, 2024). The broader context for BBNJ financing is that Sustainable Development Goal 14 ('life below water') is 'the most underfunded SDG' (UNDP, 2022), making effective new arrangements to support marine TDT especially urgent.

The agreement will come into force only after sixty parties ratify or otherwise assent to it (Article 68.1). Until then, the agreement's signatories have the opportunity to prepare for its entry into force, including by building informal consensus on how the agreement is to be operationalised.

4. Key issues in multilateral financing for environmentally sound technology development and transfer

This account has shown financing for EST technology development and transfer to be at different stages and shaped by different principles and procedures in the legal regimes under study. Nevertheless, certain issues present themselves recurrently across these regimes, suggesting that these issues concern EST technology financing in general. As such, a summary of these issues and some suggestions on how to approach them may assist the further development and implementation of EST technology financing frameworks.

First, the consensus-based and therefore voluntary nature of technology transfer has been seen to create a practical requirement for multilateral finance and other forms of support to assist recipient states. With compulsory technology transfer decisively off the agenda in the studied regimes, there will often be a requirement for financing and other forms of support (such as capacity-building) to enable poorer states to access ESTs on concessional (better-than-market) terms (Lee et al., 2023). Multilateral mechanisms have been mobilising such support through several decades of trial-and-error and institutional experimentation.

Second, the particular relationship between legal context and the scope for multilateral technology support will condition what is possible in any given regime. As different treaties enshrine different principles and provide for different procedures, it has not been possible for a single approach to multilateral financing for TDT to emerge. Rather, it has been and will continue to be necessary to evolve bespoke approaches that account for the relevant international legal context. Where the legal context recognises the principle of CBDR-RC or something like it, and the special circumstances of developing countries and subcategories of developing countries, the creation of dedicated technology and financial mechanisms has followed as a logical corollary. Where, however, the legal order acknowledges different principles that militate against differentiated treatment, as in the case of the IMO and the ICAO, there is less scope for the creation of dedicated structures. Greater reliance on ad hoc and legally non-binding 'initiatives' may be required (Chen, 2021).

Third, the design of multilateral mechanisms is a key factor to consider regarding mobilisation of finance for TDT. This issue emerges both from the experience of the UNFCCC regime but also from the choices made by negotiators in the drafting of the BBNJ agreement. In particular, the creation of separate technology and financial mechanisms can be effective but also generates several challenges. These include the potential lack of steady funding for the technology bodies, the need to develop functioning linkages between the technology and financial bodies and the mismatches in organisational cultures and procedures that can sometimes arise (see, e.g., Oh, 2020). Questions of decision also include the structuring of regulatory dialogue between the particular bodies and the main decision-making body of the relevant regime, e.g., the UNFCCC COP, and the incorporation of modalities to mobilise external expertise, financial and in-kind capacity, e.g., through the creation of a 'network'.

Fourth, the incorporation of technology support into the general programming of financial bodies presents as an opportunity for ramping up support. There are arguments of efficiency and scale in favour of incorporating technology financing into the overall funding of bodies such as the GEF and GCF, rather than having dedicated technology 'windows' or programmes. To be effective, such mainstreaming of technology support needs to be built into the activity requirements, documentation and reporting of financial bodies. Against these arguments, however, is the expressed preference of some developing countries to have dedicated channels of technology support and the desire to have decisions on technology finance made by bodies such as the COP rather than by the World Bank or associated institutions. It is likely that these debates will re-emerge if and when the BBNJ agreement enters into force and its COP convenes for the first time.

Fifth, the creation of enabling environments in recipient states is of vital importance (TEC, 2022). There is an ongoing need for financial support not only to facilitate the transfer of particular technologies but also to strengthen the enabling environments of recipient states, including policy and legal frameworks, as well as the capacity of government and other actors, so that their capacity to develop and access technology improves. There is, however, a tension between the need for such support and the focus of some on the implementation of 'hardware' transfers.

Sixth, and finally, the place of multilateral mechanisms in the broader transition of finance flows merits urgent attention. Even greatly expanded multilateral mechanisms would be able to mobilise only a minority of the funding necessary for technological uptake to bring the goals of the legal regimes discussed within reach (SCF, 2022, pp. 7ff). Therefore, actions to strengthen multilateral funding arrangements should be coordinated within the broader agenda to make financing in general sustainable, as reflected in Article 2.1(c) of the Paris Agreement and the growing body of national and regional sustainable finance frameworks (see also Bowman and Tayler, this volume). Practically, this will require a growing focus on co-financing and innovative finance. These modalities will be required not just to finance ESTs but to support the phase-out of environmentally harmful technologies in a manner acceptable to states with pressing developmental challenges.

Certain questions arise from these issues, the consideration of which is beyond the scope of this chapter, and which would merit research. These questions range from the conceptual to the stolidly practical. At the conceptual level, one wonders whether a contemporary reinterpretation of principles such as CBDR-RC would assist in broadening the financial donor base to reflect current international political economy. The deepening contradiction between the 1992 bifurcation of developed and developing countries and the contemporary global distribution of capital continues to operate as a handbrake on multilateral EST financing, despite ameliorating measures such as the exclusion of lists of countries from the Paris Agreement. There is scope for scholarship to inform such a reinterpretation, which would more likely be realised through informal understandings than formal negotiation.

Another broad question would be how multilateral technology financing fits into the larger agenda of transforming global finance flows. This concerns the Paris Agreement 2.1(c) goal but also the broader push to make finance environmentally sustainable. As I have written elsewhere, achieving such goals would 'amount to a normative reorientation of the financial system away from traditionally dominant (at least in the West) accounts of its purpose as a neutral and efficient allocator of resources' (Minas, 2022, p. 378). The privileging of sustainability objectives in the redirection of finance flows should bolster financing for ESTs. However, there is an ongoing need to translate overarching finance flows goals into institutional strategies and programming criteria. This is ultimately a question of transnational legal process: effecting the necessary feedbacks between broad goals adopted in treaties and decisions of international conferences, and operational policies developed through international institutional law, implementation on the plane of domestic law, and the alignment of financial standards including through both regulatory and voluntary measures.

At the levels of intergovernmental negotiation and multistakeholder coordination, there is the question of whether an institutional 'home' can be found for the periodic exchange of experiences and lessons learned concerning EST financing under various treaty-based and other processes. The potential value of such a process increases with the ongoing addition of new technology and financial mechanisms resulting from multilateral negotiation. Research might focus on precedents for cross-process stocktaking and inter-institutional learning in the international system, how such precedents could be adapted for the specific issue of EST financing, and where such a process could be mandated and hosted.

There is scope for research to inform the production of a practical toolkit to assist states in crafting legal and regulatory conditions that can facilitate inbound financing for ESTs. Such research could build on previous scholarship concerning contextual factors for national legislation (e.g., Scotford and Minas, 2018) but with greater focus and depth on domestic frameworks to enable technology development and transfer.

Finally, it would be Panglossian to imagine that the major geopolitical upheavals of current times will leave EST financing untouched. There is an evident need for research to probe both the risks and the opportunities that geopolitical change presents for multilateral EST financing. At a practical level, this is a question not just of 'keeping the show on the road' in the UN system and international financial institutions, but also exploring the scope for other formats, such as the BRICS, to contribute. At the normative level, there is a growing need for research (perhaps drawing on Cold War precedents) to identify bases for privileging certain 'existential' issues (such as the preservation of planetary boundaries) as exceptions to major power and bloc confrontation.

5. Conclusion

This chapter has traced the development of multilateral technology financing from the contest over a 'New International Economic Order' and compulsory technology transfer to the implementation of less sweeping technology transfer provisions in three regimes at different stages of development and under different normative frameworks: the UNFCCC system, the ICAO and IMO arrangements for international transport emission regulation, and the long-negotiated BBNJ agreement. This study has enabled the identification of certain key issues that will continue to bear on the success of financing mechanisms for technology transfer in a variety of different contexts.

When set against the vast needs of the climate transition and ocean conservation, the level of finance provided by these multilateral mechanisms for technology development and transfer may indeed seem like a drop in the ocean. What emerges from this study, however, is that choices in design and implementation can strengthen the outputs of these mechanisms, especially in the context of iterative governance systems which provide the opportunity for regular review and decision-making. At the same time, it is necessary to be realistic about the scale of multilateral mechanisms and to have appropriate focus on their capacity to act as a lever for the broader financial transition, unlocking vaster finance flows than will be forthcoming from donors alone.

References

Anderson, S.O., Sarma, M.K. and Taddonio, K.N. (2007) (eds) *Technology transfer for the ozone layer: lessons for climate change*. Earthscan.

Bowman, M. and Minas, S. (2019) 'Resilience through interlinkage: The Green Climate Fund and climate finance governance', *Climate Policy*, 19(3), pp. 342–353.

Brunnée, J. (2002) 'COPing with consent: law-making under multilateral environmental agreement', *Leiden Journal of International Law*, 15(1), pp. 1–52.

Chen, Y. (2021) 'Reconciling common but differentiated responsibilities principle and no more favourable treatment principle in regulating greenhouse gas emissions from international shipping', *Marine Policy*, 123, 104317, pp. 1–9.

COP/CMA (2023) *Decision 1/CP.28 and Decision 5/CMA.5, Operationalization of the new funding arrangements, including a fund, for responding to loss and damage referred to in paragraphs 2–3 of decisions 2/CP.27 and 2/CMA.4*.

Council of the European Union (2023) *Proposal for a Directive of the European Parliament and of the Council amending Directive 2003/87/EC establishing a system for greenhouse gas emission allowance trading within the Union, Decision (EU) 2015/1814 concerning the establishment and operation of a market stability reserve for the Union greenhouse gas emission trading scheme and Regulation (EU) 2015/757, 6210/23.* Brussels, 8 February 2023.

CTCN (2024) *Technology solutions & innovation for climate action: 10th anniversary report.* https://www.ctc-n.org/sites/default/files/resources/CTCN%2010%20year%20progress%20report.pdf

GCF (2023) *Twelfth report of the Green Climate Fund to the Conference of the Parties to the United Nations Framework Convention on Climate Change.*

GEF (2023) *The GEF to expand ocean support under new high seas treaty* [Press release]. 6 March 2023. Available at: https://www.thegef.org/newsroom/press-releases/gef-expand-ocean-support-under-new-high-seas-treaty

GEF (2024) *Initial guidelines for enabling activities and ratification support projects for the Agreement under the United Nations Convention on the Law of the Sea on the Conservation and Sustainable Use of Marine Biological Diversity of Areas beyond National Jurisdiction (BBNJ).*

ICAO (2022) *Resolution A41-21: Consolidated statement of continuing ICAO policies and practices related to environmental protection – Climate change.*

IMO (2013) *Resolution on the promotion of technical co-operation and transfer of technology relating to the improvement of energy efficiency of ships.*

IMO (2020) *Fourth IMO GHG study 2020: executive summary.*

IMO (2023) *Strategy on reduction of GHG emissions from ships.*

IMO (2025) *Draft revised MARPOL Annex VI.*

Lee, N. *et al.* (2023) *Concessional climate finance: is the MDB architecture working?* Center for Global Development.

Long, R. (2022) 'Striking an equitable balance under the Biodiversity Agreement: the elusive case of new technologies, maritime genetic resources and the Global South', in Kraska, J. and Park, Y.K. (eds) *Emerging technology and the law of the sea.* Cambridge University Press.

Minas, S. (2021a) 'Paris Agreement's technology framework and the need for transformational change', *Carbon and Climate Law Review,* 14(4), pp. 241–254.

Minas, S. (2021b) 'Technology transfer for the high seas: potential modalities for technology transfer under the international legally binding instrument', in Zou, K. and Telesetsky, A. (eds) *Marine scientific research, new marine technologies and the law of the sea.* Brill.

Minas, S. (2022) 'Financing climate justice in the European Union and China: common mechanisms, different perspectives', *Asia Europe Journal,* 20(4), pp. 377–401.

Oh, C. (2020) 'Contestations over the financial linkages between the UNFCCC's Technology and Financial Mechanism: using the lens of institutional interaction' *International Environmental Agreements,* 20(3), pp. 559–575.

Proceedings of the United Nations Conference on Trade and Development (1964), A.IV.26 Annexes 57, U.N. Doc. E/CONFA6/141, Vol. I.

Ringbom, H. (2021) 'Regulating greenhouse gases from ships: some light at the end of the funnel?' in Johansen, E., Busch, S.V. and Jakobsen, I.U. (eds) *The law of the sea and climate change: solutions and constraints.* Cambridge University Press.

Sand, P.H. (1992) 'UNCED and the development of international environmental law', *Yearbook of International Environmental Law,* 3(1), pp. 3–17.

Scotford, E. and Minas, S. (2018) 'Probing the hidden depths of climate law: analysing national climate change legislation', RECIEL, 28(1), pp. 67–81.

Standing Committee on Finance (SCF) (2022) *Fifth biennial assessment and overview of climate finance flows.*

Technology Executive Committee (TEC) (2022) *Enabling environments and challenges to technology development and transfer.*

UNCED (1992) *Agenda 21.*

UNCTAD (1985) *Draft international code of conduct on the transfer of technology as of 5 June 1985*. TD/CODE/TECHNOLOGY TRANSFER/47.

UNDP (2022) *The ocean and the blue economy are fundamental to addressing the triple planetary crisis – says UNDP* [Press release] 8 June 2022. Available at: https://www.undp.org/press-releases/ocean-and-blue-economy-are-fundamental-addressing-triple-planetary-crisis-says-undp

UNFCCC (2023) *Second biennial communications in accordance with Article 9, paragraph 5, of the Paris Agreement*. Revised compilation and synthesis report by the secretariat, 25 August.

UNGA (1974) *Programme of action on the establishment of a new international economic order*. G.A. Res. 3202, S-VI U.N. GAOR, Supp. (No. 1), U.N. Doc. A/9559.

5

Law and the International Financial Architecture: pathways and pivot points for achieving Paris objectives

Megan Bowman and Tom Tayler[1]

1. Introduction

The 2015 Paris Agreement under the United Nations Framework Convention on Climate Change (UNFCCC) contains three objectives that can be summarised as the *temperature guardrail*, the *adaptation ambition*, and the *finance imperative*. These objectives are set out in Article 2 and exhort countries to, respectively: limit global warming to well below 2°C and pursue efforts towards 1.5°C above pre-industrial levels (Article 2.1(a)); increase climate resilience through adaptation (Article 2.1(b)); and make finance flows consistent with a pathway towards a low carbon and climate resilient world (Article 2.1(c)), all in the context of sustainable development and efforts to eradicate poverty (Article 2.1).

The problem is that we are not on track to meet these objectives. The first Global Stocktake of progress towards achieving Paris Agreement commitments was held in 2023 pursuant to Article 14 of that Agreement. That Global Stocktake confirmed that global emissions are not consistent with the temperature guardrail and that there is a 'rapidly narrowing window' to implement commitments and increase ambition (UNFCCC, 2023). More starkly, recent scientific conclusions of the Intergovernmental Panel on Climate Change (IPCC, 2022) and the United Nations Environment Programme (UNEP, 2022) present a world on track for 3°C warming by the end of the century *unless* global greenhouse gas emissions are reduced by 43 per cent by 2030 (IPCC, 2022; Ripple et al., 2024). The 2023 Global Stocktake identified key implementation activities as rapidly deploying cleaner technologies, particularly for the benefit of developing countries, transitioning away from fossil fuels in energy systems, enhancing capacity-building and needs-based cooperation, and scaling up and strategically deploying international public and private finance. In short, it will require multi-sectoral and multi-scalar efforts, behavioural and technological changes, and the investment of vast amounts of money.

Specifically regarding investment, the 2023 Global Stocktake expressly identified that '[m]aking financial flows – international and domestic, public and private – consistent with a pathway toward low greenhouse gas emission and climate resilient development *entails creating opportunities to unlock trillions of dollars and shift investments to climate action across scales*' (emphasis added) (UNFCCC, 2023, item 15). Implicit in this sentence is the acknowledgement that mobilising finance at scale to flow in the same direction *toward* a low-carbon and climate-resilient world and, concomitantly, *away from* high-emissions activities will require concerted input from *all* actors within the global financial system. It further recognised 'the role of the private sector and the need to strengthen policy guidance, incentives, regulations and enabling conditions to reach the scale of investments required to achieve a global transition towards low greenhouse gas emissions and climate-resilient development' (UNFCCC, 2024a, item 70).

Accordingly, the global financial system and the way it is governed, regulated, and supervised is critical to the achievement of the *finance imperative* of the Paris Agreement. This system, known as the 'International Financial Architecture', is framed by the United Nations (UN) as the governance arrangements that safeguard the stability and function of global monetary and financial systems (UN, 2023). Yet a precise and consistent definition remains elusive, and the architecture can be perceived in different ways depending on one's ideological and jurisdictional standpoints, which belies a lack of common understanding about whether, how, and even *if* the system needs to adapt to contemporary priorities. Many commentators limit their conception of the International Financial Architecture to Multilateral Development Banks (MDBs) and International Finance Institutions (IFIs). Historically, the main focus of the global climate finance system has been MDBs and this remains the case in many forums. Multilateral and bilateral channels of finance are traditionally accepted as the way of moving development aid and debt between advanced economies and emerging economies or, using Paris Agreement parlance, developed countries and developing countries. Indeed, some prominent calls for reviews of the International Financial Architecture have been limited to this public milieu, as exemplified by the *Bridgetown Initiative for the Reform of the Global Financial Architecture* (Barbados Government, 2022) which proposes reforms to World Bank and International Finance Corporation (IFC) processes and structures for the benefit of indebted developing countries.

Nonetheless, we argue that the International Financial Architecture must also be understood as including capital markets, their regulators and supervisors, and private institutions that participate in these markets. These are the engines, channels, and allocators of much of the finance around the world, and can be the facilitators of the required amount of investment to help deliver on Paris Agreement goals and the net zero transition as identified in the 2023 Global Stocktake. We understand that this proposition is contentious. Capital markets continue to overwhelmingly invest in, lend to, and underwrite a global economy that is out of alignment with the Paris Agreement's three objectives due to reasons ranging from the banal (market imperfections and business case heuristics) to the unjust (structural inequalities and historical legacies). This fundamental misalignment perpetuates the status quo and impedes a timely transition. Acknowledging that global annual financial flows to address climate mitigation across sectors are a factor of three to six times below the investment needed up to 2030 (IPCC, 2022), and that re-alignment could potentially redirect some US$500 trillion of assets (McKinsey, 2021) toward Paris objectives, it is clear that misalignments need systemic rectification. Indeed, the Sharm El-Sheikh Implementation Plan, representing the outcome text of climate talks at COP27 in 2022, explicitly noted that financing the transition will itself '*require a transformation of the financial system and its structures and processes*, engaging governments, central banks, commercial banks, institutional investors and other financial actors' (emphasis added) (UNFCCC, 2022), a sentiment that has also been expressed in earlier scholarly and policy work (Chenet et al., 2019; Minas, 2021; Robins, 2022).

Yet it is critical to understand that capital markets and private financial institutions will not magically self-mobilise or self-reform to fulfil public interest objectives. Market distortions and failures – such as monopoly power, information asymmetry, or externalities – are now accepted as barriers to effective self-regulation (Hahn, 1981; Greenwald and Stiglitz, 1986). As such, in the absence of government and regulatory action to incentivise activity that aligns with Paris and other sustainability objectives, markets are unlikely to be a powerful force in supporting their delivery. In short, the lack of a coherent global economic framework of legal, regulatory, and fiscal policy measures that all point *in the same direction* to implement Paris imperatives means that financial flows of all types remain fundamentally misaligned.

Harnessing, steering, and especially commanding private capital for public benefit requires proactive leadership from governments, legislators, and regulators (Bowman, 2015, 2022; Tayler, 2023). As such, we argue for a further expansion of the International Financial Architecture to include key national and transnational legal and regulatory actors that are tasked with steering domestic financial market participants, namely Treasuries and finance ministries, legislators, central banks, and prudential and financial regulators. In other words, there is a need not only for greater investment to support the transition but also for 'fit for purpose' law and regulation that animates Article 2.1(c) to ensure that finance is flowing systematically and at scale to where it is needed most.

The complex and contested nature of this space must also be articulated. Thorny themes of transparency, accountability, collaboration, and coordination intermesh (and clash) in ways that highlight how finance sits at the heart of the equity debate between developed and developing countries, and how law and regulation can either enable or obfuscate a timely transition. Arguably, providing and facilitating flows of climate finance can be regarded as more than just a legal imperative or instrumental necessity; it also embodies a symbol of trust between advanced and emerging economies, which in turn influences the actual and perceived role of private sector actors. For reasons of historical legacy and intra-generational justice on the one hand, and counter-tactics of gaming and procrastination on the other hand, there is currently a trust deficit alongside financial gaps within the Architecture. So this chapter highlights the need for a 'trust transition' to embrace a spirit of collective responsibility and accountability and a fair division of labour regarding which actors and channels need to be engaged. These are the qualitative dimensions of climate finance (Naidoo et al., 2023), and mobilizing them belies a collective action problem that needs cooperation and collaboration to address.

The aim of this chapter is to analyse and substantiate the above claims and to raise some big picture ideas for addressing systemic change that extends beyond our previous work and complements other chapters in this book that focus on discrete legal tools and areas such as company law (Foerster, 2026), trade law (Getachew, 2026), tax law (Latif, 2026), public procurement rules (Lesniewska, 2026), digital currencies (Raisey-Skeats et al., 2026), and corporate litigation (Knoepfel, 2026).

This chapter proceeds as follows. Section 2 analyses the legal intricacies of the Paris Agreement objectives before identifying gaps and challenges in their implementation in section 3. We then explore two macro-level areas in section 4 that could redress these gaps and challenges: renewal of the International Financial Architecture, and mandating corporate and national-level transition planning. Section 5 concludes the chapter with thoughts for a forward-looking research agenda.

2. The Paris Agreement: 'living law' for climate finance flows

To date, there is still no internationally agreed definition of 'climate finance'. This is despite earlier calls for an agreed definition by some developing countries and regional bodies (e.g., Item 16, European Committee of the Regions, 2017) and a recent exploration of types of definitions by the United Nations Framework Convention on Climate Change (UNFCCC) Standing Committee on Finance (2023). Nonetheless, we can identify traditional *narrow conceptions* of that finance as focusing on state-directed public funding, usually in the form of development aid flowing from developed countries to emerging economies through bilateral or multilateral channels (UNFCCC, 2014). From there we can chart how the 'thinking and doing' of climate finance has evolved by necessity to include private sector finance given that public finance alone cannot implement Paris Agreement imperatives.

2.1 Historical perspectives and traditional conceptions

By way of historical analysis, the 1992 UNFCCC provides in Articles 4(3) and 4(4) that developed countries 'shall provide' financial resources to help developing countries implement the Convention and meet adaptation costs (UNFCCC, 1992). The 2015 Paris Agreement reaffirmed this financial commitment in its Article 9:

> *Developed country Parties shall provide financial resources* to assist developing country Parties with respect to both mitigation and adaptation in continuation of their existing obligations under the Convention. (Art 9(1), emphasis added)[2]

The traditional channels of these 'financial resources' have been bilateral arrangements and/or regional and multilateral development banks and IFIs, such as the World Bank and International Finance Corporation (IFC). It may also occur through the formal channel of the UNFCCC Financial Mechanism (under Article 11 of the UNFCCC) which in turn comprises stipulated 'operating entities' – the Global Environment Facility (GEF) and the Green Climate Fund (GCF). These financial operating entities are therefore creatures of the UNFCCC and subject to COP processes, policies, and politics, with the GCF in particular having a specific mandate to support the Paris Agreement (per Art 9(8) of the Paris Agreement) (Bowman and Minas, 2018).

Thus, in the context of climate law negotiations, climate finance has been regarded as financial assistance from Parties with advanced economies to more vulnerable Parties with the aim of facilitating implementation of the UNFCCC at the national level. In this light, the financial commitment of developed countries as enshrined in Article 9 of the Paris Agreement can be viewed as central to the climate law regime and at least symbolic of state obligation on their part (see e.g., Zhang, 2019; Zahar, 2017; Yamineva, 2016).

Nonetheless, the 2010 Cancun Agreements referred to funds as coming from a 'wide variety of sources, public and private, bilateral and multilateral' (UNFCCC, 2010), and there is increasing recognition amongst states and scholars alike that the trillion dollar investments needed to implement Paris objectives cannot be met by multilateral or public finance alone (see e.g., Pauw et al., 2022; Buchner et al., 2024). The dilemma becomes very clear in the context of the failed promise by developed countries to provide US$100 billion per year by 2020 to address the needs of developing countries and facilitate their treaty implementation (UNFCCC, 2011). The OECD estimated that an annual US$100 billion total was finally reached in 2022 (OECD, 2024a); however, Oxfam calculated that the 'true value' of public climate finance provided was only US$28 billion once market rate loans were excluded (Oxfam, 2024). Either way, the promise was not met. Moreover, the range of estimates of investment *actually* needed to achieve a timely net zero transition is well beyond any of those figures. Estimates sit between US$6.2 trillion and $9.2 trillion per annum up to at least 2030, which McKinsey notes will require a US$3.5 trillion per annum increase on what is flowing today (CPI and Allen & Overy, 2023; McKinsey, 2022).

2.2 Article 2.1(c) of the Paris Agreement: inviting a new approach

Despite the prevalence of Article 9 in discourse about climate finance, recent attention has turned to Article 2.1(c) of the Paris Agreement, which sits in the objectives section and is framed as follows:

> 2.1 This Agreement ... aims to strengthen the global response to the threat of climate change, in the context of sustainable development and efforts to eradicate poverty, including by:
>
> (c) Making finance flows consistent with a pathway towards low GHG emissions and climate resilient development.

Article 2.1(c) garnered little attention from legal scholars or policymakers in the years immediately after 2015.[3] There may be structural reasons for this initial oversight by legal specialists. First, attention was captured by the temperature guardrail in Article 2.1(a), the inclusion of which was momentous as it represented the first time in negotiating history that a concrete temperature had been designated as the benchmark of our collective efforts. Further, Article 2.1(c) was not *explicitly* cross-referenced in obvious places of the Paris Agreement, such as the finance provisions in Article 9 or the transparency framework in Article 13. Moreover, questions of legal bindingness and individual state obligation were the initial focus for legal scholars (e.g., Bodansky, 2016; Bodle and Oberthür, 2016); whereas 2.1(c) is a *collective* goal and of itself does not prescribe specific actions for *individual* Parties.

Nonetheless, given that the entire Paris Agreement is framed around the objectives in Article 2, it can be argued that Article 2.1(c) is pivotal to the treaty's implementation. More specifically, it can be argued that individual Parties and the collective Conference of the Parties (COP) have a legal mandate to bring Article 2.1(c) to life by reference to their obligations which exist elsewhere in the text of the Agreement, and to the explicit and implicit linkages to Article 2 that occur throughout the Agreement.[4] Notably, this is evident in Articles 3 and 4 regarding the multiple obligations associated with Nationally Determined Contributions to Paris implementation (known as NDCs); Article 13 which establishes a 'transparency framework' to 'build mutual trust and confidence and to promote effective implementation' (Art 13.1); and Article 14 which establishes the Global Stocktake requirement to assess collective progress to achieve the goals of the treaty (as described in our Introduction).

It is explicitly cross-referenced with regard to content, communication, and implementation of countries' NDCs, as follows:

- Article 3 provides that 'As nationally determined contributions [NDCs] to the global response to climate change, all Parties are to undertake and communicate ambitious efforts as defined in Articles 4, 7, 9, 10, 11 and 13 *with the view to achieving the purpose of this Agreement as set out in Article 2 …*' (emphasis added).
- Article 13.5 states that the purpose of the transparency framework 'is to provide a clear understanding of climate change action in the light of the objective of the Convention *as set out in its Article 2*' (emphasis added). It further specifies that such actions include 'clarity and tracking of progress towards achieving Parties' individual nationally determined contributions under Article 4, and Parties' adaptation actions under Article 7, including good practices, priorities, needs and gaps, to inform the global stocktake under Article 14'.

It is also implicitly referenced in provisions regarding the role of NDCs in the Global Stocktake and subsequent Paris work programmes, as follows:

- Art 14.1 provides that parties 'shall periodically take stock of the implementation of this Agreement to *assess the collective progress towards achieving the purpose of this Agreement and its long-term goals* (referred to as the "global stocktake")' (emphasis added). By definition this includes Article 2 which enshrines the long-term goals of the Paris Agreement.

- This is buttressed by Article 4.9, which requires that NDCs 'be informed by the outcomes of the global stocktake', and Article 4.2 which states that NDCs must be supported by implementing measures: 'Parties shall pursue domestic mitigation measures, with the aim of achieving the objectives of [NDCs].' As noted in our Introduction to this chapter, the first Global Stocktake in 2023 identified that 'creat[ing] "opportunities to unlock trillions of dollars and shift investments to climate action" is now urgently required globally and also domestically' (UNFCCC, 2023) thereby implicating national-level NDC content and implementation.
- Moreover, Article 15.1 established a Compliance Committee 'to facilitate implementation of and promote compliance with the provisions of this Agreement'. The terms of reference of the Compliance Committee were subsequently decided at the Katowice climate talks in 2018 and stipulate that this Committee 'shall be guided by the provisions of the Paris Agreement, *including its Article 2*' (emphasis added) (UNFCCC (2018) Decision 20/CMA.1, Annex, para 2). Indeed, although Art 2.1(c) was not explicitly mentioned in the Paris Work Programme, it was subsequently cross-referenced in work programmes and decisions under COP24 held in Katowice in 2018 just three years after Paris.

Seven years after the conclusion of the Paris Agreement, the negotiating spotlight finally pinned Article 2.1(c) as an official item of interest. The 2022 Sharm el-Sheikh Implementation Plan arising from COP27 tabled the need to discuss not only the scope of Article 2.1(c) but also its complementarity with Article 9 of the Paris Agreement in future climate talks (Decision 1/CMA.4, par 68). Although it will be for Parties to agree what this Article may allow in the context of implementing and meeting Paris objectives, the remainder of this chapter elucidates its potential for instigating necessary reform in the 'rapidly closing window' to 2030 and the role of law and regulation in facilitating those efforts.

2.3 Evolving conceptions of climate finance

From the preceding analysis, it becomes clear that Article 2.1(c) is pivotal to the implementation of the Paris Agreement. Indeed, it is hard to imagine how the temperature guardrail in Article 2.1(a) can be maintained or the adaptation goal in Article 2.1(b) can be achieved without actualising Article 2.1(c) on finance flows.

As such, we argue that the traditional conception of climate finance has expanded by necessity. The consistent finance flows anticipated by Article 2.1(c) must eventually encompass all flows of finance: domestic and international; public and private; multilateral, bilateral, and market. Unless such a holistic approach to finance is taken, the necessary realignment of the global economy to meet the temperature guardrail and adaptation goal in Article 2.1(a) and (b) will not be possible. Whilst the UNFCCC process recognises the *complementarity* between Article 2.1(c) and Article 9 of the Paris Agreement, particularly under the Sharm el-Sheikh Dialogue, we also argue that as Article 9 specifically reaffirms the commitment of developed country parties to provide financial resources to assist developing parties, Article 2.1(c) must necessarily have a broader and more holistic intention.

Therefore, alongside multilateral and national public finance, it is becoming increasingly clear that markets and private sector actors have a critical role to play in bridging the investment gap that is required for a low carbon transition and climate resilient world (Bowman, 2015; Tayler, 2023). For example, for the first time in climate law negotiating history, the COP26 agenda in 2021 included 'finance' as a discrete agenda item (being the agenda of the 26th Conference of the Parties to the Convention held in Glasgow). This agenda item was framed in terms well beyond Article 9 to embrace private sector finance and the drive to a whole-of-economy transition with the resulting Glasgow Climate Pact referencing 'the need to mobilise climate finance from all sources to reach the level needed to achieve the goals of the Paris Agreement' (UNFCCC, 2021). Moreover, the UNFCCC Secretariat website now describes climate finance as:

> local, national or transnational financing – drawn from public, private and alternative sources of financing – that seeks to support mitigation and adaptation actions that will address climate change. (UNFCCC, n.d.)

This broader and evolving conception of climate finance, whilst not uncontroversial as discussed in section 3 below, remains a standing item on COP agendas.

We posit that Article 2.1(c) ought to be interpreted expansively as a call to action that *all finance for all things*, whether public spending, private investment, mainstream finance, niche projects, domestic or transnational, must start flowing in a consistent direction, namely, towards green, sustainable, and resilient development. Support for this view is (cautiously) found in the recent summary and recommendations of the Sixth Biennial Assessment of the UNFCCC Committee on Finance (2024), which provides an overview of public and private climate finance flows and finds that 'it is also important to ensure the *consistency of finance flows as a whole (and of capital stock)* pursuant to Article 2.1(c) … [such that] *all finance flows … must reduce the likelihood of negative climate outcomes*' (at par 49, emphasis added) and 'encourage[s] Parties to engage with private sector actors in a nationally determined manner on opportunities for implementing Article 2, paragraph 1(c)' (at par 55(d)). Arguably, these statements support an expansive interpretation of 2.1(c) whereby all finance should avoid undermining climate goals, even if not designated as explicitly 'green'. On the ground, we can see initiatives such as *Mainstreaming Climate Change into Banks* as a clear attempt by private financial institutions to animate this expanded logic of Article 2.1(c) through new ways of doing business (Mai, 2026).

In short, we argue that the combined impact of Article 9 with an expansive interpretation of Article 2.1(c) could – and should – instigate fundamental change to 'business as usual' globally. Doing so will not be met without resistance; yet it will be critical to implementing Paris Agreement goals and averting tragedy (Bowman, 2023; Tayler, 2023).

3. Current challenges

Nonetheless, there are current challenges to animating Article 2.1(c) in this expansive way, and to mobilising finance to flow at scale towards green targets in sectors and economies where it is needed most whilst also diverting away from polluting entities and activities.

3.1 Structural misalignments

Despite the Polluter Pays Principle being embedded into the Rio Convention on Environment and Development as a principle that nation states should endeavour to promote (Principle 16), (UN, 1992) and being an OECD-endorsed principle since 1972 (OECD, 1992) there has been a lack of widespread measures at national or international levels that properly cost, let alone penalise, the full impacts of greenhouse gas emissions arising from business as usual. This means that the 'costs' associated with emissions (such as pollution and human rights contraventions) are not reflected on corporate balance sheets and therefore not accurately priced into transactions or assets. As such, money continues to flow around the world to high-emission, low-resilience activities and assets.

The overarching issue is that priorities, rules, and incentives that govern both private and public finance have created a 'persistent misallocation of capital' (IPCC, 2022). The current system encourages an indiscriminate accumulation of capital mostly around the Global North because investment into developing and low-income countries often comes – or is perceived to come – with undesirable risks. High interest rates and high public debt deter conservative private sector investors (such as banks, insurers, and institutional investors); and even the potential for higher returns is not regarded as compensating for such risks. The reason is that flows of market finance will principally be determined by assessment of future profitability via returns. This often involves an ex post and comparative process of 'risk-adjusted return' calculations that compare risks and volatility of investments with a benchmark portfolio, and potentially also a calculation of future anticipated value by estimating cash flows and discounting them into a current valuation (known as 'discounted cashflow analysis'). To risk-averse private sector investors and financiers, these processes create a structural bias *against* climate-related investments that are untested and/or operate in a high-risk policy environment or jurisdiction (UK Government, 2020).

Importantly, regulatory treatment of assets is also a key factor in how financial institutions are incentivised or disincentivised to allocate capital. This is because regulation influences the perceived risk of an asset or country and thus an investor's mindset. For example, for European insurers subject to the Solvency II Directive (Directive 2009/138/EC), an amount of 'prudential capital' must be held by the insurer to guard against the risk of investment default and, if default does occur, to ensure the solvency of the insurer in order to protect its consumers. In this prudential framework, holdings of the sovereign debts of all EU countries in the portfolios of relevant insurers are 'free', such that no capital needs to be held by the insurer against its default; but for investment by the same insurers into the sovereign debt of other (non-EU) countries, the amount of capital to be reserved is impacted by the credit rating ascribed to the country of issue. Developed countries predominantly have higher credit ratings (and are therefore deemed as 'investment grade') and so less prudential capital is required to hold their sovereign debt than is the case for developing countries with lower credit ratings. As prudential capital is set aside and cannot be used for productive investment, insurers will generally seek to invest in financial instruments that require less prudential capital to be held, and as sovereign bonds are a key asset class for insurers, this regulation creates an incentive to keep capital in European and other investment grade countries, rather than to invest in developing countries.

Similarly, the advent of mandatory disclosure reporting in many jurisdictions around the world is forcing financial institutions to identify and report on ex ante risk assessments of investment products, portfolios, and business strategies to account for climate risks and opportunities. Prime examples include amendments to the Listing Rules of the Singapore Exchange Regulation that incorporate the International Financial Reporting Standards (IFRS) Sustainability Disclosure standards into its corporate reporting regime, and the UK roll-out of reporting for companies that are large, listed, and regulated by the Financial Conduct Authority (FCA) that is aligned with the Taskforce on Climate Related Financial Disclosure (TCFD) recommendations. The actual and perceived risks attached to developing country investments and their generally higher carbon intensity can mean that these disclosure regimes have inadvertently created a disincentive for financial firms to invest. This is because firms that wish to show progress in decarbonising their own portfolios under these disclosure regimes may therefore avoid or sell investments that might facilitate development or the climate transition in developing countries, even if no real-world reductions occur from such divestment (a process known as 'paper decarbonisation').

3.2 Trust deficits

In addition to the structural misalignments explored above, the climate finance space is also compromised by trust deficits. As set out in the Introduction, finance sits at the heart of the climate equity debate and its provision and facilitation embody a symbol of trust between developed and developing countries. Putting it simply, the fossil fuel-based economic trajectory of developed countries is the chief cause of the climate crisis, which is threatening the development and even existence of countries that have contributed the least to it. As such, many developing country governments staunchly defend the traditional conception of climate finance as public finance coming directly from developed countries due to reasons of state responsibility and intra-generational justice. Therefore, there can be a wariness by some developing countries of non-state actors entering into multilateral processes (Leggett, 2000) and the more specific concern that market capital may become a substitute for state-directed finance and thus undermine the responsibility owed by advanced economies (see e.g., Khan et al., 2020). This is despite the fact that, as articulated throughout this chapter, while governments have primary responsibility for meeting Article 2 objectives, they will not be able to do so without the critical delivery role of non-party stakeholders, including private sector finance actors.

A less obvious repercussion of such historical legacies is the *trust deficit* thereby created, which expands every time a country or group of countries stalls or derails treaty implementation in the present day. For example, when advanced economies missed the US$100 billion annual target (described earlier in section 2), the trust deficit between developed and developing countries grew larger. Similarly, when Saudi Arabia's energy minister described the COP28 agreement to transition away from fossil fuels as an 'a la carte menu' from which governments could choose which provisions to implement or ignore (Climate Home News, 2024), the trust deficit got deeper.

Trust deficits are invisible, which makes them hard to name and therefore hard to transform. Unlike financial deficits, they do not tangibly appear on a ledger or balance sheet for measurement and management. Instead, they show up as unresolved tensions and intractable positions in negotiating rooms. As documented by observers, a low-trust environment creates opportunity for unscrupulous gaming and even male fides by any Party, regardless of their advanced or emerging economy status (Tsvetov, 2024; Wamsler et al., 2020). The rub is that how law is made or interpreted in those rooms has real-world repercussions for the rest of us.

Moreover, addressing a global collective action problem like climate change requires mutual trust that each actor will implement their commitments and ambitions. For example, the NDC process is premised on all Parties contributing their share, and that both unconditional and conditional elements of NDCs will be implemented. Many developing country Parties include elements in their NDCs that are conditional on receiving finance from developed countries, so those NDCs are prepared, trusting that support will be forthcoming. Similarly, commitments made by non-state actors about their net zero transition ambitions tend to be premised on the expectation that governments will fulfil their Paris obligations and create the enabling conditions for those ambitions to be fulfilled and transition opportunities to be realised (UN Climate Change High Level Champions, 2022).

The global implications of structural misalignments and trust deficits were brought into sharp relief during COP29 climate negotiations in November 2024 to determine a New Collective Quantified Goal on Climate Finance (NCQG) to supplant the failed US$100 billion commitment. Within the NCQG negotiation at COP29 in Baku, several core issues were hotly disputed: the overall quantum of climate finance to be agreed; the distinction between 'provision' of finance in the form of grants and grant-equivalent public finance versus the 'mobilisation' of finance from all sources; the contributor base for the goal including the role of voluntary contributions; access to finance; and the time period over which the NCQG should run. In the final hours of COP29, a decision was made to establish the NCQG (UNFCCC, 2024). It sets out the new goal of at least $300 billion per year by 2035 for the benefit of developing countries and their climate action, with developed countries taking the lead, to cover mitigation and adaptation action; that the sources of that finance will come from a wide variety of sources, public and private, bilateral and multilateral, and that it is to also include all climate-related outflows from and climate finance mobilised by MDBs. It also calls on all actors to work together to scale up financing to developing countries from all sources, public and private, to at least $1.3 trillion per year by 2035. This sounds promising, but many Parties were left disappointed with the outcome (Watson et al., 2024). For some, there is a sense that the NCQG is not just a monetary amount but also represents a spirit of collective responsibility and a division of labour and accountability that includes not just the 'what' of climate finance but also the 'how, who, and when' regarding which actors and channels need to be engaged (Bowman and Tayler, 2024). These are the qualitative elements of climate finance (Naidoo et al., 2023), and mobilising them belies a collective action problem that needs cooperation and collaboration to address.

Nonetheless, it is crucial not to conflate the NCQG with Article 2.1(c). The NCQG is but one important mechanism within a suite of mechanisms to fulfil the wider ambition represented by Article 2.1(c). Certainly, the NCQG can open the door for a reinvigorated discussion about Article 2.1(c) and its complementarity with Article 9 within the Sharm el-Sheikh dialogue that was launched at COP27.[5] However, due to the importance of CMA texts (being texts of the Conference of the Parties serving as the meeting of the Parties to the Paris Agreement) in shaping the interpretation and application of the Paris Agreement, from a public international law perspective, the minimum goal must be to 'do no harm' to the potential meaning and breadth of Article 2.1(c) as embracing *all* financial flows: domestic and international; public and private; multilateral, bilateral, and market. In short, aligning global stocks of assets and capital as well as the 'flows' of public finance is essential to making the necessary shift beyond business-as-usual for the global economy. To be clear, if Article 2.1(c) is limited solely to grants and equivalent public finance, then its effectiveness as a supportive mechanism for the delivery of the other goals of Article 2 – the temperature guardrail and the adaptation ambition, all in the context of sustainable development and the eradication of poverty – will be undermined, which thus undermines the entire Paris Agreement alongside hopes for a liveable planet.

As testimony to the importance of reducing trust deficits in order to move forward, the COP30 Presidency urged a 'healing and upgrading' of multilateral process to 'rebuild a *global infrastructure of trust* for accelerated and scaled outcomes' (Correa do Lago, 2025, emphasis included). In so doing, he invited 'all negotiators to engage as co-builders of this global infrastructure of trust' by shifting away from 'zero-sum' confrontation or 'tactical manoeuvring' that has 'been damaging mutual trust year by year' to approaches of 'empathy and solidarity' that can lead to meaningful impact for people on the ground as we head towards 2030 (Correa do Lago, 2025).

In other words, we need a trust transition.

4. Big picture thinking for ways forward

We posit that, outside of the multilateral COP process, big picture approaches to help shrink both structural misalignments and trust deficits could include, first, a re-examination and renewal of the International Financial Architecture and, secondly, thoughtful law and regulation that not only promotes economic activity that is aligned with the transition (and disincentivises or penalises that which is not) but also positions accountability and transparency as central tenets to the transition. Each is explored below.

4.1 Renewing the International Financial Architecture

4.1.1 *Purpose and composition*

Rather than being designed holistically and in a forward-looking way, the current Architecture has evolved piecemeal since the Second World War in response to successive financial crises. Its beginnings may be traced to the 1944 Bretton Woods Agreement aimed at helping to 'restore and sustain the benefits of global integration, by promoting international economic cooperation' (IMF, 2002), which bequeathed key legacies of the current system: the World Bank, the IMF, the International Bank for Reconstruction and Development, and the gold-exchange standard.

For this reason, MDBs have traditionally sat at the heart of the International Financial Architecture, especially given their crucial role in providing concessional finance, guarantees, blending in private capital and, importantly, providing technical assistance and capacity building to developing countries for development-related projects and purposes. Whilst they were not built to deal with problems such as the climate crisis, it has been natural to look to MDBs to fill climate finance gaps, even to the point of nuancing their roles and mandates to fit this task. For example, in 2023 the World Bank's vision was expanded from 'creating a world free of poverty' to add the words 'on a liveable planet' (World Bank, 2024). Moreover, MDBs have explicitly incorporated the language of Article 2.1(c) verbatim into their operations (World Bank, 2021). As articulated by Rossati and Zahar (2024), this signals a shift in the norms governing development finance and potentially reinforcing legal expectations that could crystallise into customary international law. In so doing, MDBs have extended the Paris Agreement's reach beyond state parties to the broader architecture of global finance. As such, it is understandable that some reform movements such as the Bridgetown Initiative focus on the role of MDBs and the IMF in particular.

However, there are two limitations when defining the International Financial Architecture solely by reference to MDBs. The first limitation relates to equity and representation. The respective percentage shareholdings and proportion of capital contributed by countries (or 'owners') to MDBs and IFIs often determine a country's influence in their governance, which in turn is driven by the respective size of a country's economy. As such, the power to influence the regulation and governance of public finance still sits with the wealthiest countries. Developing countries are often not well represented, which leads to a lack of global coordination on economic issues, including tackling climate change. In the words of UN Secretary-General Guterres: 'the global financial system perpetuates and even exacerbates inequalities. In 2021, and we applaud this decision, the International Monetary Fund allocated over $650 billion in special drawing rights. European Union countries, including my own, received $160 billion. African countries: $34 billion' (United Nations, 2023).

The second limitation is instrumental. In the UNFCCC process, the Sharm el-Sheikh Implementation Plan (agreed at COP27) stated that 'a global transformation to a low-carbon economy is expected to require investment of at least USD 4–6 trillion per year' (UNFCCC, 2022). Yet MDBs self-assess their climate finance contribution to low and middle-income countries as US$85 billion (World Bank, 2024) and estimate this rising to US$120 billion per year by 2030 (World Bank, 2024), which they estimate mobilises a further US$65 billion per year in private capital at an implied ratio of 1:0.54 (Thwaites, 2024). This gap shows that reforming MDBs alone cannot create sufficient financial flows to mobilise the required investment to achieve the transition, let alone pivot the whole global economy towards the vision of Article 2.1(c).

The problem is not a lack of capital per se. Global GDP stands at approximately US$110 trillion (IMF, 2024), which indicates there is plenty of financial and economic capital in the world to meet investment needs. Rather, as demonstrated in section 3 of this chapter, the primary issue is the misalignment of the flows of capital and the sources of economic productivity (which remain linked to the fossil fuel-biased economy) and the stock as well as flows of capital that have very limited alignment with the finance imperative of Paris (OECD, 2024b).

Therefore, it is important that an up-to-date conception of the International Financial Architecture includes not just MDBs and IFIs but also the supervisory bodies and regulatory instruments that steer and shape finance alignments. This was recognised in the UAE Consensus agreed at COP28, which identified an urgent '*need to strengthen policy guidance, incentives, regulations and enabling conditions* to reach the scale of investments required to achieve a global transition towards low greenhouse gas emissions and climate-resilient development' (emphasis added) (UNFCCC, 2023). This broader conception includes the bodies that are part of the Financial Stability Board (FSB), the prudential supervisors of banking within the Basel Committee on Banking Supervision (BCBS), of insurance within the International Association of Insurance Supervisors (IAIS), and the regulators of securities markets and insurers and pension funds as part of the International Organisation of Securities Commissions (IOSCO) and European Insurance and Occupational Pensions Authority (EIOPA). Central banks are also critical given their influence over supervised firms and mandate to ensure financial and price stability, as exemplified by the ongoing work and collaboration of the Supervisors' Network for Greening the Financial System (NGFS). Similarly, finance ministries in national governments are central to the operation of domestic economies and financial systems and therefore can 'play a leading role by incentivising climate-informed public expenditure and utilising climate fiscal tools such as carbon taxes and emissions trading systems to cut emissions and prioritize low-carbon growth' (CFMCA, 2023), a reality acknowledged by the creation of the Coalition of Finance Ministers for Climate Action.

4.1.2 Reform proposals

Some would argue that the International Financial Architecture was built to serve a global North agenda comprising Keynesian logic for tackling inflation (such as the creation of MDBs for rebuilding and full employment) and promoting competition rather than collaboration (exemplified by the Washington Consensus as a response to the oil price shock in the 1970s and the rise of Wall Street dominance in the 1980s). Through this lens, the system aptly serves the purpose for which it was created; it is not broken. However, in seeking solely to deliver profit maximisation outcomes, the current International Financial Architecture is delivering a trajectory to 3°C of global warming whilst increasing inequality and catastrophic depletion of nature.

Recent calls for reform have targeted debt reduction and restructuring to help vulnerable countries meet their climate priorities. In addition to the Bridgetown Agenda noted earlier, the *African Leaders Debt Relief Initiative* was launched on the sidelines of the 2025 G20 finance ministers meeting in South Africa to pinpoint how the climate crisis has exacerbated African debt (and therefore the expense of servicing that debt) as countries are forced to borrow ever larger sums to address the devastating impacts of wild weather (ALDRI, 2025). For example, the annual climate adaptation needs of African governments have been estimated at US$227 billion yet they receive only US$30 billion for those purposes whilst servicing US$163 billion of debts per annum (AFDB, 2024). In short, in honouring debt repayment obligations to avoid default, Global South countries have an untenable choice to make: either under-invest in necessary climate adaptation measures that protect their country or take on more loans to do so and sink deeper into the debt spiral.

Other reform proposals have recognised a broader need for a more representative financial architecture. For example, the 2024 *Pact for the Future* agreed by the UN General Assembly recognised the need for holistic reform:

> We will accelerate reform of the international financial architecture to: address the challenges of today and tomorrow; to strengthen the voice and representation of developing countries; to mobilise additional financing for the sustainable development goals, respond to the needs of developing countries, and direct financing to those most in need; so that countries can borrow sustainably to invest in their long-term development; to strengthen its capacity to support developing countries more effectively and equitably during systemic shocks and make the financial system more stable; so that it can meet the urgent challenge of climate change. (UN, 2024)

4.2 Regulatory frameworks for transition planning

Truly systemic reform will need to engage a broader set of actors as well as fit-for-purpose legal and fiscal policy tools. In other words, we need a comprehensive vision of a *viable alternative* to business-as-usual to align with Article 2.1(c) as a matter of design and purpose. Yet it would be flawed to assume that all regulatory principles designed in the wake of previous financial crises since 1944 are necessarily suitable to support the forward-looking net zero transition. Due to the irreversible nature of runaway climate change once tipping points are crossed, this is one crisis that requires precautionary actions (ex-ante) and not just reactions (ex-post) to bridge the chasm of mismatched incentives between present and future generations as identified in the seminal 'Tragedy of the Horizon' speech given in 2015 by Mark Carney as then-Governor of the Bank of England (Bank of England, 2015). In other words, 'fit for purpose' national and international financial regulation that embeds climate change and other sustainability-related considerations is required.

Given that the International Financial Architecture ought to comprise multiple national actors (notably Treasuries, central banks, and regulators) and their transnational networks (such as the Coalition of Finance Ministers and the NGFS), the role of law and regulation also needs to be multi-scalar. This includes public international law (such as the Paris Agreement, the UN Convention on the Law of the Sea, the Biodiversity Convention, and SDGs) and also private international law topics concerning trade, tax, procurement, and intellectual property rights. Moreover, it includes domestic and regional law and regulation that shifts incentives and internalises the true costs of doing business, as per Bowman's typology (2023) of 'financial mechanisms' (such as carbon pricing, tax incentives, and subsidies removal) and 'facilitative modalities' (such as disclosure, due diligence, prudential supervision, and taxonomies).

We seek to add to this suite of regulatory tools by exploring the emerging phenomenon of mandatory transition planning for both private sector firms and national governments around the world.

4.2.1 *The advent of transition planning*

At COP26 in Glasgow, the then UK Chancellor, Rishi Sunak, set out that the UK would lead the rewiring of the global financial system for net zero and that the UK intended to become the world's first net zero-aligned financial centre (UK Government, 2021). A key aspect of this vision related to requiring firms to publish 'a clear deliverable plan setting out how they will decarbonise and transition to net zero' (UK Government, 2021), which responded to calls from the private sector and civil society to mandate such plans from regulated financial institutions (Aviva/WWF, 2021). The logic is that 'transition plans', as they became known, help a firm to walk its talk about the net zero transition. Unlike backward-looking financial or sustainability reporting, transition plans and the process of transition planning are forward-looking strategies to assess, communicate, and evidence how an entity intends to evolve its business in a carbon-constrained economy and achieve a net zero transition by 2050.

The UK Treasury then set up the Transition Plan Taskforce (TPT) to produce recommendations for corporate and financial firms' transition plans and sectoral guidance (TPT, 2023). The resulting TPT Framework for private sector transition plans sets out the ingredients of a 'gold standard' transition plan: strategic ambition (something to transition towards), with analysis of the impacts of implementation on business model and value chain, and explicit assumptions and dependencies. It should also show over time that operational and capital expenditure, or portfolios in the case of financial entities, align with that strategic ambition; and include an implementation strategy, engagement strategy, metrics and targets (against which progress can be monitored), and governance and accountability mechanisms. The International Financial Reporting Standards Foundation (IFRS) has now assumed responsibility for the TPT Framework as part of the work of the International Sustainability

Standards Board (ISSB) to require the disclosure of an entity's transition plan (where it has one) and to streamline and consolidate international standards on transition planning (Deloitte, 2024).

In short, transition plans contain essential information to guide informed decision-making by investors, lenders, underwriters, regulators, and civil society. As such, transition planning needs to be mandated into law and regulation to ensure sufficient quantity and quality of uptake by firms and financial institutions. Several key economies are setting the direction of travel here. For example, the UK government has undertaken to make transition planning mandatory for the largest UK companies and UK-regulated financial entities (Labour Party, 2024) with implementing regulation anticipated. The EU *Corporate Sustainability Due Diligence Directive* (EU 2024/1760) requires relevant companies to adopt a transition plan compatible with the EU's climate ambition for net zero by 2050 (a measure that is expected to survive the changes to corporate reporting under the Omnibus proposals to simplify corporate disclosure requirements). The Monetary Authority of Singapore has similarly issued guidance to financial institutions including expectations for entities to have a sound transition planning process to enable effective mitigation and adaptation measures in the transition to a net zero economy and to prepare for the expected physical effects of climate change (MAS, 2023). As at the time of writing, adoption of the ISSB Sustainability Standards (which integrate the TPT Framework) accounts for around 75 per cent of global market capitalisation excluding the United States, and is increasing (IFRS, 2024). This means that transition plans and transition planning will increasingly be situated within financial regulation and corporate reporting requirements around the world.

4.2.2 *National-level transition planning and International Financial Architecture renewal*

In addition to corporate transition plans, national-level transition planning is required to provide a strategic 'whole of economy' roadmap by building a bridge between private sector ambitions and government pledges under international treaties (such as the Paris Agreement) and to increase long-term planning for and within entire countries (rather than just individual firms). As conceptualized by Manning et al. (2024), such national-level planning is required to inform and coordinate corporate transition planning, to create credible sectoral pathways that are underpinned by a system of law and regulatory governance, and to enable transparency of policies and accountability of government processes. In this way, national-level transition planning can build upon countries' NDCs and Long-Term Low Emission Development Strategies (LT-LEDS) and connect them – and the responsible ministries – together under one canopy. In effect, this is a step towards creating a 'transition plan ecosystem' (Tayler, 2023). This buttresses and extends the call by UNFCCC Executive Secretary, Simon Steill, that 'NDCs 3.0 are the investment plans for the future' (UNFCCC, 2024) and roadmaps for investment and delivery of decarbonisation ambitions (IIGCC, 2024; Haber et al., 2024; We Mean Business Coalition, 2024).

Government transition planning that sets out the legal, regulatory, and normative shifts to implement their NDC ambitions as required by Article 4.2 of the Paris Agreement is a necessary corollary to private sector transition planning. We argue, in common with Manning et al., that as well as transition planning from private sector entities and governments, regulator transition plans from the bodies that make up and are informed by the International Financial Architecture are also essential to creating the enabling environment to achieve the finance imperative in Article 2.1(c) in support of the wider purposes of Article 2 to eradicate poverty and promote sustainable development. The essential updating of NDCs to meet the findings of the Global Stocktake as anticipated by Article 4.9 will create the conditions under which economic incentives and the profit motive for business and financial institutions align with climate and sustainability action.

For a country, a transition plan that sets out the key areas it will focus on in its development and decarbonisation journey can be a tool to connect global commitments to domestic priorities that can attract private capital to supplement domestic resource mobilisation. A forward-looking plan that is reported upon annually to give confidence in its implementation and has long-term aims to build in resilience against exogenous shocks, can be a powerful tool to attract investment. Creating such a transition plan and reporting on its implementation can also provide confidence to potential investors that robust governance and structures are in place. Credit rating agencies can also take this information into account, especially if their methodologies evolve to look forward and to the longer term.

Similarly, key actors within the International Financial Architecture ought to produce transition plans that cover their own operations and also include the influence they have over the financial system and regulation. As acknowledged by the UN, this 'would include the multilateral development banks, as well as regulators and standard setters and the financial institutions within their purview' (UN, 2023). Indeed, a whole-of-economy approach to transitioning necessarily includes the institutions that oversee financial, price, and market stability and regulation, namely central banks, prudential supervisors, and market and conduct regulators that have a critical role in connecting government policy trajectories to financial system operation and regulation. Indeed, many central banks around the world have begun to integrate transition policy objectives into their strategies in a forward-looking manner, including the Bank of England, which issued a transition plan in 2023, and the Banco do Brasil, which has run scenario simulations in line with the NGFS scenarios to test their SAMBA model (Stochastic Analytical Model with a Bayesian Approach) (Banco Central do Brasil, 2024). Such documents serve to 'green' the operations of central banks and to signal commitment to market participants (Manning et al., 2024).

For finance ministries and central banks tasked with overseeing economic and financial stability, encouraging and supporting well-informed and comprehensive plans will mitigate risk during the transition. As explained earlier, the transition is currently disincentivised due to market failures, including the failure to make emitters pay the cost of their activity and the lack of comprehensive information to support accurate pricing of climate risks. Therefore, clear plans for how and when those failures will be corrected could avoid economic shocks and market panic. It could also reduce litigation risk. For example, due to a lack of an adequate transition plan, the UK government's *Net Zero Strategy* and *Carbon Budget Delivery Plan* were both challenged via judicial review in the High Court and found to be in breach of the UK *Climate Change Act 2008* and insufficient to meet legally required net zero targets by 2050 (*Friends of the Earth v. Secretary of State for Energy Security and Net Zero*, 2024). Similarly, the German government's approach was deemed to contravene the rights of young people due to a lack of planning for timely milestones that left decarbonisation too far into the future (*Neubauer et al v. Germany*, 2021).

In all these ways, a comprehensive national transition plan and investment roadmap, covering sectoral decarbonisation as well as adaptation and development, can be a means of improving national credit ratings and escaping sovereign debt traps, lowering the cost of capital for countries in emerging markets and developing countries, and mitigating litigation risk for developed country governments. These plans can also have positive reinforcing feedbacks with the dependencies and assumptions set out in private sector plans, allowing sectoral roadmaps to be informed by sectoral actors.

Moreover, transition planning can promote long-termism and also enhance accountability and transparency, which is so important for bridging the distrust divide identified in section 3 of this chapter. This is especially important in the face of political pushback against 'woke ESG' and the advent of unexpected external stresses such as war and pandemic. Long-term transition planning can promote resilience and confidence in the face of such short-term pressures and fiscal shocks. Learning from history, the COVID-19 pandemic and the Russia-Ukraine war – along with the concomitant food and energy crises, inflation, and climate impacts – have delayed and constrained progress towards the achievement of the Paris goals and UN Sustainable Development Goals (SDGs) (Ranger et al., 2023). Specifically, the lack of long-term planning for the achievement of those goals likely contributed to the failure by many nations to align their fiscal stimulus packages with the acceleration of the transition. For example, adopting a 'market-neutral' response to quantitative easing inadvertently supported capital-intensive, high-emitting economic activity (Matikainen et al., 2017). In times of stress, it is instinctive to revert to the comfort of the familiar; in the case of the energy and inflationary crisis, this has meant using more fossil fuels, despite their misalignment with climate goals. Now, however, reactive approaches are no longer tenable. As shocks become more frequent and extreme, a forward-looking plan that inspires and incentivises state and corporate decision-making to lean into less familiar, but ultimately more productive, courses of action is not only prudent but necessary (Tayler et al., 2023).

5. Conclusion

The orthodoxy of what was agreed in Paris a decade ago remains the starting point and the clearest roadmap for the transition to a sustainable global economy. The objectives within Article 2, supported by the country-led commitments in NDCs under Article 4 and informed by the ambition ratchet and stocktake processes in Articles 13 and 14, with financial support for developing countries under Article 9, can all provide the foundation for the necessary systemic transition.

Addressing the climate crisis and achieving the net zero transition is a whole-of-system problem, requiring a systemic response that engages all countries and all actors. As such, to address the current lack of progress in peaking and reducing emissions and the misalignment of incentives for the private sector, a response that encompasses interlinked legal, regulatory, financial, and wider economic systems is needed. We have argued that the International Financial Architecture, understood more broadly to include private finance institutions and regulators involved in the supervision of the global financial system rather than just focusing on MDBs and IFIs, is also an essential part of this whole-of-system response. Further, we have argued that the achievement of the financial imperative of Article 2.1(c), again in its widest sense to encompass all financial flows be they public, private, international, domestic, multilateral, bilateral, and market, requires the catalyst of an aligned system of financial regulation that connects with the real economy in which it invests, underwrites and lends. These changes must also include representation and acknowledgement of the needs and requirements of all countries, especially developing countries, to support the achievement of the NCQG and the tackling of the trust deficit for a just transition in its broadest sense.

As posited throughout this chapter, if we observe the flows of finance around the world, not just flows labelled as climate finance but *all* financial flows, we see the result of narrow political and financial choice-making over time within the global economy. Thus, to achieve different outcomes, dominant market norms regarding resource exploitation, short-termism, and obeisance to 'commercial, contractual, compliance' logics also need to change. As highlighted by the Independent Expert Group of the G20: 'Reforms … will only work with a change of mindsets and attitudes' (G20 Independent Expert Group, 2023).

There are many questions that emerge from the analysis in this chapter that, together with gaps in current research and literature, raise generative research opportunities for well-evidenced studies to help decision-makers understand and implement this holistic delivery of the Paris vision. Here are just some questions that occur to us; there are many more. How can transition-informed regulation be designed to ensure better alignment and coordination of instruments, agencies, and processes within countries and across the International Financial Architecture? What is the interplay between the regulation of finance and the real economy, and the right balance of focus between them for the most impactful change? What are the ways and spaces in which law, especially related to finance and investment, protects the status quo and impedes

Paris goals and the net zero transition? How effective are the predominant regulatory tools to date and what are their optimal combinations for most impact? If we need better oversight and coordination mechanisms to sit above the Architecture to ensure accountability and spot unintended consequences, who or what might best fill this role? In addition to a 'just' transition, what are the necessary ingredients and enabling conditions for a 'trust' transition? How could qualitative indicia of 'value' (not just quantitative metrics) be inculcated into mindset and processes within the International Financial Architecture? For example, could incorporating a 'duty of care and dignity' into climate finance help to restore agency to the Global South? What other indicia (such as dignity, transparency, access, accountability) might help to shrink the trust deficit rather than ignore or exacerbate it? How best to reorient towards humanity and collaboration in International Financial Architecture processes and go beyond a focus on 'mindsets' to embracing 'a change of heart'; to expand 'rational' decision-making to include empathy and human connectedness?

There is no doubt that in a world with so much change occurring and yet, paradoxically, so much more needed, there is great uncertainty and volatility. Yet what is certain is that systems that are misaligned to Paris goals and that perversely incentivise our own demise have been created by human thought and action. And therein lies the key. What has been created by humans can be deconstructed and reconstructed to produce different and better outcomes. As stated by Capra and Luisi (2016): 'human values can change; they are not natural laws' and 'the current form of economic globalization has been consciously designed and thus can be reshaped' (p. 398); and therefore 'we have the agency – the power to redesign [our economies] to put people and planet first' (Mazzucato, 2024). Importantly, in the words of seminal legal philosopher Lon Fuller, this constructivist approach includes the law, 'not [as] a datum, but [as] an achievement that needs ever to be renewed' (Fuller, 1954, p. 467). This chimes with our description of the Paris Agreement as *living law* that can evolve and adapt over time to address challenges in its own implementation, including the finance imperative of Article 2.1(c). The 'how' of doing so will take effort and encounter resistance, but the 'why' is undeniable.

Notes

1. The authors co-convened expert workshops at King's College London with Aviva Investors in 2020, 2022, and 2024 on topics regarding law and regulation for Paris Agreement finance implementation and reforming the international financial architecture. The aim was to stimulate knowledge exchange and collaborations between public and private sectors in emerging and advanced economies. We would like to acknowledge the constructive and courageous contributions of participants from those workshops for inspiring our own thinking for this chapter. We would also like to thank Hernan Sanchez Almendro, undergraduate law student at King's College London, for valuable research assistance.
2. The advisory opinion of the International Court of Justice on the Obligations of States in respect of Climate Change, dated 23 July 2025, confirms, at paragraph 264, that the use of the word 'shall' in Article 9.1 'indicates the legally binding character of the

provision'. The Court also notes, at paragraph 265, that parties are to implement their obligations under Article 9 in a manner and at a level that allows for the achievement of the objectives listed in Article 2, which would include the *temperature guardrail*, the *adaptation ambition*, and the *finance imperative*. See https://www.icj-cij.org/case/187#:~:text=The%20International%20Court%20of%20Justice%20(ICJ)%20delivered,opinion%20is%20available%20in%20English%20and%20French.

3. Noting some exceptions, such as Bodle and Noens (2018), and that the potential of Article 2.1(c) was first identified by practitioners, such as Robins (2018); Whitley (2018); Rydge (2020).
4. As detailed in par 121(q): (Decision 18/CMA.1) at UNFCCC, 'Report of the Conference of the Parties serving as the meeting of the Parties to the Paris Agreement on the third part of its first session, held in Katowice from 2 to 15 December 2018: Addendum: Part two: Action taken by the Conference of the Parties serving as the meeting of the Parties to the Paris Agreement' 19 March 2019 FCCC/PA/CMA/2018/3/Add.2. Also Katowice Decision 4/CP.24 (para 10) and Decision 14/CMA (para 2) at UNFCCC, 'Report of the Conference of the Parties serving as the meeting of the Parties to the Paris Agreement on the third part of its first session, held in Katowice from 2 to 15 December 2018: Addendum: Part two: Action taken by the Conference of the Parties serving as the meeting of the Parties to the Paris Agreement' 19 March 2019 FCCC/PA/CMA/2018/3/Add.2. Also UNFCCC, 'Report of the Conference of the Parties on its twenty-fourth session, held in Katowice from 2 to 15 December 2018: Addendum: Part two: Action taken by the Conference of the Parties at its twenty-fourth session' 19 March 2019 FCCC/CP/2018/10/Add.1.
5. At COP30 in Belem, Parties agreed in the Global Mutirao decision to convene a high-level ministerial roundtable to reflect on the implementation of the NCQG and to establish a two-year work programme on climate finance, including on Article 9.1. It was also decided at COP30 to establish the Veredas Dialogue on the implementation of Article 2, paragraph 1(c), of the Paris Agreement and its complementarity with Article 9 ofthe Paris Agreement, building on the Sharm el-Sheikh dialogue.

Bibliography

African Development Bank (2024) *Annual Meetings 2024: Old debt resolution for African countries – the cornerstone of reforming the global financial architecture*. Available at: https://www.afdb.org/en/news-and-events/annual-meetings-2024-old-debt-resolution-african-countries-cornerstone-reforming-global-financial-architecture-70791 (Accessed: 30 April 2025).

African Leaders Debt Relief Initiative (2025) 'African leaders demand debt relief as continent battles climate crisis', *Green Central Banking*, 5 March.

Aviva/WWF (2021) *Transition plans for a net-zero future*. Available at: https://static.aviva.io/content/dam/aviva-corporate/documents/socialpurpose/pdfs/communities/transition-plans-for-a-net-zero-future.pdf (Accessed: 12 December 2025).

Banco Central do Brasil (2024) *Report on social, environmental and climate-related risks and opportunities*. Banco Central do Brasil.

Bank of England (2015) *Breaking the tragedy of the horizon – climate change and financial stability – speech by Mark Carney*. Available at: https://www.bankofengland.co.uk/speech/2015/breaking-the-tragedy-of-the-horizon-climate-change-and-financial-stability (Accessed: 12 December 2025).

Bodansky, D. (2016) 'The legal character of the Paris Agreement', *Review of European, Comparative & International Environmental Law*, 25(2), pp. 142–150.

Bodle, R. and Noens, V. (2018) 'Climate finance: too much on detail, too little on the big picture?', *Carbon & Climate Law Review*, 3, pp. 248–257.

Bodle, R. and Oberthür, S. (2016) 'Legal form and nature of the Paris outcome', *Climate Law*, 6(1–2), pp. 40–57.

Bowman, M. (2015) *Banking on climate change: how finance actors and transnational regulatory regimes are responding*. Wolters Kluwer.

Bowman, M. (2022) *Regulatory leadership for a net zero transition: central banks and financial regulators: levers and limits*. King's College London.

Bowman, M. (2023) 'Polaris and pluralism: presenting a legal analytical framework for climate finance', *Carbon & Climate Law Review*, 17(1), pp. 3–26.

Bowman, M. and Minas, S. (2018) 'Resilience through interlinkage: the Green Climate Fund and climate finance governance', *Climate Policy*, 18(3), pp. 342–353.

Bowman, M. and Tayler, T. (2024) *Legal roundtable report: law and regulation as tools to accelerate implementation of Paris Agreement finance goals*. King's College London and Aviva Investors.

Capra, F. and Luisi, P.L. (2016) *The systems view of life*. Cambridge University Press.

Chenet, H., Zamarioli, L., Kretschmer, B. and Narvaez, R. (2019) *From transformational climate finance to transforming the financial system for climate*. COP21 Ripples and Horizon 2020 Societal Challenge 5.

Climate Home News (2024) '"A la carte menu": Saudi minister claims Cop28 fossil fuel agreement is only optional', 10 January.

Climate Policy Initiative and Allen & Overy (2023) *How big is the net zero financing gap?* Available at: https://www.climatepolicyinitiative.org/wp-content/uploads/2023/09/How-big-is-the-Net-Zero-financing-gap-2023.pdf (Accessed: 18 May 2025).

Coalition of Finance Ministers for Climate Action (2023) *Strengthening the role of ministries of finance in driving climate action: Synthesis Report*. Available at: https://www.financeministersforclimate.org/sites/cape/files/inline-files/Synthesis%20Strengthening%20the%20Role%20of%20Ministries%20of%20Finance.pdf (Accessed: 30 April 2025).

Correa do Lago (2025) *Letter from André Aranha Correa do Lago, COP30 President Designate* (COP30 Brasil Amazonia Belem 2025, 23 May).

Deloitte LLP (2024) 'IFRS Foundation to assume responsibility for the disclosure-specific materials developed by the UK's Transition Plan Taskforce', *IAS Plus*, June.

European Committee of the Regions (2017) 'Climate finance: an essential tool for the implementation of the Paris Agreement', in *125th CoR plenary session: European Committee of the Regions met in the 125th plenary session*, 9 October.

Foerster, A. (2026) 'From climate risk to net-zero and beyond: is ecologically rational regulation emerging in the finance sector?', in Bowman, M. and Mai, L. (eds) *A research agenda for law, finance and the environment*. Edward Elgar Publishing, pp. 125–151.

Friends of the Earth v. Secretary of State for Energy Security and Net Zero [2024] EWHC 995.

Fuller, L. (1954) 'American legal philosophy at mid-century', *Journal of Legal Education*, 6(4), pp. 457–485.

G20 Independent Expert Group (2023) 'The triple agenda (vol. 2): strengthening multilateral development banks'. Available at: https://icrier.org/g20-ieg/pdf/The_Triple_Agenda_G20-IEG_Report_Volume2_2023.pdf (Accessed: 12 December 2025).

Getachew, H. (2026) 'Financing Africa's just transition with reparations distributed through the African Continental Free Trade Area Agreement', in Bowman, M. and Mai, L. (eds) *A research agenda for law, finance and the environment*. Edward Elgar Publishing, pp. 209–229.

Government of Barbados (2022) *The 2022 Bridgetown initiative for the reform of the global financial architecture*. Barbados Government Information Service.

Greenwald, B.C. and Stiglitz, J.E. (1986) 'Externalities in economies with imperfect information and incomplete markets', *The Quarterly Journal of Economics*, 101(2), pp. 229–264.

Haber, S., Guilanpour, K. and Huang, J. (2024) 'What are "investable" NDCs?'. *Center for Climate and Energy Solutions, Discussion paper*. Available at: https://www.c2es.org/wp-content/uploads/2024/07/20240723-C2ES-Investable-NDCs-FINAL.pdf (Accessed: 12 December 2025).

Hahn, F.H. (1981) *Reflections on the invisible hand*. Warwick Economic Research Papers, No. 196. University of Warwick, Department of Economics.

IFRS Foundation (2024) 'Jurisdictions representing over half the global economy by GDP take steps towards ISSB Standards'. Available at: https://www.ifrs.org/news-and-events/news/2024/05/jurisdictions-representing-over-half-the-global-economy-by-gdp-take-steps-towards-issb-standards/ (Accessed: 30 April 2025).

IIGCC (2024) 'Making NDCs investable – the investor perspective'. Available at: https://www.iigcc.org/hubfs/POLICY/IIGCC_Making%20NDCs%20investable%20-%20the%20investor%20perspective_June2024.pdf (Accessed: 12 December 2025).

Intergovernmental Panel on Climate Change (IPCC) (2022) *Climate change 2022: impacts, adaptation and vulnerability*. Working Group II contribution to the Sixth Assessment Report of the Intergovernmental Panel on Climate Change. Cambridge University Press.

Intergovernmental Panel on Climate Change (IPCC) (2022) *Climate change 2022: mitigation of climate change*. Contribution of Working Group III to the Sixth Assessment Report of the Intergovernmental Panel on Climate Change. Cambridge University Press.

International Monetary Fund (IMF) (2002) *Globalization: A framework for IMF involvement*. Available at: https://www.imf.org/external/np/exr/ib/2002/031502.htm (Accessed: 30 April 2025).

International Monetary Fund (IMF) (2024) 'World economic outlook: policy pivot, rising threats'. Available at: https://www.imf.org/-/media/files/publications/weo/2024/october/english/text.pdf (Accessed: 12 December 2025)

Khan, M., Robinson, S.-A., Weikmans, R., Ciplet, D. and Roberts, J.T. (2020) 'Twenty-five years of adaptation finance through a climate justice lens', *Climatic Change*, 161(2), pp. 251–269.

Knöepfel, L. (2026) 'Corporate climate change litigation as a new business risk', in Bowman, M. and Mai, L. (eds) *A research agenda for law, finance and the environment*. Edward Elgar Publishing, pp. 153–168.

Labour Party (2024) 'Change: Labour Party manifesto 2024'. Available at: https://labour.org.uk/change/ (Accessed: 12 December 2025).

Latif, L. (2026) 'Placing Zakat in African tax policy: a pathway to sustainable finance', in Bowman, M. and Mai, L. (eds) *A research agenda for law, finance and the environment*. Edward Elgar Publishing, pp. 191–207.

Leggett, J. (2000) *The carbon war*. Penguin.

Lesniewska, F. (2026) 'Tapping into public procurement to fund a transition to a circular construction economy in Europe: opportunities and challenges', in Bowman, M. and Mai, L. (eds) *A research agenda for law, finance and the environment*. Edward Elgar Publishing, pp. 251–268.

Mai, L. (2026) 'Out of time: voluntarism and the temporality of climate finance', in Bowman, M. and Mai, L. (eds) *A research agenda for law, finance and the environment*. Edward Elgar Publishing, pp. 35–48.

Manning, M., Bowhay, R., Bowman, M., Knaack, P., Sachs, L., Smolenska, A., Stewart, F., Tayler, T., Toledano, P. and Walkate, H. (2024) 'Taking the lead on climate action and sustainable development'. Available at: https://cetex.org/publications/taking-the-lead-on-climate-action-and-sustainable-development/ (Accessed: 12 December 2025).

Matikainen, S., Campiglio, E., Zenghelis, D. (2017) ' The climate impact of quantitative easingThe climate impact of quantitative easingThe climate impact of quantitative easing'. Available at: https://www.lse.ac.uk/granthaminstitute/wp-content/uploads/2017/05/ClimateImpactQuantEasing_Matikainen-et-al-1.pdf (Accessed: 12 December 2025).

Mazzucato, M. (2024) 'Policy with purpose', *IMF Finance and Development Magazine*. Available at: https://www.imf.org/en/publications/fandd/issues/2024/09/policy-with-a-purpose-mazzucato (Accessed: 12 December 2025).

McKinsey & Company (2022) *The net-zero transition: what it would cost, what it could bring*. Available at: https://www.mckinsey.com/capabilities/sustainability/our-insights/the-net-zero-transition-what-it-would-cost-what-it-could-bring (Accessed: 30 April 2025).

McKinsey Global Institute (2021) *The rise and rise of the global balance sheet: how productively are we using our wealth?* McKinsey & Company.

Minas, S. (2021) *The Paris Agreement goal on finance flows*. Legal Response International.

Monetary Authority of Singapore (2023) *MAS proposes guidelines for financial institutions on transition planning*. Available at: https://www.mas.gov.sg/news/media-releases/2023/mas-proposes-guidelines-for-financial-institutions-on-transition-planning (Accessed: 30 April 2025).

Naidoo, C., Lehmann-Grube, P., Sheehama, A., Beaumont, J., Watson, C. and Pettinotti, L. (2023) *Exploring the intersection of equity and Article 2.1(c) towards an improved Global Stocktake*. Rabia Transitions Initiative and Overseas Development Institute.

Naran, B., Buchner, B., Price, M., Stout, S., Taylor, M. and Zabeida, D. (2024) *Global landscape of climate finance 2024: insights for COP29*. Climate Policy Initiative.

Neubauer et al. v. Germany (2021) Federal Constitutional Court of Germany 1 BvR 2656/18.

Organisation for Economic Co-operation and Development (OECD) (1992) *The polluter-pays principle*. OCDE/GD(92)81.

Organisation for Economic Co-Operation and Development (OECD) (2024a) *Climate finance provided and mobilised by developed countries in 2013–2022*. Available at: https://www.oecd.org/en/publications/2024/05/climate-finance-provided-and-mobilised-by-developed-countries-in-2013-2022_8031029a.html (Accessed: 12 December 2025).

Organisation for Economic Co-Operation and Development (OECD) (2024b) *OECD review on aligning finance with climate goals*. Available at: https://www.oecd.org/en/publications/oecd-review-on-aligning-finance-with-climate-goals_b9b7ce49-en.html (Accessed: 12 December 2025).

Organisation for Economic Co-Operation and Development (OECD) (2024c) *Climate Finance and the USD 100 billion goal*. Available at https://www.oecd.org/en/topics/sub-issues/climate-finance-and-the-usd-100-billion-goal.html

Oxfam (2024) 'Climate finance short changed'. Available at: https://oxfam.app.box.com/s/q32guouexhj6proorwm8f14sv6nvan77 (Accessed 12 December 2025).

Pauw, W.P., Moslener, U., Zamarioli, L.H., Amerasinghe, N., Atela, J., Affana, J.P.B., Buchner, B., Klein, R.J.T., Mbeva, K.L., Puri, J., Roberts, J.T., Shawoo, Z., Watson, C. and Weikmans, R. (2022) 'Post-2025 climate finance target: how much more and how much better?', *Climate Policy*, 22(9–10), pp. 1241–1251.

Ranger, N., Marotta, F., Fankhauser, F., O'Callaghan, B., (2023) Reforming the Global Financial Architecture to Drive a Resilient Net-Zero Transition

Ripple, W.J., Wolf, C., Gregg, J.W., Rockström, J., Mann, M.E., Oreskes, N., Lenton, T.M., Rahmstorf, S., Newsome, T.M., Xu, C., Svenning, J.-C., Pereira, C.C., Law, B.E. and Crowther, T.W. (2024) 'The 2024 state of the climate report: perilous times on planet Earth', *BioScience*, 74(12), pp. 812–824.

Robins, N. (2018) *Making finance climate-consistent: how could the UK implement Article 2.1.c of the Paris Agreement?* Grantham Research Institute on Climate Change and the Environment, London School of Economics and Political Science.

Robins, N. (2022) 'The $468 trillion climate question: how the financial system is starting to shift', *LSE Business Review.*

Rossati, D. and Zahar, A. (2024) 'Governing international climate finance and investment: the Paris Agreement and related international and transnational mechanisms', in Zahar, A. (ed.) *Research handbook on the law of the Paris Agreement.* Edward Elgar Publishing, pp. 296–322.

Rydge, J. (2020) *Aligning finance with the Paris Agreement: an overview of concepts, approaches, progress and necessary action.* Grantham Research Institute on Climate Change and the Environment, London School of Economics.

Tayler, T. (2023) *The tipping point for climate finance: making financial flows consistent with the Paris Agreement.* Aviva Investors.

Thwaites, J. (2024) 'Getting from here to there: scaling up climate finance for the NCQG', *NRDC* (24 November). Available at: https://www.nrdc.org/bio/joe-thwaites/getting-here-there-scaling-climate-finance-ncqg (Accessed: 12 December 2025).

Transition Plan Taskforce (TPT) (2023) 'Discourse framework'. Available at: https://www.ifrs.org/content/dam/ifrs/knowledge-hub/resources/tpt/disclosure-framework-oct-2023.pdf (Accessed: 12 December 2025).

Tsvetov, A. (2024) 'Overcoming a climate of mistrust', *Observer Research Foundation.* Available at: https://www.orfonline.org/expert-speak/overcoming-a-climate-of-mistrust (Accessed: 30 April 2025).

UK Government (2020) *Aligning your pension scheme with the TCFD recommendations: a guide for trustees on integrating climate-related risk assessment and management into decision making and reporting.* Public Consultation, Version 16.

UK Government (2021) 'COP26 Finance Day speech'. Available at: https://www.gov.uk/government/speeches/cop26-finance-day-speech (Accessed: 30 April 2025).

UN Climate Change High Level Champions (2022) *The pivot point.* Available at https://globalabc.org/resources/publications/pivot-point-report (Accessed: 30 April 2025).

United Nations (1992) 'Rio Declaration on Environment and Development', in *Report of the United Nations Conference on Environment and Development*, UN Doc. A/CONF.151/26 (Vol. I).

United Nations (2023) *Our common agenda policy brief 6: reforms to the international financial architecture.* Available at: https://digitallibrary.un.org/record/4012088 (Accessed: 30 April 2025).

United Nations (2023) *Secretary-General's remarks at the summit for a new global financing pact.* SG/SM/21855.

United Nations (2024) *Pact for the* future: outcome *document of the Summit of the Future.* Actions 47–52.

United Nations Environment Programme (UNEP) (2022) *Emissions gap report 2022: the closing window – climate crisis calls for rapid transformation of societies.* UNEP.

United Nations Environment Programme (UNEP) (2023) *Emissions gap report 2023: broken record – temperatures hit new highs, yet world fails to cut emissions (again).* UNEP.

United Nations Framework Convention on Climate Change (UNFCCC) (n.d.) *Introduction to climate finance.* Available at: https://unfccc.int/topics/introduction-to-climate-finance (Accessed: 30 April 2025).

United Nations Framework Convention on Climate Change (UNFCCC) (1992) *What is the United Nations Framework Convention on Climate Change?* Available at: https://unfccc.int/process-and-meetings/what-is-the-united-nations-framework-convention-on-climate-change (Accessed: 30 April 2025).

United Nations Framework Convention on Climate Change (UNFCCC) (2010) *Report of the Conference of the Parties on its sixteenth session. Part two: action taken by the Conference of the Parties at its sixteenth session.* FCCC/CP/2010/7/Add.1.

United Nations Framework Convention on Climate Change (UNFCCC) (2011) *Report of the Conference of the Parties on its sixteenth session, held in Cancun from 29 November to 10 December 2010: Addendum:* part two: action *taken by the Conference of the Parties at its sixteenth session*. FCCC/CP/2010/7/Add.1, Article 98.

United Nations Framework Convention on Climate Change (UNFCCC) (2016) *Paris Agreement*. FCCC/CP/2015/L.9/Rev.1. Adopted on 12 December 2015, entered into force on 4 November 2016.

United Nations Framework Convention on Climate Change (UNFCCC) (2018) *Modalities and procedures for the effective operation of the committee referred to in Article 15, paragraph 2, of the Paris Agreement: Decision 20/CMA.1, Annex, para. 2*. Available at: https://unfccc.int/sites/default/files/resource/cma2020_01E.pdf (Accessed: 30 April 2025).

United Nations Framework Convention on Climate Change (UNFCCC) (2021) *Glasgow Climate Pact: Decision -/CP.26*.

United Nations Framework Convention on Climate Change (UNFCCC) (2021) *26th session, Glasgow 31 October–12 November 2021, adopted agenda*. Available at: https://unfccc.int/sites/default/files/resource/COP26_adopted_agenda_0.pdf (Accessed: 23 March 2023).

United Nations Framework Convention on Climate Change (UNFCCC) (2022) *Sharm el-Sheikh Implementation Plan: Decision -/CP.27*, paras 30–31.

United Nations Framework Convention on Climate Change (UNFCCC) (2022) *Sharm el-Sheikh Implementation Plan: Decisions 1/CP.27 and 1/CMA.4, Article XI*. Available at: https://unfccc.int/sites/default/files/resource/cop27_auv_2_cover%20decision.pdf (Accessed: 30 April 2025).

United Nations Framework Convention on Climate Change (UNFCCC) (2023) *Key findings from the technical dialogue of the first global stocktake*. Available at: https://unfccc.int/documents/631857 (Accessed: 30 April 2025).

United Nations Framework Convention on Climate Change (UNFCCC) (2024a) *Report of the Conference of the Parties serving as the meeting of the Parties to the Paris Agreement on its fifth session, held in the United Arab Emirates from 30 November to 13 December 2023* (15 March 2024). FCCC/PA/CMA/2023/16/Add.1.

United Nations Framework Convention on Climate Change (UNFCCC) (2024b) *Decision 1/CMA.6: new collective quantified goal on climate finance*. Baku Climate Unity Pact.

UNFCCC Standing Committee on Finance (2014) *2014 biennial assessment and overview of climate finance flows report*. United Nations Framework Convention on Climate Change.

UNFCCC Standing Committee on Finance (2023) *Report on clustering types of climate finance definitions in use*. United Nations Framework Convention on Climate Change.

UNFCCC Standing Committee on Finance *(2024) Sixth biennial assessment and overview of climate finance flows*. United Nations Framework Convention on Climate Change.

Wamsler, C., Brink, E. and Rantala, S. (2020) 'Enabling new mindsets and transformative skills for negotiating and activating climate action: lessons from UNFCCC conferences of the parties', *Environmental Science & Policy*, 112, pp. 227–235.

Watson, C., Tan, E., Pettinotti, L. and Colenbrander, S. (2024) *Did COP29 end up with a good New Collective Quantified Goal Decision?* Overseas Development Institute.

We Mean Business Coalition (2024) 'Time to deliver: business call to action for ambitious and investable NDCs'. Available at: https://www.wemeanbusinesscoalition.org/wp-content/uploads/2024/09/WMBC_NDCs-call-to-action-16-09-24.pdf (Accessed: 12 December 2025).

Whitley, S. (2018) *Making finance consistent with climate goals: insights for operationalising Article 2.1(c) of the UNFCCC Paris Agreement*. Overseas Development Institute.

World Bank (2018) *Joint Declaration: MDBs' alignment approach to the objectives of the Paris Agreement: working together to catalyse low-emissions and climate-resilient development*. Available at: https://thedocs.worldbank.org/en/doc/784141543806348331-0020022018/Joint

-Declaration-MDBs-Alignment-Approach-to-Paris-Agreement-COP24-Final (Accessed: 30 April 2025).

World Bank (2021) '2020 joint report on multilateral development banks' approach to climate finance'. Available at: https://thedocs.worldbank.org/en/doc/9234bfc633439d0172f6a6eb8df1b881-0020012021/original/2020-Joint-MDB-report-on-climate-finance-Report-final-web.pdf (Accessed: 12 December 2025).

World Bank (2024) 'World Bank annual report 2024: a better bank for a better world'. Available at: https://documents.worldbank.org/en/publication/documents-reports/documentdetail/099101824180532047 (Accessed: 12 December 2025).

Yamineva, Y. (2016) 'Climate finance in the Paris outcome: why do today what you can put off till tomorrow?', *Review of European, Comparative & International Environmental Law*, 25(2), pp. 174–185.

Zahar, A. (2017) *Climate change finance and international law*. Routledge.

Zhang, H. (2019) 'Implementing provisions on climate finance under the Paris Agreement', *Climate Law*, 9(1–2), pp. 21–39.

PART II

Building a groundswell: enabling modalities

6 Gender equality and climate finance: state policy and practice

Phoebe A. Bower

1. Introduction

In 2018, UN Women criticized the pace of progress towards achieving gender equality and empowerment for all women and girls, describing it as 'unacceptably slow and uneven' (UN Women, 2018, p. 5). It is estimated that it will take 169 years to close economic opportunity and participation gender gaps; at least 50 years to close legal rights-related gender gaps; and 300 years for there to be gender equality more generally (Badel and Goyal, 2023, p. 3). Climate change is already disproportionately impacting women and girls, further worsening existing gender gaps (Alston, 2014; Atrey, 2023; Neumayer and Plümper, 2007). Accordingly, the urgency for countries to work towards adapting to the climate crisis concomitant with gender inequality cannot be overstated.

State investment is critical to achieving both climate resiliency and gender equality. It provides the money needed to finance projects and initiatives that implement development goals, policies, and commitments. However, the cost of achieving climate resiliency and gender equality is significant. The United Nations Conference on Trade and Development (UNCTAD) estimated that it would cost $5.5 trillion annually to fight climate change, protect biodiversity, and cut pollution and US$6.4 trillion annually to achieve gender equality in 48 developing economies (UNCTAD, 2024).[1] Yet, finance flows for climate adaptation 'fall short of the levels needed to meet climate goals across all sectors and regions' (IPCC, 2023, p. 10). Similarly, investments into gender equality '[lag] behind investments for most other goals' (OECD, 2020, p. 6).

Despite these funding gaps, the Intergovernmental Panel on Climate Change (IPCC) posits that there is 'sufficient global capital and liquidity to close global investment gaps' relating to climate needs, which also means there is sufficient capital to fund significant progress towards gender equality (IPCC, 2023, p. 111). States, however, have finite capital and competing budgetary needs. One solution is to recognize the relationship between gender and climate change, acknowledging that it makes sense for governments to use climate finance to further both climate and gender ambitions. This dualist approach makes each dollar spent go further. It also recognizes that climate change exacerbates gender inequality, and gender inequality further intensifies the impact of climate change.

Drawing on the correlation between gender inequality and climate change, this chapter explores the question of why should and how can State climate finance policy and practice respond to the relationship between gender inequality and climate change. It adopts a feminist research approach to do this, which considers gender as a category of experience, recognizing the importance of focusing on women's lives to understand and address their unique challenges and vulnerabilities, particularly in the context of the climate crisis (Morawski, 1997, p. 667). This approach posits that, without the incorporation of a feminist approach to climate finance, half the world's population may not be adequately reflected within State policy and practice.

While there is no agreed definition of 'climate finance', it is broadly described by the United Nations Environment Programme as referring to 'all financial flows addressing the causes and consequences of climate change' (Bowman, 2023, p. 3; United Nations Environment Programme, 2023). One particular type of climate finance is green bonds. These are financial instruments, where the State (or other issuer) borrows money from an investor, similar to 'taking a loan or getting credit to be repaid in the future' (Puaschunder, 2023, p. 8). Sovereign green bonds play a role in funding State initiatives aimed at mitigating and adapting to climate change, or other environmental projects. Accordingly, they would be a good starting point for channelling funds to both climate change initiatives and gender equality.

The first sections of this chapter focus on the 'why', discussing the relationship between women, climate change, and finance before turning to State commitments at this intersection. This is followed by an illustrative case study on women's inclusion within sovereign green bonds, examining green bond frameworks, which set out the methodology for allocating the funds raised from green bonds to assess whether and how they include gender considerations, before turning to 'how' climate finance policy and practice can recognize gender. Finally, the last sections consider how to include more gender equality considerations within climate finance to make it more responsive to the relationship between women and climate change.

The purpose of this chapter is to map the connection between climate change and gender to encourage States to consider investing in gender and climate change concomitantly using climate finance as a platform for this. It also aims to develop foundational arguments for why and how State climate finance should focus more on gender equality and inclusion. By highlighting the disproportionate impact of climate change on women and girls and the important role of finance in achieving both climate resilience and gender equality, the chapter urges practitioners and policymakers to recognize the connection between these issues. This brings together multiple strands of literature, from discussions on climate and gender justice to international environmental and gender law, while reiterating the need to foster more inclusive and effective approaches to tackling the interconnected global crises of climate change and gender inequality.

2. Gender, climate change, and finance

Shreya Atrey explains that, while climate change impacts 'the planet as a whole, and thus arguably … everyone', climate change is not impacting 'everyone equally or in the same way' (Atrey, 2023, pp. 17–18). In this chapter, the discussion is focused on how a specific group – women – experience climate change. As Atrey notes, climate change impacts more widely and across a broader, non-binary definition of gender. However, much of this chapter focuses on international commitments, which often adopt a binary approach to gender (Rosenblum, 2011; O'Connor et al., 2022). A central focus of this chapter is the Convention on the Elimination of Discrimination Against Women (CEDAW), often referred to as the women's bill of rights. CEDAW, like other areas of international law, has faced criticism for its binary approach.

Rosenblum argues that CEDAW's exclusive focus on women impedes efforts to achieve gender equality, stating that such efforts cannot succeed 'if [CEDAW] continues to focus so narrowly and exclusively on women' (Rosenblum, 2011, p. 100). This binary focus has been replicated in more recent international commitments, including within climate change law, which often fails to define 'gender', let alone adopt an inclusive and non-binary definition. By only mentioning 'women' and not providing a broader definition of gender or acknowledging non-binary and transgender individuals, the Paris Agreement (for instance) overlooks other diverse experiences and identities that fall outside of the binary. This narrow focus can lead to exclusionary practices and policies that fail to address the needs and rights of all individuals affected by climate change. To ensure a fair and just response to the climate crisis, it is essential to expand gender concepts beyond traditional binary distinctions and incorporate all gendered experiences into climate change and gender-related laws and policies – a book chapter in itself.

Against this backdrop, this chapter adopts a feminist research approach, which aims to illuminate the connections between women, climate change, and finance. This feminist approach draws on the belief that 'gender is a primary category of experience' and therefore it should be analyzed and understood (Morawski, 1997, p. 667). Equally, the focus on women is a nod to Reinharz and Davidman, who explain that feminist research supports the viewpoint that 'women's lives are important' and deserve specific and separate attention (Reinharz and Davidman, 1992, p. 241).[2] Finally, feminist methods provide a better understanding of what causes and contributes to gender-specific harms and differentiated experiences which can provide more informed solutions that are better able to mitigate and reduce harm and negative experiences, including those of the climate crisis (Morawski, 1997, p. 667).

The focus on women in this chapter is intended to narrow its scope and does not disregard the importance of research beyond women (including for the reasons mentioned above). Using this feminist research perspective, this chapter provides an overview of three key factors influencing women's distinct experience of climate change (social structural inequalities, access to resources, and gender disparities, including poverty). This aims to illustrate, by way of specific examples, some of the ways women are disproportionately impacted by climate change, before highlighting some benefits of connecting women, climate change, and finance.

2.1 Structural gender inequalities, access to resources, and poverty

Social, political, and economic systems exacerbate gender inequality while worsening the severity of women's poverty and their access to resources (Andrijevic et al., 2020, p. 2; Djoudi et al., 2016). These relationships often exhibit circular and interconnected dynamics. For instance, economic systems may restrict women's access to capital by imposing collateral requirements for loans, and social and legal systems may diminish women's land ownership rights, which limit women's ability to provide collateral (OECD-DAC, 2015, p. 1). Because of these systems, women encounter restricted financial access, exacerbating poverty and impeding their capacity to diversify livelihoods, establish enterprises, and fortify their climate resilience.

Political systems can impede women from effectively addressing or removing these barriers, curtailing their climate resilience and capacity. In 2015, only 7 per cent of Finance Ministers worldwide were women and women occupied only 22 per cent of climate fund board positions on average (Habtezion, 2016, p. 4). Consequently, women's voices and perspectives are missing or underrepresented in government and other forms of decision-making. The result is that policy often fails to fully reflect a feminist viewpoint. Acknowledging and disrupting the harms of these interconnected systems is imperative for fostering inclusive and gender-responsive climate change responses.

Access to resources is vital for climate resilience. Bradshaw and Fordham argue that disparities in resource access, such as income, education, health, and social networks, contribute to the unequally distributed impact of disaster based on gender (Bradshaw and Fordham, 2015, p. 234). UN Women also highlights the role of limited access to information, mobility, decision-making, and training in worsening women's experiences of disasters, emphasizing how gender-specific barriers increase risks further for women (UN Women, 2022). The relationship between resource access and gender norms is cyclical. Discriminatory social constructs and norms result in women having fewer resources (including financial assets) and less capacity than men to prepare and adapt to weather shocks and climate change (Adams et al., 2014, p. 1; Bradshaw and Fordham, 2015, p. 234). These factors aggregate, reducing resilience to the impacts of climate change and leaving women worse off in relation to recovery, rehabilitation, and reconstruction (Turquet et al., 2023, p. 7). Poverty and limited access to income and financial resources are critical indicators of women's experience of climate change.

Climate change makes women poorer. UN Women estimates that by 2050, climate change will 'push up to 158 million more women and girls into poverty and lead to 236 million more women into hunger' (UN Women, 2023). Globally, 10 per cent of women already live in extreme poverty (Turquet et al., 2023, p. 11). Gender gaps, including wealth gaps, contribute significantly to climate vulnerability. This is also not a static phenomenon; climate change exacerbates vulnerability by further depleting already limited resources in a downward spiral. The link between land ownership, poverty, and resources before and after a climate event illustrates this dynamic.

Globally, women's land ownership is limited, with less than 20 per cent of land owned by women and unequal land rights for female farmers in 90 countries (Villa, 2017; Turquet et al., 2023, p. 7). After a disaster, land remains intact, while other possessions and resources, particularly those owned by women, may be irreparably damaged or lost (Erman et al., 2021, p. 8). Further economic harm is caused by women's dependence on sectors heavily affected by climate disasters (such as agriculture, forestry, and water) (Adams et al., 2014, p. 1). Moreover, infrastructure damage from climate events increases domestic workload and women's unpaid work (Fruttero et al., 2023, p. 2). Climate disasters often cause women to suffer greater economic harm than men – pushing more women into extreme poverty.

One final takeaway is that women's vulnerability to climate change stems mostly from structural inequalities (e.g., socio-economic status), rather than inherent biological differences (Neumayer and Plümper, 2007; Andrijevic et al., 2020). Instead, systemic discrimination, perpetuated through various social, political, and economic mechanisms over time, consolidates the marginalization of women, relegating them to positions of poverty and resource scarcity. Consequently, women bear disproportionate and discriminatory burdens from climate change.

2.2 Examples: women encountering climate change

The preceding paragraphs focused on how marginalization and socio-economic status impact women's experience of climate change. The next paragraphs thematically build on this, concentrating on how the climate crisis is discriminatorily impacting women, through the examples of resource scarcity, ecosystem degradation, and climate events (such as floods, hurricanes, or droughts).

While the examples in this section represent a finite list of women's encounters with climate change, many more factors further entrench women's inequality and reduce their coping capacity, while also reducing their opportunity to achieve their ambitions and aspirations. For instance, in relation to education, climate change will prevent 12 million girls annually from completing their education by 2025 (Hassani, 2022). This further deprives women and girls of the opportunities they need to fulfil their potential and contribute fully to their communities and economies.

Other gendered impacts related to climate change that could be discussed include the more significant risks of child marriage, higher rates of gender-based violence, higher levels of sex and other trafficking, more limited access to health services (including reproductive health services), worsened maternal and neonatal outcomes, and extreme labour exploitation (Hassani, 2022; Turquet et al., 2023, pp. 7–8, 11). These all play a role in understanding the far-reaching impacts of climate change on women.

Resource scarcity is exacerbated by climate change (European Commission, 2023a; Rothkopf and Casey, 2014). Resource scarcity has significant impacts on women. For example, in regions where resource scarcity is prevalent, families facing a cultural preference for boys may allocate limited resources disproportionately to male offspring (Fruttero et al., 2023, p. 2). This resource allocation bias can exacerbate gender disparities in education, increase rates of early marriage among girls, and limit their participation in productive agricultural activities.

The depletion of resources, compounded by biodiversity loss attributed to climate change, not only diminishes available resources but also escalates the burden of women's unpaid labour. This is evident in their increased time spent seeking scarcer resources, exemplified by tasks like fuelwood collection and water retrieval. Notably, statistics indicate that women undertake approximately 80 per cent of unpaid fuelwood collection worldwide and dedicate 200 million hours daily to water-gathering globally (Malgorzata Buszko-Briggs, 2022; UN Women, 2022; Turquet et al., 2023, p. 11). Resource scarcity is a pertinent example of climate change specifically and negatively impacting women's experiences.

Continuing with ecological degradation. This element of climate change also disproportionately impacts women's jobs and livelihoods (Huyer et al., 2020, p. 572). Forest deterioration affects the income of approximately one billion women globally who depend on forests for their livelihoods, and it is increasing due to climate change-related events, such as wildfires or flooding (Malgorzata Buszko-Briggs, 2022). Soil degradation and water scarcity diminish food productivity and job opportunities in the agricultural sector, which is a crucial sector for women in low-income countries (Bryan et al., 2024; Lecoutere et al., 2023). Ecological degradation from climate change plays a significant role in further impoverishing women, limiting their educational and economic opportunities, increasing their unpaid work, and heightening their exposure to climate risks. This cycle preserves poverty and deepens the impact of climate change on women. Similar impacts on women materialize from weather shocks, which are becoming more prevalent due to climate change.

Gendered impacts manifest during and following weather shocks, such as floods, hurricanes, or droughts. These impacts encompass various dimensions, spanning from increased mortality rates to economic losses and further heightened workloads. In some circumstances, research has found that women are more vulnerable to mortality and injury during weather shocks, such as in extreme heat, drought, and typhoons (Fruttero et al., 2023, pp. 5, 7, 8). Similarly, Neumayer and Plumper found that, where women's socio-economic status is low, disasters kill more women than men (Neumayer and Plümper, 2007, p. 27). Their research also notes that the correlation between biological sex and mortality rates 'vanishes with the rising socio-economic status of women' (Neumayer and Plümper, 2007, p. 27). This highlights, once again, that poverty is a key contributor to climate harm (rather than biological factors).

Increasing the socio-economic status of women increases climate change resilience, allows for faster recovery from climate events, and responds to the greater economic harms from climate change faced by women. This is essential as the negative impacts of climate change are only expected to worsen, for instance, with increasing resource scarcity, higher levels of ecological degradation, and the escalating frequency and severity of weather events and disasters (Intergovernmental Panel on Climate Change, 2023).

2.3 Connecting women, climate change, and climate finance

Turning from the connection between climate change impacts and harm to briefly mention the role women have in climate solutions. It is important to recognize that climate adaptation methods are more effective when they prioritize 'equity, climate justice, social justice, inclusion and just transition processes' (IPCC, 2023, p. 31). Using the example of agriculture, climate change is increasing food insecurity and women farmers produce between 45–80 per cent of food in developing countries (UN WomenWatch, 2009, p. 1). Given women's importance for food supply, women farmers are integral to climate solutions in the agriculture industry. Yet, the world rarely turns to this group to inform climate policies and practices.

It is essential to recognize and value the experiences of women. Their experiences make them well-placed to shape solutions. In the agricultural landscape, gendered knowledge and experiences are indispensable for informing climate solutions and should be integrated into government and other levels of decision-making and project design, but also climate finance. Broadening perspectives fosters innovation and inclusion, enhancing the robustness of solutions. This approach acknowledges that women are instrumental in creating and developing effective climate change coping strategies and resilience (OECD, 2020, p. 1).

Just as women are integral to climate change solutions, so is climate finance. Climate finance could play a critical role at the nexus of gender and climate change, which would be more equitable, efficient, and effective than non-gender inclusive climate finance (Habtezion, 2016, p. 2; Adams et al., 2014).

From an equity standpoint, the symbiotic connection between climate change and women requires climate finance to incorporate women's voices and experiences to be responsive to the realities of climate change harm (OECD-DAC, 2015, p. 1). Equally, inclusive climate finance offers the chance to upend the harmful gender and exclusionary constructs within traditional systems, including the financial system. This is possible since climate finance is a relatively new and developing category of finance, providing a blank canvas for inclusivity. This is particularly true of climate finance at the State level, which plays a substantial role in financing gender-climate projects, while also setting nationwide (or even international) standards.

Beyond equity, using finance for both climate and gender maximizes the impact of each dollar spent by progressing both gender equality and climate resiliency. This is more efficient. In terms of being effective, it is increasingly clear that promoting gender equality leads to higher economic growth; more sustainable development; more impactful environmental conservation; and other Sustainable Development Goal (SDG) benefits, such as poverty reduction (Habtezion, 2016, p. 4). Accordingly, Adams and others proposed that incorporating gender considerations into climate policy and financing mechanisms is 'smart climate finance', recognizing that gender equality can lead to improved growth and development outcomes (Adams et al., 2014, p. 4). Furthermore, there is emerging evidence that 'supporting women's empowerment builds climate resilience and reduces the negative effects of climate change on outcomes such as hunger and food security' (Bryan et al., 2024). It is more effective and efficient to invest at the nexus of gender equality and climate change mitigation and adaptation.

Climate finance is an important means of mitigating the gendered harms of climate change. Climate finance mechanisms and strategies can include gender considerations, such as target performance outcomes linked to gender, or specific earmarking to projects that reflect women's differentiated experience of the climate crisis. There are clear benefits to recognizing the intersection of gender and climate within climate finance. Nonetheless, while investing with dual purpose is more equitable, effective, and efficient, an argument could also be made that States have an obligation to consider gender within climate finance.

3. International commitments

Now that the relationship between climate change, gender, and climate finance has been outlined, the discussion will turn to responsibility, focusing on State responsibility under international law and policy to determine if States have a responsibility to recognize this relationship and to use climate finance to mitigate the gendered harms of the climate crisis. Starting with the home of women's rights, this section commences with State obligations under CEDAW, followed by the United Nations' 2030 Agenda for Sustainable Development, before closing with climate-related commitments within the United Nations Framework Convention on Climate Change (UNFCCC) and the Paris Agreement. The list is not intended to consider every angle of State responsibility, but rather to provide a foundational map charting the key areas where States have obligations to mitigate the harms to women emanating from climate change, while drawing out any references to finance that are relevant for the discussions in the following sections.

3.1 State obligations under CEDAW

Discussions on gender and climate change cannot overlook the significance of CEDAW. Often referred to as the 'international bill of rights for women', CEDAW was adopted in 1979 (United Nations General Assembly, 1979). CEDAW does not explicitly address the connection between climate change and gender; however, this is not surprising. When CEDAW was adopted, climate change discussions were more limited than today. Importantly, States that ratify CEDAW have committed to prohibiting all forms of discrimination against women. This is a broad obligation, which includes, by implication, addressing the discriminatory impacts of climate change, making it an essential part of discussions on gender and climate change.[3] While silent on the gender-climate change nexus, integrating even the broad-brush principles of CEDAW in relation to equality and non-discrimination within climate finance policy and practice can create more equitable and inclusive responses to the climate crisis.

Recognizing the evolving nature of climate discussions within the context of CEDAW took some time. As Huyer and others note: 'the integration of gender equality into climate policy has been slow at both global and national levels' – it is possible to say the same on climate change inclusion in gender policy (Huyer et al., 2020, p. 573). To remedy CEDAW's silence on climate change, the CEDAW Committee issued General Recommendation 37 (GR37) in 2018 (Committee on the Elimination of Discrimination against Women, 2018). While General Recommendations are not binding, they offer authoritative guidance on CEDAW's application.[4]

GR37 discusses the gender-related harms of disasters stemming from climate change, emphasizing the need for States to mitigate climate change and reduce disaster risk urgently. GR37 also recognizes the critical role of women's participation at all levels of decision-making in addressing climate change, as well as the need to empower women through all climate activities. Connecting gender and climate has taken time. However, despite the time taken for the CEDAW Committee to issue further guidance connecting women to climate change, CEDAW, as supplemented by GR37, provides a clear obligation for State parties to mitigate the discriminatory impacts of climate change on women.[5]

3.2 The 2030 Agenda for Sustainable Development

Similar prohibitions on discrimination appear in the 2030 Agenda for Sustainable Development (United Nations General Assembly, 2015). Adopted in 2015, the Agenda created the SDGs and established objectives for countries to 'improve health and education, reduce inequality, and spur economic growth – all while tackling climate change' (United Nations, 2024a). While the 2030 Agenda is non-binding, 'governments are expected to take ownership and establish national frameworks for the achievement of the 17 Goals' (United Nations, 2024b). Moreover, the Agenda specifically calls for gender equality – SDG5 is dedicated to this. SDG5 targets ending discrimination against women and girls, reiterating the anti-discrimination messages of CEDAW, and further delineating some of the most prevalent barriers to gender equality.

SDG5 does not join all the dots between gender and climate change. However, when considering the SDGs holistically, it is possible to view barriers to gender inequality within their wider context, including through the lens of the climate crisis. Through a more detailed review of SDG5, it is apparent that the discriminatory nature of climate change is a significant obstacle to achieving gender equality, even if this is not explicitly spelled out. For instance, while SDG 5.2 on the elimination of gender-based violence (GBV) does not mention climate change, many studies have found 'an increase in one or several GBV forms during or after extreme events', linking this to 'economic instability, food insecurity, mental stress, disrupted infrastructure, increased exposure to men, tradition, and exacerbated gender inequality' (van Daalen et al., 2022, p. 504).

Similarly, other SDG 5 targets are negatively impacted by climate change, such as reducing child marriage rates (SDG 5.3), promoting the equitable distribution of unpaid care work (SDG 5.4), and ensuring women's access to natural resources (SDG 5(a)) (United Nations General Assembly, 2015). While the overarching message of SDG 5 is ending gender-based discrimination, these more granular targets are impeded by climate change. This hints at the complex and multifaceted nature of gender discrimination and inequality at the intersection of climate change. Further, this holistic approach that looks across SDGs is important – the SDGs only make sense when viewed together, at least if the mandate for women's equality is to be achieved (OECD-DAC, 2015, p. 2).

The 2030 Agenda also contains important commitments to increasing women's access to finance, and it encourages inclusive climate action at SDG 13. Starting with access to finance, SDG 5(a) calls on States to increase women's access to economic resources and financial services, recognizing that gender equality cannot be achieved if women lack resources (United Nations General Assembly, 2015). Increasing women's access to finance is particularly pertinent for building climate resilience. Further, SDG 13(b) on climate action explicitly highlights the need to build capacity for climate change planning and management in the least developed countries, with a requirement that this focus on women (United Nations General Assembly, 2015). Achieving this goal also requires funding and resources.

To meet these cross-cutting SDG commitments, States should support climate financing that includes women, increasing women's economic resources and financial service access.[6] The 2030 Agenda's recognition of the interconnected nature of all SDGs results in the entwining of gender commitments throughout the SDGs. The interconnectedness of the SDGs should not be overlooked by States, by their implementing them in isolation, SDG by SDG. Instead, State implementation strategies must respond to the interdependence of all SDGs, recognizing that progress in one goal often hinges upon progress in others.

3.3 The UNFCCC and the Paris Agreement

SDG 13 on climate action prompts readers to turn to the 1994 UNFCCC as the 'primary international, intergovernmental forum for negotiating the global response to climate change' (UN General Assembly, 1992; United Nations General Assembly, 2015). While the UNFCCC does not expressly mention gender, it established the Conference of the Parties (COP) and is the foundation of climate finance mechanisms.[7]

The issue of gender and climate change has been an ongoing talking point at COP, as evidenced by COP decisions over the years.[8] Initial COP discussions centred on the need for more gender representation and leadership within the UNFCCC framework, per decisions 36/CP.7 of COP7 and 1/CP.16 of COP16 (UNFCCC, 2001, 2010). Yet, even with such calls for inclusion, women remained underrepresented in climate policy resulting in a renewed commitment at COP18 (in Decision 23/CP.18) to strengthen gender representation and leadership 'to inform more effective climate change policy that addresses the needs of women and men equally' (UNFCCC, 2012b, p. 48).

Additionally, climate change and gender became a standing agenda item for COP, reflecting a growing recognition of the importance of gender in climate change discussions and the need for ongoing attention to this critical issue (UNFCCC, 2012b, p. 48).

In 2014, the 'Lima work program on gender' was launched by Decision 23/CP.18. It focused on gender mainstreaming throughout all climate policies, goals, and activities. This transitioned COP Decisions from being focused on representation only to the comprehensive inclusion of gender across all areas (UNFCCC, 2014). This was a significant step, which could be seen as indirectly encouraging gender mainstreaming within climate finance. Subsequently, the following year, the Paris Agreement was agreed at COP21. The legally binding Paris Agreement's preamble encourages Parties to consider 'gender equality, empowerment of women, and intergenerational equity' in their actions to address climate change (United Nations, 2015, p. 2). Gender also appears under Articles 7(5), 7(9)(c), and 11(2) of the Agreement, reiterating the message of SDG 13 by requiring gender considerations to be incorporated into climate change planning and implementation, but also for States to develop gender-responsive climate policies and actions (United Nations, 2015, pp. 8, 13, 15). These developments provide strong encouragement for States to recognize gender harms from climate change and to include gender in climate policies, goals, and activities, including sovereign climate finance.

Post-Paris Agreement, gender and finance are addressed in the 2016 COP Decision 21/CP.22, emphasizing the need to improve the implementation of gender-responsive climate policies and actions, along with the means of implementation, such as financing (UNFCCC, 2016, p. 17). This Decision also calls for UNFCCC financing mechanisms to report on 'gender considerations in all aspects of their work' (UNFCCC, 2016, p. 19). A further pivotal moment was the 2017 COP in Bonn, which established the Gender Action Plan (GAP) (UNFCCC, 2019).[9] Among its priorities, the GAP tasked the UNFCCC Standing Committee on Finance with organizing a dialogue on gender-responsive access to finance for climate action (UNFCCC, 2019). Additionally, it urged States to incorporate gender-responsive budgeting into climate policies. The GAP also mandates State parties to monitor and report on the integration of gender considerations within their adaptation and mitigation policies, plans, and actions (UNFCCC, 2019). These developments acknowledge the challenge of implementing gender-responsive climate policies without dedicated funding.

Subsequent COPs, including the 2019 session, have urged 'public and private entities to increase the gender-responsiveness of climate finance to strengthen the capacity of women' (UNFCCC, 2019, p. 7). This call has been reiterated in the most recent COPs, indicating a stronger international commitment to funding gender-responsive climate adaptation and mitigation. Yet, the effectiveness of these commitments by States remains uncertain. At COP 28, parties agreed to revisit the challenges, gaps, and priorities of the GAP at the 2024 COP.

What remains though, is a need to strengthen the linkage between gender harm from climate change and the need to finance projects that mitigate this harm at an international level. The strongest obligation on States discussed here in relation to more gender-inclusive climate finance seems to emerge from commitments to gender equality and non-discrimination under CEDAW, which binds State parties who have ratified the treaty. However, while the legal obligations under General Recommendation 37, the 2030 Agenda, and COP Decisions remain more ambiguous under international law, even instruments with a non-binding nature can have 'political force' (Maljean-Dubois et al., 2015, p. 72). Therefore, viewing these in aggregate, there is a strong foundational argument for State responsibility to pursue gender equality and non-discrimination in sovereign climate finance policy and practice.

4. Gender and climate finance

In 2021, the global green bond market was estimated at just over half a trillion US dollars (US$517.4 billion), with some estimates that the market will increase to US$5 trillion by 2025 (Climate Bonds Initiative, 2022). This section aims to provide an overview of a subset of green bonds – those issued by sovereign States - with a focus on gender to highlight some areas where climate finance could be more responsive to the connections between gender and climate change.

Effective action on gender and climate requires significant financial investments from both the public and private sectors. The costs of implementing projects and initiatives to reduce the gendered impacts of climate change are substantial. Nonetheless, there is a significant funding gap for meeting climate targets alone. According to the OECD, the total amount of climate finance provided by developed countries to developing countries was US$89.6 billion in 2021, falling short of the US$100 billion target set by the UNFCCC, despite showing an 8 per cent increase over 2020 (UNFCCC, 2024a; OECD, 2023, p. 3). Similarly, the funding gap affects financing that targets both gender and climate. Of the total amount allocated to climate-related projects and programmes, only a small portion is directed toward initiatives that address both climate change and SDG5 on gender equality.

Research underscores significant disparities in funding allocation and gender integration within climate finance initiatives. Habtezion's research notes that, on a global level, only 0.01 per cent of funding is allocated to initiatives supporting climate change and women's rights (Habtezion, 2016, p. 4). Similarly, Zagema and others note that only one-third of climate finance projects integrate gender equality considerations (Zagema et al., 2023, p. 4). In relation to Zagema's findings, it is important to recognize that referencing or mentioning gender equality within a climate finance project does not necessarily translate into relevant and proportional gender action and inclusion within climate projects and initiatives. The integration of gender into climate finance must be meaningful and result in real impact. Addressing the climate-gender funding gap through effective gender inclusion is imperative – it should be a priority within

State climate finance. It is essential to achieving the climate and gender equality goals and obligations outlined in the previous section.

Funding gaps for climate adaptation and resiliency make it difficult for States to finance their climate commitments, notwithstanding their gender commitments. One way States often reduce their funding gaps is through sovereign debt, including through the bond market. Climate bonds, often called 'green bonds', have become increasingly popular, providing a fundraising mechanism for a country's investment into climate projects.

4.1 Climate finance design

Issuers of green bonds usually prepare and publish frameworks that detail four key components: the use of proceeds; the process for project evaluation and selection; the management of proceeds; and reporting (The International Capital Market Association, 2021). Essentially, these frameworks determine how the money borrowed from an investor by the issuer can be spent (i.e., the type of projects and programmes). Given their purpose, the frameworks are a useful indication of how green bond financing is allocated, with green bond issuers (including States) aligning their green bond issuances with the relevant framework. Therefore, for this chapter, sovereign green bond frameworks were reviewed for their inclusion of gender.[10]

Based on the commitments of States discussed in the preceding section, green bonds could provide a method of finance at the gender-climate nexus. However, within the sovereign green bond market, gender is distinctly missing from State issuer frameworks. At least nineteen sovereigns have issued green bonds, yet, in almost all green bond frameworks surveyed, there is no mention of gender or its relationship with climate change (OECD, 2021).[11] All the countries surveyed have ratified CEDAW and the Paris Agreement – highlighting a missed opportunity for sovereigns to access the funding needed to close gaps relating to their obligations and their climate actions under these agreements through green bond finance. By failing to ensure adequate funds for women's projects and general climate resiliency, States perpetuate the existing gender-based inequalities and discrimination that international commitments aim to eliminate, such as those under Article 2 of CEDAW.

While it is noted that gender may appear in other thematic bond areas, such as sovereign social bonds, which focus on funding social initiatives, the point is that climate change is a gender issue. Not expressly referencing gender in green bond frameworks is not representative of the disproportionately borne gendered harms of climate change and the need to finance projects at this intersection. This is a design problem – a fact that was recognized by a 2023 IPCC Report, which also posited that the design of regulatory and economic instruments is critical for increasing equity (IPCC, 2023, p. 31). The non-inclusive design of climate finance instruments may also feed into why Habtezion and Zagema's research found limited funding directed toward the nexus of climate and gender.

4.2 Non-inclusion of women

Ultimately, however, the lack of gender within climate finance is not limited to the limited gender inclusion within the sovereign green bond market. Other areas fail to include gender adequately, with many perpetuating gender inequality, norms, and stereotypes. At the project or programming level, women's experiences are improperly addressed too, possibly because of a lack of requirements to include gender considerations at the financial instrument level. To demonstrate this, two examples are discussed, firstly, the sectoral focus of climate projects, followed by climate adaptation and mitigation.

There are sectoral biases within climate projects that have gender-related impacts and reinforce gender norms and constructs. For instance, while gender equality is 'quite well integrated' in areas typically associated with women, such as agriculture and water, for other important sectors it is 'poorly addressed', such as in the economic infrastructure sectors that are critical for women's socio-economic development (OECD-DAC, 2015, pp. 1, 4). Similarly, areas traditionally associated with men fail to include gender equality adequately, with climate aid to sectors such as energy and transport seldom prioritizing gender equality despite receiving the largest amount of climate aid (OECD-DAC, 2015, pp. 1, 4). This crowds women out of key areas of the just transition and green economy movement. It is also contrary to CEDAW's GR37, which requires States to empower women through all climate activities. This underlines the need for gender-responsive climate finance that is cognizant of (and aims to counter) entrenched gender biases in allocating climate-related funding, with gender equality a consideration in all sectors. A similar phenomenon arises with climate mitigation and adaptation.

Two pivotal domains within climate finance, namely mitigation and adaptation, often overlook critical gender considerations. In this context, mitigation efforts target the root causes of climate change, seeking to mitigate its impacts, while adaptation aims to focus on adjusting to (or adapting to) the effects of climate change. The OECD notes that, while adaptation funding tends to address gender issues more than mitigation funding, less than half of aid in this area specifically addresses 'women's specific needs and contributions' (OECD-DAC, 2015, p. 4). The imperative for gender inclusion across both mitigation and adaptation strategies is highlighted in GR37. GR37 states that: 'Any mitigation or adaptation measures should be designed and implemented in accordance with the human rights principles of substantive equality and non-discrimination ...' (Committee on the Elimination of Discrimination against Women, 2018, p. 13). This neglect to include women's needs and contributions within climate adaptation and mitigation efforts is troubling; it is contrary to GR37, and it fails to reflect women's disproportionately negative experience of climate change impacts, as discussed earlier.

Beyond important principles of equality and non-discrimination, there are advantages to including women in mitigation and adaptation efforts. For instance, in relation to mitigation efforts, Adams and others argue that women can actively contribute to emission reduction and mitigation efforts and should thus be central to mitigation finance (Adams et al., 2014, pp. 3–4). Their policy brief highlights the importance of including women as 'essential stakeholders' for more effective climate change initiatives. They provide the example that, since women often manage household energy use, providing them with more efficient technology is crucial for reducing household emissions (Adams et al., 2014, p. 4). For effective mitigation and adaptation, gender must be a key consideration. Failing to include women in all aspects of climate finance reinforces gender stereotypes and diminishes the effectiveness of efforts to create a more climate-resilient world. The equitable allocation of resources across sectors and climate action is essential, and more research is needed at this intersection to document the need for fair climate finance distribution.[12]

While there is a need for more research, current evidence strongly suggests that sovereign climate finance needs to consider more comprehensively gender considerations, without perpetuating harmful gender norms and constructs. Ultimately, the current limited inclusion of gender within the broad spectrum of climate finance (and its regulation) perpetuates and increases the discriminatory impacts of the climate crisis, undermining resiliency and mitigation methods. Gender inequality and climate change are inherently intertwined, and all types of climate finance need to recognize this. Building on earlier discussions relating to international commitments towards climate change, gender, and climate finance, the next section considers how to increase gender equality considerations within climate finance.

5. Gender equality through climate finance

This section focuses on some initial steps to make climate finance more gender equality-focused and to mitigate the risk that it feeds the discriminatory impacts of the climate crisis. It is not a finite list, but aims to support some foundational thinking on supporting gender equality through climate finance, before the chapter's concluding remarks.

5.1 Revisiting existing law and policy

Starting at the top with climate commitments, there is scope for international climate commitments to boost the recognition of gender-climate financing. For instance, under Article 9(4) of the Paris Agreement, there is recognition of the need to scale up financial resource provision for countries that are most in need, financing climate adaptation and mitigation that prioritizes Parties that 'are particularly vulnerable to the adverse effects of climate change' (United Nations, 2015, p. 8). This includes small island developing nations and less developed countries. Commitments, such as those in Article 9(4), need to be more granular in their objectives at the intersection of climate harm and finance to recognize both state-level injustice and the injustice within States. This would better recognize that inequality exists at multiple levels and inequality within borders must also be addressed.

Creating economic and political environments that promote equality in the face of climate change is vital. Commitments should also extend more clearly to climate finance planning, implementation, policy, and action – this is a crucial foundation for promoting equality in response to the climate crisis. Despite existing commitments, there appear to be several gender-related oversights or gaps in existing climate finance systems, policies, and laws. For example, as discussed, sovereign green bond frameworks. If States are committed to progressing SDG 5 and CEDAW, as well as their Paris Agreement and COP commitments, they should mandate that all climate finance specifically further gender inclusionary principles, including in their own financing arrangements (e.g., sovereign green bonds). Moreover, plans should be implemented to close gaps in policy and practice, including areas that continue to be overlooked, such as limited views of gender that are focused on the binary. The obligations sitting at an international level must feed into State climate finance policy and practice.

Recognition and joining of the dots on gender and climate finance would be well-placed in upcoming COP agendas. It is also something that the CEDAW Committee could consider within a new General Recommendation. Noting that CEDAW General Recommendations are more sporadic and are unlikely to focus on the theme of gender and climate so soon after GR37. Including more granular commitments on gender and climate finance in the next COP agenda could encourage States to use climate finance more concretely in a way that is responsive to the uneven distribution of climate change-related harm within that State's population.

5.2 Private sector role

Private institutions also play a role in State policy and practice. Organizations, such as industry bodies, have an impact on public and private climate finance practice. In the green bond space, two key players are the International Capital Markets Association (ICMA) and the Climate Bonds Initiative (CBI), whose work further guides the formulation of green bond standards and principles.

Both ICMA and CBI do not mention gender in their green bond guidance (Climate Bonds Initiative, 2022; The International Capital Market Association, 2021). However, their guidance is often referred to in green bond frameworks, with many frameworks noting their alignment with these industry standards. Equally, many sovereign green bond frameworks have second-party opinions from private sector companies (such as S&P). These opinions certify the green bond issuer's compliance with the industry guidelines. As there is no gender requirement in the ICMA or CBI guidance, there is no mention of gender (or certification on its inclusion) in second-party opinions.

The non-inclusion of gender is becoming baked within climate finance. Both policy and secondary methods of guidance (such as that from ICMA and CBI) should expressly include gender to recognize the relationship between climate and gender. Currently, if the sovereign green bond issuers (or indeed any issuers) refer to international policy, market practice, or industry bodies for guidance, climate finance and the projects funded may not sufficiently incorporate gender considerations. A just and inclusive transition requires both the private and public sectors to advocate for gender equality within climate finance.

5.3 Gap filling: inspiration and accountability

International organizations can serve as a source of inspiration for sovereign climate finance practice. Many of the climate financing mechanisms established by the UNFCCC are encouraged to be gender-inclusive and require gender-sensitive approaches in all their activities. The Green Climate Fund (GCF), established at COP17, is a leader in prioritizing gender perspectives as an essential element of its decision-making process for deploying climate finance resources. From the outset of its operations, it has integrated gender considerations, making it the first climate finance mechanism to do so (Green Climate Fund, 2023).

Moreover, GCF projects require inclusive decision-making for the affected communities, specifically women. This is essential as there is an absence of gender representation in climate finance decision-making, with the role of women's groups 'often very limited' with a lack of 'significant engagement of women's organizations and [civil society organizations]' (Price, 2021, p. 2). Other public finance entities, such as the Adaptation Fund, have similar requirements relating to gender equality within their climate finance operations. There is no need to reinvent the wheel, and important lessons can be shared and learned from the international organization space.

In building better policy and practice, States must fulfil their commitments and be held accountable when they fail to do so. There is an accountability gap at the intersection of climate and gender. A good example of this is the biennial reporting mechanism of the UNFCCC, which requires developed States to outline the actions they have taken to implement the UNFCCC (UNFCCC, 2012c, pp. 31–35, 2012a, pp. 3–42). The form and substance of the reports are set out in the COP Decision 2/CP.17 Guidelines.

Notably, while the Guidelines for the biennial reports require details of climate finance commitments, they do not require information on the portion allocated to gender-related projects. Currently, the Guidelines only encourage parties to detail the 'social consequences of response measures' – there is no mandatory obligation to do so (UNFCCC, 2012c, p. 32). This gap in the Guidelines is particularly unfortunate since another Decision, at the same COP, concerns 'promoting gender balance and improving the participation of women' (UNFCCC Secretariat, 2013, p. 47). A sign that gender needs to be considered a cross-cutting issue rather than left in a vacuum.

Reporting on gender and climate is crucial for accountability and directing funding towards gender-inclusive projects. The Biennial Reports provide an opportunity to generate more accountability. A lack of reporting makes it challenging to hold States accountable and misses an opportunity to incentivize gender-responsive funding and the generation of better data in this area. Some countries, like Australia and the UK, voluntarily include gender considerations in their biennial reports, demonstrating a positive trend. Nonetheless, explicitly requiring gender as part of the UNFCCC Reporting Guidelines would prompt the relevant States to integrate gender considerations more effectively and consistently into their reports, as well as into their just transition finance, policies, and programmes. This would enhance the tracking of progress, the comparison of countries, and the identification of issues, while enabling a more effective accountability system that recognizes gendered climate impacts and allocates capital accordingly.

6. Conclusion

Gender equality and climate change are intertwined, and multifaceted approaches are required to address the injustices that stem from the disproportionate effects that women are experiencing from climate change due to discriminatory social constructs and norms. This principle is enshrined within international commitments, such as CEDAW and its General Recommendation 37, the 2030 Agenda establishing the SDGs, and the Paris Agreement and COP Decisions. These interconnected frameworks demonstrate international commitments to gender equality, climate action, and finance, particularly through a broad-brush requirement for equality and non-discrimination. Nevertheless, despite these commitments, a gap between commitment and action is emerging, with obligations not trickling into climate finance policy and practice. This is witnessed through the lack of gender-climate finance across sectors, but also between climate change mitigation and adaptation, and within the sovereign green bond market. This failure to provide adequate financing to mitigate climate change-related gender discrimination perpetuates existing inequalities and fails to recognize the opportunities that more inclusive climate finance offers.

As climate finance continues to grow exponentially, this becomes a question of equity, efficiency, and efficacy in reducing climate change harm in a just and proportionate manner. Creating economic and political environments that promote equality across all systematic levels is crucial. Separately, just as supranational bodies have the power to encourage better State practice, States can require better private sector practice. States should not ignore the role of the private sector in furthering gender equality. Instead, the private sector should be seen as an opportunity to provide more funding at this intersection, with countries encouraging private sector climate finance to specifically further gender inclusionary principles.

In the future, gender-related gaps in existing climate finance systems, policies, and laws must be closed, including in areas that continue to be based on outdated concepts of gender. While a binary view of gender harms from climate change focusing on women has been discussed in this chapter, it is essential to acknowledge that gender impacts are not as simple as a male and female binary. This area appears little explored, but, in the key agreements relating to gender and climate change, it is possible to see a dangerous precedent for the binary being established.

CEDAW is the treaty on 'the elimination of discrimination against women', and the Paris Agreement references the 'empowerment of women' (United Nations, 2015; United Nations General Assembly, 1979). Similarly, the 2030 Agenda seeks to 'achieve gender equality and empower all women and girls'. This reinforces a narrow view of gender, with no exploration of a broader, more inclusive definition. Indeed, more attention is paid to the 'biological characteristics' of fish in the 2030 Agenda than the important distinction between sex and gender (United Nations General Assembly, 2015).[13] More research and discussion are needed to ensure that non-inclusive views of gender are not baked within climate finance.

Another critical area of development is the need for further research on the current subject, focusing on the allocation of climate finance based on gender considerations to chart further the disconnect between gender harm from climate change and the proportion of climate finance allocated to mitigate that harm. Such research could be used to encourage more concrete action from States to combat climate change's gendered impacts through increased gender-climate finance. More research is also needed at the intersection of inclusion. There is space for a more thorough investigation into how to progress climate finance towards more inclusion, not only in terms of gender, but other areas, such as socio-economic status, race, disability, and other considerations that reflect the differentiated harms emanating from climate finance. This would enable more dialogue on holding States accountable for failing to incorporate gender and other social considerations within their climate finance mechanisms.

Investment at the nexus of gender and climate presents a pivotal opportunity to begin dismantling the barriers impacting women's resilience to climate change. Gender-inclusive climate finance should be seen as a vital tool for gender equality and non-discrimination, while providing the resources for women to safeguard themselves and their communities more effectively against the climate crisis and the harms therefrom. Moreover, such investments signal a tangible commitment by States to fulfil their obligations in meeting gender and climate commitments and targets.

Neglecting to acknowledge and rectify the current course of State climate finance practice not only contravenes State obligations to uphold principles of non-discrimination and equality but also exacerbates existing social and economic inequities. The far-reaching and profound gendered impacts of climate change highlight the imperative to act decisively and to act now. By embracing a more inclusive approach to the climate crisis and allocating mitigation and adaptation resources commensurate with the gendered dimensions of climate harm, States can pave the way for climate solutions that leave no one behind.

Notes

1. Approximately 18 per cent and 20.5 per cent of their collective GDP, respectively. These forty-eight countries cover approximately 68 per cent of the people living in developing economies worldwide.
2. There is limited space within this chapter to discuss the different gender theories or broader discussions on climate change, gender justice, and human rights. Each of these areas, while missing in this chapter, is a critical area for future discussion and research development. For further information on the broader gender impacts of climate change, please see: Fruttero et al., 2023.

3. Much of CEDAW focuses on eliminating discrimination against women, with the most broad-brush obligations set out in Article 2, which states that 'States Parties condemn discrimination against women in all its forms, agree to pursue by all appropriate means and without delay a policy of eliminating discrimination against women …'. Article 2 also lists the measures that State Parties agree to undertake to achieve this, from the recognition of equality within law and policy to refraining from practices that are discriminatory.
4. For more information, please see UN Women, 2023.
5. Only State parties to CEDAW are bound by its obligations.
6. One sidenote to this is the focus on women and girls in the 2030 Agenda and not gender more generally, which fails to recognize broader gender harms from climate change.
7. The Convention, under Article 11, established the Global Environment Facility (GEF), which was later supplemented by the Green Climate Fund (GCF) at COP17. The Kyoto Protocol, under Article 11, also notes the need for financial mechanisms to finance developing countries' climate resiliency needs. Finally, the Paris Agreement, under Article 9, requires financial resources to be provided for developing countries for climate mitigation and adaptation. For more information, please see UNFCCC, at page 7, Article 7 (*Conference of Parties*) and Article 11 (*Financing Mechanism*); UNFCCC, 2024a and United Nations, 2015, p. 13.
8. The UNFCCC has since noted that it has established 'a dedicated agenda item under the Convention addressing issues of gender and climate change' (UNFCCC, 2024b).
9. This was part of the 'Enhanced Lima Work Programme on Gender and its Gender Action Plan'.
10. Bonds and green bond frameworks are also the focus of the chapter as they are fairly transparent financial instruments, with many of the relevant documents publicly available. The survey involved a search of the terms '*Equity*', '*Gender*', '*Woman*', and '*Women*' within the relevant green bond framework. It is appreciated that there may be additional policy or legislation focusing on gender; however, that was not considered within this initial research. Moreover, this initial research does not look at other types of bonds, such as sustainability or SDG bonds, which may be more intersectional.
11. The following green bond frameworks were reviewed: Belgium's Green OLO Framework dated June 2022, Chile's Green Bond Framework dated 2020, Egypt's Sovereign Green Financing Framework dated September 2020, Fiji's Green Bond Framework dated October 2017, France's Framework for the Green OAT dated January 2017, Germany's Green Bond Framework dated 24 August 2020, Hong Kong's Green Bond Framework dated 22 February 2022, Hungary's Green Bond Framework dated May 2020, Ireland's Sovereign Green Bond Framework dated 2018, Italy's Framework for the issuance of green bonds dated February 2021, Korea's Green Bond Framework dated 2017 (through KDB, the policy bank of the Korean Government), Lithuania's Green Bond Framework dated 2017, and the Netherlands' Green Bond Framework dated 2022. The Netherlands includes a reference to the minimum social safeguards that it employs in its project and programme financing.
12. It is worth raising here that GR37 notes that: 'Any mitigation or adaptation measures should be designed and implemented in accordance with the human rights principles of substantive equality and non-discrimination, participation and empowerment, accountability and access to justice, transparency and the rule of law' (Committee on the Elimination of Discrimination against Women, 2018, p. 13).
13. See Goal 14.4 of the 2030 Agenda for more details on the relevance of the biological characteristics of fish.

References

Adams, L. Zusman, E., Sorkin, L. and Harms, N. (2014) *Making climate finance work for women*. Gender & Climate Finance. Policy Brief. Publication Stock No. ARM146800-2. Asian Development Bank (ADB), pp. 1–15. Available at: https://www.adb.org/publications/making-climate-finance-work-women (Accessed 5 April 2024).

Alston, M. (2014) 'Gender mainstreaming and climate change', *Women's Studies International Forum*, 47(B), pp. 287–294. Available at: https://www.sciencedirect.com/science/article/pii/S0277539513000204 (Accessed: 2 April 2024).

Andrijevic, M., Crespo Cuaresma, J., Lissner, T. and Thomas, A. (2020) 'Overcoming gender inequality for climate resilient development', *Nature Communications*, 11(6261). Available at: https://www.nature.com/articles/s41467-020-19856-w (Accessed: 4 April 2024).

Atrey, S. (2023) 'The inequality of climate change and the difference it makes', in Albertyn, C., Campbell, M., Alviar García, H., Fredman, S. and Rodriguez de Assis Machado, M. (eds), *Feminist frontiers in climate justice*. Edward Elgar Publishing, pp. 17–39. Available at: https://www.elgaronline.com/edcollchap-oa/book/9781803923796/book-part-9781803923796-6.xml (Accessed: 27 November 2023).

Badel, A. and Goyal, R. (2023) *When will global gender gaps close?* IMF working papers 2023, 189. Available at: https://www.imf.org/-/media/Files/Publications/WP/2023/English/wpiea2023189-print-pdf.ashx#:~:text=On%20the%20current%20track%2C%20UN,from%20the%20pre%2Dpandemic%20period.

Bowman, M. (2023) 'Polaris and pluralism: presenting a legal analytical framework for climate finance', *Carbon & Climate Law Review (CCLR)*, 17(1), pp. 3–25. Available at: https://papers.ssrn.com/sol3/papers.cfm?abstract_id=5000253 (Accessed: 15 March 2024).

Bradshaw, S. and Fordham, M. (2015) 'Chapter 14 – Double disaster: disaster through a gender lens', in Shroder, J.F. *et al.* (eds), *Hazards, risks, and disasters in society*. Hazards and Disasters Series. Academic Press, pp. 233–251. Available at: https://www.sciencedirect.com/science/article/pii/B9780123964519000147 (Accessed: 3 April 2024).

Bryan, E., Alvi, M., Huyer, S. and Ringler, C. (2024) Addressing gender inequalities and strengthening women's agency to create more climate-resilient and sustainable food systems. *Global Food Security*, 40, 100731. Available at: https://linkinghub.elsevier.com/retrieve/pii/S2211912423000615 (Accessed: 4 April 2024).

Buszko-Briggs, M. (2022) *International Women's Day: empowering women in forest communities is key to achieving climate goals and SDGs*. SDG Knowledge Hub. Available at: http://sdg.iisd.org/commentary/guest-articles/international-womens-day-empowering-women-in-forest-communities-is-key-to-achieving-climate-goals-and-sdgs/ (Accessed: 1 April 2024).

Climate Bonds Initiative (2022) *Climate bonds initiative green bond database methodology*. Available at: https://www.climatebonds.net/data-insights/publications/climate-bonds-initiative-green-bond-database-methodology

Committee on the Elimination of Discrimination against Women (2018) *General recommendation No.37 on gender-related dimensions of disaster risk reduction in a changing climate*. CEDAW/C/GC/37. Available at: https://www.ohchr.org/en/documents/general-comments-and-recommendations/general-recommendation-no37-2018-gender-related (Accessed: 2 April 2024).

Djoudi, H., Locatelli, B., Vaast, C., Asher, K., Brockhaus, M. and Basnett Sijapati, B. (2016) Beyond dichotomies: gender and intersecting inequalities in climate change studies. *Ambio*, 45(3), 248–262. Available at: https://doi.org/10.1007/s13280-016-0825-2 (Accessed: 14 January 2024).

Erman, A., De Vries Robbe, S.A., Thies, S.F., Kabir, K. and Maruo, M. (2021) *Gender dimensions of disaster risk and resilience: existing evidence*. World Bank. Available at: http://elibrary.worldbank.org/doi/book/10.1596/35202 (Accessed: 7 April 2024).

European Commission (2023a) *Aggravating resource scarcity*. Available at: https://knowledge4policy.ec.europa.eu/aggravating-resource-scarcity_en (Accessed: 1 May 2024).

Fruttero, A., Halim, D., Broccolini, C., Coelho, B., Gninafon, H. and Muller, N. (2023) *Gendered impacts of climate change: evidence from weather shocks*. Available at: https://wrd.unwomen.org/practice/resources/gendered-impacts-climate-change-evidence-weather-shocks (Accessed: 3 April 2024).

Green Climate Fund (2023) *Gender*. Available at: https://www.greenclimate.fund/projects/sustainability-inclusion/gender (Accessed: 2 April 2024).

Habtezion, S. (2016) Gender and climate finance. *United Nations Development Programme*. Gender and Climate Change. Available at: https://www.undp.org/sites/g/files/zskgke326/files/publications/UNDP%20Gender%20and%20Climate%20Finance%20Policy%20Brief%205-WEB.pdf.

Hassani, U. (2022) 'Why we must engage adolescent girls in climate change solutions', *World Bank Blogs*, 10 October. Available at: https://blogs.worldbank.org/en/climatechange/why-we-must-engage-adolescent-girls-climate-change-solutions (Accessed: 1 April 2024).

Huyer, S., Acosta, M., Gumucio, T. and Ilham, J.I.J. (2020) Can we turn the tide? Confronting gender inequality in climate policy. *Gender & Development*, 28(3), pp. 571–591. Available at: https://doi.org/10.1080/13552074.2020.1836817 (Accessed: 5 April 2024).

Intergovernmental Panel on Climate Change (ed.) (2023) 'Weather and climate extreme events in a changing climate', in *Climate change 2021 – the physical science basis: Working Group I contribution to the sixth assessment report of the Intergovernmental Panel on Climate Change*. Cambridge University Press, pp. 1513–1766. Available at: https://www.cambridge.org/core/books/climate-change-2021-the-physical-science-basis/weather-and-climate-extreme-events-in-a-changing-climate/5BCB24C5699F1D42B2DE379BDD4E2119 (Accessed: 1 May 2024).

IPCC (2023) *AR6 synthesis report: climate change 2023*. Available at: https://www.ipcc.ch/report/sixth-assessment-report-cycle/ (Accessed: 15 March 2024).

Lecoutere, E., Mishra, A., Singaraju, N., Koo, J., Azzarri, C., Chanana, N., Nico, G. and Puskur, R. (2023) 'Where women in agri-food systems are at highest climate risk: a methodology for mapping climate–agriculture–gender inequality hotspots', *Frontiers in Sustainable Food Systems*, 7. Available at: https://www.frontiersin.org/articles/10.3389/fsufs.2023.1197809 (Accessed: 4 April 2024).

Maljean-Dubois, S., Spencer, T. and Wemaere, M. (2015) 'The legal form of the Paris Climate Agreement: a comprehensive assessment of options', *Carbon & Climate Law Review*, 9(1), pp. 68–84. Available at: https://www.jstor.org/stable/43859674 (Accessed: 1 May 2024).

Morawski, J. (1997) 'The science behind feminist research methods', *Journal of Social Issues*, 53(4), pp. 667–681. Available at: https://spssi.onlinelibrary.wiley.com/doi/10.1111/j.1540-4560.1997.tb02455.x (Accessed: 2 April 2024).

Neumayer, E. and Plümper, T. (2007) 'The gendered nature of natural disasters: the impact of catastrophic events on the gender gap in life expectancy, 1981–2002', *Annals of the Association of American Geographers*, 97(3), pp. 551–566. Available at: https://www.tandfonline.com/doi/full/10.1111/j.1467-8306.2007.00563.x (Accessed: 14 January 2024).

OECD (2020) *Putting finance to work for gender equality and women's empowerment: the way forward*. 25. Available at: https://www.oecd-ilibrary.org/development/putting-finance-to-work-for-gender-equality-and-women-s-empowerment_f0fa4d91-en (Accessed: 1 April 2024).

OECD (2021) *Increasing sovereign green bond issuance, helping to promote green growth.* Available at: https://www.oecd.org/coronavirus/en/data-insights/increasing-sovereign-green-bond-issuance-helping-to-promote-green-growth (Accessed: 2 April 2024).

OECD (2023) *Climate finance provided and mobilised by developed countries in 2013–2021: aggregate trends and opportunities for scaling up adaptation and mobilised private finance.* Climate Finance and the USD 100 Billion Goal. Available at: https://www.oecd-ilibrary.org/environment/climate-finance-provided-and-mobilised-by-developed-countries-in-2013-2021_e20d2bc7-en (Accessed: 2 April 2024).

OECD-DAC (2015) *Making climate finance work for women: overview of the integration of gender equality in aid to climate change.*

Price, R. (2021) *Access to climate finance by women and marginalised groups in the Global South.* Available at: https://opendocs.ids.ac.uk/opendocs/handle/20.500.12413/16622 (Accessed: 2 April 2024).

Puaschunder, J.M. (2023) 'Funding climate justice: taxation transfers and green bonds', in Boubaker, S. and Le, T.-H. (eds), *Handbook of environmental and green finance. Transformations in banking, finance and regulation.* World Scientific (Europe), pp. 107–150. Available at: https://www.worldscientific.com/doi/abs/10.1142/9781800614451_0004 (Accessed: 29 March 2024).

Reinharz, S. and Davidman, L. (1992) *Feminist methods in social research.* Oxford University Press.

Rosenblum, D. (2011) *Unsex Cedaw, or what's wrong with women's rights.* Available at: https://papers.ssrn.com/abstract=1545302 (Accessed: 2 April 2024).

Rothkopf, D. and Casey, C. (2014) Impacts of climate change, resource scarcity and foreign policy. *World Wildlife Fund Magazine.* Available at: https://www.worldwildlife.org/magazine/issues/winter-2014/articles/impacts-of-climate-change-resource-scarcity-and-foreign-policy (Accessed: 1 May 2024).

The International Capital Market Association (2021) *Green bond principles.* Available at: https://www.icmagroup.org/assets/documents/Sustainable-finance/2022-updates/Green-Bond-Principles_June-2022-280622.pdf.

Turquet, L., Tabbush, C., Staab, S., Williams, L. and Howell, B. (2023) *Feminist climate justice: a framework for action.* Available at: https://dspace.ceid.org.tr/xmlui/handle/1/2306 (Accessed: 29 March 2024).

UN General Assembly (1992) *United Nations Framework Convention on Climate Change resolution adopted by the General Assembly.* A/RES/48/189. Available at: https://www.refworld.org/legal/resolution/unga/1994/en/26583.

UN Women (2018) 'Why gender equality matters across all SDGs', in *Turning promises into action: gender equality in the 2030 Agenda for Sustainable Development.* UN Women. Available at: https://www.unwomen.org/sites/default/files/Headquarters/Attachments/Sections/Library/Publications/2018/SDG-report-Chapter-3-Why-gender-equality-matters-across-all-SDGs-2018-en.pdf.

UN Women (2022) *Explainer: how gender inequality and climate change are interconnected.* Available at: https://www.unwomen.org/en/news-stories/explainer/2022/02/explainer-how-gender-inequality-and-climate-change-are-interconnected (Accessed: 1 April 2024).

UN Women (2023) *As climate change pushes millions of women into poverty, UN Women calls for a new feminist climate justice approach.* Available at: https://www.unwomen.org/en/news-stories/press-release/2023/12/as-climate-changes-pushes-millions-of-women-into-poverty-un-women-calls-for-a-new-feminist-climate-justice-approach (Accessed: 4 April 2024).

UN WomenWatch (2009) *Women, gender equality and climate change.* Available at: https://www.un.org/womenwatch/feature/climate_change/ (Accessed: 1 April 2024).

UNCTAD (2024) *The costs of achieving the Sustainable Development Goals*. Available at: https://unctad.org/sdg-costing (Accessed: 2 April 2024).

UNFCCC (2001) *Decision 36/CP.7 – Improving the participation of women in the representation of Parties in bodies established under the United Nations Framework Convention on Climate Change or the Kyoto Protocol*. FCCC/CP/2001/13/Add.4, p. 26. Available at: https://unfccc.int/files/bodies/election_and_membership/application/pdf/decision_36_cp7.pdf.

UNFCCC (2010) *Decision 1/CP.16 – The Cancun Agreements*. FCCC/CP/2010/7/Add.1, Annex I. Available at: https://unfccc.int/documents?f%5B0%5D=conference%3A3452

UNFCCC (2012a) *19/CP.18 – Common tabular format for 'UNFCCC biennial reporting guidelines for developed country Parties'*. FCCC/CP/2012/8/Add.3, pp. 3–42. Available at: https://unfccc.int/resource/docs/2012/cop18/eng/08a03.pdf#page=3.

UNFCCC (2012b) *Decision 23/CP.18 – Promoting gender balance and improving the participation of women in UNFCCC negotiations and in the representation of Parties in bodies established pursuant to the Convention or the Kyoto Protocol*. FCCC/CP/2012/8/Add.3, pp. 47–49. Available at: https://unfccc.int/sites/default/files/cop18_gender_balance.pdf.

UNFCCC (2012c) *Report of the Conference of the Parties on its seventeenth session, held in Durban from 28 November to 11 December 2011*.

UNFCCC (2014) *Decision 18/CP.20 – Lima work programme on gender*. FCCC/CP/2014/10/Add.3, pp. 35–37. Available at: https://unfccc.int/resource/docs/2014/cop20/eng/10a03.pdf#page=35%22.

UNFCCC (2016) *Decision 21/CP.22 – Gender and climate change*. FCCC/CP/2016/10/Add.2, pp. 17–20. Available at: https://unfccc.int/files/gender_and_climate_change/application/pdf/pages_17-20_from_10a02.pdf (Accessed: 1 April 2024).

UNFCCC (2019) *Decision 3/CP.25 – Enhanced Lima work programme on gender and its gender action plan*. FCCC/CP/2019/13/Add.1, pp. 6–15. Available at: https://unfccc.int/sites/default/files/resource/cp2019_13a01E.pdf (Accessed: 2 April 2024).

UNFCCC (2024a) *Climate finance in the negotiations*. Available at: https://unfccc.int/topics/climate-finance/the-big-picture/climate-finance-in-the-negotiations (Accessed: 2 April 2024).

UNFCCC (2024b) *Introduction to gender and climate change*. Available at: https://unfccc.int/gender (Accessed: 2 April 2024).

UNFCCC Secretariat (2013) *Report of the Conference of the Parties on its eighteenth session*. Available at: https://unfccc.int/documents/7644 (Accessed: 2 April 2024).

United Nations (2015) *The Paris Agreement. U.N. Doc. FCCC/CP/2015/L.9/Rev/1*. Available at: https://treaties.un.org/pages/ViewDetails.aspx?chapter=27&clang=_en&mtdsg_no=XXVII-7-d&src=TREATY#:~:text=%3A-,Certified%20true%20copy,-United%20Nations%2C.

United Nations (2024a) *The 17 goals – sustainable development*. Available at: https://sdgs.un.org/goals (Accessed: 2 April 2024).

United Nations (2024b) *United Nations sustainable development agenda*. Available at: https://www.un.org/sustainabledevelopment/development-agenda-retired/ (Accessed: 4 April 2024).

United Nations Environment Programme (2023) *Climate finance*. Available at: http://www.unep.org/topics/climate-action/climate-finance (Accessed: 16 March 2024).

United Nations General Assembly (1979) *Convention on the Elimination of All Forms of Discrimination Against Women*. Treaty Series, vol. 1249. Available at: https://www.ohchr.org/en/instruments-mechanisms/instruments/convention-elimination-all-forms-discrimination-against-women (Accessed: 2 April 2024).

van Daalen, K.R., Kallesøe, S.S., Davey, F., Dada, S., Jung, L., Singh, L., Issa, R., Emilian, C.A., Kuhn, I., Keygnaert, I. and Nilsson, M. (2022) Extreme events and gender-based violence: a mixed-methods systematic review. *The Lancet Planetary Health*, 6(6), e504–e523. Available at: https://www.thelancet.com/journals/lanplh/article/PIIS2542-5196(22)00088-2/fulltext (Accessed: 2 April 2024).

Villa, M. (2017) *Women own less than 20% of the world's land. It's time to give them equal property rights.* World Economic Forum. Available at: https://www.weforum.org/agenda/2017/01/women-own-less-than-20-of-the-worlds-land-its-time-to-give-them-equal-property-rights/ (Accessed: 1 April 2024).

Zagema, B., Kowalzig, J., Walsh, L., Hattle, A., Roy, C. and Dejgaard, H.P. (2023) *Climate finance shadow report 2023: Assessing the delivery of the $100 billion commitment.* Available at: https://policy-practice.oxfam.org/resources/climate-finance-shadow-report-2023-621500/ (Accessed: 2 April 2024).

7 From climate risk to net-zero and beyond: is ecologically rational regulation emerging in the finance sector?

Anita Foerster

1. Introduction

In response to the multiple ecological crises facing the planet, Parker and Haines (2018) argue for a new approach to regulatory studies that explicitly recognises the fundamental ecological underpinnings of all social and economic activity in respect of planetary boundaries (Rockström et al., 2009; Steffen et al., 2015) and reflecting post-capitalist, de-growth approaches to economics (Raworth, 2017). An *ecologically rational approach to regulation* challenges traditional, instrumentalist approaches to regulation which treat social and environmental issues as externalities of economic activity, which tend to address these issues in isolation, ignoring cumulative impacts and often privileging economic considerations, and which rely heavily on the authority of the State (Parker and Haines, 2018, pp. 140–145). *Ecologically rational regulation* also moves beyond more recent theories of responsive regulation which recognise the regulatory role of non-State actors and the regulatory effect of a wide range of measures beyond direct regulation in helping to mitigate the social and environmental harms of economic activity, but which have not succeeded in addressing unsustainable patterns of resource extraction and consumption (Parker and Haines, 2018, pp. 145–149). Ecologically rational regulation takes responsive regulation as a foundation, but adds a critical normative element, aiming to disrupt dominant forms of production and consumption and change business as usual to achieve alignment and consistency with planetary boundaries and social justice objectives. In advancing an agenda for *ecologically rational regulation*, Parker and Haines invite scholars and practitioners to explore emerging regulatory spaces from an ecological perspective, questioning whether these spaces are generating holistic solutions to complex environmental and social problems and whether they are challenging dominant forms of activity and organisation in capitalist systems, while guarding against perverse consequences, such as entrenching existing or creating new inequalities.

Thus far, the contribution of ecologically rational regulation has been largely theoretical. However, this chapter posits that the rise of sustainable finance initiatives can provide a fruitful testing ground for the theory of ecological regulation. At first glance, this may seem counter-intuitive. Traditionally, market-based financial systems focus on exchanging capital to grow assets and wealth and have served to embed unsustainable patterns of resource extraction and consumption which contribute to planetary poly-crises, including climate change (Wheeler, 2017). Moreover, while financial systems are already heavily regulated, much of this regulation focuses narrowly on protecting market participants and maintaining financial stability as a foundation for continued economic growth, relegating environmental and social externalities to other regulatory systems such as environmental law and human rights law which struggle to effectively address associated social and environmental harms. Yet, the advent of sustainable finance initiatives represents a potential shift in this regulatory agenda. A core aim of these initiatives is to re-align capital flows to help address environmental and social harms (e.g., European Commission, n.d.b). As such, they introduce new regulatory objectives that challenge and broaden the existing focus of financial regulation.

This chapter argues that there are two discernible dimensions of progress in the development of sustainable finance initiatives to date: an initial 'constrained' approach, characterised by significant, but conservative regulatory efforts within the boundaries of existing frameworks for financial risk regulation; and a more recent 'expansive' approach, involving a more ambitious regulatory agenda oriented to addressing social and environmental harms. The *constrained* approach was initiated by the recognition of the financial risk implications of climate change. Central banks and financial regulators warned of the systemic financial risks posed by climate change (Carney, 2015), urged prudent risk management (Armour, 2021; Summerhayes, 2017) and, in some jurisdictions, reformed risk disclosure laws to make climate reporting mandatory (e.g., HM Treasury & UK Dept of Business, Energy and Industrial Strategy, 2021). Institutional investors, recognising their own risk exposure, pushed investee companies to disclose and manage climate-related risks (Climate Action 100+, n.d.a); and banks and insurers began to integrate climate risk considerations into lending and underwriting activities (UNEPFI, n.d.). Yet these developments took place within existing frameworks for financial risk regulation, which are not designed to address complex environmental and social problems like climate change, but rather to supervise the management of financial risks to protect market stakeholders and promote stable, efficient markets. While recognition and treatment of climate change as a financial risk represents a significant shift in discourse and practice within these systems, it does not, of itself, mark a radical divergence from traditional ways of regulating.

More recently, however, a more *expansive* approach can be discerned. Regulatory activity has started to coalesce around substantive standards that do have their roots in ecological realities and planetary boundaries. This has been achieved largely through the activities of non-State actors, using a diverse array of regulatory strategies including advocacy, investor engagement, and strategic litigation. For example, best practice standards for climate risk disclosure and management are now based on the net zero and temperature goals of the international Paris Agreement (developed from international scientific consensus on 'safe' levels of climate change) (UNFCCC, 2015).[1] Civil society, industry bodies, and investor coalitions are all involved in developing these standards and engaging with companies to drive their uptake; and in some cases, also litigating to embed best practice expectations and hold companies accountable on their climate performance. In these more recent developments, it is possible to discern the early seeds of a more ecologically rational approach to financial regulation.

This chapter uses the theory of *ecologically rational regulation* as a frame to explore the potential and the limits of these recent developments in sustainable finance, reflecting on whether this fast-developing body of regulation is establishing new limits on economic activity that reflect the ecological realities of the global climate system. As a foundation for this inquiry, section 2 outlines the ecologically rational approach to regulation, noting its expansion on previous theories of responsive regulation and its links to the burgeoning scholarship on planetary boundaries and Earth Systems Law. Section 3 explores the two dimensions of regulatory developments in the fast-evolving regulatory space of sustainable finance (constrained and expansive), focusing on the finance sector and climate change and using the jurisdiction of Australia to illustrate regulatory trends common to Anglo-American jurisdictions. Section 4 reflects on whether and how these regulatory developments might embody a more ecologically rational approach to regulating the finance sector. Section 5 concludes by considering the value of ecologically rational regulation as a frame for progressing the development of the finance sector's response to climate change and other sustainability challenges, and highlighting important areas for future research inquiry.

2. Ecologically rational regulation

Ecologically rational regulation is posited by Parker and Haines as a new approach to regulatory studies which responds to the multiple ecological crises facing the planet and which recognises that all social and economic activity is embedded within, and limited by, the biophysical systems of the Earth (Parker and Haines, 2018; Parker, 2022). It draws inspiration and impetus from the earth system sciences, particularly the highly influential planetary boundaries scholarship which has aimed to define a 'safe operating space' for human societies to develop and thrive (Rockström et al., 2009). Based on an understanding of the functioning and resilience of nine interconnected earth system domains (including climate, biosphere, nutrient cycles, and freshwater), this scholarship sets out quantified boundaries for each domain, intended to designate limits to the human impacts that can be sustained by the Earth without resulting in undesirable, often irreversible change and associated adverse impacts for human wellbeing (Rockström et al., 2009). Of these, climate change and biosphere integrity are recognised as core boundaries which interact with, and underpin, all other earth system domains (Steffen et al., 2015). Recent iterations of the planetary boundaries move beyond what is considered 'safe' and add multi-layered justice criteria to the delineation of limits to human activity (interspecies, intergenerational, and intragenerational justice). This recognises that the 'stability and resilience of the Earth system and human wellbeing are inseparably linked' and 'contributions to earth system change and the consequences of its impacts vary greatly among social groups and countries' (Rockström et al., 2023, p. 102).

In concluding their most recent work on safe *and just* earth system boundaries, Johan Rockström and co-authors call for the practical application of earth systems science at different institutional scales: 'nations, cities, businesses and other key actors need to set and achieve science-based targets for reducing their environmental impacts based on translating the safe and just Earth System Boundaries to actor fair shares' (Rockström et al., 2023, p. 109). Climate is currently the only earth system domain with relatively well-established methods for translating global limits to science-based targets at different scales, from the nation state to subnational jurisdictions to corporate entities (Rockström et al., 2023, p. 109). This translation effort has been aided by the fact that climate-related planetary boundaries were used as a basis for the core mitigation goals of the international Paris Agreement (Ebbesson, 2014, p. 8), which aims to hold global average temperature rise to 'well below 2°C' above pre-industrial temperatures, and pursue efforts to limit temperature rise to no more than 1.5°C, so as to significantly reduce the risks and impacts of climate change' and achieve net-zero emissions as soon as possible in order to achieve this 'long-term temperature goal' (UNFCCC, 2015, Arts 2.1, 4.1). However, as Rockström et al.'s latest work suggests, while the more ambitious 1.5°C temperature goal may meet the 'safe' earth systems criteria at a global scale, it does not meet associated justice thresholds: 'if exposure of tens of millions of people to significant harm is to be avoided, the just boundary should be set at or below 1.0°C', a threshold which has already been overstepped (Rockström et al., 2023, p. 105).

The articulation of planetary boundaries has catalysed and contributed to a growing body of social sciences scholarship exploring the limits and the potential of the planetary boundaries concept to guide the future development of social institutions, including law and regulation, to help avert socio-ecological collapse (Bleby et al., 2021, pp. 30–32). It is here that the ecologically rational approach to regulatory studies sits, alongside and linked to the broader project of Earth System Law, which rests on the fundamental concept that humans are part of nature, the Earth is a single, interconnected system, and human activities should be limited by reference to the laws of nature (Cullinan, 2011; Maloney, 2014; Kotzé and Kim 2019; Kim and Kotzé 2021; Kotzé et al., 2022).

In explaining and justifying the need for an ecologically rational approach to regulation, Parker and Haines begin by pointing out the limitations of existing approaches. They describe *instrumentally rational* approaches which treat the social and environmental harms of commercial activity as market externalities, and which tend to address these issues in isolation, ignoring cumulative impacts. Here, the regulation of social and environmental harms is more typically conducted *by* formal State-based regulators *to* regulated entities. In practice, environmental regulation is often undermined and weakened by dominant discourses and associated (non-ecologically oriented) regulation that privileges competitive markets and economic growth as the pathway to human wellbeing (Haines and Parker, 2017, pp. 83–85; Parker and Haines,

2018, pp. 140–145). More recent theories of *responsively rational* regulation challenge instrumentally rational models, recognising that networks of actors beyond the State, including civil society, play a role in influencing the behaviour of businesses and helping to mitigate social and environmental harms. Here, regulation is broadly conceived to include pricing, information, and participatory approaches, alongside direct regulation, often coordinated by the State through a process of meta-regulation (Parker and Haines, 2018, pp. 145–149). Yet, despite this broader framing and stronger democratic basis, responsive regulation has not succeeded in addressing unsustainable resource extraction and consumption. Indeed, it relies heavily on civil society to advocate for environmental interests, positing the environment as one of many stakeholders, rather than recognising that all social and economic activity is fundamentally reliant on healthy ecological systems (Parker and Haines, 2018, pp. 148–149).

An ecologically rational approach to regulation takes *responsive regulation* as a foundation and adds a critical normative element. Recognising that 'the production of both ecological crisis and social inequality is to a large degree tied to the way in which capitalism and business activity are organised and governed' (Parker, 2021, p. 44), an ecologically rational approach aims to disrupt dominant forms of production and consumption and change business as usual to achieve alignment and consistency with planetary boundaries and social justice objectives. In theory, ecologically rational regulation offers opportunities for holistic solutions to intersecting ecological and social challenges. For example, in exploring complex water-energy-food nexus issues such as meat consumption (Parker et al., 2018), and food system issues such as the dominance of ultra-processed foods with adverse human health and environmental implications (Northcott et al., 2023), advocates of ecologically rational regulation argue that elegant solutions with a range of environmental and social benefits demand alternative regulatory approaches guided by ecological limits and social justice norms.

Parker and Haines recognise that realising an ecologically rational approach in practice is unlikely to be swift and clean, but instead will require plural normative and legal strategies (Haines and Parker, 2018, p. 102), and involve extensive contestation and conflict (Parker and Haines, 2018). They draw attention to the strategy of 'bracing' ecological limits and social justice norms onto existing (non-ecologically oriented) regulatory regimes such as corporate law and related business regulation (Haines and Parker, 2018, pp. 88–89). In this context, bracing refers to introducing norms and rules that are grounded in ecological limits through regulatory interventions such as advocacy, investor engagement, and strategic litigation, typically led by non-State actors, but potentially also through the formal regulatory enforcement and law reform activities of the State. However, this 'bracing' strategy comes with attendant risks that business behaviour will only shift within the boundaries of the existing (non-ecologically oriented) regulatory context, or that market actors will adapt to regulatory interventions in ways that can serve to maintain the status quo and favour their interests (Haines and Parker, 2018, p. 102).

As such, the ecologically rational approach to regulation suggests two main areas of inquiry to guide this chapter's investigation of climate-related regulatory developments in the finance sector:

- Bracing: Is there evidence that regulatory regimes governing the finance sector are being 'braced' with ecological limits (and social justice norms)? What types of actors are involved and what types of regulatory activities are leading to this bracing?
- Alignment: Is this regulatory activity shifting the behaviour of the finance sector towards substantive alignment with ecological limits and social justice norms (and beyond the boundaries of the existing regulatory regime)? Will it help to limit business activity that contributes to climate change and explicitly redirect this activity to achieving global climate goals?

Following the characterisation of the different dimensions of regulatory developments in sustainable finance in section 3, the discussion will return to these concepts of bracing and alignment in section 4, drawing on available empirical evidence and considering the potential for law reform to further embed ecological and social limits and norms within the regulation of the finance sector to strengthen and hasten alignment with planetary boundaries.

3. Charting the rise of sustainable finance initiatives and characterising the Regulatory Space

Using climate change as a touchstone, this part characterises two dimensions of regulatory developments in sustainable finance in Australia: an initial *constrained* approach whereby climate change has been introduced to existing legal and regulatory frameworks as a source of financial risk which must be disclosed and managed; and a subsequent more *expansive* approach whereby diverse non-State actors are developing substantive standards for climate risk management that reference planetary boundaries and use corporate law tools to drive their uptake and hold companies accountable to them.

Developments in Australia mirror common regulatory trends across Anglo-American jurisdictions (which have similar legal traditions and comparable underlying corporate law and prudential regulation). Indeed, sustainable finance agendas are developing in broadly similar ways around the world,[2] with the most advanced implementation in the European Union (European Commission, n.d.). As such, the two-dimensional characterisation set out in this part should resonate at a general level across a range of diverse jurisdictions, particularly Anglo-American jurisdictions, noting that there will be differences in the nature and pace of developments and acknowledging that Australia does not represent the most progressive of jurisdictions, rather, a middle-runner.

3.1 Dimension 1 - constrained regulation of climate change within existing corporate law and prudential frameworks

In the lead-up to the Paris Agreement in 2015, Mark Carney's speech to Lloyd's of London (Carney, 2015) is often marked as a turning point for private sector approaches to climate change, helping to catalyse a shift from treating climate change as a matter of corporate social responsibility to recognising it as a source of material financial risk. The work of the Task Force on Climate-Related Financial Disclosures (TCFD) was instrumental in this shift. Established in 2015 by the international Financial Stability Board (FSB, n.d.), the TCFD brought together a group of powerful, non-State market actors (representatives from leading global businesses, including many in the finance sector), to develop recommendations for climate-risk disclosures to underpin more informed investment, credit, and insurance underwriting decisions. Through the work of the TCFD and others (e.g., Bank of England, 2017), there are now well-accepted categories of climate-related financial risks (physical, transition, litigation) and a good general understanding of the way in which these risks may result in lower revenue, reduced asset value, or stranded assets for operating companies, with flow-on implications for finance sector entities (banks, insurers, and institutional investors), which lend to, insure, or invest in these companies (TCFD, 2017, pp. 7–12).

Recognising climate change as a source of financial risk has the effect of enlivening existing legal obligations under corporate law and prudential regulation. In Anglo-American jurisdictions, obligations to identify, disclose, and manage material financial risks to company interests are central to corporate law frameworks. An additional layer of prudential regulation applies to finance sector entities, designed to ensure adequate risk management and governance, so that these entities can meet their obligations to policy and deposit holders and beneficiaries (Black, 2004; Gunningham, 2020).

For example, under Australian law, annual company reports must include financial statements which provide a 'true and fair view' of the company's financial position and performance (Corporations Act 2001 (Cth), ss. 295–297, 307, 308); as well as a director's report discussing the operations of the entity, its financial position, business strategies, and future prospects (Corporations Act 2001 (Cth), s. 299A(1)). Regulatory guidance provides that 'it is likely to be misleading to discuss prospects for future financial years without referring to the *material business risks* that could adversely affect the achievement of the financial prospects described for those years' (Australian Securities and Investment Commission (ASIC), 2019). Serious penalties apply for false or misleading disclosure (see e.g., Corporations Act 2001 (Cth) ss. 674, 1311, 1317E; see also Barker, 2018, pp. 37–38). Following the work of the TCFD, corporate regulators and accounting standard-setting bodies have clarified that these rules apply to climate-related risks where they are material to company interests (Australian Accounting Standards Board & Australian Audit Standards Board (AASB & AUASB), 2019; ASIC, 2019). Although regulators have not brought legal action to enforce disclosure obligations in relation to climate change, they have increased their scrutiny of climate disclosures (Armour, 2021; ASIC, 2018), including cautioning companies regarding misleading or non-disclosure of climate risks in annual reports (ASIC, 2023; Roddan, 2021).

Company directors also have broader legal duties to act in the best interests of the company (Corporations Act 2001 (Cth), s. 181) and with due care and diligence (Corporations Act 2001 (Cth), s. 180(1)). It is now widely accepted that, as part of their duty of due care and diligence, directors are required to inform themselves of foreseeable risks posed to company interests by climate change and must take proportionate measures to manage these risks (Hutley and Hartford-Davis, 2016; Hutley and Hartford-Davis, 2019; Hutley and Hartford-Davis, 2021; see also Australian Institute of Company Directors (AICD), 2020; ASIC, 2018; Barker, 2015; Peel et al., 2020, pp. 24–29). A failure to do so which harms, or which could potentially harm, company interests could expose directors to liability for breach of duty (Hutley and Hartford-Davis, 2016). Understanding of the standard of care required of a reasonable director is also developing rapidly in light of evolving market expectations which reinforce the foreseeability and materiality of the financial impacts of climate change. In a recent legal opinion, high-profile Australian commercial law barrister Noel Hutley and colleagues concluded, 'it is no longer safe to assume that directors adequately discharge their duties simply by considering and disclosing climate-related trends and risks; in relevant sectors, directors of listed companies must also take reasonable steps to see that positive action is being taken: to identify and manage risks, to design and implement strategies, to select and use appropriate standards, to make accurate assessments and disclosures, and to deliver on their company's public commitments and targets' (Hutley and Hartford-Davis, 2021, pp. 2–3).

For finance sector entities, the prudential regulatory regime establishes similar legal duties and explicitly requires certain risk management processes and activities. For example, trustee directors of pension funds must exercise their powers in the best interests of the fund's beneficiaries and exercise due care, skill, and diligence in carrying out their duties and functions (Superannuation Industry Supervision Act 1993 (Cth) ('SIS Act'), s. 52(2)(c) (trustee) and s. 52A(2)(c) (trustee directors); Hutley and Mack, 2017, pp. 7–8). Governing legislation mandates the formulation, regular review, and implementation of an investment strategy having regard to the level of risk, likely return, diversification, and availability of reliable information (SIS Act, s. 52(6); Australian Prudential Regulatory Authority (APRA), 2023); the development and maintenance of a risk management strategy to address risks that may have a material impact on their operations (SIS Act, s. 52(8); APRA, *Prudential Standard SPS 220 – Risk Management*); and the implementation of a comprehensive stress-testing programme that assesses the performance of each investment option against prescribed scenarios covering a range of factors that could lead to extraordinary losses (APRA, *Prudential Practice Guide SPG 530*). It is now broadly accepted that climate-related financial risks can and should be considered by pension funds and their directors in the exercise of their duties and functions to the extent that those risks intersect with the financial interests of beneficiaries (APRA, 2019, p. 7; Hutley and Mack, 2017, p. 2; Summerhayes, 2017). Prudential regulators have also increased their oversight of climate risk management and governance and developed regulatory guidance to assist regulated entities to comply with existing standards as they apply to climate change (APRA, 2020; APRA, 2021).

This legal framework is designed to protect the interests of market stakeholders with underpinning objectives to maintain a stable, efficient, and competitive financial system (Gunningham, 2020, pp. 460–462; Black, 2004). It relies heavily on process-based risk regulation (or meta-regulation) and informational regulation (Gunningham, 2020, p. 468; Sinclair, 2019, pp. 154–158; Baldwin and Black, 2016). These regulatory approaches aim to raise awareness about risks, ensure transparent sharing of risk information, and oversee risk management activities to ensure that material risks are considered and priced in financial decisions (Black and Baldwin, 2010, p. 202; Gunningham, 2020, p. 468). Regulators frame their role as ensuring well-informed decision-making and appropriate risk management practices, not as seeking to determine the financial decisions of regulated entities (APRA, 2021, p. 5).

It is important to emphasise that this legal framework does not create obligations for companies and their directors to respond to climate change in a particular way. Rather, entities have the latitude to take their own context into account and exercise their judgement in assessments of materiality and treatment of risks. For example, it is reasonably open for company directors to decide to continue to pursue climate-damaging activities as part of their business model if the financial risks associated with these activities can be appropriately managed (e.g., through diversification of business activities and investment in developing alternatives over time). For some finance sector actors – for example, pension funds – which are diversified investors with longer-term investment horizons, financial returns depend on the overall performance of the economy, not only profits from individual assets (Alexander et al., 2020, p. 16). Diversified investors therefore have a financial imperative and implied legal duty to mitigate sustainability-related systemic risks through capital allocation and stewardship. As such, in theory, they should place expectations on investee companies to disclose information about their climate change impacts which threaten the stability of the economy and to demonstrate how they are managing these impacts. However, the financial imperative to address sustainability-related systemic risks is not fully understood across the financial sector and other counter-incentives are also powerful (e.g., shorter-term returns from continued investment in climate-damaging activities) (Freshfield Bruckhaus Deringer, Principles for Responsible Investment, United Nations Environment Programme Finance Initiative, and the Generation Foundation, 2021; Principles for Responsible Investment, 2022).

In summary, the recognition of climate change as a financial risk issue, which enlivens legal obligations to identify, disclose, and manage these risks, represents a significant shift in discourse and practice within these systems. Yet the predominant focus on financial risk to market participants, as it manifests at the entity scale, means that it does not amount to the substantial shift and realignment envisaged by ecologically rational regulation.

3.2 Dimension 2 – expansive regulation of climate change via substantive standards for climate risk management, investor engagement, and strategic litigation

The legal framework outlined above has provided a foundation for a range of associated regulatory activities, involving different constellations of non-State actors, which are coalescing around norms of Paris alignment and net-zero emissions. Non-State actors have differing motivations for these interventions: civil society is engaging strategically with the tools of corporate law and prudential regulation to influence and shift private sector behaviour; whereas institutional investors are driven by their own risk management imperatives and obligations, as well as by more normative pressures which intersect with reputational concerns regarding the role that the private sector can and should play to address climate change.

3.2.1 *Voluntary industry standards*

The role of the TCFD in establishing climate change as a source of material financial risk for companies and investors was outlined above. The TCFD has also played a significant role in developing substantive best practice expectations for climate risk management that expand upon what are otherwise principles-based legal obligations. The TCFD explicitly refers to the Paris Agreement as a critical reference point for measuring risk exposure and for guiding risk management responses. Entities are recommended to disclose detailed information on the direction and ranges of potential financial implications under different climate-related scenarios, including emissions reduction scenarios that align to the Paris Agreement (TCFD, 2017, pp. 25–32; TCFD, 2021b). They should also use metrics to measure risk exposure over time (including greenhouse gas (GHG) emissions) (TCFD, 2021b, pp. 16–17), set quantified targets using these metrics, and report regularly on progress (TCFD, 2017, p. 14; TCFD, 2021b; TCFD 2021c). As such, the TCFD gently encourages alignment of strategy with Paris goals and the setting of targets to reflect this.

Setting Paris-aligned emissions targets at the scale of a corporate entity requires translation of *global* temperature goals to the entity scale, and therefore involves complex assumptions about the timing and magnitude of emissions reduction required and how this should be allocated to companies and sectors (Krabbe et al., 2015, pp. 1057–1061). To provide rigorous and transparent methods to calculate a company's 'fair share' of emissions reductions against these global goals, voluntary standards and associated target certification platforms are developing (Dietz et al., 2018, pp. 1072–1075; Krabbe et al., 2015, pp. 1057–1061). These have been developed by a broader range of stakeholders than the TCFD, with strong participation from civil society and investor organisations focused on environmental and social issues (Dietz et al., 2018, pp. 1072–1075; SBTi, 2019).

For example, the Science-based Target Setting Initiative (SBTi) provides an accreditation platform to certify that corporate climate targets are aligned with the Paris Agreement (SBTi, n.d.). To be accredited under the SBTi Net-Zero Standard (which is aligned to the 1.5°C temperature goal) (SBTi, 2021a), companies must commit to reducing Scope 1, Scope 2, and where relevant, Scope 3 (value chain) emissions[3] to zero or to a residual level that is consistent with Paris-aligned pathways and set near-term (5–10 years) and long-term (2050 or earlier) targets to achieve this (SBTi, 2021, pp. 20–32). The pace and magnitude of emissions reductions expected differs between industries and sectors in recognition of their various contributions to global emissions as well as their mitigation potential (SBTi, 2021, p. 15). For example, heavy emitting sectors (e.g., power generation, energy forestry, agriculture) should use a sectoral target-setting approach, but others should use an absolute approach (equating to a requirement to reduce emissions by 4.2 per cent annually). Signatory companies commit to report company-wide emissions and disclose progress annually against targets (SBTi, 2021b; SBTi, 2022b).

Similar, more targeted initiatives for finance sector entities provide guidance for setting Paris-aligned targets for attributable *financed* or *portfolio* emissions (i.e., emissions associated with lending, finance, or investment activities) (SBTi, 2022a). For example, for banks, the United Nations Environment Programme Finance Initiative (UNEPFI) has developed *Guidelines for Climate Target Setting for Banks* (UNEPFI, 2021) and the associated Net-Zero Banking Alliance commitment platform (UNEPFI, n.d.) to address financed emissions (UNEPFI, 2021; see also Investor Group on Climate Change, 2021). These recommend that banks prioritise 2030 lending and finance targets for GHG-intensive and GHG-emitting sectors, as well as setting targets for financing climate solutions. For institutional investors like pension funds, the *Net Zero Investment Framework* (Institutional Investors Group on Climate Change, 2021) developed by the European Institutional Investors Group on Climate Change and the United Nations' convened *Net Zero Asset Owner Alliance Target Setting Protocol* (Net Zero Asset Owners Alliance 2021, UNEP Finance Initiative and UN PRI 2024) both emphasise the need to decarbonise investment portfolios while concurrently increasing investment in climate solutions, and underscore that net-zero strategies must be designed to drive emissions reductions in the real economy, not only shift emissions from a particular portfolio to other asset owners via divestment. As such, they recommend targets be set for the portfolio as a whole and for each asset class (based on the SBTi method) with an initial focus on the highest emitting sectors, targets for financing the energy transition, and targets for corporate engagement and policy engagement (Net Zero Asset Owners Alliance, 2021, pp. 11, 27–67). Signatories to the Net Zero Asset Owners Alliance commit to publishing interim targets every five years and to report regularly on progress (Net Zero Asset Owners Alliance, 2021, p. 8).

As the discussion below illustrates, voluntary standards like the TCFD and the SBTi have been taken up as reference points for investor engagement and strategic litigation activities in Australia.

3.2.2 *Investor engagement*

Large institutional investors in Australia and other jurisdictions are increasingly engaging with investee companies on climate change, working together in coalitions to amplify their influence and to undertake more transparent, public-facing engagement activities. Over time, the focus of investor engagement has shifted from requests for improved risk disclosure following the TCFD standards to more substantive demands to cut GHG emissions in line with the Paris Agreement. While these activities are framed as necessary to address risks to investment portfolios (including systemic, market-wide risks) and to create long-term shareholder value (ACSI, 2021); their ambition and their alignment with global climate goals also suggest a more normative recognition that the private sector can and should play a more central role in society's efforts to address climate change.

For example, *Climate Action 100+* is an engagement initiative backed by hundreds of global investors, including large Australian pension funds and fund managers (Climate Action 100+, n.d.a). The initiative targets 171 companies which are high GHG emitters, or which have significant opportunities to drive the clean energy transition (Climate Action 100+, n.d.b). Climate Action 100+'s *Net Zero Company Benchmark* measures the performance of target companies against select climate indicators. The indicators draw on the industry standards outlined above and include corporate emissions reduction targets aligned to Paris goals using SBTi methodologies; disclosure of a decarbonisation strategy to deliver on targets; strong climate governance including clear board oversight of climate-related risks as well as sufficient competencies to assess and manage these risks; and executive remuneration incentives incorporating climate performance (Climate Action 100+, n.d.c).

Shareholder resolutions have also been used by civil society and institutional investors in Australia to pressure companies on their approach to climate change (Peel et al., 2020, pp. 31–37). Early resolutions focused on disclosure, seeking to drive the uptake of TCFD standards or to pressure companies to address corporate lobbying activities that were inconsistent with their stated climate goals. More recent resolutions explicitly address the systemic nature of climate risk and focus on aligning corporate risk management and mitigation of corporate climate impacts with global climate goals. Examples include resolutions that pressure companies to set Paris-aligned emissions reduction targets accompanied by decarbonisation plans that demonstrate alignment of company strategy and capital allocation to these targets;[4] to disclose liabilities associated with decommissioning oil and gas infrastructure in line with Paris-aligned net zero scenarios;[5] to disclose how their capital allocation to fossil fuel assets aligns with Paris goals;[6] and to bring forward closure dates for coal assets in alignment with Paris goals.[7] These resolutions largely target companies in the energy, mining, and finance sectors (especially banks). Climate resolutions in Australia are typically lodged by civil society groups such as the Australasian Centre for Corporate Responsibility (ACCR) and Market Forces, but have at times been co-filed by institutional investors, a practice more common in other jurisdictions to date (ACCR, n.d.). As large institutional investors become more active in climate engagement, these resolutions are now receiving significant (albeit variable) levels of the shareholder vote (ACCR, n.d.), amplifying their potential influence on company behaviour.

3.2.3 *Strategic litigation*

Strategic climate litigation that targets the private sector is on the rise around the world, including in Australia (Markey-Tower and Peel, 2021; Setzer and Higham, 2021), with a growing number of cases seeking to enforce legal obligations to disclose and manage climate-related risks as a strategy to drive companies and investors to shift capital and resources away from climate-damaging activities (Setzer and Higham, 2021; see also Foerster, 2019). Early Australian cases helped establish that underlying risk management and disclosure obligations apply to climate change, both in the context of corporate risk disclosure obligations (*Guy Abrahams v. Commonwealth Bank of Australia* (2017); Hutchens, 2017), and in relation to the duties of pension fund trustees (*Mark McVeigh v. Retail Employees Superannuation Pty Ltd* (2019); REST, 2020). More recent claims address the substance of company and investor approaches to climate risk management and seek to hold entities accountable for delivering on their climate commitments and targets.

For example, in 2021, retail shareholders (represented by public interest law firm Equity Generation Lawyers) brought proceedings against the Commonwealth Bank of Australia (one of Australia's largest banks) (CBA) seeking to access internal company documents (Corporations Act 2001 (Cth), s. 247A), to examine the truth of the bank's commitments on climate change (Abrahams and Abrahams, 2021). In 2019, CBA had stated that, 'We ensure our business lending policies support the responsible transition to a net zero emissions economy by 2050, by only providing Banking and Financing activity to new oil, gas or metallurgical coal projects if supported by an assessment of the environmental, social and economic impacts of such activity, and in line with the goals of the Paris Agreement'. The applicants sought documents relating to several of the bank's loans to gas and other fossil fuel projects (Abrahams and Abrahams, 2021). The Federal Court granted the application ordering CBA to produce the documents for inspection. In finalising the proceedings in April 2023, the Court ordered that the applicants could use certain documents to pursue further litigation against the bank and could forward such documents to relevant corporate and prudential regulators (*Abrahams & Abrahams v. Commonwealth Bank of Australia* (2023)). It is possible that the documents received would have provided a strong foundation for further claims of misleading or deceptive disclosure, although this now appears unlikely in the near term given the CBA's response to the litigation. The bank has recently updated its climate policy, committing to new restrictions on fossil fuel financing including no direct financing of new or expanded oil and gas projects or associated enabling infrastructure such as pipelines (Commonwealth Bank of Australia, 2023).

In 2022, the ACCR brought proceedings against Santos (a leading Australian oil and gas company) in *Australasian Centre for Corporate Responsibility v. Santos*, alleging that the company had engaged in misleading and deceptive conduct relating to claims made in its 2020 Annual Report (Competition and Consumer Act 2010 (Cth), ss. 4, 18; ASIC Act 2001 (Cth), ss. 12BB, 12DA; Corporations Act 2001 (Cth), ss. 796C). At issue in this ongoing case are representations made in the annual report that the company had a clear and credible pathway to achieve its long-term and interim emissions reduction targets; that the company is a producer of 'clean energy'; that natural gas is a 'clean fuel'; and that hydrogen produced from natural gas with carbon capture and storage is 'clean' and produces 'zero emissions'. In relation to targets, ACCR alleges that Santos failed to disclose that it intends to pursue oil and gas growth beyond 2025, which would increase its overall emissions and further that Santos failed to disclose that its net zero plans depend on a range of undisclosed and unreasonable qualifications or assumptions. In relation to natural gas, ACCR alleges that Santos falsely conveyed that natural gas has no material adverse effect on the environment nor releases material greenhouse gas emissions. On hydrogen, ACCR alleges that Santos has failed to disclose how its hydrogen production activities will increase its scope 1 and 2 emissions and that it is not practically or commercially viable to capture all emissions with carbon capture and storage.

Similar litigation strategies are being used to target the climate risk management strategies of other large Australian energy companies such as Woodside Energy (leading Australian oil and gas company) and Energy Australia (large Australian electricity generator with significant coal assets). For example, in *Greenpeace Australia v. Woodside Energy*, Greenpeace alleges that Woodside Energy has made misleading statements in relation to the GHG emissions reductions it claims to have achieved and in relation to its plan to attain net zero by 2050. In *Australian Parents for Climate Action v. Energy Australia*, it is alleged that Energy Australia has made misleading statements in relation to the use of carbon credits to offset GHG emissions associated with green-labelled energy products.

Litigation seeking to enforce directors' duties as they relate to climate change has not yet emerged in Australia. However, recent developments in the United Kingdom, which has very similar corporate law frameworks, provide an indication of the significant obstacles that this may face in Australia. In *ClientEarth v. Shell's Board of Directors*,[8] civil society group ClientEarth filed a derivative action against Shell's directors, arguing that by failing to adopt and implement a robust and credible climate transition strategy in line with the *Paris Agreement*, the directors were in breach of their duties to act with due care and diligence in the best interests of the company under UK company law. The claim argued, *inter alia*, that Shell's ongoing allocation of capital to new oil and gas projects, as well as high reliance (and lack of transparency) on their use of negative emissions technology and offsets to meet climate targets, did not establish a reasonable basis for achieving the company's net-zero target (ClientEarth n.d.).

This case was unsuccessful. In deciding that the derivative action should not proceed, the UK High Court noted that Shell did have a plan to manage climate-related risks and it is for the directors (and not the courts) to consider how best to promote the success of a company. This result highlights that courts in Anglo-American jurisdictions are likely to be very careful to avoid infringing on the considerable discretion granted to company directors in the exercise of their legal duties. The court also highlighted that ClientEarth was a minority shareholder and noted that over 80 per cent of shareholders had voted in favour of Shell's climate strategy in 2021 and 2022. As such, ClientEarth's interests did not align with the best interests of the body of shareholders, which directors are required to consider when discharging their legal duties. This also suggests that courts may interpret directors' duties and the best interests of the company in ways that prioritise the short-term, profit-focused interests of current shareholders above the interests of longer-term or even future shareholders. Further, it highlights that institutional shareholders balance competing short-term considerations (investment returns) with longer-term considerations of climate risk management and may not always pressure companies to adopt longer-term strategies.

In summary, to the extent that it introduces norms and substantive compliance expectations that move beyond the narrow focus on financial risk at the entity scale (evident in the first dimension) towards aligning risk management to global climate goals, this second regulatory dimension certainly reflects further progress towards an ecologically rational approach to financial regulation. The potential of these developments to shift and constrain corporate and market behaviour is considered below.

4. Bracing and alignment: moving towards ecologically rational regulation of the finance sector and climate change?

As noted in section 2, in considering whether ecologically rational regulation is developing in the finance sector, it is useful to consider progress in bracing and alignment. The discussion in section 3 highlighted that through the regulatory activities of institutional investors, civil society and, to a lesser degree, State-based regulators, the goals of the Paris Agreement (and the ecological limits that they represent) are being 'braced' onto the regulatory regime for financial risk management in Australia.

Yet while there is some evidence of bracing occurring through the second *expansive* dimension of regulatory developments, there is less evidence of substantive alignment away from harmful activities in line with the Paris Agreement. Indeed, there is evidence to suggest that the behaviour shift that is possible and foreseeable within the current regulatory space in Australia remains constrained by persistent, narrow understandings of financial materiality and a regime which accords considerable discretion to companies, pension funds, and their directors in the management of these risks. Despite early signs of bracing, this is not a regime that effectively limits market activity in accordance with ecological (and social) boundaries or which reorients market activity to achieving global climate and other sustainability goals.

For example, while there is ostensibly high uptake of TCFD standards among Australian companies (Australian Council of Superannuation Investors (ACSI), 2022, p. 6) in practice, companies only partly implement the TCFD recommendations, with highly variable, poor-quality reporting against the more substantive aspects of the standard (e.g., risk quantification against Paris-aligned scenarios, targets, and transition plans) (AASB and AUASB, 2019; Foerster and Spencer, 2023; TCFD, 2021a). While corporate net-zero commitments and claims of Paris-alignment are prolific, few companies have targets accredited by the SBTi (with numbers especially low in high-emitting sectors), nor are many companies setting out comprehensive transition strategies, using relevant targets and metrics to measure progress and performance

(Foerster and Spencer, 2023). A recent benchmarking exercise measuring the net-zero commitments of major Australian banks against best practice standards is illustrative. This assessment found all banks to be underperforming against best practice expectations, particularly in terms of transparent and comprehensive targets to phase out fossil fuel lending and finance and accountability measures, such as linking executive remuneration to meeting climate targets (Australian Conservation Foundation, 2023). Targeted benchmarking of Australia's largest pension funds reveals similar patterns: most large pension funds have now committed to net-zero, Paris-aligned investment portfolios. Yet beyond the high-level commitments, evidence of changed investment practice in line with best practice net-zero standards for the finance sector is mixed. For example, Australia's five largest pension funds continue to hold substantial equity in fossil fuel companies which are pursuing major expansion plans and disclose little effective stewardship of these companies (MarketForces, 2023).

Strategic litigation led by civil society is certainly seeking to address these gaps by specifically targeting companies that continue to invest in, lend to, or directly pursue climate-damaging activities. However, as the outcome in *ClientEarth v. Shell's Board of Directors* illustrates, the broad discretions embodied in corporate law frameworks in Anglo-American jurisdictions may make it difficult to use directors' duties to hold companies accountable for continued investment of capital and resources in fossil fuels which run counter to Paris Agreement goals. Indeed, courts may consider it sufficient that directors have taken *some* action in response to the risks posed by climate change rather than taking a course of action to align business activities with the goal of limiting temperatures to 1.5°C.

Nonetheless, there are also encouraging signs of the direction of travel in this regulatory space. In jurisdictions beyond Australia, most notably the EU, there has been a recent wave of sustainable finance law reform, which has introduced stronger ecological and social foundations to relevant regulatory regimes, using regulatory approaches with more potential to align corporate and market behaviour with these foundations. For example, mandatory disclosure regimes have been strengthened and enhanced through the *Corporate Sustainability Reporting Directive* ('CRSD') and associated *European Financial Reporting Standards* which now clearly require companies to report not only on risks posed by climate change (and other environmental and social issues) to the company, but also on the material environmental and social impacts caused by the companies' activities (double materiality) (European Financial Reporting Advisory Group, n.d.a, para 3.3, 3.4). The reporting standards also require companies to disclose climate transition plans that demonstrate how the business model and strategy is or will become compatible with the 1.5°C temperature goals of the Paris Agreement (European Financial Reporting Advisory Group, n.d.b, para E1-1). In 2024, the EU Parliament passed the *Corporate Sustainability Due Diligence Directive*, which will require environmental and human rights due diligence to be undertaken by the biggest firms operating in the EU. Specific requirements to publish *and implement* Paris-aligned transition plans with emissions reduction targets for scope 1, 2, and 3 emissions (CSDDD, 2024, art. 22) may however be wound back in forthcoming reforms (European Commission, 2025). The *EU Green Taxonomy* has also established categories of 'sustainable' economic activities to facilitate the allocation of capital to meet environmental and social objectives (European Commission, n.d.). Moreover, the need for substantive reforms to directors' duties to clarify that acting in the best interests of the company requires consideration of human rights, climate change, and environmental consequences of the company's activities in the short, medium, and long term has also been seriously debated, although not yet implemented (Sjåfjell and Mähönen 2026; European Commission and EY, 2020).

Similar law reform is now developing in Australia. The Australian Government released its *Sustainable Finance Roadmap* in 2024 (Australian Government, 2024) and has amended the Corporations Act 2001 (Cth) to explicitly require large public and private companies to provide climate risk disclosures in the annual report in line with a reporting standard developed by the Australian Accounting Standards Board (Corporations Act 2001 (Cth) ss. 292A, 296A, 296B, 296C, 296D; AASB, 2024). However, at this stage, the ambition is lower, and the scope is narrower than these recent EU developments, suggesting that the boundaries of this regulatory regime (with its focus on market efficiency and stability) remain fairly rigid. For example, new mandatory climate risk disclosure rules will require covered entities to report on their risk exposure and management, irrespective of the entity's materiality assessment. Yet reporting standards focus predominantly on reporting financially material risks posed to company interests and do not adopt an explicit double materiality approach like the EU. While the government has committed to support more transparent, credible, and ambitious transition planning (Australian Government, 2024, pp. 6–7), there appears to be no immediate intention to mandate their development and disclosure. Instead, the proposed approach is to require companies to disclose a transition strategy where they have one, and to report on self-determined transition targets, with no clear regulatory direction for companies to align their climate risk management with Paris Agreement goals.

5. Concluding remarks

As cross-cutting regimes with a significant influence on corporate behaviour and market activity, corporate law and prudential regulation are important focal points for the project of ecologically rational regulation. They provide a rich context for considering whether and how regulatory regimes which are not explicitly designed to achieve environmental and social ends might nonetheless be braced with ecological limits and social norms to help bring business activity in line with planetary boundaries.

By exploring climate-related financial regulation in Australia, this chapter has highlighted how and where preliminary bracing has occurred. Yet business behaviour is unlikely to shift at the pace and scale required to meet Paris Agreement goals, due in part to the rigid focus of corporate law and prudential regulatory regimes on financial risk management and the protection of market stakeholders. As the programme of sustainable finance reform rolls out in Europe and around the world, empirical research measuring its impact and highlighting opportunities for stronger ecologically rational regulation will be critical. Reforms which embed sustainability into corporate law frameworks as a way to counter a short-term focus on profit generation at the expense of inadequately regulated social and environmental externalities have been debated in academic circles for many years (Grant, 2015; Maskill, 2016; Quinn, 2019; Sjåfjell et al., 2015; Sjåfjell, 2018, pp. 58–61). The time may have finally come for more fundamental law reform along these lines, through the introduction of novel sustainability-focused due diligence duties for companies and their directors embedded in corporate law, or introduced as supplementary business regulation (Foerster et al., 2023). Academics and practitioners can play important roles in reinvigorating and expanding these important debates and shaping law reform pathways.

Akin to the regulatory trajectory explored here in relation to climate change, we are now seeing similar developments in the field of nature and biodiversity risk. There are certainly challenges associated with bracing financial regulation with ecological limits that address biodiversity loss and degradation. For example, biodiversity loss is less easily understood and quantified as a financial risk, particularly at the entity scale. Some biodiversity dependencies and impacts (e.g., pollinator collapse) pose clear financial risks to companies in some sectors, but others (e.g., ecosystem decline and species extinctions) might pose minimal financial risks, especially in the short term (Irvine-Broque and Dempsey, 2023). Moreover, there is generally a lack of comprehensive data on biodiversity impacts, and models to translate this data into measurements of financial risk are in their infancy (Almeida et al., 2023). Nonetheless, regulatory activities framing biodiversity loss as a financial risk issue are developing in very similar ways to climate change: new voluntary disclosure standards (Task Force on Nature-Related Financial Disclosures, 2023), standards for science-based targets at different scales (SBTN, 2020, pp. 35–39), and increased market expectations for companies to set and deliver on nature-related targets as part of their risk management, with leading jurisdictions already embarking on associated law reform (Triantafilidis, 2021).[9]

In this context, it is important that academics and practitioners closely scrutinise and intervene in these unfolding regulatory trajectories, drawing on lessons learnt from the climate change context. Just as recent regulatory activity around climate risk management has encountered some rigid boundaries that may only be surmountable with comprehensive targeted law reform, similar limits and challenges are likely in the context of biodiversity and other sustainability-related issues. The regulatory trajectories observed in a climate change context suggest that while non-State actors can play a formative role in introducing ecological bracing to financial systems, there remains a critical role for the State in firming up these social and ecological foundations in ways that effectively constrain economic activity through clear legal obligations and accompanying oversight and enforcement.

Indeed, as sustainable finance regulation develops around the world, academics and practitioners alike should also remain alert to the risks of diverting public and private sector attention and resources to regulatory 'solutions' in the sustainable finance space to the detriment of direct *substantive* environmental law measures. Regulating adverse environmental impacts through licensing and approval regimes or pricing instruments may be less politically palatable than sustainable finance incentives, but ultimately more effective in bringing business into line with planetary boundaries in a timely fashion. This is particularly so given the heavy reliance on information instruments that seek to regulate reporting to inform robust risk management by market stakeholders, rather than regulating risk management more directly to also contribute to social and environmental goals. The next step in the project of ecologically rational regulation of the finance sector will be advancing sustainable finance reforms beyond disclosure, towards measures that regulate corporate conduct more directly (e.g., directors' duties and due diligence regimes), while continually improving the body of substantive laws which more directly address social and environmental harms.

Notes

1. Art 2.1(a) sets out the 'long-term temperature goal' to hold global average temperature rise to 'well below 2°C' above pre-industrial temperatures and pursue efforts to limit temperature rise to no more than 1.5°C, to significantly reduce the risks and impacts of climate change. Art 4.1 provides that to achieve this goal, parties should aim to 'reach global peaking of greenhouse gas emissions as soon as possible ... and undertake rapid reductions thereafter ... so as to achieve a balance between anthropogenic emissions by sources and removals by sinks of greenhouse gases in the second half of this century', an objective commonly interpreted as requiring net zero emissions globally in the second half of the century.
2. International initiatives include: the *Network for Greening the Financial System* (NGFS) (a group of central banks and supervisors from around the world sharing best practices and contributing to the development of environmental and climate risk management in the financial sector and the mobilisation of mainstream finance to support the transition to a sustainable economy); the European Commission Sustainable Finance initiative as part of the European Green Deal; the Asia Sustainable Finance Initiative; and the Canadian Expert Panel on Sustainable Finance.
3. Scope 1 refers to direct emissions from owned or controlled sources. Scope 2 refers to indirect emissions from the generation of purchased electricity, steam, heat, and cooling consumed. Scope 3 refers to all other indirect emissions that occur in a company's value chain. The SBTI recommends setting scope 3 targets where value chain emissions are significant, and a company has significant influence over its value chain and visibility of value chain emissions.
4. For example, see resolution put to Origin Energy's AGM in 2021: https://www.accr.org.au/news/accr-shareholder-resolutions-to-origin-energy-ltd-on-climate-related-lobbying-and-paris-aligned-capital-expenditure/
5. For example, see resolution put to Woodside Energy's AGM in 2022: https://www.accr.org.au/posts/accr-shareholder-resolutions-to-woodside-petroleum-ltd-on-climate-related-lobbying-decommissioning/
6. For example, see resolution put to BHP's AGM in 2021: https://www.marketforces.org.au/wp-content/uploads/2021/08/BHP-2021-resolution.pdf
7. For example, see resolution put to AGL's AMG in 2020: https://www.accr.org.au/news/agl-energy-ltd-resolution-2020/
8. *ClientEarth v. Shell's Board of Directors* [2023] EWHC 1137(Ch); EWHC 1897 (Ch).

9. For example, biodiversity reporting standards are being developed under the EU *Corporate Sustainability Reporting Directive*. The draft *ESRS E4 – Biodiversity and Ecosystems* mandates covered entities to disclose a transition plan that demonstrates how their business model and strategy is or will become compatible with the planetary boundaries of biosphere integrity and land-system change as well as relevant targets with the Kunming-Montreal Global Biodiversity Framework and the EU's own biodiversity strategy. Further, under the reformed French Law on Energy and Climate, financial institutions (banks, insurers, and investors) must disclose how their financial activities depend on climate and biodiversity as well as how their financial activities impact on climate and biodiversity. They must also disclose their strategy for reducing biodiversity impacts, including specific targets and a measure of alignment with international biodiversity goals. There is limited information on the impact of these reforms as they have only recently come into force in 2022.

References

Abrahams, G. and Abrahams, K. (2021) Originating process. Submission in *Abrahams & ors v. Commonwealth Bank of Australia*, NSD864/2021, 26 August 2021. Available at: https://equitygenerationlawyers.com/wp/wp-content/uploads/2021/08/210826-Originating-Process-stamped.pdf

Abrahams G & Abrahams K as Trustee for the Guy and Kim Abrahams Family Trust v. Commonwealth Bank of Australia (Consent Order, Justice Markovic) (2023). Available at: https://comcourts.gov.au/file/Federal/P/NSD864/2021/3921677/event/31377494/document/2089025

Alexander, R., Ensign-Barstow, H., Palladino, L. and Kassoy, A. (2020) *From shareholder primacy to stakeholder capitalism*. B Lab and The Shareholder Commons.

Almeida, E., Senni, C.C. and Dunz, N. (2023) *Building blocks for central banks to develop nature scenarios 11* [Policy Briefing]. INPSIRE Central Banking Toolbox. https://www.lse.ac.uk/granthaminstitute/wp-content/uploads/2023/01/INSPIRE-Sustainable-Central-Banking-Toolbox_Policy-Briefing-Paper-11.pdf

Armour, C. (2021) 'Managing climate risks for directors', *Company Director Magazine*, 1 February. Available at: https://www.asic.gov.au/about-asic/news-centre/articles/managing-climate-risk-for-directors/

Australasian Centre for Corporate Responsibility (n.d.) *Australian ESG shareholder resolutions*. Available at: https://www.accr.org.au/research/australian-esg-resolution-voting-history/

Australasian Centre for Corporate Responsibility v. Santos, NSD858/2021 (Federal Court of Australia, commenced August 2021).

Australian Accounting Standards Board (2024) *S2* – climate-related disclosures. Available at: https://standards.aasb.gov.au/aasb-s2-sep-2024.

Australian Accounting Standards Board and Auditing and Assurance Standards Board (2019, April). *Climate-related and other emerging risks disclosures: assessing financial statement materiality using AASB/IASB*. Available at: https://www.aasb.gov.au/admin/file/content102/c3/AASB_AUASB_Joint_Bulletin_Finished.pdf.

Australian Conservation Foundation (2023) *From laggards to leaders: an assessment of Australian bank's climate commitments*. Available at: https://assets.nationbuilder.com/auscon/pages/22443/attachments/original/1691718063/Banks_Net_Zero_Benchmarking_Report.pdf

Australian Council of Superannuation Investors (2021) 'Climate change policy', *Australian Council of Superannuation Investors*, 26 April. Available at: https://acsi.org.au/policies/climate-change/.

Australian Council of Superannuation Investors (2022) *Promises, pathways & performance: climate change disclosures in the ASX200*. Available at: https://acsi.org.au/wp-content/uploads/2022/08/WEBSITE-VERSION-ACSI-Climate-Change-Disclosure-in-ASX200-designed-1.pdf.

Australian Government, The Treasury (2024) *Sustainable finance roadmap*. Available at:https://treasury.gov.au/sites/default/files/2024-06/p2024-536290.pdf.

Australian Institute of Company Directors (2020) 'Coming to terms with the global climate crisis', *Company Director Magazine*, 1 April. Available at: https://aicd.companydirectors.com.au/membership/company-director- magazine/2020-back-editions/april/coming-to-terms-with-climate-change.

Australian Parents for Climate Action v. Energy Australia, NSD833/2023 (Federal Court of Australia, commenced 9 August 2023).

Australian Prudential Regulation Authority (2019) *Information paper: climate change – awareness to action*. Available at: https://www.apra.gov.au/sites/default/files/climate_change_awareness_to_action_march_2019.pdf

Australian Prudential Regulation Authority (2020, January) *Prudential Standard SPS 220 – Risk management pursuant to superannuation (prudential standard) determination No. 3 of 2019* (Cth). Available at: https://www.apra.gov.au/sites/default/files/sps_220_risk_management_december_2018_1.pdf

Australian Prudential Regulation Authority (2021, November) *Prudential practice guide CPG 229 climate change financial risks*. Available at: https://www.apra.gov.au/sites/default/files/2021-11/Final%20Prudential%20Practice%20Guide%20CPG%20229%20Climate%20Change%20Financial%20Risks.pdf

Australian Prudential Regulation Authority (2023, July) *Prudential* practice guide *SPG 530* investment governance. Available at: https://www.apra.gov.au/sites/default/files/2023-07/Prudential%20Practice%20Guide%20SPG%20530%20Investment%20Governance%20Integrated%20version%20-%20clean.pdf

Australian Securities and Investments Commission Act 2001 (Cth).

Australian Securities and Investments Commission (2018) *Climate risk disclosure by Australia's listed companies*. Commonwealth Agency. Available at: https://download.asic.gov.au/media/4871341/rep593-published-20-september-2018.pdf

Australian Securities and Investments Commission (August 2019) *Effective disclosure in an operating and financial review – regulatory guide 247, RG247*. Available at: https://download.asic.gov.au/media/5230063/rg247-published-12-august-2019.pdf

Australian Securities and Investments Commission (2023) *ASIC's recent greenwashing interventions*. Commonwealth Agency. Available at: https://download.asic.gov.au/media/aoolzoid/rep763-published-10-may-2023.pdf

Baldwin, R. and Black, J. (2016) 'Driving priorities in risk-based regulation: what's the problem?', *Journal of Law and Society*, 43(4), pp. 565–595. Available at: https://doi.org/10.1111/jols.12003

Bank of England (2017) *The Bank of England's response to climate change*.

Barker, S. (2015) 'Directors' personal liability for corporate inaction on climate change', *Governance Directions*, 67(1), pp. 21–25. Available at: https://search.informit.org/doi/10.3316/informit.943602113626710

Barker, S. (2018) *Director's liability and climate risk: Australia country paper*. Commonwealth Climate and Law Initiative. Available at: https://www.smithschool.ox.ac.uk/sites/default/files/2022-04/CCLI-Australia-Paper-Final.pdf.

Black, J. (2004) *The development of risk based regulation in financial services: Canada, the UK and Australia*. ESRC Centre for the Analysis of Risk and Regulation, London School of

Economics and Political Science. Available at: https://ideas.repec.org/h/elg/eechap/3769_8.html

Black, J. and Baldwin, R. (2010) 'Really responsive risk-based regulation', *Law & Policy*, 32(2), pp. 181–213.

Bleby, A., Holley, C. and Milligan, B. (2021) Exploring the planetary boundaries and environmental law: historical development, interactions and synergies. In French, D. and Kotzé, L.J. (eds) *Research handbook on law, governance and planetary boundaries*. Edward Elgar Publishing, pp. 21–44.

Carney, M. (2015) *Breaking the tragedy of the horizon – climate change and financial stability* [Speech]. Lloyd's of London. 29 September 2015.

ClientEarth (n.d.) *Our ground-breaking case against Shell's Board of Directors*. Available at: https://www.clientearth.org/latest/latest-updates/news/we-re-taking-legal-action-against-shell-s-board-for-mismanaging-climate-risk/ (Accessed: 11 December 2023).

Climate Action 100+ (n.d.a) *About Climate Action 100+*. Available at: https://www.climateaction100.org/about/ (Accessed: 11 December 2023).

Climate Action 100+ (n.d.b) *Companies*. Available at: https://www.climateaction100.org/whos-involved/companies/ (Accessed: 11 December 2023).

Climate Action 100+ (n.d.c) *Climate Action 100+ Net Zero Company Benchmark*. Available at: https://www.climateaction100.org/wp-content/uploads/2021/03/Climate-Action-100-Benchmark-Indicators-FINAL-3.12.pdf

Commonwealth Bank of Australia (2023) *Environmental and social framework*. Available at: https://www.commbank.com.au/content/dam/commbank/about-us/download-printed-forms/environment-and-social-framework.pdf (Accessed: 11 December 2023).

Competition and Consumer Act 2010 (Cth) sch 2 ('Australian Consumer Law')

Corporations Act 2001 (Cth).

Cullinan, C. (2011) 'A history of wild law', in Burdon, P. (ed.) *Exploring wild law: the philosophy of Earth jurisprudence*. Wakefield Press, pp. 12–24.

Dietz, S., Fruitiere, C., Garcia-Manas, C., Irwin, W., Rauis, B. and Sullivan, R. (2018) 'An assessment of climate action by high-carbon global corporations', *Nature Climate Change*, 8(12), pp. 1072–1075. Available at: https://doi.org/10.1038/s41558-018-0343-2

Directive (European Union) 2022/2464 of the European Parliament and of the Council of 14 December 2022 amending Regulation (EU) No 537/2014, as regards corporate sustainability reporting (Text with EEA relevance), EP, CONSIL, 322 OJ L (2022) ('CRSD'). Available at: http://data.europa.eu/eli/dir/2022/2464/oj/eng

Directive (European Union) 2024/1760 of the European Parliament and of the Council on Corporate Sustainability Due Diligence and Amending Directive (EU) 2019/1937 and Regulation (EU) 2023/2859 [2024] OJ L 2024/1760, ('CSDDD').

Ebbesson, J. (2014) 'Planetary boundaries and the matching of international treaty regimes', *Scandinavian Studies in Law*, 59, pp. 260–284.

European Commission (n.d.a) *EU Taxonomy for sustainable activities*. Available at: https://finance.ec.europa.eu/sustainable-finance/tools-and-standards/eu-taxonomy-sustainable-activities_en#:~:text=The%20taxonomy%20is%20a%20classification,the%20European%20green%20dealEN (Accessed: 11 December 2023).

European Commission (n.d.b) *Sustainable finance*. Available at: https://ec.europa.eu/info/business-economy-euro/banking-and-finance/sustainable-finance_en(Accessed: 11 December 2023).

European Commission (2025) *Commission proposes to cut red tape and simply business environment* [Media Release]. 26 February. Available at: https://commission.europa.eu/news/commission-proposes-cut-red-tape-and-simplify-business-environment-2025-02-26_en (Accessed: 16 April 2025).

European Commission and EY (2020) *Study on directors' duties and sustainable corporate governance*. Available at: https://op.europa.eu/en/publication-detail/-/publication/e47928a2-d20b-11ea-adf7-01aa75ed71a1/language-en# (Accessed: 11 December 2023).

European Financial Reporting Advisory Group (n.d.a) *ESRS 1 General Principles.*

European Financial Reporting Advisory Group (n.d.b) *ESRS E1 climate change.*

Financial Stability Board (FSB) (n.d.) *About the FSB*. Available at: https://www.fsb.org/about/ (Accessed: 31 July 2022).

Foerster, A. (2019) 'Climate justice and corporations', *King's Law Journal*, 30(2), pp. 305–322. Available at: https://doi.org/10.1080/09615768.2019.1645447

Foerster, A., House, M., Landau, I. and Chen, V. (2023) *Net zero, nature positive and socially responsible? Exploring corporate law reform opportunities in Australia*. Australian Conservation Foundation and Jubilee Australia. Available at: https://issuu.com/monashbusinessschool/docs/mbus_corporate_law_reform_report_v2?fr=sODFjOTY2MDEwMzk

Foerster, A. and Spencer, M. (2023) 'Corporate net zero pledges: a triumph of private climate regulation or more greenwash?', *Griffith Law Review*, 32(1), 110–142. Available at: https://doi.org/10.1080/10383441.2023.2210450

Freshfield Bruckhaus Deringer, Principles for Responsible Investment, United Nations Environment Programme Finance Initiative and the Generation Foundation (2021) *A legal framework for impact: sustainability impact in investor decision-making.*

Grant, N. (2015) 'Mandating corporate environmental responsibility by creating a new directors' duty', *Environmental Law Review*, 17(4), pp. 252–265. Available at: https://doi.org/10.1177/1461452915611772

Greenpeace Australia v. Woodside Energy, NSD1520/2023 (Federal Court of Australia, commenced 13 December 2023).

Gunningham, N. (2020) 'Roadmaps and regulation: sustainable finance in Australia', *Environmental and Planning Law Journal*, 37(4), pp. 459–476.

Guy Abrahams v. Commonwealth Bank of Australia, VID879/2017 (2017).

Haines, F. and Parker, C. (2017) 'Moving towards ecological regulation: the role of criminalisation', in Holley, C. and Shearing, C. (eds) *Criminology and the Anthropocene*. Taylor and Francis (pp. 103–128).

HM Treasury and UK Dept of Business, Energy and Industrial Strategy (2021) UK to enshrine mandatory climate disclosures for largest companies in law [Press release]. 29 October. Available at: https://www.gov.uk/government/news/uk-to-enshrine-mandatory-climate-disclosures-for-largest-companies-in-law

Hutchens, G. (2017) 'Commonwealth Bank shareholders drop suit over nondisclosure of climate risks', *The Guardian*, 21 September. Available at: https://www.theguardian.com/australia-news/2017/sep/21/commonwealth-bank-shareholders-drop-suit-over-non-disclosure-of-climate-risks

Hutley, N. and Hartford-Davis, S. (2016) *Climate change and directors' duties* [Memorandum of Opinion]. Centre for Policy Development. Available at: https://cpd.org.au/wp-content/uploads/2016/10/Legal-Opinion-on-Climate-Change-and-Directors-Duties.pdf (Accessed: 11 December 2023).

Hutley, N. and Hartford-Davis, S. (2019) *Climate change and directors' duties* [Supplementary Memorandum of Opinion]. 26 March. Centre for Policy Development. Available at: https://cpd.org.au/wp-content/uploads/2019/03/Noel-Hutley-SC-and-Sebastian-Hartford-Davis-Opinion-2019-and-2016_pdf.pdf

Hutley, N. and Hartford-Davis, S. (2021) *Climate change and directors' duties* [Further Supplementary Memorandum of Opinion]. 23 April. Centre for Policy Development. Available at: https://cpd.org.au/wp-content/uploads/2021/04/Further-Supplementary-Opinion-2021-3.pdf

Hutley, N. and Mack, J. (2017) *Superfund trustee duties and climate change risk* [Memorandum of Opinion]. 15 June. Market Forces. Available at: https://www.marketforces.org.au/wp-content/uploads/2020/01/170615-Market-Forces-Memorandum-Superannuation-Trustee-Duties-and-Climate-Change-Risk-Hutley-Mack-.pdf

Institutional Investors Group on Climate Change (2021) *Net zero investment framework: implementation guide*. Available at: https://www.parisalignedassetowners.org/media/2021/03/PAII-Net-Zero-Investment-Framework_Implementation-Guide.pdf

Investor Group on Climate Change (2021) *Aligning the banking sector with the goals of the Paris Agreement*. Available at: https://www.localpensionspartnership.org.uk/Portals/0/Documents/Responsible%20Investment/IIGCC%202021%2002%20Banks%20IE%20v16.pdf?ver=2021-05-10-102650-267 (Accessed: 11 December 2023).

Irvine-Broque, A. and Dempsey, J. (2023) 'Risky business: protecting nature, protecting wealth?', *Conservation Letters*, 16(4), e12969. Available at: https://doi.org/10.1111/conl.12969

Kim, R.E. and Kotzé, L.J. (2021) 'Planetary boundaries at the intersection of Earth system law, science and governance: A state-of-the-art review', *Review of European, Comparative & International Environmental Law*, 30(1), pp. 3–15. Available at: https://doi.org/10.1111/reel.12383

Kotzé, L.J. and Kim, R.E. (2019) 'Earth system law: the juridical dimensions of earth system governance', *Earth System Governance*, 1, 100003.

Kotzé, L.J., Kim, R.E., Blanchard, C., Gellers, J.C., Holley, C., Petersmann, M., van Asselt, H., Biermann, F. and Hurlbert, M. (2022) 'Earth system law: exploring new frontiers in legal science', *Earth System Governance*, 11, 100126.

Krabbe, O., Linthorst, G., Blok, K., Crijns-Graus, W., Van Vuuren, D.P., Höhne, N., Faria, P., Aden, N. and Pineda, A.C. (2015) 'Aligning corporate greenhouse-gas emissions targets with climate goals', *Nature Climate Change*, 5(12), pp. 1057–1060. Available at: https://doi.org/10.1038/nclimate2770

Maloney, M. (2014) 'Ecological limits, planetary boundaries and Earth jurisprudence', in Maloney, M. and Burdon, P. (eds) *Wild law: in practice*. Routledge, pp. 193–212.

Mark McVeigh v. Retail Employees Superannuation Pty Ltd (2019) FCA 14 [Concise Statement].

MarketForces (2023) *Stewards of climate disaster*. Available at: https://www.marketforces.org.au/campaigns/super/stewards-of-climate-disaster/ (Accessed: 11 December 2023).

Markey-Tower, R. and Peel, J. (2021) *Trends in Australian climate litigation 2021*. University of Melbourne. Available at: https://law.app.unimelb.edu.au/climate-change/assets/Trends-in-Australian-Climate-Litigation-2021.pdf

Maskill, J. (2016) 'Extending directors' duties to the natural environment: perfect timing for greener companies in Aotearoa New Zealand?', *Te Mata Koi: Auckland University Law Review*, 22, pp. 281–314. Available at: https://search.informit.org/doi/10.3316/agis_archive.20181412

Net Zero Asset Owners Alliance (2021) *Inaugural 2025 target-setting protocol*. Available at: https://www.unepfi.org/wordpress/wp-content/uploads/2021/01/Alliance-Target-Setting-Protocol-2021.pdf

Northcott, T., Lawrence, M., Parker, C. and Baker, P. (2023) 'Ecological regulation for healthy and sustainable food systems: responding to the global rise of ultra-processed foods', *Agriculture and Human Values*, 40(3), pp. 1333–1358. Available at: https://doi.org/10.1007/s10460-022-10412-4

Parker, C. (2021) 'From responsive regulation to ecological compliance: meta-regulation and the existential challenge of corporate compliance', in Rooij, B. and Sokol, D.D. (eds) *The Cambridge handbook of compliance*. Cambridge University Press, pp. 37–49.

Parker, C. (2022) *From corporate governance to ecological regulation: flipping the regulatory story on climate change* [Special issue]. UCL Research Paper Series, Climate Change and the Rule of Law (10/2022).

Parker, C. and Haines, F. (2018) 'An ecological approach to regulatory studies?', *Journal of Law and Society*, 45(1), pp. 136–155. Available at: https://doi.org/10.1111/jols.12083

Parker, C., Haines, F. and Boehm, L. (2018) The promise of ecological regulation: the case of intensive meat. *Jurimetrics*, 59, pp. 15–42. Available at: https://papers.ssrn.com/abstract=3338233

Peel, J., McDonnell, B., Osofsky, H.M., Foerster, A. and Markey-Towler, R. (2020) *Corporate energy transition: legal tools for shifting companies towards clean energy practices*. University of Melbourne.

Principles for Responsible Investment (2022) *A legal framework for impact: Australia*. Available at: https://public.unpri.org/download?ac=16940

Quinn, J. (2019) 'The sustainable corporate objective: rethinking directors' duties', *Sustainability*, 11(23), 6734. Available at: https://doi.org/10.3390/su11236734

Raworth, K. (2017) *Doughnut economics: seven ways to think like a 21st century economist*. Chelsea Green Publishing.

REST (2020) *Rest reaches settlement with Mark McVeigh*. Available at: https://rest.com.au/why-rest/about-rest/news/rest-reaches-settlement-with-mark-mcveigh (Accessed: 11 December 2023).

Rockström, J., Gupta, J., Qin, D., Lade, S.J., Abrams, J.F., Andersen, L.S., Armstrong McKay, D.I., Bai, X., Bala, G., Bunn, S.E., Ciobanu, D., DeClerck, F., Ebi, K., Gifford, L., Gordon, C., Hasan, S., Kanie, N., Lenton, T.M., Loriani, S. … Zhang, X. (2023) 'Safe and just Earth system boundaries', *Nature*, 619(7968), pp. 102–111. Available at: https://doi.org/10.1038/s41586-023-06083-8

Rockström, J., Steffen, W., Noone, K., Persson, Å., Chapin, F.S., Lambin, E.F., Lenton, T.M., Scheffer, M., Folke, C., Schellnhuber, H.J., Nykvist, B., De Wit, C.A., Hughes, T., Van Der Leeuw, S., Rodhe, H., Sörlin, S., Snyder, P.K., Costanza, R., Svedin, U., Foley, J.A. (2009) 'A safe operating space for humanity', *Nature*, 461(7263), pp. 472–475. Available at:https://doi.org/10.1038/461472a

Roddan, M. (2021) 'ASIC targets fossil fuel companies over climate change', *Australian Financial Review*, 1 June. Available at: https://www.afr.com/companies/financial-services/asic-targets-fossil-fuel-companies-over-climate-change-20210531-p57wq4 (Accessed: 31 July 2022).

SBTi (n.d.) *About us*. Available at: https://sciencebasedtargets.org/about-us (Accessed: 31 July 2022).

SBTi (2019) *Foundations of science-based target setting*. Available at: https://sciencebasedtargets.org/resources/files/foundations-of-SBT-setting.pdf (Accessed 11 December 2023).

SBTi (2021a) *SBTi corporate net zero standard*. Available at: https://sciencebasedtargets.org/resources/files/Net-Zero-Standard.pdf (Accessed 11 December 2023).

SBTi (2021b) *From ambition to impact: how companies are reducing emissions at scale with science-based targets – science-based targets initiatives annual progress report 2020*. Available at: https://sciencebasedtargets.org/resources/files/SBTiProgressReport2020.pdf.

SBTi (2022a) *Financial sector science-based targets guidance*. Available at: https://sciencebasedtargets.org/resources/files/Financial-Sector-Science-Based-Targets-Guidance.pdf

SBTi (2022b) *Science-based net zero: scaling urgent corporate climate action worldwide*. Available at: https://sciencebasedtargets.org/resources/files/SBTiProgressReport2021.pdf

Setzer, J. and Higham, C. (2021) *Global trends in climate change litigation: 2021 snapshot*. Available at: https://www.lse.ac.uk/granthaminstitute/wp-content/uploads/2021/07/Global-trends-in-climate-change-litigation_2021-snapshot.pdf

Sinclair, D. (2019) 'Speak loudly and carry a small stick: prudential regulation and the climate, energy, and finance nexus', *Jurimetrics: Journal of Law, Science and Technology*, 59(2), pp. 141–166. Available at: https://www.americanbar.org/groups/science_technology/publications/jurimetrics/2019/winter-2019-volume-59no-2/

Sjåfjell, B. (2018) 'Beyond climate risk: integrating sustainability into the duties of the corporate board', *Deakin Law Review*, 23, pp. 41–62. Available at: https://doi.org/10.21153/dlr2018vol23no0art805

Sjåfjell, B., Johnston, A., Anker-Sørensen, L. and Millon, D. (2015) 'Shareholder primacy: the main barrier to sustainable companies', in Sjåfjell, B. and Richardson, B.J. (eds) *Company law and sustainability*. 1st edn. Cambridge University Press, pp. 79–147. Available at: https://doi.org/10.1017/CBO9781107337978.005

Sjåfjell, B. and Mähönen, J. (2026) 'Reimagining corporate purpose for a safe and just world', in Bowman, M. and Mai, L. (eds) *A research agenda for law, finance and the environment*. Edward Elgar Publishing, pp. 169–187.

Steffen, W., Richardson, K., Rockström, J., Cornell, S.E., Fetzer, I., Bennett, E.M., Biggs, R., Carpenter, S.R., De Vries, W., De Wit, C.A., Folke, C., Gerten, D., Heinke, J., Mace, G.M., Persson, L.M., Ramanathan, V., Reyers, B. and Sörlin, S. (2015) 'Planetary boundaries: guiding human development on a changing planet', *Science*, 347(6223), 1259855. Available at: https://doi.org/10.1126/science.1259855

Summerhayes, G. (2017) *Australia's new horizon: climate change challenges and prudential risk* [Speech]. APPRA. 17 February. Available at: https://www.cpd.org.au/wp-content/uploads/2017/02/ICA-Speech-Geoff-Summerhayes-17-February-2017.pdf

Summerhayes, G. (2020) 'Understanding and managing the financial risks of climate change', Letter to APRA-regulated entities, 24 February. *Australian Prudential Regulation Authority*. Available at: https://www.apra.gov.au/understanding-and-managing-financial-risks-of-climate-change

Superannuation Industry Supervision Act 1993 (Cth).

Task force on Climate-Related Financial Disclosures (n.d.) *Taskforce members*. Available at: https://www.fsb-tcfd.org/members/

Task force on Climate-Related Financial Disclosures (2017) *Final report: recommendations of the Task Force on Climate-Related Financial Disclosures.*

Task force on Climate-Related Financial Disclosures (2021a) *2021 status report: Taskforce on Climate-Related Financial Disclosures*. Available at: https://www.fsb.org/2021/10/2021-status-report-task-force-on-climate-related-financial-disclosures/#:~:text=The%20latest%20status%20report%20finds,50%25%20of%20firms%20disclosed%20their

Task force on Climate-Related Financial Disclosures (2021b) *Guidance on metrics, targets and transition plans.*

Task force on Climate-Related Financial Disclosures (2021c) *Implementing the recommendations of the Taskforce for Climate-Related Financial Disclosures*. Available at: https://assets.bbhub.io/company/sites/60/2021/07/2021-TCFD-Implementing_Guidance.pdf

Task force on Nature-Related Financial Disclosures (2023) *The TNFD nature-related risk and opportunity management and disclosure framework, final draft – beta v0.4*. March.

The Science Based Targets Network (2020) *Science-based targets for nature: internal business guidance*. September.

Triantafilidis, B. (2021) 'France's Article 29: biodiversity disclosure requirements sign of what's to come', *Global Canopy*, 17 March. Available at: https://globalcanopy.org/insights/insight/frances-article-29-biodiversity-disclosure-requirements-sign-of-whats-to-come/ (Accessed: 5 December 2023).

United Nations Environment Programme Finance Initiative (UNEPFI) (n.d.) Net Zero Banking Alliance – industry led, UN convened. Available at: https://www.unepfi.org/net-zero-banking/

United Nations Environment Programme Finance Initiative (UNEPFI) (2021) *Guidelines for climate target setting for banks*. Available at: https://www.unepfi.org/wordpress/wp-content/uploads/2021/04/UNEP-FI-Guidelines-for-Climate-Change-Target-Setting.pdf.

United Nations Environment Programme Finance Initiative (UNEPFI) and United Nations Principles of Responsible Investment (UN PRI) (2024) Net Zero Asset Owner Alliance Target Setting Protocol Fourth Edition.
United Nations Framework Convention on Climate Change (2015) *Report of the Conference of the Parties on its twenty-first session.* Paris Agreement. UN Doc FCCC/CP/2015/10/Add.1.
Wheeler, S. (2017) 'The corporation and the Anthropocene', in Kotzé, L.J. (ed.) *Environmental law and governance for the Anthropocene.* Hart Publishing, pp. 289–309.

8 Corporate climate change litigation as a new business risk

Laura Knöpfel

1. Introduction

The Swiss television coverage of the first climate case against a company in a Swiss court opens with the following statement by a fisherman on the Indonesian island of Pari: 'We used to know where the winds came from. We could read nature. Today that is no longer possible. Storms come suddenly and the water with them' (SRF, 2023). The programme follows the fisherman and portrays the impacts of rising sea levels on both the natural environment and the daily lives of the island's inhabitants. The island of Pari has been gradually subsiding as a result of sea-level rise occurring at a rate exceeding the global average.[1]

Midway through the programme, a sudden shift in scene and setting occurs – from the island of Pari to the headquarters of the Swiss cement company Holcim Ltd in Zug – achieved through a 'smash cut', a cinematic technique in which one scene abruptly transitions to another. This abrupt cut creates a sense of tension and intrigue, encouraging viewers to contemplate the potential connection between the dramatic effects of sea-level rise on the island and the activities of the Swiss corporation.

Shortly thereafter, the programme reveals that this stark juxtaposition signifies a tangible relationship between the inhabitants of Pari and Holcim Ltd, a relationship shaped by the global, yet locally experienced consequences of the company's historical carbon dioxide (CO_2) emissions. While the smash cut visually accentuates the striking contrast between two ostensibly unrelated contexts, suggesting that transitioning from one to the other can only be abrupt, it simultaneously reveals a connection between them through the emission of CO_2 and its resulting impacts.

In the specific context of a local courtroom in Switzerland, the aforementioned smash cut, juxtaposing the rising sea levels in Pari with the parent company of Holcim enterprises, is currently under legal scrutiny. In the case of *Asmania et al. v. Holcim Ltd*,[2] the fisherman introduced at the beginning of this chapter, along with three other residents of Pari Island, has filed a civil lawsuit against Holcim Ltd. The plaintiffs seek compensation for damages suffered as a result of rising sea levels, as well as commitments to future reductions in CO_2 emissions. At the heart of the case lies the question of whether the relationship depicted in the smash cut can be construed as a legal relationship, or whether it remains solely a moral or political connection. The answer will depend on the extent to which legal doctrines are sufficiently 'open' to accommodate the harms, relationships, and responsibilities elicited by climate change.

This chapter argues that climate litigation of this kind challenges the traditional boundaries of legal reasoning. Legal systems are being called upon to address harms that are global in their production but local in their effects (Eckert and Knöpfel, 2020, p. 1), requiring legal doctrines to engage with transnational flows of capital, scientific models of causation, and complex chains of responsibility. The chapter therefore examines how legal relationships are constructed through a process of translation between different systems: law, finance, science, and politics.

By focusing on *Asmania et al. v. Holcim Ltd*, the chapter offers a theoretical framework for understanding how law can (or cannot) accommodate the novel challenges posed by climate change. Legal relationships can only be constructed before a court if effective translations are made between the systems of finance and law, politics and law, and science and law. These translational processes mobilise diverse forms of knowledge about 'the climate' to produce representations that are legible within legal discourse. The success of such translations is critical, as it directly influences the likelihood of attributing legal and financial liability for climate-related harms. Moreover, these translations form the conceptual and normative basis for constructing legal responsibilities that connect historical flows of extractive capital with the transnational production of harm – harm that is ultimately experienced at the local level. The chapter thus contributes to ongoing debates about the adaptability of legal institutions in the face of environmental disruption (Fisher, Scotford and Barritt, 2017, p. 177), and about the extent to which legal accountability can be extended to encompass the long-term, distributed consequences of corporate activity on the climate. The argument put forward is based on a study of decisions as well as the positions of claimants and defendants in recent corporate climate change litigation cases.[3]

2. The state of corporate climate litigation and its effects on firm value

The rise of economic globalisation has created complex interconnections and new forms of proximity between nations, corporations, and individuals. Multinational enterprises and global value chains intricately link geographically distant actors and jurisdictions, meaning that political and business decisions made in one country may have profound consequences for consumers, workers, and communities in another. Corporations operate across complex governance systems (Ruggie, 2013) and multiple, intersecting legal frameworks (Zumbansen, 2010, p. 148) that regulate their responsibilities across borders. These frameworks encompass legal, procedural, and normative components, structuring transnational corporate activity. At the core of these operations lie financial flows, which connect locations of investment with locations of profit. Such flows have generated global relationships of harm, particularly between investors, typically located in the Global North, and affected communities, often situated in the Global South.

In the context of corporate climate change litigation, claimants aim to establish legal linkages between these financial flows and the harm experienced by individuals and communities due to corporate greenhouse gas emissions. These linkages are presented in legal terms, drawing on doctrines from tort law, human rights law, and company law.

The case of *Asmania et al. v. Holcim Ltd* is one of several cases seeking to establish a legally enforceable connection between financial flows and transnational harm. According to a 2023 report by the Grantham Research Institute on Climate Change and the Environment at the London School of Economics, approximately sixty cases were filed globally against 'carbon majors' – companies involved in oil, gas, coal, and cement production – within that year alone (Grantham Research Institute, 2023, p. 5). The central legal issue in these cases is whether a binding legal relationship exists between carbon majors and affected individuals or communities, such that liability for past harm and obligations for future emissions reductions may be imposed. Given the inadequacy of existing legislation to address these questions comprehensively, courts have become the primary venue for advancing climate accountability claims against corporations.

The legal frameworks governing corporate climate litigation vary according to jurisdiction and case-specific context. Claimants may include affected individuals or communities, non-governmental organisations (particularly environmental advocacy groups), and local governments. Defendants may include corporations[4] or their directors.[5] Venues range from domestic courts in host and home states to quasi-judicial bodies such as the National Contact Points under the OECD Guidelines for Multinational Enterprises.[6]

Legal arguments in these cases often rely on traditional tort law claims for damages,[7] supported by references to international human rights standards and soft law instruments such as the UN Guiding Principles on Business and Human Rights and the OECD Guidelines. These references help define corporate responsibility for climate-related harms. An early example is *Luciano Lliuya v. RWE*,[8] initiated in 2015, in which a Peruvian farmer filed suit against Germany's largest electricity producer, RWE, in the District Court of Essen. The claimant sought compensation for the costs of flood defences necessitated by glacial melt near his hometown, arguing that RWE's share of historical emissions (estimated at 0.47 per cent) should determine its share of liability. While the court of first instance dismissed the claim due to the complexity of establishing linear causation, the Higher Regional Court of Hamm admitted the case to the evidentiary phase. A site visit took place in Huaraz, Peru, in 2022, and a ruling on the merits is still pending.

More recently, litigation has expanded to include claims related to the failure of companies to disclose climate risks and adopt adequate emissions reduction strategies.

These actions have been facilitated by new legal requirements around non-financial reporting. For example, under the French Duty of Vigilance Law (Articles L. 225-102-4 and L. 225-102-5 of the French Commercial Code), the case of *Notre Affaire à Tous, Les Amis de la Terre, and Oxfam France v. BNP Paribas* challenges the adequacy of the bank's climate risk mitigation plan (Fornasari, 2023).[9] Unlike tort-based cases, these disclosure-related claims are often brought by shareholders and investors seeking to protect firm value rather than by individuals suffering direct harm. A prominent example of this shift is *ClientEarth v. Shell Board of Directors*,[10] in which plaintiffs argue that the board breached its statutory duty to promote the long-term success of the company by failing to implement a credible climate strategy (Lord Carnwath, 2024).

Legal trends in corporate climate litigation are also shifting from retrospective claims for compensation to prospective demands for emissions reductions. While damages for past harm remain a component, recent cases increasingly seek injunctions requiring private actors to reduce future emissions. *Asmania et al. v. Holcim Ltd* exemplifies this trend. The landmark case of *Milieudefensie et al. v. Royal Dutch Shell*,[11] decided by the Hague District Court, ordered Shell to reduce its global emissions by 45 per cent by 2030 (relative to 2019 levels), including emissions from end-use of its products. The ruling was declared provisionally enforceable and has been widely cited as a turning point in corporate climate accountability (Macci and van Zeben, 2021; Paiement, 2021). It builds on the earlier *Urgenda* decision, in which Dutch courts held the government accountable for insufficient climate action.[12]

These lawsuits pose an increasing challenge to established legal doctrines, testing the limits of what is deemed possible within the law and prompting the legal system to adapt in response to the climate crisis. They establish a link between financial flows and climate change impacts, a coupling that manifests not only within legal reasoning but also independently within the financial system, as reflected in fluctuations in firm value. The link between corporate litigation and firm value is particularly relevant in shareholder-driven governance systems. As long as corporate behaviour is primarily governed by shareholder value, changes in firm valuation provide a key indicator of litigation risk. A recent study by researchers at the Grantham Institute and the Centre for Climate Change Economics and Policy (Sato et al., 2023) shows that even the filing of a climate case can negatively affect stock performance. Based on an analysis of 108 lawsuits filed between 2005 and 2021 against publicly listed US and European firms, the study found that filings and adverse rulings decreased firm value by an average of 0.41 per cent. The effect was greater for carbon majors, whose valuation declined by 0.51 per cent on filing and by 1.5 per cent following negative decisions. Notably, the market reacted most strongly to novel cases, whether in terms of legal argument or jurisdiction. No measurable effects were observed prior to 2019, indicating a growing sensitivity among investors to climate litigation risk.

Insurance markets are also beginning to respond. In 2021, the Lloyd's Market Association published a model exclusion clause for climate-related risks in liability policies. Other insurers have begun linking coverage to companies' disclosure of net-zero targets and climate risk exposure (The Chancery Lane Project, n.d.).

3. The case: *Asmania et al. vs Holcim Ltd*

The claimants in this case are four residents of Pari Island, located in the Java Sea approximately 40 km north of Jakarta, Indonesia. The island is low-lying, with its highest point only 1.5 metres above sea level. In recent years, it has experienced increasingly frequent and severe flooding, which has disrupted the daily lives and livelihoods of the claimants, who rely on fishing, small-scale farming, and tourism. The impacts of climate change are already undermining the viability of these activities, and the plaintiffs anticipate that they will be unable to sustain themselves through these means in the near future.

Holcim Ltd., one of the world's largest cement manufacturers, operates subsidiaries in over 70 countries and manages more than 250 cement and grinding plants globally. While historically focused on cement and concrete, Holcim has recently expanded its operations to include a broader range of construction materials (Holcim, 2021).[13] The company discloses its Scope 1, 2, and 3 emissions annually through its Sustainability Performance Report, which covers all its consolidated subsidiaries.[14] Although Holcim has pledged to achieve net-zero emissions by 2050 and has set relative reduction targets per tonne of cement produced (Holcim, 2020, 2021), it has not adopted absolute reduction targets – rendering total emissions reduction contingent upon production volumes (HEKS/EPER, 2023).

According to a study by attribution scientist Richard Heede, Holcim and Lafarge produced 7.26 billion tonnes of cement between 1950 and 2021, representing 6.5 per cent of global cement production during that period (Heede, 2022). Heede's analysis attributes 7.15 billion tonnes of CO_2 emissions to Holcim over the same period (Heede, 2022),[15] equivalent to 0.48 per cent of total industrial emissions between 1950 and 2021, and 0.42 per cent of all global industrial emissions from 1751 to 2021 (Heede, 2022, p. 24).

In autumn 2022, the four claimants filed a pre-trial conciliation request with the conciliation authority of the Canton of Zug, Switzerland, where Holcim Ltd. is headquartered. The claimants seek several forms of relief: (1) a reduction of the company's emissions in line with the 1.5°C target of the Paris Agreement; (2) compensation for both financial and non-financial losses caused by flooding; and (3) contributions to adaptation measures, including flood barriers and water purification systems. The conciliation hearing ended without resolution, permitting the claimants to bring their case to the Cantonal Court of Zug.

The legal claim is grounded in Article 28 et seq. of the Swiss Civil Code (SCC),[16] which protects personality rights. The plaintiffs argue that Holcim has unlawfully infringed their rights by contributing to climate change through its CO_2 emissions.

Under Article 28a(1) SCC, courts may issue orders to prohibit ongoing or threatened infringements and declare such infringements unlawful. The claimants assert that Holcim's climate strategy – developed and implemented in Switzerland – is central to the company's identity and operations, justifying the application of Swiss law. Although Indonesian law might otherwise be applicable under Article 133 of the Swiss Federal Act on Private International Law, the claimants successfully argued that the relevant conduct occurred in Switzerland.

Holcim contests the legal admissibility of the claim. The company argues that the plaintiffs lack a legitimate legal interest, a procedural precondition for bringing a claim. It maintains that questions regarding corporate climate responsibility are political, not legal, and therefore beyond the jurisdiction of the courts. At Holcim's request, the court has agreed to first adjudicate the question of legal interest in interlocutory proceedings before addressing the merits of the case.

In response, the claimants emphasise the need for judicial intervention. They argue that their personality rights are at risk of future infringement if Holcim fails to align its emissions with the 1.5°C trajectory. Consequently, they request an injunction to compel emissions reductions, in addition to compensation for harm already suffered. They contend that the company's current emissions strategy falls short of the commitments it has publicly endorsed, including through the UN-backed Race to Zero Campaign.

The claimants present a clear and measurable basis for their demands. They rely on Heede's estimate that Holcim is responsible for 0.42 per cent of global industrial CO_2 emissions since 1751 and argue that the company should therefore be held accountable for 0.42 per cent of the losses and costs associated with climate change impacts on Pari Island. This includes a proportional share of adaptation costs and damages. In doing so, the claimants aim to make the object of the claim legible to the court by quantifying the relationship between emissions and harm in a precise, evidence-based manner.

They further request prospective relief: a 43 per cent reduction in CO_2 emissions by 2030 and a 69 per cent reduction by 2040, relative to 2019 levels. These targets are based on the Intergovernmental Panel on Climate Change's (IPCC) 2022 assessment report. The plaintiffs argue that Holcim's climate pledges implicitly recognise these targets and that failure to meet them would constitute an ongoing infringement of their rights.

A further complexity lies in the legal identity of the defendant. The claim is directed at Holcim Ltd., a Swiss entity, but the emissions in question originate from its global subsidiaries. Swiss law does not explicitly recognise the legal concept of a corporate group or 'enterprise' in the context of liability. However, under Article 963 CO, parent companies are required to prepare consolidated financial statements for controlled entities. The claimants invoke this framework to argue that Holcim Ltd., as the ultimate decision-maker for the group's climate strategy, should be held liable for the consolidated emissions of its subsidiaries.

The legal argument centres on the theory of 'actual control'. The claimants point to Holcim's own sustainability reports and corporate structure, which present the group as a unified entity governed by a single climate strategy. They argue that this internal boundary-setting should determine the scope of legal responsibility. Accordingly, Holcim Ltd. is, in their view, jointly and severally liable under Article 50(1) CO for the emissions and harms caused by the group's operations.

4. Translations, representations, and legal responsibility

The global financial flows of investment and profit have had tangible and often detrimental effects on both people and ecosystems. These flows have given rise to transnational relationships of harm, particularly where the benefits of capital accumulation are geographically and temporally removed from the environmental and social costs they generate.

A central challenge in contemporary corporate climate litigation – such as *Asmania et al. v. Holcim Ltd* –is to legally connect historical capital flows and carbon dioxide (CO_2) emissions to locally experienced harms. The legal task is to translate this relationship into a form that is enforceable before a court. Specifically, it involves constructing a legal relationship between a polluting corporation and the individuals and communities affected by climate change.

This challenge is visually and conceptually encapsulated in the 'smash cut' introduced at the beginning of the chapter: a cinematic technique that juxtaposes the lives of fishermen and other residents of Pari Island, Indonesia, who are increasingly affected by rising sea levels, with the operations of Holcim, a multinational cement company headquartered in Switzerland. The *smash cut* creates a factual relationship between two seemingly unrelated scenes. The legal question that follows is whether this factual juxtaposition can be matched by a legally significant relationship.

The plaintiffs' principal aim in the *Asmania* case is to convince the court that such a legal relationship does, in fact, exist. Their position is that the court in Zug has both the jurisdiction and the obligation to adjudicate the claim. The defendants, by contrast, argue that any perceived relationship between Holcim and the people of Pari Island is moral or political at best, but not legal. They contend that the issues raised do not fall within the scope of judicial competence and should instead be addressed through international diplomacy or public policy.

The *smash cut* is thus not merely a rhetorical or narrative device; it symbolises what Fisher, Scotford and Barritt (2017) describe as a 'legal disruption'. Climate change disrupts conventional legal reasoning because it cannot be adequately addressed using standard doctrinal tools. It challenges foundational concepts such as standing, legitimate interest, causation, and responsibility – requiring the law to evolve in response to new, complex realities (Fisher, Scotford and Barritt, 2017, p. 177).

This legal disruption is not unique to the *Asmania* case; rather, it lies at the heart of corporate climate litigation more broadly. In such cases, claimants attempt to render relationships between geographically and temporally distant actors legally relevant and enforceable. They seek to overcome the spatial remoteness between the site of emissions (Switzerland) and the site of impact (Indonesia), as well as the temporal gap between historical emissions and current or future harms.

4.1 From the politics of the climate to climate law

The primary argument advanced by the defendant is that the claims brought by the residents of Pari Island fall outside the realm of law and belong, instead, to the domain of political deliberation. According to this view, 'the climate' – as framed within the political system – constitutes a matter of negotiation between states, concerning issues such as historical responsibility and the creation of compensation mechanisms.[17] The defendant thus characterises the dispute not as one of legal rights and obligations, but as a political issue requiring intergovernmental resolution rather than judicial intervention.

In their request for interlocutory proceedings, the defendant emphasised the difficulty of translating the factual context of the case – specifically the flooding experienced on Pari Island and its adverse effects on the claimants – into legal terms. The argument presented is that such a translation is not possible, as the matters raised do not correspond to legally protected interests. Consequently, the claimants, in the defendant's view, lack standing, and the court should refrain from making determinations on questions of responsibility or liability. Notably, similar arguments have been made by corporate defendants in other climate litigation cases, underscoring the broader relevance of this legal-political divide.[18]

In common law jurisdictions, this distinction is often formalised through the 'political question doctrine'. A prominent example is the case of *Native Village of Kivalina v. ExxonMobil Corp.*,[19] in which native Alaskans sought damages from twenty-four oil and power companies for the impacts of climate change on their community. The claim, filed in 2008, was dismissed the following year on the basis that it raised non-justiciable political questions. The court concluded that, by pursuing this lawsuit, the plaintiffs were effectively asking the judiciary to determine which of the defendants should bear responsibility for global warming. Such a decision, the court argued, fell within the purview of the legislative or executive branches, not the judiciary. As a result, the court held that the case was 'political' rather than 'legal' in nature, and it declined jurisdiction. The *Kivalina* decision illustrates the challenge claimants face in persuading courts to accept their framing of climate harms as legal wrongs rather than political grievances. It highlights the limits of legal translation – when courts are unwilling or unable to receive scientific and political representations of climate change within legal categories, claims may be dismissed without consideration of their substantive merits.

This (im)possibility of legal translation raises fundamental questions about the role of law in today's global society. Can courts, the central institutions of the legal system, respond meaningfully to the defining crisis of our time? The answer depends on whether the legal system is capable of receiving and processing the concept of 'climate', as it is constructed within political discourse, into legally cognisable claims. This process requires the transformation of political language and normative expression into clearly articulated legal issues, legal relations, legal subjects, and legal objects.

4.1.1 *Making translations: defining legal relations, their subjects, and objects*

The issue of translation foregrounds the legal system's capacity to recognise and process climate-related harm as it is embedded within global political and economic relationships. Global relationships are difficult to isolate and localise. This disconnect complicates the attribution of legal responsibility. As anthropologist Marilyn Strathern has observed, Western legal systems operate by cutting through complex social relations in order to produce clearly defined legal subjects and boundaries (Strathern, 1996). The law thus constructs subjects, objects, and relationships in ways that allow rights and responsibilities to be attributed. Clear delineation is a prerequisite for the imposition of liability.

In the case of *Asmania et al. v. Holcim Ltd*, an essential part of this delineation lies in the localisation of harm within the framework of Swiss law. This involves translating a materially and geographically distant harm – climate-induced flooding in Indonesia – into a tangible legal claim filed in the district court of Zug. To effect this translation from the site of harm to the site of law, the claimants submitted not only legal arguments but also evidentiary materials intended to render the reality of their experiences legible to the court. These included headshots of the claimants, satellite images from Google Maps showing their homes, and photographs of their everyday lives as fishers and small-scale business owners. These visual representations aim to bridge the spatial and epistemic distance between Pari Island and the Swiss legal forum, rendering the impacts of climate change perceptible within the courtroom, even if only temporarily.

To clearly define the object of their claim, and their relationship to it, the plaintiffs needed to attribute a quantifiable portion of CO_2 emissions to Holcim and demonstrate the effects of these emissions on their livelihoods. They did so by drawing on a study conducted by climate attribution scientist Richard Heede, commissioned by the NGO HEKS, which supports the plaintiffs through a public climate justice campaign. Heede's study estimates that the Holcim group is responsible for approximately 0.42 per cent of global cumulative CO_2 emissions since 1751.

On the basis of this estimate, the plaintiffs argue that Holcim should be held accountable for a corresponding share, 0.42 per cent, of the damages caused by climate change. Their legal reasoning follows a proportional liability approach: they request only 0.42 per cent of the costs for climate adaptation measures, such as the planting of mangroves and the construction of wave breakers, and similarly claim 0.42 per cent of the personal and economic losses they have already suffered. This precise definition of the emissions attributable to Holcim serves to materialise the object of the claim and to establish a clear causal relationship, albeit indirect, between the company's emissions and the plaintiffs' harm. Whether this form of proportional attribution will be accepted by the Swiss courts remains uncertain. It is possible that the court may instead require a more stringent demonstration of causation, demanding further elaboration on the chain of responsibility.

While parts of the claim concern adaptation and compensation for past harm, the principal relief sought is prospective. The plaintiffs request that Holcim be ordered to reduce its CO_2 emissions by 43 per cent by 2030 and by 69 per cent by 2040, relative to its 2019 emission levels. These targets are derived from the IPCC's Sixth Assessment Report (IPCC, 2022), which outlines the emission reductions necessary to remain within the 1.5°C global warming threshold. The plaintiffs assert that Holcim has endorsed these objectives by participating in the United Nations' Race to Zero Campaign, a voluntary initiative in support of the Paris Agreement.[20] The requested emissions reductions are therefore framed not only as scientifically grounded but also as aligned with Holcim's own public commitments.

The boundary-making and definition effort also extends to the subject of the defendant itself. Holcim Ltd, a Swiss-domiciled legal entity, is the named defendant. However, the emissions in question were largely produced by subsidiaries within the broader Holcim group. Under Swiss law, neither the concept of a 'group of companies' nor the 'enterprise' has an independent legal status. Nevertheless, the Swiss Code of Obligations (CO) addresses corporate control in the context of financial reporting. Article 963(1) CO obliges a controlling entity to prepare consolidated annual accounts for all undertakings under its control. Control, according to Article 963(2) CO, is presumed where a company holds the majority of voting rights, appoints a majority of board members, or exercises dominant influence through statutes, contracts, or comparable means.

The plaintiffs acknowledge that Holcim Ltd is not directly responsible for the majority of the emissions. Instead, they circumvent the formal issue of corporate separateness by focusing on the climate strategy developed at the group level. Their argument rests on the notion that had Holcim's group-wide climate strategy aligned with the 1.5°C target, the subsidiaries would have implemented emissions reductions, thereby mitigating the adverse impacts experienced by the plaintiffs.

Holcim's own reporting practices support this view. The company's Sustainability Performance Report consolidates emissions data across its entire group, presenting the Holcim Group as a unified actor. According to the Holcim Integrated Annual Report (2021), the Board of Directors of Holcim Ltd is responsible for setting and overseeing the group's climate strategy. On this basis, the plaintiffs argue that Holcim's own internal governance structure, as reflected in its reporting practices, defines the relevant boundaries for legal liability. The plaintiffs therefore assert that Holcim Ltd should be held jointly and severally liable under Article 50(1) CO for the emissions and resulting harms caused by its subsidiaries. Their reasoning is that the boundaries drawn by

Holcim itself – through its integrated climate strategy and consolidated reporting – should be mirrored in the attribution of legal responsibility. This approach reframes internal corporate governance as a normative basis for liability, thereby transforming corporate climate strategy into a potential source of legal obligation.

4.2 Legal representations of climate science

In addition to the challenge of translating complex, multi-jurisdictional relationships into clearly defined legal subjects and claims, corporate climate litigation must also grapple with a further form of translation: that between scientific and legal knowledge. In order for scientific findings to be rendered actionable in legal terms, the concept of 'climate', as it is produced, understood, and represented within the scientific domain, must be made intelligible within the legal system. In *Asmania et al. v. Holcim Ltd*, this translation centres on the material component of the claim, which rests heavily on scientific findings related to the impacts of climate change on the island of Pari and on the lives of the four claimants. The claim presents the effects of climate change not only as lived experiences but also as scientifically verified realities.

To introduce the court to the relevant body of climate science, the claimants rely primarily on the Intergovernmental Panel on Climate Change (IPCC) Assessment Reports. First, the claim outlines the history, mandate, and authority of the IPCC and its reports. It then links rising sea levels directly to anthropogenic climate change. Between 1901 and 2018, global sea levels rose by approximately 20 centimetres, a rise metaphorically equated to the width of a sheet of paper, thereby framing the data in a format familiar to legal institutions. This juxtaposition is emblematic of the broader goal: to materialise the lived experience of climate change within the formal structure of legal procedure.

The claim further notes that the rate of sea-level rise has accelerated significantly in recent decades, with projected consequences including more frequent and severe coastal flooding, accelerated coastal erosion, and the retreat of coastlines. These phenomena contribute to the degradation of coral reefs, rendering them uninhabitable, and to a cascade of socio-economic consequences, such as loss of livelihood, infrastructure damage, groundwater salinisation, and the permanent loss of habitable land. To visually communicate these linkages, the plaintiffs submitted a schematic diagram illustrating the causal relationship between CO_2 emissions, rising sea levels, and their concrete effects.

Following this scientific contextualisation, the claim turns to the specific impacts of coastal flooding and erosion on the island of Pari. It includes individualised accounts of how each claimant's life has been affected, supported by reference to a working paper on the island's vulnerability to sea-level rise. This paper states that it is 'almost certain' ('so gut wie sicher') that anthropogenic climate change has caused rising sea levels and the resultant adverse impacts on Pari. The claim then shifts focus to Holcim's historical contribution to global CO_2 emissions. It is argued that Holcim is responsible for 0.42 per cent of cumulative industrial emissions since 1750, and that the company has been aware of the environmental consequences of its emissions since at least 1958. These assertions are grounded in studies by attribution scientist Richard Heede and other publicly available databases that estimate corporate responsibility for climate change.

Only after this extensive discussion of the scientific evidence does the claim turn to the legal arguments. This structure, placing scientific detail before legal framing, raises a critical question: How should the law respond? The sheer volume and specificity of the facts presented create a normative pressure on the legal system. If no legal redress can be offered in the face of such facts, the legitimacy of law itself as a system of accountability and justice is called into question.

On the crucial issue of causation, the plaintiffs again rely on scientific findings. They argue that CO_2 emissions were a *conditio sine qua non* – a 'but for' cause – of the harm suffered. Furthermore, they assert that it is *gerichtsnotorisch* (a fact known to the court and not requiring further proof) that climate change leads to sea-level rise and that such rise causes flooding and coastal erosion. Acknowledging that Holcim is not solely responsible for global emissions, the plaintiffs do not attempt to establish exclusive liability. Instead, they assert that Holcim bears partial responsibility and is thus partially liable. This argument is supported by Heede's attribution studies, which quantify Holcim's share of total emissions at 0.42 per cent. In line with this, the plaintiffs request compensation amounting to only 0.42 per cent of the total damages and adaptation costs, thereby performing a legal translation of scientific attribution into a concrete damages calculation.

Beyond the IPCC reports, the claimants also cite a working paper by researchers at the Global Climate Forum in Berlin (Hinkel et al., 2023), which investigates the current and projected impacts of sea-level rise on Pari Island. Commissioned by the Swiss NGO HEKS, which supports the plaintiffs, the study does not explicitly reference the legal case but was introduced as supporting evidence in the proceedings. This document exemplifies the growing reliance on scientific expertise in climate litigation. While the law alone cannot determine whether rising sea levels are caused by anthropogenic climate change, science increasingly can. The challenge, then, is to translate scientific representations of climate harm into legally cognisable claims.

4.3 Law's co-production of climates

This chapter has so far adopted the perspective of the legal system, focusing on the steps necessary for law to absorb and translate the concept of climate – as produced in financial, political, and scientific domains – into legally cognisable relationships, objects, and subjects. This perspective is shaped by the nature of corporate climate litigation, where courts are called upon to respond to disputes brought by claimants and defendants. Inevitably, this raises the question of whether, and how, the legal system is capable of responding to the systemic disruptions posed by climate change.

However, viewing law solely as a reactive system risks overlooking its formative role in shaping the very conditions under which climate change has occurred. Law, particularly corporate, contract, investment, and environmental law, has not only responded to climate change but has also actively participated in its production. Especially, law has played a key role in shaping the legal concept of 'climate' (Mai, 2023). This is most evident in instruments such as the Paris Agreement and, earlier, the United Nations Framework Convention on Climate Change (UNFCCC) of 1992. These frameworks have given legal form to scientific and political understandings of climate, embedding them within the normative and procedural structures of international law. As such, when legal systems are asked to adjudicate disputes concerning climate-related harm, they are not simply interpreting external scientific or political knowledge. Rather, they are confronted with the re-entry of their own prior legal constructions of 'climate' into the adjudicative process. Hence, as socio-legal scholar Laura Mai has emphasised, the climate cannot be simply located or found; rather, it is actively produced as 'climates' through discursive, scientific, and legal practices (Mai, 2023). For the climate to become legally relevant, it must first be represented within law through a process of conceptual and doctrinal integration. This representation is not straightforward. The law must therefore develop representational strategies capable of accommodating this multiplicity. For legal relationships to be constructed, the legal system must engage with and represent these 'multiple climates' in forms that are legible to legal doctrine. This includes developing frameworks for reasoning about causation, responsibility, and harm that reflect the complexity of climate science and climate politics. In this way, law functions not merely as an arena for climate adjudication, but as a co-producer of the very epistemic and normative realities it is asked to govern.

5. Concluding remarks

Corporate climate litigation presents significant financial risks for companies beyond the prospect of compensatory damages or reputational harm. Shareholders, investors, and insurers increasingly respond to such lawsuits even before judicial decisions are rendered. This chapter has argued that such financial reactions depend on a belief in the viability of translating the empirical facts of climate change into an emergent body of climate law. In turn, the development of this body of law is itself contingent on the success of such translations.

To illustrate this point, the chapter examined the case of *Asmania et al. v. Holcim Ltd*, currently pending before the Cantonal Court of Zug. As the first climate litigation case brought against a corporation in Switzerland, it centres on the proposed (by the claimants) and contested (by the defendant) translations between law and politics, and between science and law.

The purpose of these translation processes is to establish legal linkages between historical and ongoing financial flows and relations of legal responsibility. As legal discourse evolves, it becomes apparent that courts must move beyond traditional doctrinal categories and engage with the complex dynamics of the globalised economic order. Yet it remains uncertain whether judges and legal practitioners in the Global North – who are, for the moment, less exposed to the direct consequences of climate change than their counterparts in the Global South – are willing to adapt their inherited legal frameworks. These frameworks are shaped by doctrines and reasoning developed decades ago and may be ill-suited to respond to the challenges presented by climate litigation today.

Meanwhile, the claimants from the island of Pari continue to confront the very real impacts of climate change, including worsening floods, as they await a first-instance judgment – a process that may take years. This situation underscores that, beyond translating between geographies and epistemologies, climate litigation also necessitates translation between temporal registers. As the effects of climate change become increasingly immediate and irreversible, the pressure will grow on courts to reconcile the temporal rhythms of legal adjudication with the accelerating pace of environmental transformation.

The question, therefore, is not only whether law can respond to climate change, but whether it can do so in time.

Notes

1. Average global sea level rose by 0.2 (range: 0.15–0.25) metres, or 20 cm, between 1901 and 2018. The average rate of sea-level rise has also increased massively. Between 1901 and 1971, the rise was 1.3 [0.6 to 2.1] mm per year; from 1971 to 2006 it was 1.9 [0.8 to 2.9] mm per year, and from 2006 to 2018 already 3.7 [3.2 to 4.2] mm per year (IPCC, 2021; Hinkel et al., 2023).
2. *Asmania et al. v. Holcim Ltd.*, pending before the Cantonal Court of Zug (Switzerland), claim submitted January 2023.
3. An overview of present and past corporate climate litigation cases can be found in the database of the Sabin Centre for Climate Change Law at Columbia Law School, available at: https://climatecasechart.com/ (Accessed: 24th April 2024).
4. *Hugues Falys, FIAN, Greenpeace, Ligue des droits humains v. TotalEnergies*, pending with the Commercial Court of Tournai, Belgium.
5. *ClientEarth v. Shell's Board of Directors* [2023] EWHC 1137 (Ch); [2023] EWHC 1897 (Ch); [2023] EWHC 2182 (Ch).
6. See for a global overview of corporate climate lawsuits: Columbia Law School and Sabin Centre for Climate Change Law, Climate Change Litigation Database, available at: https://climatecasechart.com/ (Accessed: 17th July 2024).
7. *Municipalities of Puerto Rico v. ExxonMobil Corp.*, pending before the United States District Court, District of Puerto Rico.
8. *Luciano Lliuya v. RWE AG*, Case No. 2 O 285/15, Essen Regional Court, pending appeal.
9. *Notre Affaire à Tous Les Amis de la Terre, and Oxfam France v. BNP Paribas*, pending before the judicial court of Paris.
10. *ClientEarth v. Shell's Board of Directors* [2023] EWHC 1137 (Ch); [2023] EWHC 1897 (Ch); [2023] EWHC 2182 (Ch).
11. *Milieudefensie et al. v. Royal Dutch Shell plc*, Case C/09/571932 / HA ZA 19-379, District Court of The Hague, 26 May 2021.
12. *Urgenda Foundation v. State of the Netherlands* [2015] HAZA C/09/00456689, The Hague District Court.

13. Holcim (2021) *Strategy 2025 – Accelerating green growth* [Media release]. 18 November. Available at: https://www.holcim.com/investors/publications/capital-markets-day (Accessed: 28 April 2024).
14. See all the sustainability reports available on Holcim under https://www.holcim.com/sustainability/esg/esg-policies-documents-reports (Accessed: 28 April 2024). Holcim holds 100 per cent of the shares in the majority of the subsidiaries included in the consolidated reports on non-financial information.
15. Of this total, scope 1 operational emissions account for 5.33 GtCO2 (74.6 per cent), scope 2 emissions 0.40 GtCO2 (5.5 per cent), and scope 3 indirect emissions 1.42 GtCO2 (19.8 per cent).
16. The author was provided with the claim in *Asmania et al. v. Holcim Ltd* and further legal information by the claimants for academic purposes.
17. At the 2023 United Nations Climate Change Conference of the Parties, commonly known as COP28, the decision was taken to formally establish a loss and damage fund to support vulnerable countries dealing with the effects of climate change. See for more information on the climate compensation fund: UNFCC (n.d.) *Fund for responding to loss and damage*. Available at: https://unfccc.int/loss-and-damage-fund-joint-interim-secretariat#:~:text=In%20this%20context%2C%20the%20COP,economic%20and%20non%2Deconomic%20loss (Accessed: 18 April 2024).
18. See for example *Martin Kaiser, Roland Hipp and Clara Mayer v. Volkswagen AG* (Az. 6 O 3931/21) 6. Zivilkammer des Landgerichts Braunschweig vom 14. Februar 2023.
19. *Native Village of Kivalina v. ExxonMobil Corp.*, 663 F. Supp. 2d 863 (N.D. Cal. 2009), affirmed 696 F.3d 849 (9th Cir. 2012), cert. denied 569 U.S. 1000 (2013).
20. Climate High-Level Champions, *Race to Zero*. Available at: https://www.climatechampions.net/campaigns/race-to-zero/ (Accessed: 10 December 2025).

References

Eckert, J. and Knöpfel, L. (2020) 'Legal responsibility in an entangled world', *Legal Anthropology*, 4, pp. 1–16.

Fisher, E., Scotford, E. and Barritt, E. (2017) 'The legally disruptive nature of climate change', *Modern Law Review*, 80(2), pp. 173–201.

Fornasari, R. (2023) 'French NGOs target bank's activities contributing to climate change', *Climate Law Blog*, Sabin Centre for Climate Change Law. Available at: https://blogs.law.columbia.edu/climatechange/2023/03/03/french-ngos-target-banks-activities-contributing-to-climate-change/ (Accessed: 10 December 2025).

Grantham Research Institute on Climate Change and the Environment (2023) *Global trends in climate change litigation: 2023 snapshot*. Policy publication. Available at: https://www.lse.ac.uk/granthaminstitute/publication/global-trends-in-climate-change-litigation-2023-snapshot/ (Accessed: 17 July 2024).

Heede, R. (2022) *Carbon history of Holcim Ltd: Carbon dioxide emissions 1950–2021*. Climate Accountability Institute, 7 September, pp. 20–23. Available at: https://climateaccountability.org/pdf/CAI%20Holcim%20Rpt%20Jul22.pdf (Accessed: 28 April 2024).

HEKS/EPER (2023) *Holcim's climate strategy: too little – too late*. Zurich. Available at: https://callforclimatejustice.org/wp-content/uploads/HEKS-EPER_Climate-Analysis_Summary_EN_DEF.pdf (Accessed: 28 April 2024).

Hinkel, J., Gussmann, G., Lincke, D. and Völz, V. (2023) *Heutige und zukünftige Auswirkungen des Klimawandels und Meeresspiegelanstiegs auf der Insel Pari*. GCF Working Paper.

Available at: https://globalclimateforum.org/wp-content/uploads/2023/01/GCFwp1_2023.pdf (Accessed: 18 July 2024).

Holcim (2020) *Holcim unterzeichnet Net-Zero Pledge* [Press release]. Available at: https://www.holcim.ch/de/lafargeholcim-unterzeichnet-net-zero-pledge#:~:text=Als%20erstes%20globales%20Baustoffunternehmen%20unterzeichnet,(SBTI)%20wissenschaftlich%20best%C3%A4tigt%20wurden (Accessed: 28 April 2024).

Holcim (2021) *Holcim's net-zero journey: climate report 2021*. Available at: https://www.holcim.com/sites/holcim/files/2024-02/08042022-holcim-climate-report-2021.pdf (Accessed: 28 April 2024).

IPCC (2021) 'Summary for Policymakers', in Masson-Delmotte, V., Zhai, P., Pirani, A., Connors, S.L., Péan, C., Berger, S., Caud, N., Chen, Y., Goldfarb, L., Gomis, M.I., Huang, M., Leitzell, K., Lonnoy, E., Matthews, J.B.R., Maycock, T.K., Waterfield, T., Yelekçi, O., Yu, R. and Zhou, B. (eds), Climate Change 2021: The Physical Science Basis. Contribution of Working Group I to the Sixth Assessment Report of the Intergovernmental Panel on Climate Change. Cambridge University Press.

IPCC (2022) 'Summary for Policymakers', in Shukla, P.R., Skea, J., Slade, R., Al Khourdajie, A., van Diemen, R., McCollum, D., Pathak, M., Some, S., Vyas, P., Fradera, R., Belkacemi, M., Hasija, A., Lisboa, G., Luz, S. and Malley, J. (eds), Climate Change 2022: Mitigation of Climate Change. Contribution of Working Group III to the Sixth Assessment Report of the Intergovernmental Panel on Climate Change. Cambridge University Press.

Lord Carnwath, R. (2024) *Client Earth v Shell: What future for derivative claims?* Grantham Research Institute on Climate Change and the Environment & Climate Change Laws of the World, pp. 1–6.

Macci, C. and van Zeben, J. (2021) 'Business and human rights implications of climate change litigation: Milieudefensie et al. v Royal Dutch Shell', *Review of European, Comparative & International Environmental Law*, 30(3), pp. 409–415.

Mai, L. (2023) 'What is the climate? Notes on a critical legal methodology', *Tilburg Law Review*, 28, pp. 20–25.

Paiement, P. (2021) 'Reimagining the energy corporation: Milieudefensie and Others v Royal Dutch Shell Plc', in *Netherlands Yearbook of International Law*, pp. 281–299. Springer.

Ruggie, J.G. (2013) *Just business: multinational corporations and human rights*. W.W. Norton & Company.

Sato, M., Gostlow, G., Higham C., Setzer, J. and Venmans, F. (2023) Impacts of climate litigation on firm value. Centre for Climate Change Economics and Policy Working Paper 421/ Grantham Research Institute on Climate Change and the Environmenta Working Paper 397. London School of Economics and Political Science.

SRF (2023) *Inselbewohner verklagen Zementkonzern Holcim*. Available at: https://www.srf.ch/news/international/wegen-klimaschaeden-inselbewohner-verklagen-zementkonzern-holcim (Accessed: 17 July 2024).

Strathern, M. (1996) 'Cutting the network', *The Journal of the Royal Anthropological Institute*, 2, pp. 517–535, 526.

The Chancery Lane Project (n.d.) Insurance: disclosure and mitigation of pending climate change litigation. Available at: https://chancerylaneproject.org/climate-clauses/insurance-disclosure-and-mitigation-of-pending-climate-change-litigation/ (Accessed 28 April 2024).

Zumbansen, P. (2010) 'Transnational legal pluralism', *Transnational Legal Theory*, 141, pp. 141–189, 148.

9

Reimagining corporate purpose for a safe and just world

Beate Sjåfjell and Jukka Mähönen[1]

1. Introduction

Practically all people have some degree of involvement with business. We may be employed by a business or be members of a business, or we may be entrepreneurs or contractual partners as creditors, debtors, or buyers ('consumers'). Businesses produce the essential commodities and services that most people depend on. Business affects us all directly or indirectly through the way that production, transport, sales, and follow-up are organized. They are an integral part of most societies and communities and contribute to creating wealth and prosperity. Yet, businesses are in aggregate a main driver of the extreme unsustainabilities of our time, exploiting people, destroying the environment, and undermining the economic and governance bases for well-functioning societies. Conversely, business has the potential to contribute to the fundamental transformation of economies and societies of which it is a part. As legal scholars, much of our work over more than a decade has been committed to investigating the role of law, and specifically company law, in this fundamental transformation. Drawing on multijurisdictional comparative company law analyses, we have a sound basis for identifying the barriers to change and the possibilities for sustainable business law, that is, business law that contributes to that fundamental transformation towards sustainability.

We start out in section 2 by explaining what a company is and what the role of finance is in it; why corporate purpose is important for both finance and corporate governance, and accordingly why we cannot discuss sustainable business law without discussing the sustainability of the corporate purpose. In section 3, we explore corporate purpose in comparative company law and theories. We concentrate on European companies, and distinguish between what we see as specific to these companies and what we see as being of general relevance to other forms for organizing business in other legal cultures and jurisdictions. With all this as our backdrop, we discuss in section 4 how we reimagine corporate purpose for sustainability. Section 5 concludes the chapter with brief reflections.

2. The company and the Anglo-Saxon influence on its theorizations

Production of a broad range of goods and services from food and clothes to software is organized through businesses. They range from Indigenous businesses, such as the Sámi *siida*, to partnerships, cooperatives, and companies; from small and medium-sized enterprises to global platform multinational companies; from sole entrepreneurs to state-owned enterprises. Businesses cooperate with each other, forming value chains and networks. Common to all businesses is that they require resources. This includes that which is sometimes denoted as 'human capital' – the work of members and employees, and 'financial capital' – from members, creditors, and investors that the company uses to acquire factors of production.[2] The core of a business organization is its *purpose* which dictates the duties of the leadership and management of the business, for instance, a company board.

The leading business form in Europe is the company; a creation of nineteenth-century European capitalism (e.g., British, French, and German), and United States (US) capitalism, which has become predominant in businesses all over the world. As a creation of law, the company has been granted separate legal personality, and its members (the shareholders) are given so-called limited liability, which is to say that they are not responsible for the company's debts and obligations. This has generally meant no liability if company law rules were respected. This limitation of liability for shareholders creates additional risk to other investors, such as creditors, and to the employees and local communities where the company is situated and carries out its activities. In addition, the majority of shareholders normally decide, through the general meeting, who sits on the board. The legal creation of the company, a 'creature of national (company) law', as it has been repeatedly denoted by the Court of Justice of the European Union (e.g., *The Queen v. H M Treasury and Commissioners of Inland Revenue, ex parte Daily Mail and General Trust plc*, 1988), has both positive and negative consequences. It enables entrepreneurs to obtain funding from a range of investors, while investors can rely on the protection of limited liability. And yet, the company also serves as a mechanism for externalizing negative impacts onto other involved parties and affected interests, notably those who are not in a position to control or influence the decision-making in the company.

When company law was created in nineteenth-century Europe and the United States (US), important goals were to establish the rules of the game between the shareholders and the company, and to protect the creditors against shareholders' opportunism. In the twentieth century, increasing attention was given to the employees, in recognition of their need for protection. From the 1960s the tide changed, with a neoclassical economics turn away from societal purpose to the shareholders and towards their alleged role as 'residual' investors, calling for a specific protection of their interests (Sjåfjell and Mähönen, 2020). In direct contradiction to the law, neoclassical economists propagated the idea that the purpose of the company is the maximization of shareholder 'welfare' and that the main duty of the board and senior executive management is to ensure that this happens. This strand of economic theory also affected discourses about company law and corporate governance, creating the false idea that boards are 'agents' of shareholders (rather than the company itself) with a duty to create value for the company. This particular view has become so dominant that it has influenced perspectives on the duties of the board, the role of company law in the economy, and also how the company is perceived as an entity; not as a legal person owning its own assets but as property of the shareholders (Sjåfjell and Mähönen, 2020).

This neoclassical 'new economic theory' was not based on economic thinking alone. It borrowed the nineteenth-century idea of a company as a 'legal fiction' from legal theory but employed it only to serve as a 'nexus' (Jensen and Meckling, 1976) for a set of contracting relationships among individuals, concealing the real transactions that constitute it. According to the 'nexus of contracts' theory, company law is a set of default rules hypothetically accepted by a majority of shareholders in all companies, designed to reduce the costs of contracting with each other and other corporate constituencies. All constituents are assumed to be protected through their contracts with the company, or through 'extra-corporate' regulation such as environmental law or labour law.

Examples of the influence on company law by economic theory include Frank Easterbrook and Daniel Fischel's *The Economic Structure of Corporate Law* (Easterbrook and Fischel, 1991) and Kraakman et al.'s *The Anatomy of Corporate Law* (Kraakman et al., 2017). In Kraakman et al., agency theory as the basis for company law and corporate purpose appears to be purely instrumental: to reduce agency conflicts and increase market efficiency. In corporate governance, this economic theory reduces the role of law to a mere application of agency theory to corporate relationships. This does not match legal reality, not even in the US, which is commonly regarded as the birthplace of the theory.

This new legal-economic mainstream was so strong that it not only prevented new theoretical approaches from flourishing, but it also sidelined the previous rich theories of company law that integrated societal benefit and purpose. Similar flaws as those seen in the economic theory can be identified in the alternative legal competitors of the mainstream economic theory, such as the various versions of 'stakeholder' theories. We will mention here just two seminal examples: Edward Freeman's *Strategic Management: A Stakeholder Approach* (Freeman, 1984) and the 'team production' theory by Margaret Blair and Lynn Stout (Blair and Stout, 1999). Freeman (1984) posits, mainly on non-legal ethical grounds, that business should attempt to maximize the positive impact not only for shareholders but also for other 'stakeholders', notably employees and customers. Blair and Stout (1999) rely heavily on Kraakman et al.'s specific approach to agency theory and present a variant of the same legal agency theory, yet give little guidance on what should be done and how.

These different agency-based theorizations do not engage with and often contradict company law. They also do not engage with the various alternative ways of creating and controlling business organizations, such as Indigenous businesses, cooperatives, partnerships, foundations, and associations, or other ways of organizing business such as corporate groups, networks, franchises, platforms, and so on. These alternative business forms are not encompassed by the dominating theory, or its past or current competitors. This limits theoretical understandings of which elements and impacts should be integrated into business decision-making.

After decades of this instrumental and narrow focus on the role of company law in business, with the dominant view identifying the company with its shareholders, we are now seeing a reawakening of the debate on corporate purpose. Unfortunately, the debate is constrained by the Anglo-American shareholder versus stakeholder dichotomy, created as a part of the neoclassical agency drive. Business policy statements, based on (narrow) stakeholder thinking, notably that from the US-based Business Roundtable (Business Roundtable, 2019), have been given a lot of attention both in the US and Europe. Yet, in European countries and European Union (EU) institutions, the discussion on how to integrate sustainability into company law and corporate governance has spearheaded a renewed debate on corporate purpose and the societal significance of businesses (Sjåfjell and Taylor 2019; Fleischer, 2021; Knapp, 2021; Möslein and Sørensen, 2021; Sjåfjell, 2021). Corporate purpose in this sense has been brought to the forefront more or less clearly and explicitly through a variety of initiatives in European countries and the EU, ranging from legislative interventions such as the 2019 PACTE Law (Action Plan for Business Growth and Transformation) which amended Articles 1833 and 1835 of the French Civil Code to, among other things, encourage companies to consider social and environmental issues in their business purpose and strategies, through reforms of soft law, notably Corporate Governance Codes in the Netherlands (2016), the UK (2018), Denmark (2020), France (2020), Belgium (2020), Austria (2021), Norway (2021), and Germany (2022) (Sjåfjell and Tsagas, 2023). In the EU, the issue became especially topical with the European Commission's Sustainable Corporate Governance initiative (European Commission, 2020).

Our analysis draws on and is situated within these developments in the EU and, more broadly, the European Economic Area, including the twenty-seven EU Member States, and three of the four European Free Trade Association member states: Iceland, Liechtenstein, and Norway. In our approach to corporate purpose, we draw on over a decade of multijurisdictional comparative company law analyses (Sjåfjell et al., 2015; Bruner and Sjåfjell, 2019; see also Sjåfjell and Mähönen, 2023). With 'corporate purpose' we mean the overarching aim of the company. Accordingly, our analysis is delimited against the objects of the company, which legislation may require to be set out in a company's constitutional documents. We posit that companies as 'creatures of national law' cannot be properly understood without engaging with a variety of company law approaches and theories. Further, in our research aiming to contribute to sustainability, we undertake interdisciplinary analyses, drawing on legal theory, law and economics, and sustainability science and research. That gives us a rich basis for reimagining corporate purpose for a safe and just world in a way that transcends dichotomies and jurisdictional differences. We recognize, of course, the variations between jurisdictions and corporate forms, and that political ontologies (Ehrnström-Fuentes and Böhm, 2023) of good business regulation will vary, for example, Indigenous, Western, or Shariah worldviews. However, we believe that some general recommendations for a sustainable corporate purpose can be made based on a conceptualization of sustainable value creation (Sjåfjell and Tsagas, 2023; Sjåfjell and Cornell 2024) as a response to the global challenges humanity faces. Our detailed recommendations for implementation are intended for European companies and reflect their organization, notably in our proposal for revised duties of the board.

Our analysis is based on a research-based concept of sustainability as a safe and just world, which requires securing social foundations for humanity now and for the future while mitigating pressures on planetary boundaries (Raworth, 2012; Leach, Raworth and Rockström, 2013; Sjåfjell and Cornell, 2024). We choose to use this research-based understanding of sustainability, which we have worked with over the past decade, as it is well established and increasingly referenced by business and policymakers. It is also, in the way we use it, an open and inclusive concept, which responds to the full range of the extreme unsustainabilities of our time. In this way, our proposal for a sustainable corporate purpose leaves plenty of room for further jurisdiction-specific developments of company law, and for different implementations in local contexts and worldviews.

3. Comparing corporate purpose in company law theories over time

The discussion of corporate purpose and especially the relationship between corporate purpose and sustainability is – or should be – jurisdiction-specific. Corporate purpose is embedded in the core of national company law regulation. However, Anglo-American approaches to company law have become embedded around the world due to the dominance of Anglo-American business law scholars in legal-economic discourse, a prime example being the attention given to the US Business Roundtable (Business Roundtable, 2019). This dominance sidelines the variety of discussion on corporate purpose and sustainability in jurisdictions across the world, such as in Southeast Asia (Puchniak, 2022), in the Nordics (Sjåfjell and Mähönen, 2023), in the EU (Möslein and Sørensen, 2021), and in broad comparative work (Sjåfjell and Bruner, 2019).

However, when conducting a comparative analysis of company law across various jurisdictions, it becomes clear that, although popular in discourse, sustainability is seldom taken seriously. The discussion is going in circles *around* corporate purpose without *addressing* it directly. Our analysis exposes and underlines the need for a coherent approach to regulating for sustainability, which does not exclude an area of law from the regulatory toolbox based on path-dependent approaches in that area.

The modern company was created in the nineteenth century to serve the normative societal needs of industrialization, modernization, and democratization. It arose from the socio-economic transformation from a sovereign-led economy in which large business was supported by the state to a market-based economy with an unfettered right to establish companies. This led to legal innovations of separate legal personality and limited liability and a normative theory of company law to provide justification for this new business form. This justification was partly economic, reflecting the changing economic environment from state-led economy to market-based economy, and partly historical, given that the Roman (and Canon) concept of legal fiction (*persona ficta*) formed the basis for legal personality.

Further, the 'new' company law theory provided a basis for understanding and defining the role of shareholders and the board in this legal 'person'. It did not, however, encompass the relationship of this entity to the outer world, with the exception of direct financial creditors. Other affected parties, such as employees, customers, and local communities, were left out of the entity (with some notable exceptions such as codetermination in, most famously, German public companies). Other affected parties were expected to be governed by the (liberal) market-based contract law of the nineteenth century, notably labour and competition legislation, extending in the twentieth century to protection of the environment and consumers.

This theorization did not grasp other business forms and so no comprehensive legal theory of 'business' was ever developed. Legal theories of company law were replaced in the early 1930s with managerialist institutional economics by Adolf Berle and Gardiner Means (e.g., Berle and Means, 1933). Berle and Means contributed an economic-political picture of the management-controlled company which prevailed in academic legal discussions until the new contractual microeconomic theory of the firm, sometimes denoted the 'new economic theory of the firm', which appeared to challenge it around 1980. In short, the societal ethos of company law theory was replaced with the economic ethos of efficiency.

Societal purpose was historically clear in European and US company law, with the right to establish a company granted only to activities that also served the interests of society (Gierke, 1954; Muchlinski, 2013; Davoudi, McKenna and Olegario, 2018). While company law seldom sets such explicit requirements today, we see it as underpinning current company law in the form of a legislative presumption that companies in aggregate still contribute to societal welfare in the pursuit of their business. Indeed, it is hard to imagine that societies around the world would continue to enable and encourage the use of the legal form of the company without an underpinning presumption that this is beneficial for society.

During the last decades, this societal underpinning of company law has been pushed to the side and even forgotten under the influence of efficiency-based, law-and-economics inspired, and privatized approaches to company law. We use the economics-based concept of *shareholder primacy* (coined by David Millon and Lyman Johnson in 1989; Millon, 2013) as a short form for a complex mix of perceived market signals and economic incentives, informed by path-dependent corporate governance assumptions and postulates from legal-economic theories (Sjåfjell, 2019). While Millon used radical and traditional shareholder primacy to distinguish between the economics-based social norm and the legal norm (Millon, 2013), we (together with Millon in later work) use shareholder *primacy* exclusively to describe the social norm and shareholder *value* to describe the legal norm (Sjåfjell et al., 2015). Originating in the US, shareholder primacy is based on US economic theory and developed as such a strong social norm as to become a legal myth (Sneirson, 2008, 2019; Stout, 2012, Bruner and Sjåfjell, 2019). Shareholder primacy equates corporate purpose with maximizing returns to shareholders. Under the shareholder primacy view, maximizing returns to shareholders is the duty of corporate boards and senior executive management (Smith, 1998; Sneirson, 2019).

From the US, shareholder primacy has spread all over the world, suppressing the societal purpose of the company. We see this illustrated in *The Anatomy of Corporate Law* (Kraakman et al., 2017) where the international Anglo-American oriented group of company law scholars concedes that 'non-contractual stakeholders' of a company deserve legal protection, but argue that protection of interests extraneous to the firm should come (only) from other areas of law, such as environmental law, human rights law, antitrust law, or financial regulation (Kraakman et al., 2017, p. 93). The basis for their reluctance to include company law in the regulatory toolbox for dealing with sustainability is their view that company law should not be employed to 'tackle concerns which reach far beyond the agency problems that form its core competency' (p. 108), thereby using their own definition of company law as a basis for excluding it from the sustainability discussion (Sjåfjell, 2025).

Isolating and insulating company law from the broader discussion of the impact companies have on society and narrowing their thinking in enforcement of company law obligations (Kraakman et al., 2017, p. 107) jars with *The Anatomy*'s own identification of a range of legal strategies (p. 31) that can be employed where needed. Even *The Anatomy* perceives company law as having the broad goal of 'serv[ing] the interests of society as a whole' and particularly 'the aggregate welfare of all who are affected by a firm's activities, including the firm's shareholders, employees, suppliers, and customers, as well as third parties such as local communities and beneficiaries of the natural environment' (Kraakman et al., 2017, pp. 23–24). Yet in their analysis, the authors set aside this broad understanding of the societal purpose of companies to concentrate on what they perceive to be the core role of company law as resolving agency issues (Sjåfjell, 2025).

Nonetheless, discussion of the societal purpose of the company has re-emerged with the advent of Anglo-American company law and corporate governance scholars (re) discovering the sociological concept of 'social licence to operate'. It was introduced by Jim Cooney, a Canadian mining executive, at a World Bank conference in 1997, to describe the challenges of mining companies in managing the political and social risks of their projects (Cooney, 2017). It has been subsequently discussed as the need for societal legitimacy, and specifically social acceptance from affected communities and peoples (Stuart et al., 2023). As such, it has been used to reduce legal discussion of societal purpose to voluntary 'corporate social responsibility' approaches, thereby fitting seamlessly within the realm of shareholder primacy.

The Anglo-American discussion on stakeholderism, a variation of 'social licence to operate', should also be seen in the light of shareholder primacy. As noted above, the 'stakeholder' approaches that attempt to challenge shareholder primacy have had very little success. They do not represent a fundamentally different way of conceptualizing business or good company law, but rather, a reaction to the mainstream shareholder primacy thinking by attempting to bring more people into the group of decision-makers that is prioritized by the board and senior executive management. As a reactive approach, stakeholder theories have not provided a credible alternative view of corporate purpose to maximizing returns for shareholders (see also Jensen, 2001).

The shareholder primacy norm and the shareholder versus stakeholder dichotomy are not merely questions of theory as an academic exercise. Shareholder primacy is firmly positioned at the heart of the *un*sustainability of business and constitutes a systemically entrenched barrier to the contribution of business to sustainability. As such, these questions of theory infect the whole company *law* discourse. The discussion about section 172 of the UK Companies Act 2006 and its 'enlightened shareholder value' is a prime example. Section 172 of the Companies Act 2006 explicitly requires 'directors' (members of the corporate board) to take account of environmental impacts, along with other matters such as employee interests, in deciding how to promote the success of the company for the benefit of shareholders. The duty requires boards to at least try to anticipate, for example, the environmental consequences of their decisions within the limits of the information available to them. However, the way in which a company trades off, for example, employment and environmental considerations, would normally not be justiciable, provided that this represents the 'director's subjective judgment, exercised in good faith' as to how best to promote the success of the company for the benefit of its shareholders (Sjåfjell et al., 2015).

Generally speaking, company law gives broad discretionary space for boards and senior executive management to shift companies onto a more sustainable path across jurisdictions. This applies to jurisdictions such as the UK, with its company law norm of (enlightened) shareholder value, and also to jurisdictions with more pluralistic approaches such as the Netherlands and Norway. Yet, across jurisdictions, the social norm of shareholder primacy takes over that discretionary space and continues to keep companies on a path of maximization of returns to investors.

Instead of discussing the role of company law in ensuring that corporate governance contributes to a safe and just world, much of the academic and political discussions have been derailed through an overly strong focus on the shareholder versus stakeholder dichotomy. Advocates of shareholder primacy claim that the only alternative is a stakeholder model, and then outline the (perceived) problems of a stakeholder regime (Jensen, 2001; Krüger Andersen et al., 2020). One main reason for the narrow and binary nature of this debate, limiting it to these two choices only, is that both critics and proponents are constrained by the US-centric economic agency model.

The shareholder versus stakeholder dichotomy is not only misleading; it is dangerous. Firstly, it tends to take company law proper out of the legal discussion of corporate purpose and corporate governance, and thereby reinforces the shareholder primacy drive. The shareholder primacy drive continues to constrain – in Christopher Bruner's pen – 'our collective sense of the possible – even for many who favour pursuing corporate sustainability in the abstract' (Bruner, 2013; Bruner and Sjåfjell, 2019).

Secondly, well-intended efforts at dismantling shareholder primacy by introducing stakeholder framing risk diluting a core company law principle that the board is responsible to the *company*. Shareholder primacy proponents argue that their way of seeing the boards as solely agents of shareholders is the only way to ensure that companies are run efficiently. Similarly, under a 'stakeholder primacy' view, boards would be responsible for the private interests of various interest groups rather than the interests of the company as a whole (as the law stipulates).

We therefore reject the shareholder versus stakeholder dichotomy and rather discuss corporate purpose as a matter of modern company law. Our starting point is the role of company law in setting an overarching purpose that resonates with a research-based concept of sustainability (Sjåfjell and Cornell, 2024).

4. Corporate purpose that is fit for purpose

4.1 Corporate purpose is at the heart of sustainable company law

We see corporate purpose, and company law's redefinition of that purpose, as being at the heart of the debate on how to integrate sustainability into corporate governance (Sjåfjell and Taylor, 2019; Sjåfjell and Mähönen, 2020). That gives us a basis for reimagining corporate purpose for a safe and just world in a way that transcends limiting dichotomies and national differences.

Setting out a sustainable corporate purpose (which we introduce below) is about taking back the company law space that has been displaced by economic theories and explicitly defining the overarching aim of companies. Although corporate purpose is, as we see it, such an important element of the societal basis on which company law's acceptance and promotion of the company form is based, statutory law does not generally set overarching purposes for companies. We suggest that company law should take back the power of defining why companies exist and push back against shareholder primacy to set companies on the path towards a sustainable future.

To this end, we have proposed a legislative and explicit redefinition of corporate purpose for European undertakings broadly understood to include all business forms (both public and private) (Sjåfjell et al., 2020; Sjåfjell, 2021 pp. 209–216). The corporate purpose we have suggested will not alter or replace the possibility of expressing an individual and more detailed purpose or objects for businesses, which could be set in law governing different business forms and in the firm-specific instruments of the constitution, memorandum, or articles of association. The aim of our proposal is not to dramatically change the nature of European businesses. It does not take away profit-making as an intrinsic element of the nature of for-profit companies or of their value creation and how profit is used and distributed in them. Rather, it is to put the overarching societal purpose back in the centre of company law. We suggest that it should be formulated employing the concepts of *sustainable value creation* and *planetary boundaries.*

Positioning sustainable value creation within the planetary boundaries framework is a crucial step in integrating a research-based concept of sustainability into proposals for legislative reform. Ensuring that companies contribute to the overarching societal goal of mitigating pressures on planetary boundaries is necessary if there is going to be a chance to achieve crucial environmental goals, including those of mitigating climate change and reversing biodiversity loss. When the planetary boundaries framework was first presented in 2009, three of the identified nine planetary boundaries were highlighted as boundaries that human activity on a global scale has transgressed (Rockström et al., 2009). In 2015, the number of transgressed boundaries had increased to four (Steffen et al., 2015) and then to six out of nine by 2023 (Persson et al., 2022; Richardson et al., 2023).

While the United Nations (UN) Secretary-General António Guterres has declared climate change a 'code red' for humanity (UN Press Release, 2021), planetary boundaries research shows that the reality is even more grim – we have a whole set of code reds for humanity, and they must all be dealt with simultaneously. The sustainability challenges of our time are complex and interconnected, and piecemeal and isolated elements will not work. In using the planetary boundaries framework as a part of our understanding of sustainability, we acknowledge the inherent limitations and biases in a Western scientific approach and the tensions between the framework and Indigenous and postcolonial ways of seeing the world. We do not see the planetary boundaries framework as the only approach to environmental aspects of sustainability; its usefulness is in outlining global consequences of human activity (also recognizing that 'human activity' conceals historical and current inequalities) on the Earth system processes upon which human prosperity relies.

Working towards sustainability entails questions of justice. Just as we cannot silo environmental issues into various categories to be dealt with separately, we cannot separate environmental and social issues. These are all interconnected elements, and for people's lived realities, a distinction between environmental and social makes little sense. Clean drinking water is a part of securing social foundations; polluting or exploiting drinking water for profit is social harm as much as it is environmental harm. Securing social foundations is also about preventing the undermining of economic and governance bases of well-functioning communities and states, which are deeply interconnected issues.

Sustainable value creation is already an emerging concept in company law discussions and corporate governance codes in a range of countries (Sjåfjell and Tsagas, 2023). Creating sustainable value, as we see it, encompasses issues such as fair treatment of employees as well as workers and local communities across global value chains, with respect for international human rights and core International Labour Organization conventions as a minimum, ensuring a 'living wage' and safe working conditions (Sjåfjell and Cornell, 2024). Further, sustainable value encompasses participatory aspects of the social foundations of sustainability, including all workers regardless of their labour law status, with participation being organized according to local laws and customs. Sustainable value also entails honouring Indigenous Peoples' rights, including their relationship with the land, irrespective of state law regulation of that relationship, and engaging with affected communities and Peoples based on their ways of seeing the world and how deliberations are conducted (Kimmerer, 2013; Ferdinand, 2021; Chao, 2022).

As such, avoiding the shareholder versus stakeholder trap does not mean ignoring the various interests affected by the company's business. Our point is that a mere canvassing of 'stakeholder interests' (and giving priority to the ones that make themselves heard the most) is insufficient, misleading, and potentially destructive for the overarching purpose of sustainable value creation. The backdrop must always be the interconnected complexities and the vulnerability of the often unrepresented groups, whether invisibilized workers deep in the global value chains or Indigenous or other local communities (Kotzé, 2019 pp. 62–85), and the aim of a safe and just world, which depends on mitigating pressures on planetary boundaries (Sjåfjell, 2021, p. 213).

4.2 Reimagining corporate purpose for sustainability

4.2.1 Introducing 'sustainable value' and 'planetary boundaries' to corporate purpose

An overarching corporate purpose for all corporate forms can be formulated simply in the following manner:

> The overarching purpose of the undertaking is to create sustainable value in a manner that also contributes to mitigating pressures on planetary boundaries. (Sjåfjell, 2023)

The phrase 'contributes to' in the context of planetary boundaries is a carefully chosen formulation in acknowledgement that mitigating pressures on planetary boundaries is not something that can be operationalized easily at the level of the individual company (Clift et al., 2017). Rather, the company's responsibility is envisaged in a way that encompasses the operations and activities of the business, including the full life of the products, processes, and services of the business.

We have suggested 'planetary boundaries' to be defined as:

> the scientifically recognised processes that regulate the stability and resilience of the Earth system within which humanity can continue to develop and thrive for generations to come

and that 'sustainable value' be defined as:

> creating value for the undertaking, while respecting the rights of its members, investors, employees, and other contractual parties, and promoting good governance, decent work and equality, and the human rights of its workers and affected communities and peoples.

Yet we also envisage 'sustainable value' and 'planetary boundaries' as general clauses in company law, the content of which can be gradually firmed up as practice develops. The definitions above would ensure sufficient parameters to ensure that business does not turn these two concepts into opportunities for 'sustainability washing'.

Our formulations are drafted in a European company law context. How the overarching corporate purpose and sustainable value are defined in other jurisdictions and for other corporate forms depends on the local context, legal system, and corporate form, taking into consideration their varieties discussed above.

4.2.2 *Revising board duties to operationalize a sustainable corporate purpose*

As noted in section 2, during the nineteenth century, companies were, in most jurisdictions, granted a separate legal personality, which allowed them to own property and contract in their own name (Foster, 2000; Watson, 2019). As a company does not have physical personality, it must be coordinated by humans. Companies need organs to operationalize their activities. The competence and duties of the organs are therefore core company law issues. In European companies, the boards have overarching competence to run the company, with the shareholders having control over the composition of the board by voting at the general meeting. The board's powers are normally defined in national company law and firm-specific constitutional documents.

Although the detailed competencies of the board vary between different jurisdictions and across various corporate forms, its law-based corporate governance role is crucial in fulfilling the firm's corporate purpose. In most jurisdictions, the board is compulsory, even where the board duties have been divided between several management and supervisory organs. For example, the board is central in several parts of EU company legislation, described as the 'administrative or management body' of the undertaking, as it is done, for instance, in multiple provisions in the 2017 EU Company Law Directive (European Parliament and Council, 2017, Articles 13f, 50, 60, 61, 64, 65, 72, 86d, 86e, 86j, 124, 126b, 160d, 160e, and 160j). Although there are attempts, especially in the US, to partially replace boards with artificial intelligence, they still consist mainly of human decision-makers (Bruner, 2020). Given the central role of boards in companies, it is paramount to integrate our proposal for corporate purpose into the duties of the board. Our goal is to outline these duties in a way that provides legal certainty for undertakings and to clarify the board's relationship to the company and its shareholders and other affected parties. Below we explain why and briefly how, drawing on extensive presentations and discussions of this in previous work.

The understanding of corporate purpose is not governed only by law. It is also influenced by social norms, market forces, and human-made and ecological 'architectures' (Sjåfjell and Taylor, 2019). Company law is underpinned by a societal purpose of the company and gives boards (and by extension senior executive management) a broad discretionary space to run the company in a more sustainable way. However, the social norm of shareholder primacy, signals from internationalized financial markets, and use of algorithms and artificial intelligence-based trade, reporting, and governance, send contradictory signals to boards about the importance of maximizing financial capital value.

To implement a sustainable corporate purpose and facilitate sustainable value creation, it is therefore crucial to strengthen the duties of the board. The board's company law duty to promote the interests of the company, or the 'company interest', as it is often referred to in Continental Europe, is key in this context. To clarify the board's role in a company, which has been clouded through the influence of the shareholder primacy drive, it should therefore be set clearly in law that the core duty of the board is to promote the interests of the company. In line with what we have proposed, this will not entail a harmonization of the definition of the interests of the company in European company law. Developing the understanding of what the interests of the specific company entail in a concrete instance should remain with the board to define, within the scope of national legislation, articles of association, and existing contracts and commitments. The duty of the board to promote the interests of the company should – and can – be positioned within the overarching purpose set out in section 4.2.1 above, namely:

> promoting the interests of the company in such a way as to create sustainable value that also contributes to mitigating pressures on planetary boundaries.

This should further be specified as entailing duties to assess and, as necessary, change the corporate business model and strategy, and encompass changes in risk management, with mandatory corporate sustainability due diligence as a key tool for boards to fulfil this duty. We have also proposed mechanisms for public and private enforcement, including regulating the board's liability (Sjåfjell, 2023). The company is bound by contracts made by the board on the company's behalf, and the harm caused by the board through its actions or inactions falls under the liability of the company as a legal entity. This forms the basis for potential liability for individual board members. EU law, including the Corporate Sustainability Due Diligence Directive (European Parliament and the Council, 2024), is moving in this direction. Whatever the outcome may be of the 2025 Omnibus proposals to limit this Directive (and other sustainability-oriented legislation), legal uncertainty and liability risks will continue to increase for boards that do not actively integrate sustainability into their governance (Sjåfjell and Mähönen, 2025). Legislation clarifying the duties of the board would mitigate these risks.

5. Concluding reflections

The shareholder versus stakeholder dichotomy has dominated company law discussion. This dichotomy constrains the possibilities for finding ways to mitigate the risks of continued unsustainability in business. It is time to reject the dichotomy and identify how we can secure the contribution of business to a safe and just world. We see that the key is in the societal purpose of the company and how we can rebuild company law around it.

In this chapter, we have presented our proposal for how the overarching purpose of companies could be reformed. We have written from our European perspective. In future research, we welcome a further broadening of the debate on corporate purpose, taking into consideration the jurisdictional variations and different ways of organizing business that we have touched upon.

We are convinced of the significance of corporate purpose. Without a clearly defined corporate purpose for sustainability, we believe that business will continue on the path of extreme unsustainability. All companies have a corporate purpose; explicit or implicit. So the real issue is the content of that corporate purpose. It is elementary that corporate purpose engages with sustainability, unless it is a purpose for a business in the sunset industry – and then the unsustainable purpose should also be clear (e.g., 'our purpose is to source and sell fossil fuels until we are put out of business'). It is the implicitness of the shareholder primacy version of corporate purpose that is dangerous – with all the talk of sustainability, the underlying reality of continued maximization of returns for shareholders remains a major barrier to sustainable business.

Yet, redefinition of corporate purpose is not enough. We have set out our preliminary proposal, concentrating on redefining the duties of the boards of European companies. Much research remains to be done. Research questions include how duties of the board in the context of a renewed corporate purpose are to be implemented by individual members in multiple-member boards; what individual board members' liability would be for insufficient implementation, and what would be required, procedurally and materially, for the company (or other constituents) to enforce these duties. From the perspective of the board members, an important question is also what defences board members would have at their disposal to convince courts that they have fulfilled their duties sufficiently.

Future research is also required concerning the concept of sustainable value creation. 'Value' in the corporate context is an accounting concept. Traditional financial accounting is concentrated on financial capital and its accumulation. Sustainable value therefore requires a significant reorienting of financial value-based accounting. Sustainable valuation processes should account for the complex, contextual, and multidimensional characters of sustainability that are not reflected in monetary valuation (Martinez-Alier, Munda and O'Neill, 1998; Monciardini, 2013; Ahlström and Monciardini, 2022); thereby recognizing the risks for unsustainability in financially oriented value creation.

As at writing this chapter in the Spring of 2025, we are in the time of the second Trump presidency in the US and of the Omnibus proposals to dilute some key sustainability-oriented legislation that the EU has put into place over the last years. An urgent and remaining research question is therefore how to convince policymakers that the economy and business do not exist in a bubble, separate from society and nature of which we are all a part and depend on, and that regulating for sustainability is crucial to secure a safe and just world for all of us.

Notes

1. This chapter draws on our article 'Corporate Purpose and the Misleading Shareholder vs Stakeholder Dichotomy', *Bond Law Review* (2022), 34(2), pp. 69–112, published 14 March 2024, available at: https://doi.org/10.53300/001c.94050, and segments of the text are reproduced from the article with the kind permission of the editor.
2. The concepts 'human capital' and 'financial capital' come from sustainability accounting literature, which claims that sustainability requires going beyond merely accounting for traditional financial and industrial capital and taking account of the benefits and detriments to the natural world and society. We also note that Jane Gleeson-White urges attention to four new categories of wealth: 'intellectual' (such as intellectual property), 'human' (skills, productivity, and health), 'social and relationship' (shared norms and values), and 'natural' (environment) (Gleeson-White, 2015). According to Gleeson-White, integrating these categories of wealth into financial statements and gross domestic product figures may be the only way to address the many calamities of unsustainability we face (Gleeson-White, 2015). In this joint chapter, although we understand the argumentation, we do not employ that categorization.

References

Ahlström, H. and Monciardini, D. (2022) 'The regulatory dynamics of sustainable finance: paradoxical success and limitations of EU reforms', *Journal of Business Ethics*, 177(1), pp. 193–212. Available at: https://doi.org/10.1007/s10551-021-04763-x.

Berle, A.A. and Means, G.C. (1933) *The modern corporation and private property*. Macmillan. Available at: http://books.google.com/books?id=zaZZAAAAYAAJ (Accessed: 3 February 2020).

Blair, M.M. and Stout, L.A. (1999) 'A team production theory of corporate law', *Virginia Law Review*, 85(2), pp. 247–328. Available at: https://doi.org/10.2307/1073662.

Bruner, C.M. (2013) 'Conceptions of corporate purpose in post-crisis financial firms', *Seattle University Law Review*, 36, pp. 527–561.

Bruner, C.M. (2020) 'Distributed ledgers, artificial intelligence and the purpose of the corporation', *The Cambridge Law Journal*, 79(3), pp. 431–458. Available at: https://doi.org/10.1017/S0008197320000756.

Bruner, C.M. and Sjåfjell, B. (2019) 'Corporate law, corporate governance and the pursuit of sustainability', in Sjåfjell, B. and Bruner, C.M. (eds) *The Cambridge handbook of corporate law, corporate governance and sustainability*. Cambridge University Press (Cambridge Law Handbooks), pp. 713–720. Available at: https://doi.org/10.1017/9781108658386.057.

Business Roundtable (2019) *Business Roundtable redefines the purpose of a corporation to promote 'an economy that serves all Americans'*. Available at: https://www.businessroundtable.org/business-roundtable-redefines-the-purpose-of-a-corporation-to-promote-an-economy-that-serves-all-americans (Accessed: 22 November 2023).

Chao, S. (2022) In the shadow of the palms: more-than-human becomings in West Papua. Duke University Press. Available at: https://www.dukeupress.edu/in-the-shadow-of-the-palms (Accessed: 30 April 2025).

Clift, R. *et al.* (2017) 'The challenges of applying planetary boundaries as a basis for strategic decision-making in companies with global supply chains', *Sustainability*, 9(2), pp. 279–302. Available at: https://doi.org/10.3390/su9020279.

Cooney, J. (2017) 'Reflections on the 20th anniversary of the term "social licence"', *Journal of Energy & Natural Resources Law*, 35(2), pp. 197–200. Available at: https://doi.org/10.1080/02646811.2016.1269472.

Davoudi, L., McKenna, C. and Olegario, R. (2018) 'The historical role of the corporation in society', *Journal of the British Academy*, 6(s1), pp. 17–47. Available at: https://doi.org/10.5871/jba/006s1.017.

Easterbrook, F. and Fischel, D. (1991) *The economic structure of corporate law*. Harvard University Press.

Ehrnström-Fuentes, M. and Böhm, S. (2023) 'The political ontology of corporate social responsibility: obscuring the pluriverse in place', *Journal of Business Ethics*, 185(2), pp. 245–261. Available at: https://doi.org/10.1007/s10551-022-05175-1.

European Commission (2020) *Sustainable corporate governance initiative*. Available at: https://ec.europa.eu/info/law/better-regulation/have-your-say/initiatives/12548-Sustainable-corporate-governance_en.

European Parliament and the Council (2017) 'Directive (EU) 2017/1132 of the European Parliament and of the Council of 14 June 2017 relating to certain aspects of company law (codification) (Text with EEA relevance.), OJ L'. Available at: http://data.europa.eu/eli/dir/2017/1132/oj/eng (Accessed: 22 November 2023).

European Parliament and the Council (2024) 'Directive (EU) 2024/1760 of the European Parliament and of the Council of 13 June 2024 on corporate sustainability due diligence and amending Directive (EU) 2019/1937 and Regulation (EU) 2023/2859 Text with EEA relevance. OJ L, 2024/1760, 5.7.2024'. Available at: http://data.europa.eu/eli/dir/2024/1760/oj/eng (Accessed: 5 July 2024).

Ferdinand, M. (2021) *Decolonial ecology: thinking from the Caribbean world*. Wiley. Available at: https://www.wiley.com/en-dk/Decolonial+Ecology%3A+Thinking+from+the+Caribbean+World-p-9781509546220 (Accessed: 12 May 2023).

Fleischer, H. (2021) 'Corporate purpose: a management concept and its implications for company law', *European Company and Financial Law Review*, 18(2), pp. 161–189. Available at: https://doi.org/10.1515/ecfr-2021-0008.

Foster, N.H.D. (2000) 'Company law theory in comparative perspective: England and France', *The American Journal of Comparative Law*, 48(4), pp. 573–621. Available at: https://doi.org/10.2307/840908.

Freeman, R.E. (1984) *Strategic management: a stakeholder approach*. Pitman.

Gleeson-White, J. (2015) *Six capitals: or, can accountants save the planet? Rethinking capitalism for the twenty-first century*. 1st American edn. W.W. Norton & Company.

Jensen, M.C. (2001) 'Value maximization, stakeholder theory, and the corporate objective function', *Journal of Applied Corporate Finance*, 14(3), pp. 8–21. Available at: https://doi.org/10.1111/j.1745-6622.2001.tb00434.x.

Jensen, M.C. and Meckling, W.H. (1976) 'Theory of the firm: managerial behavior, agency costs and ownership structure', *Journal of Financial Economics*, 3(4), pp. 305–360. Available at: https://doi.org/10.1016/0304-405X(76)90026-X.

Kimmerer, R.W. (2013) *Braiding sweetgrass*. 1st edn. Milkweed Editions. Available at: http://books.google.com/books?vid=isbn9781571313355 (Accessed: 3 July 2024).

Knapp, V. (2021) 'Sustainable corporate governance: a way forward?', *European Company and Financial Law Review*, 18(2), pp. 218–243. Available at: https://econpapers.repec.org/article/bpjeucflr/v_3a18_3ay_3a2021_3ai_3a2_3ap_3a218-243_3an_3a6.htm (Accessed: 21 November 2023).

Kotzé, L.J. (2019) 'The Anthropocene, Earth system vulnerability and socio-ecological injustice in an age of human rights', *Journal of Human Rights and the Environment*, 10(1), pp. 62–85. Available at: https://doi.org/10.4337/jhre.2019.01.04.

Kraakman, R. *et al.* (2017) *The anatomy of corporate law: a comparative and functional approach*. 3rd edn. Oxford University Press. Available at: https://doi.org/10.1093/acprof:oso/9780198739630.001.0001.

Krüger Andersen, P. *et al* (2020) *Response to the study on directors' duties and sustainable corporate governance by Nordic company law scholars*. Research Paper No 2020-100, University of Copenhagen, 7 October 2020. Available at:https://ssrn.com/abstract=3709762

Leach, M., Raworth, K. and Rockström, J. (2013) 'Between social and planetary boundaries: navigating pathways in the safe and just space for humanity', in *World Social Science Report 2013*. OECD Publishing, pp. 84–90. Available at: https://steps-centre.org/blog/wssr/ (Accessed: 22 November 2020).

Martinez-Alier, J., Munda, G. and O'Neill, J. (1998) 'Weak comparability of values as a foundation for ecological economics', *Ecological Economics*, 26(3), pp. 277–286. Available at: https://doi.org/10.1016/S0921-8009(97)00120-1.

Millon, D. (2013) 'Radical shareholder primacy', *University of St. Thomas Law Journal*, 10(4), pp. 1013–1044.

Monciardini, D. (2013) *Quello che conta – a socio-legal analysis of accounting for sustainable companies*. Doctoral Thesis (monograph). Department of Sociology of Law, Lund University.

Möslein, F. and Sørensen, K.E. (2021) 'Sustainable corporate governance: a way forward', *European Company Law*, 18, pp. 7–14. Available at: https://doi.org/10.2139/ssrn.3761711.

Muchlinski, P. (2013) 'The development of German corporate law until 1990: an historical reappraisal', *German Law Journal*, 14(2), pp. 339–379. Available at: https://doi.org/10.1017/S2071832200001838.

Persson, L., Carney Almroth, B.M., Collins, C.D., Cornell, S., de Wit, C.A., Diamond, M.L., Fantke, P., Hassellöv, M. MacLeod, M., Ryberg, M.W., Søgaard Jørgensen, P., Villarrubia-Gómez, P., Wang, Z. and Zwicky Hauschild, M. (2022) 'Outside the safe operating space of the planetary boundary for novel entities', *Environmental Science & Technology*, 56(3), pp. 1510–1521. Available at: https://doi.org/10.1021/acs.est.1c04158.

Puchniak, D.W. (2022) 'No need for Asia to be woke: contextualizing Anglo-America's "discovery" of corporate purpose', *RED*, 4(1), pp. 14–21. Available at: https://www.cairn-int.info/journal-red-2022-1-page-14.htm (Accessed: 22 November 2023).

Raworth, K. (2017) 'A safe and just space for humanity: can we live within the doughnut?', in Raworth, K, *Doughnut economics: seven ways to think like a 21st-century economist*. Chelsea Green Publishing.

Richardson, K., Steffen, W., Lucht, W., Bendtsen, J., Cornell, S.E., Donges, J.F., Drüke, M., Fetzer, I., Bala, G., von Bloh, W., Feulner, G., Fiedler, S., Gerten, D., Gleeson, T., Hofmann, M., Huiskamp, W., Kummu, M., Mohan, C., Nogués-Bravo, D., Petri, S., Porkka, M., Rahmstorf, S., Schaphoff, S., Thonicke, K., Tobian, A., Virkki, V., Wang-Erlandsson, L., Weber, L. and Rockström, J. (2023) 'Earth beyond six of nine planetary boundaries', *Science Advances*, 9(37), eadh2458. Available at: https://doi.org/10.1126/sciadv.adh2458.

Rockström, J., Steffen, W., Noone K., Persson, Å, Chapin, F.S.I., Lambin, E., Lenton, T., Scheffer, M., Folke, C., Schellnhuber, H.J., Nykvist, B., de Wit, C., Hughes, T., van der Leeuw, S., Rodhe, H., Sörlin, S., Snyder, P., Costanza, R., Svedin, U., Falkenmark, M., Karlberg, L., Corell, R., Fabry, V., Hansen, J., Walker, B., Liverman, D., Richardson, K., Crutzen, P. and Foley, J. (2009) 'Planetary boundaries: exploring the safe operating space for humanity', *Ecology and Society*, 14(2). Available at: https://doi.org/10.5751/ES-03180-140232.

Sjåfjell, B., Johnston, A., Anker-Sørensen, L. and Millon, D. (2015) 'Shareholder primacy: the main barrier to sustainable companies', in Sjåfjell, B. and Richardson, B.J. (eds) *Company law and sustainability*. 1st edn. Cambridge University Press, pp. 79–147. Available at: https://doi.org/10.1017/CBO9781107337978.005.

Sjåfjell, B. (2019) 'Realising the potential of the board for corporate sustainability', in Sjåfjell, B. and Bruner, C.M. (eds) *The Cambridge handbook of corporate law, corporate governance, and sustainability*. Cambridge University Press, Ch. 49.

Sjåfjell, B., Mähönen, J., Novitz, T.A., Gammage, C. and Ahlström, H. (2020) *Securing the future of European business: SMART Reform Proposals*. SMART report, 7 May. University of Oslo Faculty of Law Research Paper No. 2020-11, Nordic & European Company Law Working Paper No. 20-08, Available at: https://ssrn.com/abstract=3595048

Sjåfjell, B. (2021) 'Reforming EU company law to secure the future of European business', *European Company and Financial Law Review*, 18(2), pp. 190–217. Available at: https://doi.org/10.1515/ecfr-2021-0009.

Sjåfjell, B. (2023) 'A general corporate law duty to act sustainably', in Birkmose, H.S., Neville, M. and Engsig Sørensen, K. (eds) *Instruments of EU corporate governance: effecting changes in the management of companies in a changing world*. Kluwer Law International, pp. 39–64. Available at: https://papers.ssrn.com/abstract=4224255 (Accessed: 20 March 2023).

Sjåfjell, B. (2025) 'Revisiting agency theory: a radical rethinking of allocation of responsibility, accountability and liability', in Chevrollier, N, Argyrou, A. and Jeurissen, R. (eds) *Radical business perspectives for sustainability transitions*. Edward Elgar Publishing, Ch. 9. Available at: https://ssrn.com/abstract=4835681

Sjåfjell, B., and Cornell, S.E. (2024) 'What the actual … .? Tensions in the science-business-policy interface for global sustainability', *European Law Open*, 3(3), pp. 529–560. Available at: https://doi.org/10.1017/elo.2024.34.

Sjåfjell, B. and Mähönen, J. (2020) *Interdisciplinarising legal theory: towards a reconceptualisation of business law in an era of complexity*. SSRN scholarly paper ID 3731289. Social Science Research Network. Available at: https://papers.ssrn.com/abstract=3731289 (Accessed: 15 September 2021).

Sjåfjell, B. and Mähönen, J. (eds) (2023) *Nordic company law: broadening the horizon*. Scandinavian University Press. Available at: https://www.universitetsforlaget.no/en/nordic-company-law-broadening-the-horizon (Accessed: 22 November 2023).

Sjåfjell, B. and Mähönen, J. (2024) 'Corporate purpose and the misleading shareholder vs stakeholder dichotomy', *Bond Law Review*, 24(2), pp. 69–112. Available at: https://doi.org/10.2139/ssrn.4039565.

Sjåfjell, B. and Mähönen, J.T. (2025) 'Sustainable corporate governance for boards and their lawyers', in De Silva, S., Froggatt, A., George, D., Goldberg, S., Haigh, J., Holland, O., Krier, S., Tanna, M., Kerrigan, C. and Norman, C. (eds) *Expert essentials*. Oxford University Press. Available at: https://doi.org/10.1093/9780198972877.003.0048 (Accessed 11 December 2025).

Sjåfjell, B. and Taylor, M.B. (2019) 'Clash of norms: shareholder primacy vs. sustainable corporate purpose', *International and Comparative Corporate Law Journal*, 13(3), pp. 40–66. Available at: https://ssrn.com/abstract=3444050 (Accessed: 26 January 2020).

Sjåfjell, B. and Tsagas, G. (2023) 'Integrating sustainable value creation in corporate governance: company law, corporate governance codes and the constitution of the company', in Sjåfjell, B., Tsagas, G. and Villiers, C. (eds) *Sustainable value creation in the European Union: towards pathways to a sustainable future through crises*. Cambridge University Press, Ch. 9.

Smith, D. (1998) 'The shareholder primacy norm', *Journal of Corporation Law*, 23, pp. 277–323. Available at: https://digitalcommons.law.byu.edu/faculty_scholarship/27.

Sneirson, J.F. (2008) 'Green is good: sustainability, profitability, and a new paradigm for corporate governance', *Iowa Law Review*, 94, p. 987–1022.

Sneirson, J.F. (2019) 'The history of shareholder primacy, from Adam Smith through the rise of financialism', in Sjåfjell, B. and Bruner, C.M. (eds) *The Cambridge handbook of corporate law, corporate governance and sustainability*. Cambridge University Press (Cambridge Law Handbooks), pp. 73–85. Available at: https://doi.org/10.1017/9781108658386.011.

Steffen, W. *et al.* (2015) 'Planetary boundaries: guiding human development on a changing planet', *Science*, 347(6223), p. 1259855. Available at: https://doi.org/10.1126/science.1259855.

Stout, L.A. (2012) *The shareholder value myth: how putting shareholders first harms investors, corporations, and the public*. Berrett-Koehler Publishers.

Stuart, A. *et al.* (2023) 'Conceptualising social licence to operate', *Resources Policy*, 85, p. 103962. Available at: https://doi.org/10.1016/j.resourpol.2023.103962.

The Queen v. H M Treasury and Commissioners of Inland Revenue, ex parte Daily Mail and General Trust plc (1988). Available at: https://eur-lex.europa.eu/legal-content/EN/TXT/?uri=CELEX%3A61987CJ0081 (Accessed: 3 July 2024).

UN Press Release (2021) 'IPCC Report: "Code Red" for Human Driven Global Heating, Warns UN Chief', *UN News*, 9 August (Accessed 27 December 2021).

von Gierke, O.F. (1954) *Das deutsche Genossenschaftsrecht*. Graz, Akademische Druck-u. Verlagsanstalt. Available at: http://archive.org/details/dasdeutschegenoo2giergoog (Accessed: 3 February 2020).

Watson, S.M. (2019) 'The corporate legal person', *Journal of Corporate Law Studies*, 19(1), pp. 137–166. Available at: https://doi.org/10.1080/14735970.2018.1435951.

PART III

Chasing the rapids: turbulent actions and experiments

10 Placing zakat in African tax policy: a pathway to sustainable finance

Lyla Latif

1. Introduction

Zakat, an Islamic form of tax on wealth redistribution, represents an Indigenous form of sustainable finance that has been practised by Muslim communities for centuries. Its principles of wealth redistribution and care for the less privileged resonate strongly with the goals of sustainable finance, making it a unique model that can contribute to the broader discourse on contemporary fiscal and environmental challenges. This perspective is particularly relevant in countries with significant Muslim populations and could serve as a valuable model for integrating cultural and religious principles into modern finance practices (Latif, 2023). This chapter explores the potential of zakat to intersect with modern frameworks of tax policy and sustainable finance in the African context. By examining this intersection, the chapter opens up new avenues for addressing pressing issues around climate change mitigation and sustainable development.

Zakat is one of the five pillars of Islam, a religious obligation for Muslims to annually pay a portion of their wealth to specific beneficiaries (Al Qaradawi, 2001), with priority given to the poor and needy (Latif, 2023). The beneficiaries of zakat outlined in the Quran are the poor, the needy, zakat administrators, those in bondage, debtors, those committed to propagating Islam, and travellers. Zakat is calculated based on the value of one's possessions, traditionally including savings, livestock (only cows, goats, sheep, and camels), agricultural produce, and gold and silver, that exceed a minimum threshold (nisab). Zakat rates vary depending on the type of wealth. Generally, it is levied at 2.5 per cent on monetary wealth (such as savings and precious metals) that exceeds the nisab (minimum threshold). For agricultural produce, the rate ranges from 5 to 10 per cent, depending on the irrigation method. Livestock zakat follows a more complex system; for instance, one yearling calf is due on thirty heads of cattle (Al Qaradawi, 2001). These rates may vary slightly across different schools of Islamic jurisprudence. This wealth-based approach, focusing on assets rather than income, distinguishes zakat from many conventional tax systems.

Zakat can be paid directly to beneficiaries, given to mosques or faith-based institutions for distribution, or collected by the state in Muslim majority countries like Saudi Arabia, Sudan, and Pakistan (Powell, 2010). Through principles of wealth redistribution and community solidarity, zakat aligns closely with the goals of sustainable finance, offering a unique model of ethical wealth transfer. Within sustainable finance frameworks, directing zakat funds towards supporting small-scale farmers represents a promising area of focus, aligning with several key objectives. Firstly, many small-scale farmers in developing countries fall within the categories of zakat beneficiaries due to their economic vulnerability. Secondly, supporting agriculture through zakat addresses food insecurity, a critical issue recognised in Sustainable Development Goal 2 (Zero Hunger). Agriculture is highly sensitive to climate change impacts, with changing weather patterns, rising temperatures, droughts, and floods posing major risks to crop yields and food security (Ore, 2015). This vulnerability to climate change is especially acute for smallholder farmers in developing countries, who often lack the resources and capacity to implement climate adaptation strategies. Many African countries, in particular, face recurring droughts that exacerbate food insecurity and poverty among rural populations.

By channelling zakat funds into sustainable agriculture initiatives, this approach creates a nexus between Islamic principles of wealth redistribution, sustainable finance goals, and climate resilience strategies. It offers a means to simultaneously address poverty alleviation, food security, and climate adaptation – all key components of sustainable development. This integration demonstrates how traditional Islamic practices can be leveraged within modern sustainable finance frameworks to address pressing global challenges.

The chapter is structured to comprehensively unpack the intersections between zakat, tax policy, and sustainable finance. It begins by exploring these concepts, highlighting their unique characteristics and intrinsic linkages. This sets the stage for an examination of how tax policy can reflect zakat's wealth redistribution objectives and how sustainable finance principles can guide such policies. The discussion then delves into the complexities of integrating zakat into sustainable finance frameworks, scrutinising its potential role as a catalyst for this book's theme, and its contribution to socio-legal scholarship. The chapter emphasises the implications of zakat's religious and cultural foundations for its integration into broader fiscal systems.

Following this, the chapter considers the potential benefits of such an integrative approach for African countries, acknowledging the demographic composition of these nations and recognising the importance of aligning tax policies with religious contexts. The concluding sections explore the implications of this analysis for fiscal sociology and socio-legal studies, arguing for the potential of religious fiscal systems to drive social change and contribute to sustainable finance. The chapter ends with a reflection on key insights and potential future directions for research and practice in this innovative intersection of tax policy, sustainable finance, and zakat.

2. Tax policy and sustainable finance

Before delving into the potential role of zakat in sustainable finance and tax frameworks, it is crucial to establish a foundational understanding of the relationship between tax policy and sustainable finance. This section explores this nexus for four key reasons. Firstly, understanding the intersection of tax policy and sustainable finance provides essential context for considering how alternative fiscal approaches, such as zakat, might be integrated into existing systems. By examining how conventional tax policies can promote sustainability, we can better assess the potential complementary or alternative role of zakat. Secondly, the challenges and opportunities identified in the interaction between tax policy and sustainable finance in African nations highlight the gaps that innovative approaches like zakat might address. This analysis sets the stage for understanding why alternative or complementary fiscal tools may be necessary. Thirdly, exploring this nexus demonstrates the evolving nature of fiscal policy in response to global sustainability challenges. This evolution provides a framework for considering how traditional Islamic practices like zakat can be reimagined in the context of modern sustainable development goals. By establishing the link between tax policy and sustainable finance, this section lays the groundwork for arguing that zakat, as a form of wealth redistribution, can be viewed through a similar lens – as a tool for promoting sustainable development and addressing socio-economic challenges.

The synergy between fiscal strategy and sustainable growth is becoming increasingly apparent, necessitating a deep dive into the intersection of tax policy and sustainable finance. As an integral component of fiscal strategy, tax policy plays a fundamental role in revenue generation, serving as the financial backbone that supports a country's growth and development. Concurrently, sustainable finance, encompassing practices that integrate environmental, social, and governance (ESG) considerations, is central to contemporary discussions on economic resilience and long-term growth.

In the examination of fiscal strategies pertinent to economic and social development, tax policy emerges as a critical tool within the armamentarium of governments (Bahl and Bird, 2008). It shapes the financial landscape of nations, particularly African nations that are grappling with economic underdevelopment, poverty, and inequality (Ojo, 2016). The formulation of a robust and equitable tax policy is not merely a matter of pragmatic governance, but an urgent imperative, considering its profound impacts on revenue generation, economic stimulation, and societal welfare. The primary function of tax policy is revenue generation (Mumford, 2002), providing the financial lifeblood for government operations and public services. However, its role extends beyond this. Tax policy can stimulate economic activities, attract foreign direct investments, and serve as a mechanism for income redistribution (Njuguna, 2022). When applied progressively, it can mitigate income inequality, a pervasive issue across the African continent.

Ghana provides an illustrative example of the impact of tax policy reforms. Over the past three decades, Ghana has undertaken significant tax policy reforms aimed at boosting domestic resources mobilisation. This includes diversifying the tax base, implementing value-added tax, and strengthening tax administration. Consequently, Ghana has witnessed a steady increase in its tax to GDP ratio from around 12 per cent in the early 1990s to over 17 per cent by 2020 (Brafu-Insaidoo and Obeng, 2020). These policy reforms enabled Ghana to boost revenues, reduce donor dependence, and invest in socio-economic development programmes.

The implementation of effective tax policy in African nations, however, faces several challenges. These include weak tax administration, rampant tax evasion and avoidance, the prevalence of informal economies, and political instability (Ndikumana and Boyce, 2023). The African Development Bank Group estimates that the informal economy constitutes between 30 and 60 per cent of the total economy across the continent, a statistic that underscores the challenges faced by tax authorities (AfDB, 2019). Despite these hurdles, the necessity for robust tax policy in African countries cannot be overstated, as it is crucial for financing development aspirations and reducing dependency on foreign aid.

The discourse surrounding sustainable finance has gained significant traction, acknowledging the intertwining of economic growth and sustainability (Migliorelli, 2021; Schoenmaker, 2019). Sustainable finance refers to financial practices that factor in ESG considerations for the lasting benefit of both clients and society (Gaganis et al., 2023). Within this framework, tax policy emerges as a critical tool to shape and promote sustainable financial practices. Tax policy can incentivise sustainable business practices and disincentivise environmentally harmful activities. For instance, tax credits for renewable energy projects can stimulate investment in this sector, as demonstrated in South Africa, where such incentives helped catalyse growth in the renewable energy sector, with over 6 GW of new renewable energy capacity added over the last decade (Dippenaar, 2018). Conversely, carbon taxes can discourage polluting activities and promote cleaner technologies. Tax revenue can also directly finance sustainable development projects, linking tax policy to sustainability promotion.

The intersection of tax policy and sustainable finance creates a potential positive feedback loop towards sustainable revenue generation. Governments can utilise tax policy to stimulate sustainable finance through mechanisms such as green bonds, environmental taxes, and tax incentives for sustainable business practices (Jones et al., 2020; Lutken, 2015; Bowman, 2014). However, the prospect of harnessing tax policy for sustainable finance and revenue generation is not without challenges. First, the efficacy of such fiscal instruments is contingent on robust governance, administrative capacity, and regulatory oversight. Without these, the risk of tax evasion, regulatory capture, and misuse of funds increases substantially (Kila, 2023). Second, the application of tax policy to stimulate sustainable finance must contend with the reality of economic inequalities. While tax incentives might stimulate sustainable investments, care must be taken to ensure that the benefits of such policies are equitably distributed and do not inadvertently exacerbate wealth disparities (Bakker, 2009). Finally, the international dimension of tax policy and sustainable finance cannot be understated. As capital and businesses operate globally, a coordinated international approach to tax policy is vital to prevent tax evasion, profit shifting, and the offshoring of environmentally damaging activities.

Despite these challenges, the confluence of tax policy and sustainable finance delineates a potential pathway to engender financial systems that are not just economically sound, but also environmentally considerate and socially equitable. At its core, tax policy can be leveraged strategically to direct the financial sector towards a sustainable trajectory. This is achieved by providing incentives that encourage adherence to sustainable practices. Governments can facilitate these incentives through tax breaks or deductions for enterprises that embrace sustainable operational models, or for individuals who channel investments into sustainable funds. Through such fiscal enticements, tax policy can effectively catalyse the flow of capital towards sectors that underscore sustainability. This, in turn, consolidates the financial viability of sustainable sectors and further attracts capital investment, fostering a virtuous cycle of sustainable finance.

In the African context, some countries are already exploring innovative approaches. For instance, Kenya's Fiscal Incentives Policy Framework (The National Treasury and Economic Planning, 2022) aims to steer the economy towards a low-carbon, climate-resilient development pathway through various fiscal and economic mechanisms. The confluence of tax policy and sustainable finance delineates a potential pathway to engender financial systems that are not just economically sound, but also environmentally considerate and socially equitable. By leveraging tax policy strategically, governments can direct the financial sector towards a sustainable trajectory, catalysing the flow of capital towards sectors that underscore sustainability. These emerging policy frameworks intersect with the broader questioning of regulatory approaches examined by Foerster (2026) in this book, which explores whether ecologically rational regulation is emerging in the finance sector. The integration of environmental considerations into tax policy also relates to the analysis by Bowman and Tayler (2026) in this book of aligning international financial architecture with sustainable transition beyond the Paris Agreement.

The intersection of tax policy and sustainable finance reveals a promising landscape for shaping sustainable development trajectories, particularly in Africa. Despite inherent challenges, the potential to stimulate a shift towards sustainable economic models is immense. By developing comprehensive tax policies that resonate with the tenets of sustainable finance, African countries can edge closer to fulfilling their development goals, ensuring financial resilience, environmental sustainability, and social equity. This sets the stage for exploring innovative approaches, such as the potential integration of zakat, which will be discussed next.

3. Reimagining revenue generation with zakat as part of sustainable finance discourse

Building on the established nexus between tax policy and sustainable finance, this section proposes a paradigm shift in conceptualising revenue generation for sustainable development. It introduces zakat, an Islamic wealth redistribution system, as a potential complement to conventional fiscal mechanisms in addressing contemporary challenges of sustainable finance and tax policy, particularly in the African context. Zakat represents an Indigenous form of ethical finance that has persisted for centuries, embodying principles of social equity and community welfare that resonate strongly with modern sustainable finance objectives (Latif, 2023). By examining zakat through the lenses of fiscal sociology and socio-legal scholarship, this section argues for a more inclusive approach to fiscal policy-making – one that recognises and integrates diverse cultural and religious practices into the fabric of sustainable finance. This reimagining of revenue generation not only offers innovative solutions to pressing issues such as climate resilience and poverty alleviation but also challenges the conventional boundaries between religious obligations and secular fiscal systems. In doing so, it opens new avenues for creating more culturally attuned, socially just, and environmentally conscious fiscal frameworks, particularly relevant to the diverse socio-economic landscapes of Africa. This discussion complements the broader framing of finance and environmental challenges presented by Bowman and Mai (2026) in the introduction to this book, who conceptualise the relationship between finance and the environment, highlighting the urgency and complexity of these interconnected issues.

The diverse socio-economic landscapes of Africa present a complex tapestry of challenges and opportunities for fiscal innovation. Characterised by rapid urbanisation, demographic shifts, and uneven economic growth, many African nations grapple with the dual imperatives of fostering development and ensuring environmental sustainability. The continent's economies range from resource-dependent states to emerging service sector hubs, each facing unique fiscal pressures (Ojo, 2016). Moreover, the prevalence of informal economies, which account for a significant portion of economic activity in many African countries, poses distinct challenges for traditional tax systems. This economic informality, coupled with varying degrees of institutional capacity, necessitates innovative approaches to revenue generation and wealth redistribution.

Furthermore, the religious and cultural diversity across the continent, including sizeable Muslim populations in many countries, provides a fertile ground for exploring alternative fiscal mechanisms that resonate with local values and practices (Mati, 2017). This cultural richness, combined with the pressing need for sustainable development solutions, creates a unique environment for reimagining fiscal policies that can address both economic growth and environmental stewardship. In this context, the integration of traditional practices like zakat into modern sustainable finance frameworks offers a promising avenue for developing more inclusive and effective fiscal strategies. Such an approach not only acknowledges the cultural specificities of African societies but also aligns with the continent's aspirations for endogenous solutions to development challenges, as articulated in frameworks like the African Union's Agenda 2063.

Building upon the complex socio-economic landscapes of Africa, the concept of zakat emerges as a potential complement to existing sustainable finance strategies. Whilst contemporary sustainable finance employs various instruments such as green bonds, impact investing, and socially responsible investing (SRI), zakat offers a unique, culturally rooted approach to wealth redistribution and social welfare. Zakat aligns intrinsically with the principles of sustainable finance. Its fundamental purpose of redistributing wealth from the affluent to those in need directly addresses issues of poverty alleviation and social solidarity, which are central to sustainable development goals. This practice not only ensures a form of social security within communities but also fosters a spirit of shared responsibility and social cohesion, elements crucial for sustainable societal development (Latif, 2022).

Although traditional interpretations of zakat do not explicitly reference environmental stewardship, there is significant potential for its application in support of environmental sustainability. Zakat funds could be strategically directed towards projects that preserve the environment, promote sustainable agriculture, or help communities adapt to the impacts of climate change. Such applications would reflect the environmental consciousness that is integral to sustainable finance, thereby extending zakat's relevance to contemporary sustainability challenges.

The potential of zakat as a tool for sustainable finance is particularly salient in the context of supporting small-scale farmers, a demographic highly vulnerable to climate change impacts. In many African countries, smallholder farmers constitute a significant portion of the agricultural sector. For instance, in Kenya, over 80 per cent of agricultural output is produced by smallholders (Republic of Kenya, Ministry of Agriculture, Livestock, Fisheries and Cooperatives, 2021). These farmers face substantial climate risks, with increased frequency of droughts devastating crop yields and exacerbating food insecurity and poverty (Kibria et al., 2013).

In this context, zakat could play a pivotal role in enhancing the climate resilience and productivity of smallholder farming systems. Potential initiatives could include providing microfinancing for irrigation systems and drought-tolerant seeds, funding farmer education programmes on sustainable agriculture practices, supporting index-based crop insurance, and investing in climate information services. Such targeted interventions could simultaneously boost productivity, increase climate resilience, reduce poverty and food insecurity, and promote sustainable agriculture, aligning with key Sustainable Development Goals (SDGs) and sustainable finance principles.

The application of zakat in climate change mitigation and adaptation strategies aligns well with the broader concept of sustainable finance, which integrates Environmental, Social, and Governance (ESG) criteria into financial decision-making (Goel et al., 2022). By deploying zakat funds to support climate resilience measures for small-scale farmers, this approach directly addresses interconnected issues of climate vulnerability, food security, and rural livelihoods. However, the effective utilisation of zakat in this context necessitates careful consideration of several factors. Firstly, a robust and transparent system for collecting and distributing zakat funds must be established. Secondly, it is crucial to ensure that such applications of zakat align with religious interpretations and the beliefs of those contributing the funds. Lastly, to maximise impact, zakat-based initiatives should be coordinated with other forms of support, such as government programmes and initiatives from international organisations.

Thus, the integration of zakat into sustainable finance frameworks presents an innovative model for leveraging cultural and religious forms of finance to address pressing developmental and environmental challenges in Africa. This approach not only resonates with the cultural and religious contexts of many African societies but also offers a pathway to more inclusive and effective sustainable finance strategies. The subsequent sections delve deeper into the theoretical and practical implications of integrating this Islamic fiscal practice into contemporary sustainable finance and tax frameworks.

Section 3.1 examines the theoretical justifications for including zakat as a component of sustainable finance, introducing the concept of a 'Resilient Fiscal State' and exploring the intersections with fiscal sociology and socio-legal scholarship. This analysis reveals how religious fiscal systems can drive societal transformation and contribute to sustainable development objectives. Section 3.2 then considers the practical aspects of incorporating zakat into tax policy, addressing the complexities and opportunities that arise when attempting to align religious obligations with secular fiscal systems. Together, these discussions reveal the importance of reimagining revenue generation in the African context, highlighting the potential synergies between zakat, tax policy, and sustainable finance.

3.1 The theoretical justification in including zakat as sustainable finance

Within the confluence of tax policy and sustainable finance, the concept of what I refer to as a 'Resilient Fiscal State' is beginning to emerge. This construct refers to a state that innovatively recalibrates its fiscal system to buttress resilience against climate change impacts. Rather than introducing additional tax burdens, this could be accomplished by strategically looking towards zakat. Incorporating zakat into sustainable finance serves as an innovative fusion of religious practice and modern economic strategy, illustrating a profound confluence of socio-economic systems. Such an approach is not only instrumental in addressing pressing global challenges, but it also contributes meaningfully to advancing fiscal sociology and socio-legal scholarship.

Fiscal sociology explores the societal effects of fiscal systems, including taxation and government spending (Wagner, 2007). It is interested in how fiscal systems shape and are shaped by the broader social and economic environment. In this context, zakat, as an integral part of the Islamic fiscal system, carries significant potential for shaping societal norms and behaviours, particularly when tied to sustainable finance.

Integrating zakat into sustainable finance facilitates a more holistic understanding of fiscal systems, moving beyond the conventional lens of taxation as merely a revenue-generating tool. It propounds the concept of tax as a societal tool that can foster greater social equity, encourage sustainable practices, and spur economic development – all central tenets to sustainable finance.

This incorporation of a religious form of fiscal contribution into mainstream economic strategies enriches fiscal sociology by underscoring the potential of fiscal systems to drive societal transformation. From a socio-legal perspective, zakat presents an interesting case study in how religious and secular legal frameworks can interact (Latif, 2023). As a religious obligation, zakat is governed by Islamic law, but its integration into sustainable finance would require its alignment with secular legal systems and financial regulations. This intersection opens up new avenues for research in socio-legal studies, exploring the potential challenges and benefits of blending religious and secular legal systems in the realm of finance. Furthermore, integrating zakat into sustainable finance would require careful legal structuring to ensure compliance with both Islamic law and secular financial regulations. This would necessitate an intimate understanding of the respective legal codes, their interpretative flexibility, and their potential for mutual alignment. These dynamics could enrich socio-legal scholarship by fostering a deeper understanding of the complexities and nuances involved in synthesising religious and secular legal systems.

Moreover, zakat's incorporation into sustainable finance can highlight the potential for religious law to support and complement secular environmental law and policy. This opens up fresh perspectives on how diverse legal systems can coalesce to address global environmental challenges – a relatively underexplored field within socio-legal scholarship. Massoud's (2021), Choudhury's (2022), and Latif's (2023) work have demonstrated how a non-state legal system can maintain its autonomy not by avoiding the state legal system, but rather by depending on it. Hence, the integration of zakat into sustainable finance is not merely a practical strategy for advancing sustainability objectives. It also provides a rich, interdisciplinary context for academic investigation, offering new insights into fiscal sociology and socio-legal studies. By weaving together elements of religion, law, finance, and sustainability, this approach elucidates the multifaceted and interconnected nature of our social systems and their potential to drive meaningful change.

As we delve deeper into the argument of incorporating zakat into sustainable finance, we enter a nexus of fiscal sociology, socio-legal scholarship, and the realities of climate change and sustainable development. Integrating zakat – a religious fiscal obligation – into sustainable finance illuminates the scope of fiscal systems to transcend the mere function of revenue generation. Zakat, with its underpinnings in wealth redistribution, poverty alleviation, and social solidarity, aligns with the principles of sustainable finance, particularly social equity and economic sustainability. Through this lens, the linkage of zakat with sustainable finance brings to the fore a form of what I refer to as 'Religious Fiscal Sociology'. It posits that religious practices, such as zakat, can contribute to shaping societal norms towards sustainability and social equity. It also reveals that such practices can be successfully incorporated into modern financial systems to address contemporary challenges, such as climate change and socio-economic inequality. This conceptualisation of zakat's role in sustainable finance contributes to the 'groundswell of enabling modalities' discussed in Part II of this book, which recognises that finance must be deliberately channelled toward sustainability goals. The religious and cultural dimensions of zakat also add an important perspective to Sjåfjell and Mähönen's (2026) reimagining of corporate purpose for a sustainable future in this book, demonstrating how diverse value systems can inform financial practices.

This integration thus broadens the scope of fiscal sociology, underscoring the potential of religious fiscal systems to drive social change and contribute to sustainable development. In terms of socio-legal scholarship, the integration of zakat into sustainable finance presents a unique intersection of religious and secular legal systems. Islamic law governs zakat, yet its application within the realm of sustainable finance necessitates alignment with secular financial regulations and practices. This presents an opportunity for *A Research Agenda for Law, Finance and the Environment*, an area that can support an understanding of how different legal systems interact, overlap, and influence one another.

The challenge lies in ensuring compliance with both Islamic law, which mandates zakat, and the secular laws that govern financial systems. This necessitates meticulous legal structuring and innovative legislative design. Such a process involves thorough examination and interpretation of the respective legal codes, offering a fertile ground for legal research. The exploration and understanding of the legal nuances involved in this synthesis can contribute significantly to socio-legal studies. Furthermore, the intersection of zakat and sustainable finance highlights how religious law can support and even enhance secular environmental law and policy. It underscores the potential for religious doctrines to contribute to environmental sustainability and climate resilience. This area of study can lead to the development of a 'Green Jurisprudence' that acknowledges and harnesses the potential of religious laws to address environmental challenges.

3.2 Legal boundaries of including zakat as part of tax policy

From a tax policy perspective, the arguments made earlier carry critical significance. They prompt a re-evaluation of conventional perspectives on fiscal systems, encourage a broader appreciation of diverse revenue sources, and stress the importance of socio-cultural factors in shaping effective and sustainable tax policies. In essence, the integration of zakat into the broader discourse of sustainable finance represents an innovative way to navigate the complexity of tax policymaking. It invites policymakers to perceive tax not merely as a revenue-generating tool but as a societal tool capable of fostering greater social equity, encouraging sustainable practices, and spurring economic development. This mirrors the ethos of sustainable finance, suggesting a novel avenue for developing tax policies that are attuned to the multi-dimensional challenges of the modern world, from income inequality to climate change.

However, the question of whether zakat can be directly integrated into tax policy is complex. Zakat is a religious obligation for Muslims and is governed by specific religious rules and principles. Its collection and distribution mechanisms, as well as its underlying purposes, are inherently distinct from conventional tax systems. Therefore, integrating zakat into tax policy would require careful consideration of these religious and cultural nuances. Nevertheless, zakat can serve as a valuable reference point for tax policymaking, particularly in countries with significant Muslim populations. It can encourage the development of tax policies that are not only technically sound but also culturally relevant and socially accepted. For instance, tax policies could be designed to reflect the wealth redistribution objective of zakat, thereby fostering social solidarity and promoting income equality.

Legal pluralism offers a compelling methodological framework for addressing the complexities of integrating zakat into tax policy whilst preserving its religious integrity. This approach recognises the coexistence of multiple legal systems within a single social field (Griffiths, 1986; Merry, 1988) and provides a nuanced lens through which to view the interaction between religious and secular legal orders. In the context of zakat and tax policy, legal pluralism allows for the acknowledgement of zakat's distinct religious character whilst exploring avenues for its incorporation into broader fiscal frameworks. As Woodman (1996, 2011) argues, legal pluralism can facilitate the recognition of non-state legal orders within state legal systems, providing a pathway for the formal recognition of zakat's principles and practices within tax policy.

Further, legal pluralism's emphasis on the dynamic interaction between different legal orders aligns well with the goal of developing tax policies that are both technically sound and culturally resonant. This approach could facilitate the development of what Santos (2002) terms 'interlegality' – a complex web of legal orders and cultures that intersect in dynamic and creative ways. The application of legal pluralism to the integration of zakat into tax policy could manifest in several ways. Firstly, it could involve the creation of parallel systems within the tax framework, where zakat payments are recognised and potentially offset against certain tax obligations. This approach has been adopted to varying degrees in countries such as Malaysia and Pakistan (Powell, 2009). Secondly, it could involve the incorporation of zakat principles into the design of specific tax policies, particularly those aimed at wealth redistribution and social welfare.

Crucially, a legal pluralist approach would necessitate ongoing dialogue between religious scholars, tax experts, and policymakers to ensure that any integration respects both the religious essence of zakat and the technical requirements of effective tax policy. This aligns with Tamanaha's (2001) conception of legal pluralism as a process of negotiation and renegotiation between different normative orders. However, it is important to note that the application of legal pluralism in this context is not without challenges. As Swenson (2018) cautions, the recognition of multiple legal orders can sometimes lead to forum shopping and legal uncertainty. Therefore, any integration of zakat into tax policy through a legal pluralist approach would need to be carefully structured to ensure clarity and consistency in application.

Likewise, the principle of using zakat for socially beneficial purposes could be echoed in tax policies that incentivise environmentally friendly business practices or support social welfare initiatives. However, any attempt to integrate zakat into tax policymaking must be handled delicately to ensure respect for religious beliefs and practices. It would necessitate a comprehensive understanding of Islamic jurisprudence, as well as engagement with religious scholars and communities. Transparency, accountability, and sensitivity would be key to ensuring that any integration of zakat into tax policy is both effective and ethically sound.

The integration of zakat into sustainable finance and tax systems also requires careful consideration of local contexts, religious sensitivities, and socio-economic realities, as well as collaborative dialogue involving a wide range of stakeholders. It requires commitment and concerted effort to realise the African Union's Agenda 2063 aspirations, transforming Africa into a global powerhouse characterised by inclusive growth, sustainable development, strong cultural identity, and effective governance. A deeper analysis is presented next.

4. Zakat as a feature of tax sustainability in the African context

When we shift our lens to examine the theoretical claims under section 3.1 from an African perspective, we encounter a diverse continent marked by varying socio-economic realities, cultural backgrounds, and religious beliefs. Nonetheless, the intersection of zakat, sustainable finance, and tax policy can hold substantial relevance for many African nations, particularly those with significant Muslim populations such as Nigeria, Niger, Senegal, Egypt, Algeria, Morocco, Tunisia, Sudan, and others. African nations, like much of the Global South, grapple with myriad socio-economic challenges, such as poverty, income inequality, and inadequate access to social services. These are the very issues zakat seeks to address. Zakat's principle of wealth redistribution aligns with the African socio-cultural ethos of Ubuntu, which emphasises community solidarity and mutual assistance (Mati, 2017).

By considering zakat in tax policymaking, African nations could develop fiscal systems that not only generate revenue but also actively promote social equity and poverty alleviation. From a sustainable finance perspective, African countries face significant climate-related challenges. Agriculture, a major economic sector in many African nations, is particularly vulnerable to climate change. Sustainable finance principles can guide tax policies to incentivise climate-smart agricultural practices and investments in renewable energy, contributing to both economic growth and environmental sustainability. Zakat can potentially amplify this impact, given its stipulation to aid the poor and needy, many of whom are smallholder farmers or rural communities particularly susceptible to climate change impacts.

On the socio-legal front, African countries showcase a wide array of legal systems, from customary and religious laws to colonial and post-colonial statutory laws. The integration of zakat into sustainable finance presents an opportunity to examine how Islamic law can coexist and intersect with these diverse legal systems. Nonetheless, any attempt to integrate zakat into tax policymaking in African countries must respect the pluralistic legal and cultural landscape. Religious and cultural sensitivity, community engagement, and a thorough understanding of local contexts would be essential (Massoud, 2021; Sandberg, 2017). The involvement of religious scholars, community leaders, and local stakeholders in policy dialogues can foster a tax system that is not only economically efficient but also socially accepted and culturally attuned.

In Africa, taxation is a critical source of government revenue and plays a pivotal role in state-building, governance, and development (Latif, 2016). However, conventional tax systems often face challenges such as tax evasion, regressive tax structures, and lack of public trust. Zakat, deeply rooted in the Islamic tradition and culture, embodies the principles of social justice, generosity, and community solidarity. Incorporating elements of zakat into tax policymaking can offer an innovative approach to address these challenges. For example, given its mandatory nature and religious significance, zakat enjoys a high compliance rate among Muslims. Thus, incorporating elements of zakat into the tax system could potentially enhance tax compliance and increase public trust in the tax system. Moreover, zakat's progressive nature – being levied on wealth rather than income – can serve as a model for developing more equitable tax policies in African countries, thereby addressing income inequality and fostering social cohesion.

The sustainability component of this discourse comes into play when we consider the pressing environmental challenges that Africa faces, from climate change impacts to deforestation and biodiversity loss (Izah, 2022). By aligning tax policies with principles of sustainable finance, African countries can incentivise businesses to adopt more sustainable practices, promote investments in green technology, and support climate-resilient initiatives. Here, zakat can play a significant role. Zakat funds can be channelled towards supporting sustainable projects and initiatives, particularly those that benefit the poor and vulnerable, such as smallholder farmers and rural communities. For instance, zakat funds could be used to provide microfinance for climate-smart agriculture, renewable energy projects in rural areas, or investments in sustainable infrastructure.

Additionally, integrating zakat into sustainable finance requires navigating the interplay between Islamic law and the diverse legal systems present in Africa. This presents an intriguing domain for socio-legal research and offers potential for developing innovative legal frameworks that respect religious beliefs while promoting sustainable development. Clearly, the intersection of tax policy, sustainable finance, and zakat offers a rich tapestry of possibilities for African countries. By weaving together these threads, African nations can develop culturally relevant, socially just, and environmentally sustainable fiscal systems. However, this process requires careful consideration of local contexts, religious sensitivities, and socio-economic realities. Collaborative dialogue involving policymakers, religious scholars, local communities, and international stakeholders can facilitate the development of such innovative fiscal frameworks.

Furthermore, the African Union's Agenda 2063 is a strategic blueprint for transforming Africa into a global powerhouse of the future. It encapsulates seven key aspirations, which include a prosperous Africa based on inclusive growth and sustainable development, an Africa with a strong cultural identity and values, and an Africa whose development is people driven (AU, 2015). The integration of zakat, tax policy, and sustainable finance can directly contribute to the realisation of these aspirations. It presents a unique opportunity to create fiscal systems that not only align with Africa's socio-cultural context but also drive sustainable development and inclusive growth. Under Agenda 2063, one key goal is to modernise and increase agricultural production, improve resilience to climate change, and achieve food security. Zakat funds could be strategically channelled to support small-scale farmers, providing them with the necessary resources to adopt climate-smart agricultural practices.

Such an approach aligns with the principles of sustainable finance, which emphasises the need for financial systems to support sustainable development and resilience to environmental risks. Moreover, Agenda 2063 envisages an Africa with a strong cultural identity, values, and ethics. Incorporating zakat into the financial system speaks directly to this aspiration, as it represents an affirmation of the significant role that Islamic principles and culture play in many African societies. It also reinforces the idea that tax systems and tax policies should be closely tied to the societal values and cultural identities of a nation. The promotion of social justice and equal opportunity is another core aspiration of Agenda 2063. The principles of wealth redistribution inherent in zakat could serve as a model for tax policies that seek to reduce income inequality, foster social solidarity, and ensure more equitable economic growth.

In terms of governance and legal systems, integrating zakat into sustainable finance requires navigating the complex interplay between Islamic law and the diverse legal systems present in Africa. This not only contributes to a more nuanced understanding of Africa's socio-legal dynamics but also aligns with Agenda 2063's aspiration for an Africa with a capable and developmental state, characterised by effective and transparent institutions. Finally, by stimulating sustainable practices and environmental responsibility, the integration of zakat, tax policy, and sustainable finance contributes to the vision of Agenda 2063 for a continent that prioritises environmental sustainability and combats climate change effectively.

5. Conclusion and future research

The interplay of tax policy, sustainable finance, and zakat provides a powerful conceptual lens through which we can reimagine fiscal policymaking in Africa. This intersection enables a multi-dimensional approach to the fiscal state, one that extends beyond mere revenue generation to encompass socio-cultural resonance, sustainable development, and wealth redistribution. The incorporation of zakat principles into tax policymaking contributes to more equitable wealth distribution, which aligns with the socio-cultural ethos of many African nations. Furthermore, the alignment of tax policy with the principles of sustainable finance presents an avenue for incentivising sustainable business practices and supporting vulnerable communities, contributing to both economic growth and environmental sustainability.

Incorporating zakat into sustainable finance also enables a dynamic exploration of the interface between Islamic law and the diverse legal systems prevalent in Africa, enriching both socio-legal scholarship and the broader discourse of fiscal sociology. This perspective can contribute to a nuanced understanding of fiscal systems that respects religious beliefs while driving social change and sustainable development. Moreover, the integration of these dimensions can significantly contribute to the realisation of the African Union's Agenda 2063, supporting the vision of an economically prosperous, socially inclusive, and environmentally sustainable African continent. However, this discourse also highlights the complexity of integrating religious fiscal systems like zakat into broader tax policymaking, calling for sensitivity towards religious and cultural nuances, local engagement, and interdisciplinary collaboration. Thus, while the integration of zakat, tax policy, and sustainable finance offers an innovative and culturally attuned approach to fiscal policymaking, its implementation calls for careful navigation and context-specific adaptations.

The exploration of this nexus not only provides a template for a new discourse in fiscal policymaking, one that is economically efficient, sustainable, and deeply rooted in the socio-cultural fabric of society, but also opens up a myriad of avenues for future research. Empirical case studies could provide valuable insights into the practical implementation and impact of integrating zakat into tax and sustainable finance frameworks. Conducting comparative analyses across different African countries with varying socio-economic, legal, and cultural contexts would enrich our understanding of the contextual factors that shape the effectiveness and acceptance of such integrative approaches. Furthermore, future research could delve deeper into the philosophical and theoretical underpinnings of this intersection. Exploring questions such as the role of religious fiscal practices in shaping societal values, the ethical dimensions of wealth redistribution, and the epistemological foundations of Islamic finance in relation to sustainable development could yield novel insights and contribute to the development of a more holistic and culturally informed fiscal sociology.

Finally, the zakat-tax-sustainable finance nexus holds the potential to contribute to a more equitable, sustainable, and culturally resonant fiscal state in Africa and beyond. By pursuing these empirical and conceptual lines of inquiry, future research can refine our understanding of this nexus and contribute to the broader discourse on building fiscally innovative, socially just, and environmentally conscious societies.

References

AfDB (2019) *Jobs, growth and firm dynamism*. Africa Development Bank Group.

Al Qaradawi, Y. (2001) *Fiqh Al Zakah, Vol II: A comparative study of Zakah, regulations and philosophy in the light of Qur'an and Sunna*. Translated by Monzer Kahf Scientific Publishing Centre, Jeddah.

AU (2015) Agenda 2063. The Africa we want. Addis Ababa.

Bahl, R.W. and Bird R.M. (2008). 'Tax policy in developing countries: looking back – and forward', *National Tax Journal*, 61(2), pp. 279–301.

Bakker, A. (2009) *Tax and the environment. A world of possibilities*. IBFD.

Bowman, M. (2014) *Banking on climate change. How finance actors and transnational regulatory regimes are responding*. Wolters Kluwer Law & Business.

Bowman, M. and Mai, L. (2026) 'Introduction', in Bowman, M and Mai, L. (eds) *A research agenda for law, finance and the environment*. Edward Elgar Publishing, pp. 1–10.

Brafu-Insaidoo, W.G. and Obeng, C. (2020) *Estimating Ghana's tax capacity and effort*. AERC Research Paper 388.

Choudhury N. (2022) 'Order in the bazaar: the transformation of non-state law in Afghanistan's premier money exchange market', *Law & Social Inquiry*, 47(1), pp. 292-330. Available at: https://doi.org/10.1017/lsi.2021.41

de Sousa Santos, B. (2002) *Toward a new legal common sense: law, globalization, and emancipation*. Butterworths LexisNexis.

Dippenaar, M. (2018) 'The role of tax incentives in encouraging energy efficiency in the largest listed South African businesses', *South African Journal of Economic and Management Sciences*, 21(1), https://doi.org/10.4102/sajems.v21i1.1723

Foerster, A. (2026) 'From climate risk to net-zero and beyond: is ecologically rational regulation emerging in the finance sector?', in Bowman, M. and Mai, L. (eds) *A research agenda for law, finance and the environment*. Edward Elgar Publishing, pp. 125–151.

Gaganis, C., Pasiouras, F., Tasious, M., *et al.* (2023) *Sustainable finance and ESG*. Palgrave Macmillan.

Goel, R., Gautam, D. and Natalucci, F. (2022) *Sustainable finance in emerging markets: evolution, challenges and policy priorities*. IMF.

Griffiths, J. (1986) 'What is legal pluralism?', *Journal of Legal Pluralism*, 24(1), pp. 1–55.

Izah, S.C. (2022) *Biodiversity in Africa: potentials, threats and conservation*. Springer.

Jones, R., Baker, T., Huet, K. *et al.* (2020) 'Treating ecological deficit with debt: the practical and political concerns with green bonds', *Geoforum*, 114, pp. 49–58.

Kibria, G., Haroon, K.Y. and Nugegoda, D. (2013) *Climate change and agricultural food production – impacts, vulnerabilities, and remedies*. New India Publishing Agency.

Kila, K.O. (2023) *Corporate regulation for climate change mitigation in Africa. A case for dilute interventionism*. Routledge.

Latif, L. (2016) 'Centralized revenue redistribution as a potential cause of internal conflict in Kenya', *Modern Africa: Politics, History and Society*, 4(1), pp. 91–105.

Latif, L. (2022) 'Improving livelihood at household level with Zakat based conscious financing', *AZJAF*, 3(1), pp. 1–19.

Latif, L. (2023) *Zakat and the financing of public health in Kenya: an interdisciplinary analysis of human rights law, Islamic law and constitutional law*. Ethics Press.

Lutken, S.E. (2015) *Financial engineering of climate investment in developing countries*. Anthem Press.

Massoud, M.F. (2021) *Shar'ia, Inshallah: finding God in Somali legal politics*. Cambridge University Press.

Mati, J.M. (2017) *Philanthropy in contemporary Africa. A review*. BRILL.

Merry, S.E. (1988) 'Legal pluralism', *Law & Society Review*, 22(5), pp. 869–896.

Migliorelli, M. (2021) 'What do we mean by sustainable finance? Assessing existing frameworks and policy risks', *Sustainability*, 13(2), 975, pp. 1–17.

Mumford, A. (2002) *Taxing culture: towards a theory of tax collection law.* Routledge.

Ndikumana, L. and Boyce, J.K. (2023) *On the trail of capital flight from Africa: the takers and the enablers.* Oxford University Press.

Njuguna, A.E. and Nnadozie, E. (2022) 'Investment climate and foreign direct investment in Africa: the role of ease of doing business', *Journal of African Trade*, 9, pp. 23–46.

Ojo, E.O. (2016) 'Underdevelopment in Africa: theories and facts', *The Journal of Social, Political and Economic Studies*, 41(1), pp. 89–103.

Ore, M. (2015) 'Analysis of agricultural sustainability indicators system', in *Economic Science for Rural Development Conference Proceedings*, No. 38.

Powell, R. (2009) 'Zakat: drawing insights for legal theory and economic policy from Islamic jurisprudence', *Pittsburgh Tax Review*, 7(43), pp. 10–17.

Republic of Kenya, Ministry of Agriculture, Livestock, Fisheries and Cooperatives (2021) *Agricultural policy, Nairobi, Kenya.*

Sandberg, R. (2017) *Religion and legal pluralism.* Routledge.

Schoenmaker, D. (2019) *A framework for sustainable finance.* Erasmus Platform for Sustainable Value Creation.

Swenson, G. (2018) 'Legal pluralism in theory and practice', *International Studies Review*, 20(2), pp. 438–462.

Tamanaha, B. (2001) 'Socio-legal positivism and a general jurisprudence', *Oxford Journal of Legal Studies*, 21(1), pp. 1–32.

The National Treasury and Economic Planning (2022) *Draft national green fiscal incentives policy.* Available at: https://www.treasury.go.ke/wp-content/uploads/2023/01/Draft-Green-Fiscal-Incentives-Policy-Framework.pdf

Wagner, R.E. (2007) *Fiscal sociology and the theory of public finance.* Edward Elgar Publishing.

Woodman, G. (1996) 'Legal pluralism and the search for justice', *Journal of African Law*, 40(2), pp. 152–167.

Woodman, G. (2011) 'Legal pluralism in Africa: the implications of state recognition of customary laws illustrated from the field of land law', *Acta Juridica*, 1,pp. 35–58.

11 Financing Africa's just transition with reparations distributed through the African Continental Free Trade Area Agreement

Hannah Getachew

1. Introduction

The objective of this chapter is to connect the dots between seemingly disparate fields: African history, Africa's comparatively low economic development, the climate crisis, reparations by Europe and the United States (US) to Africa, and finance for a just transition. It presents a conceptual mapping that strives to contribute to the growing body of literatures (thus far unconnected) on how to finance Africa's just transition with reparations. In so doing, this chapter leans on the dual epistemic lens of Pan-Africanism and Afrocentricity to argue that the African Continental Free Trade Area Agreement (AfCFTA) can facilitate the realisation of a just transition in Africa by providing a channel for reparations from Africa's oppressors, notably Europe and the US. In other words, it conceives of the AfCFTA as a means of facilitating climate change adaptation and mitigation activities in Africa whilst concomitantly facilitating the distribution of potential financial reparations for harms perpetrated by the Trans-Atlantic Trade in Africans,[1] colonialism, and neo-colonialism; the effects of which still reverberate today and are epitomised and exacerbated by the global climate crisis.

Scientists have presented evidence in support of the conclusion that human activities have been altering the climate for decades (United Nations Economic Commission for Africa (UNECA), 2024). In 1938 the burning of fossil fuels (and subsequent release of carbon dioxide into the atmosphere) was linked to higher temperatures on Earth (Callendar, 1938). Since then scientific evidence proving anthropogenic (i.e., human-induced) climate change has continued to mount (Arblaster et al., 2007). In 2022, the Intergovernmental Panel on Climate Change (IPCC) published its Sixth Assessment Report, presenting science-based findings that 'human-induced climate change, including more frequent and intense extreme events, has caused widespread adverse impacts and related losses and damages to nature and people, beyond natural climate variability' (Intergovernmental Panel On Climate Change (IPCC), 2022, p. 11). Furthermore, the fourth IPCC report concluded with very high confidence that human activities since 1750 have led to anthropogenic warming of the earth. These changes in the earth's temperature have been attributed to increases in greenhouse gas emissions due to agriculture and fossil fuel use (Arblaster et al., 2007). Historical records show that the industrial revolution (which relied on fossil fuels) began in the United Kingdom (UK) circa 1750, before extending to Northern and Western Europe (Mgbemene, Nnaji and Nwozor, 2016).

Through the widely adopted Paris Agreement, state parties aim to respond to climate change, including by:

> Holding the increase in the global average temperature to well below 2°C above pre-industrial levels and pursuing efforts to limit the temperature increase to 1.5°C above pre-industrial levels. (United Nations, 2015a, Article 2.1(a))

However, a 2022 study by Climate Action Tracker found that, according to climate action outlined in Nationally Determined Contributions (NDCs) under the Paris Agreement, the world is on track for temperature increases of 2.4°C above pre-industrial levels – much higher than is considered safe (Climate Action Tracker, 2022). If the world surpasses the 1.5°C temperature target set under the Paris Agreement (United Nations, 2015a) the human, ecological, and financial implications on the African continent in particular could be devastating.[2]

Specifically, Africa is the region with the lowest per capita greenhouse gas emissions (Intergovernmental Panel On Climate Change (IPCC), 2023a) yet it is likely to experience greater rises in land surface temperatures than the global average (IPCC, 2023b). This change will increase the risks of reduced crop productivity, destruction of coral reefs, species extinction, degradation of fishery stocks, changes in the incidence and geographic range of diseases, and adverse effects on livestock, amongst others (Niang et al., n.d.). Yet IPCC data comparing the emissions of fifteen African countries in 1990 and 2019 show a clear trend of an increase in greenhouse gas emissions by all countries studied, with South Africa and Nigeria the highest emitters (Intergovernmental Panel on Climate Change (IPCC), 2023a). Thus, it is imperative for Africa's development to be sustainable in ways that both mitigate emissions and adapt to adverse climate impacts at the same time.

In short, it is imperative for the African continent to expand its economy in a climate-compatible manner in order to avoid contributing to dangerous levels of warming that will harm it. Mitchell and Maxwell define climate-compatible development as that which 'minimises the harm caused by climate impacts, while maximising the many human development opportunities presented by a low emissions, more resilient, future' (Mitchell and Maxwell, 2010, p. 1). It is a similar concept to green growth, which in turn is broadly understood as sustained economic growth that minimises environmental harm. The benefit of using the term 'climate-compatible development' over 'green growth' is that they operate from different starting points. Climate-compatible development recognises that in some regions economic growth is necessary to meet basic human needs. Green growth, by contrast, does not distinguish between the differing priorities of high- and low-income countries and assumes that infinite economic growth is possible in all regions in perpetuity. Green growth fails to consider that infinite economic growth is not possible on a finite planet (Hickel and Kallis, 2020).

Authors Mebratu and Swilling claim that there is an awareness of planetary boundaries and a paradigm shift away from the mentality that environmental degradation is a natural cost of economic growth. These changes, combined with the technological development of environmentally friendly goods and services, mean that lower-income countries can grow their economies in a more environmentally sustainable fashion compared to the carbon-intensive development path pursued by today's high-income countries (Mebratu and Swilling, 2019).

However, adequate climate finance is necessary for African countries to effectively chart a low-carbon development pathway. Although the exact figure is difficult to determine due to the unpredictability of worsening natural disasters (United Nations Development Programme (UNDP), 2018), it has been calculated that implementing the Nationally Determined Contributions (NDCs) of African countries will require US$1.3 trillion to US$1.6 trillion until 2030 (Mohammed, 2022). This is evident in part through the substantive conditional financing component in the NDCs of African countries. The same study discovered that 37 African countries have conditioned their mitigation pledges and 32 African countries have conditioned their adaptation pledges upon receiving external finance. The extent of the climate finance requested varies across the African continent, with Zambia requesting US$35 billion and São Tomé and Príncipe requesting US$59 million (African Development Bank Group, 2022). Despite this, a 2022 study by the African Development Bank (AfDB) that investigated the climate financing gap in Africa predicted an annual shortfall of US$99.9 billion to US$127.2 billion in the 2020 to 2030 period.

It is within this context that the AfCFTA agreement operates. At its core, the AfCFTA is an aspirational free trade agreement that strives to expand intra-African trade (by eliminating trade barriers) as a means towards expanding Africa's economy (AU-AfCFTA, n.d.). Importantly, the World Bank predicts that economic activity stimulated by the AfCFTA could generate an additional US$450 billion by 2035, and if so, would lift 30 million people out of extreme poverty and 68 million Africans from moderate poverty (The Statutes Project, 2020).

Long before the adoption of the African Continental Free Trade Area agreement, intellectuals called for Africa's economic integration as a means to achieve its sustainable development imperatives. Kwame Nkrumah (the first President of Ghana) wrote in 1970 that 'the total integration of the African economy on a continental scale is the only way in which the African states can achieve anything like the levels of the industrialized countries' (Nkrumah, 1970, p. 163). One way to achieve economic integration is through preferential trade agreements, or what has become known as 'free trade'. This logic has led to the rise in recent decades of reciprocal preferential trade agreements such as the AfCFTA. Through their pursuit of trade liberalisation, preferential trade agreements seek to promote economic integration between participating nations (Trebilcock et al., 2012; International Trade Administration, n.d.). Indeed, one of the AfCFTA's general objectives is to create a single African market for goods and services, thereby limiting trade barriers and facilitating trade liberalisation (African Union, 2018, Article 3(a)).

This chapter acknowledges the severity of the climate crisis and the challenges it presents for Africa. It adopts an African-centric approach (referred to dually as Pan-Africanism and Afrocentricity) to present the AfCFTA as a strong contender for the realisation of a just transition in Africa. It must be noted from the outset that 'just transition' is a broad term without universal consensus. When used in discussions pertaining to climate action, legal scholar Johansson observes that the term 'generally refers to the idea of minimising the adverse and potentially unequal socioeconomic effects that climate policies may have on various vulnerable groups and communities' (Johansson, 2023, p. 230). Yet a precise and succinct conceptualisation of a just transition is difficult to identify when applied specifically to the African continent. This point is well articulated by the African Development Bank, which writes that the terminology 'is often nebulous given that just transition is highly context-dependent' (African Development Bank Group, 2023, p. 35). The Africa-led United Nations Economic Commission for Africa (UNECA) defines a just transition in Africa as one that sets out a 'path for inclusive, low-carbon, and resource-efficient development where new technologies, infrastructure, and decision making approaches replace the past and existing ones to address and correct their negative impacts' (United Nations Economic Commission for Africa (UNECA), 2024, p. 23). This chapter adopts the UNECA's definition of a just transition as it reflects Africa's urgent need for low-carbon development and the correction of past harms. Furthermore, the UNECA insists that Africa's just transition must be led by Africans (UNECA, 2024).

The remainder of this chapter is divided into sections. Section 2 lays out the conceptual framework of the chapter, centring around Pan-Africanism and Afrocentricity. Section 3 provides a brief account of the exploitation of Africa and its impacts on achieving a just transition, with a focus on past and present atrocities against Africa by Europe and the US. Section 4 describes how climate-compatible development could be achieved through trade. Finally, section 5 connects the previous sections through an exploration of how the financing of Africa's just transition could be realised by the distribution of financial reparations through the AfCFTA.

2. Pan-Africanism and Afrocentricity

Pan-Africanism has evolved over the years, according to the needs of African peoples at that time (Williams, 2022). Aniche et al. observe that Pan-Africanism has transitioned from 'a liberation movement for eradicating oppression, slavery, and colonialism to an ideology of achieving continental unity, interdependence, self-sufficiency and economic transformation' (Aniche, Alumona and Mlambo, 2022, p. 286). Historian Hakim Adi offers an expansive view of Pan-Africanism. Drawing inspiration from numerous articulations of Pan-Africanism, he identifies a movement towards the complete liberation of Africans on the continent and in the diaspora based on the conviction that their history and destiny are interconnected as underlying principles (Adi, 2018, p. 2). Adi's conceptualisation of Pan-Africanism is useful as it offers an umbrella term for the intersectional pursuit of freedom from the forces oppressing African people, such as climate change and neo-colonialism.

Afrocentricity, in turn, can be understood as part of the epistemic lens which gives shape to Pan-Africanism (Kete Asante, 2020). At its core, Afrocentricity is a position through which African peoples and their lived experiences are placed in the centre of the discussion (Kete Asante, 2020). It stands in contrast with Eurocentrism, i.e., the theory and practice which asserts European superiority and, as a result, justifies European dominance (Hostettler, 2012).

This chapter is rooted in the dual epistemic lens of Pan-Africanism and Afrocentricity for several reasons. Firstly, both Pan-Africanism and Afrocentricity rely on the epistemological centredness of Africans in their approach (Kete Asante, 2020; Aniche, Alumona and Mlambo, 2022). Secondly, research centred on the advancement of Indigenous populations should be based on local epistemologies, and as Pan-Africanism and Afrocentricity are concerned with the economic and social advancement of Africa, it is well suited to academic research on Africa. This is especially pertinent in the African context as researchers on Africa have intentionally or unintendedly produced work that grossly misrepresents the African continent (Owomoyela, 1994).

Thirdly, the AfCFTA agreement itself is inspired by Pan-Africanism (African Union, 2018, Article 3: General Objectives). This is evident in part through Article 3 of the AfCFTA, which establishes its general objectives, and it outlines the AfCFTA's purpose to:

> Create a single market for goods, services, facilitated by movement of persons in order to deepen the economic integration of the African continent and in accordance with *the Pan African Vision* of 'An integrated, prosperous and peaceful Africa' enshrined in Agenda 2063. (African Union, 2018, Article 3: General Objectives, emphasis added)

Furthermore, the AfCFTA's inherent Pan-Africanness is also evident through the fact that it has been ratified by fifty-four out of fifty-five African Union member states (AfCFTA, n.d.). Through its ideological underpinnings and widespread support, the AfCFTA connects African people on the continent and the diaspora through trade, thereby serving as a concrete manifestation of a Pan-African project.

When adopting Afrocentricity as an epistemic lens, as this chapter does, there are seven principles by which to abide as articulated by the scholar Ama Mazama: the lived experience of Africans should guide and inform the research; the spiritual plane should be given a place; the researcher should immerse themselves in the subject; a holistic approach should be adopted; intuition should be trusted; the researcher should acknowledge that not everything can be measured; and finally, the outcome of Afrocentric research should contribute towards the liberation of Africans (Mazama, 2003). In giving life to those principles, the overarching aim of this chapter is to seek to contribute to the liberation of African peoples as follows. It gives scholarly attention to the internally driven push by African countries to achieve economic development through the AfCFTA against a background of the inter-generational trauma of the Trans-Atlantic Trade in Africans, described by Dr DeGruy as Post-traumatic Slave Syndrome (DeGruy, 2005), which entitles the descendants of enslaved Africans to financial reparations from former enslavers. Moreover, it acknowledges that the enduring harm of colonialism and neo-colonialism also entitles African countries to financial reparations, and that the harmful and worsening effects of climate change across the African continent hinder the realisation of a just transition in Africa. Finally, a holistic approach to addressing the challenges related to financing a just transition in Africa connects the AfCFTA with climate finance and the call for financial reparations.

3. Past and present exploitation of Africa

Africa's comparatively low economic development and its related challenges in responding sufficiently to the climate crisis are directly linked to the Trans-Atlantic Trade in Africans, colonialism, and neo-colonialism. This section outlines the key features of those past and present atrocities and links them to the righteous call for reparations. This discussion is relevant as it is necessary to examine the injustices that contributed to Africa's comparatively weak economic position in order to make the case that Europe and the US have a moral duty to provide reparations and that those reparations could be channelled through the AfCFTA to finance a just transition in Africa.

3.1 The impacts of Trans-Atlantic Trade in Africans, colonialism, and ongoing neo-colonialism

Africa was growing at its own pace prior to close relations with Europe, at which point the continent's development trajectory was dramatically altered (Rodney, 2018). Evidence shows that, under the Trans-Atlantic Trade in Africans, millions of Africans were enslaved and 'defined as a human chattel who is the legal property of another person' (Osabu-Kle, 2000, p. 332). The violent enslavement of Africans was so extensive it cost an estimated minimum of 15 million lives between 1492 and 1870 (Beckles and Shepherd, 2000) as reckoned by an approximation of Africans forcibly shipped to the Americas. However, when accounting for the number of Africans 'caught in the web' of the Trans-Atlantic Trade in Africans, the figure is closer to 50 million (Beckles and Shepherd, 2000, p. xxiii).

In the words of Beckles and Shepherd:

> Africa – well poised like Europe and Asia for economic development at the end of the fifteenth century – was plundered and derailed by the reign of terror known as the

trans-Atlantic trade in Africans, from which it has yet to recover. (Beckles and Shepherd, 2000, p. 98)

The economic sovereignty of Africa suffered from this inhumane trade in the following ways. First, it disrupted and diminished economic growth on the continent. Secondly, it tarnished political institutions and local governance structures. Thirdly, it promoted violence, generated fear, and disintegrated community life. Fourthly, it was an extraordinary drain of human creativity and ingenuity to other countries that would otherwise have been cultivated locally (Beckles and Shepherd, 2000). Ultimately the Trans-Atlantic Trade in Africans '… contributed to eroding, retarding and almost brought to a standstill, the capacity of Africans to develop economically' (Mushanga, 2011, p. 15).

Crucially, freedom for Africans did not follow the formal abolition of the Trans-Atlantic Trade in Africans in 1807 when an Act by the UK abolishing the Trans-Atlantic Trade in Africans received royal assent (United Kingdom Parliament, 2024). Instead, the Trans-Atlantic Trade in Africans was replaced by colonialism, a deleterious phenomenon defined as 'the direct and overall domination of one country by another on the basis of state power being in the hands of a foreign power' (Ocheni and Nwankwo, 2012).

The subsequent European colonialisation of Africa was motivated by several factors. The Trans-Atlantic Trade in Africans allowed Europe to acquire immense monetary resources through the purchase and sale of enslaved Africans. These profits were invested in European economies, which were a contributing factor to Europe's eventual industrial revolution. With the construction of large-scale manufacturing plants that accompanied the industrial revolution, Europe began to require additional raw materials from the African continent to sustain industrialisation.[3] It also sought out a consumer market to sell its surplus manufactured goods. Furthermore, European countries were experiencing rapid urbanisation which necessitated new agricultural sources to feed the urban population and Africa was an attractive agricultural investment destination (Ocheni and Nwankwo, 2012).

Many African countries formally won their independence from Europe between the 1950s and late 1970s, ushering in a wave of hope across the continent. However, neo-colonialism and economic hardship ran rampant across the vast African continent. Neo-colonialism is a form of imperialism through which many African countries remain under the heavy yoke of the West through entrenched structures of economic extraction. As penned by Osabu-Kle, 'under colonialism, the human and material resources of the (African) continent were exploited to the benefit of the West, and that exploitation continues unabated during this era of neocolonialism' (Osabu-Kle, 2000). Taylor describes neo-colonialism as:

> A system of domination and exploitation, invested and maintained by the former colonial power in which economic, financial and military instruments work for keeping in power

> well-disposed leaders and maintaining favourable policies which procure economic and financial advantages. (Taylor, n.d., p. 3)

To this day, neo-colonialism, described as 'the ongoing economic and political domination of nominally independent developing countries by external powers' (Langan, 2020), is present across Africa.

The full and brutal extent of neo-colonialism on contemporary African economies is beyond the scope of this chapter. Instead, as an illustration, French monetary neo-colonialism in Africa will be spotlighted. On 26 December 1945, France announced the creation of a new currency to be used in fourteen African countries.[4] Thus, the 'franc des colonies françaises d'Afrique' or French Colonies of Africa was born (French Senate, 2023). France's motives were not benevolent; the currency was designed to 'shore up the French economy' (Omeje, 2021, p. 71).

Since rebranded as the French Community of Africa (CFA), this currency operates through the following mechanisms:

> (i) a fixed parity against the euro, adjustable if needed, but only after consultation with Paris and the unanimous decision of all members within each monetary area; (ii) convertibility of the CFA franc into the euro; (iii) the guaranteeing of such convertibility by France through each regional central bank holding an operating account with the French Treasury in Paris; (iv) free capital mobility between the two CFA zones and France; and (v) the sharing of foreign exchange reserves of each regional monetary area. (Taylor, n.d., p. 5)

This system harms the economies of the fourteen African countries that are required to deposit a minimum of 50 per cent of their foreign exchange reserves into the French Treasury as they are unable to invest those funds to benefit their people. Instead, it grants France enormous capital to invest and accrue additional revenue. In so doing, France directly deprives fourteen nations of using their own resources to advance their national economy (Taylor, n.d.). The benefits of the CFA to France have been recognised at the highest levels of French government. In 1957, former French President François Mitterand proclaimed, 'without Africa, France will have no history in the 21st century' (Roger Lokongo, 2012). Similar statements were made by subsequent French presidents. Jacques Chirac, Mitterand's successor, said that 'without Africa, France will slide down into the rank of a third (world) power' (Roger Lokongo, 2012).

France's monetary imperialism in Africa has attracted international criticism. Luigi Di Maio, a former Italian minister of foreign affairs, has said:

> If France didn't have its African colonies, because that's what they should be called, it would be the 15th largest world economy. Instead, it's among the first, exactly because of what it is doing in Africa. (Reuters, 2019)

3.2 Africa's case for reparations

In 2022, for the first time, the Intergovernmental Panel on Climate Change (IPCC) accepted 'historical and ongoing patterns of inequality such as colonialism' as both a driver of climate change and an obstacle to climate mitigation and adaptation (Intergovernmental Panel on Climate Change (IPCC), 2023, p. 14). This acknowledgement is highly relevant to the African call for reparations for slavery, colonialism, and neo-colonialism as well as access to meaningful climate finance, as both will bolster its capacity to concomitantly implement the African Continental Free Trade Area agreement (AfCFTA) in a climate-compatible manner and sustain a just transition.

As per the final report of the Special Rapporteur of the United Nations Economic and Social Council, reparations specifically encompass 'restitution, compensation, rehabilitation, and satisfaction and guarantees of non-repetition' (Bassiouni, 2000, p. 21). Restitution strives to restore as much as possible the victims' circumstances to those that existed prior to the violation of their rights. This may include the return of property, employment, or place of residence. Monetary compensation is to be issued for physical or emotional harm and material damages. Rehabilitation provides the means for victims to obtain medical attention for physical or psychological care. Satisfaction and guarantees of non-repetition begin with the end of human rights violations and include both an official declaration and an apology with acceptance of responsibility (Bassiouni, 2000).

There is a growing body of activists and scholars demanding justice for the climate crisis through the form of climate reparations from governments and corporations that have profited from environmental degradation for centuries. Scholars such as Burkett (2009), Case and Dehm (2020), Táíwò (2022), and Case (2023), amongst others, have called for climate reparations. Broadly speaking, climate reparations demand that countries who benefited from carbon-intensive industrialisation compensate countries that have contributed the least to the climate crisis, yet suffer disproportionately from it. More specifically, Burkett defines climate reparations as 'the effort to assess the harm caused by the past emissions of the major polluters and to improve the lives of the climate vulnerable ... to assure the ability of the climate vulnerable to contemplate a better livelihood in light of future climate challenges' (Burkett, 2009, p. 523).

The approach to climate reparations is similar to that demanded for reparations for the Trans-Atlantic Trade in Africans, colonialism, and ongoing neo-colonialism. Their similarity stems from the ongoing nature of the harm such that the continued degradation of the environment by high-income nations is harming both present and future generations of Africans. With regard to climate reparations, the first step is to reduce the probability of future harm by taking action to adhere to the Paris Agreement's target of limiting temperature increases to 1.5°C above pre-industrial levels (United Nations, 2015a, Article 2.1(a)). The second step is to assess the harm suffered to date and to continue re-evaluating harm as and when disastrous climate events occur (Burkett, 2015).

In the context of reparations to Africa for the Trans-Atlantic Trade in Africans, colonialism, and neo-colonialism, the following forms of reparations are owed particularly by the US and Europe. An unequivocal public apology from their highest officials (including heads of state and senior members of royal families); the restoration of property such as stolen art and historical artefacts; the swift termination of the French Community of Africa (CFA) currency; and, most relevantly to this chapter, financial reparation for emotional harm to descendants of enslaved Africans and macroeconomic harm from the loss of labour and disruption to economic progress.

While the ecological and human toll of the Trans-Atlantic Trade in Africans, colonialism, and neo-colonialism are impossible to quantify monetarily, research has been conducted on the estimated cost of economic destruction to Africa and resulting profit to the West. (IPCC, 2022).[5] One of the highest figures for financial reparations due to Africa was reached in a 1999 'Truth Commission Conference' held in Accra, Ghana. At this conference, private individuals from nine African countries, three Caribbean countries, the US, and the UK, recommended reparations to the tune of US$777 trillion (plus annual interest) and the cancellation of existing African debt. It is worth noting that the methodology used to reach this figure was not shared (Howard-Hassmann, 2004).

Assuming similar fertility and mortality rates between Africa and Asia over the course of the Trans-Atlantic Trade in Africans, Osabu-Kle concludes that without the Trans-Atlantic Trade in Africans, Africa would have a similar population to Asia. However, the contemporary population difference between the two regions is over 1 billion. In the interest of underestimating, Osabu-Kle chooses 1 billion for his calculations. Next, he turns to the Warsaw Convention, under which the loss of a human life (in the event of an airplane crash) is valued at US$75,000. He then argues 'there is no reason why the estimated human loss to Africa should be compensated for less, for the processes of slavery crashed the aircraft of life in which Mother Africa and her children were riding' (Osabu-Kle, 2000, p. 344). A figure of US$75 trillion is reached for loss of life alone, and another US$25 trillion is added for subsequent 'mental slavery' (Osabu-Kle, 2000, p. 15), reaching a total of US$100 trillion (Osabu-Kle, 2000).

Craemer offers a number on the lower end of the spectrum. Relying on Emory University's 2013 Transatlantic Slave Trade Database,[6] he concludes that US$43.9 trillion (in 2016 currency) is owed by Europe to Africa in reparations based on the population-loss estimate employed by Osabu-Kle (Craemer, 2018). To contextualise these figures and the harm suffered by Africa, it is worth noting that the 2022 global economy was valued at US$101.33 trillion (World Bank Group, n.d.).

While these estimates vary greatly, they are unified in their grounding in law and policy at national and international levels (as reparations have been made to other groups in the past) (Craemer, 2018). The moral argument for reparations was eloquently articulated by Pope John Paul II in a speech at the Vatican on 28 May 1998, where he said 'the requirements of justice are such that wherever a wrong has been committed, wherever evil has been done, it must be acknowledged and, as far as possible, reparation made' (Mushanga, 2011, p. 1).

In a perverse development, reparations were made at the end of the Trans-Atlantic Trade in Africans to the enslavers rather than to the formerly enslaved and their descendants. In the UK, for example, Parliament passed an act in 1833 commonly referred to as the Abolition of Slavery Act. At the very start, the Abolition of Slavery Act concomitantly acknowledged that enslaved persons are entitled to their freedom, yet categorises them as property that enslavers are being deprived of by the government. In so doing, the Abolition of Slavery Act sets the groundwork for parliament to allocate funds to enslavers as compensation.[7] In the end, the British government took out a loan amounting to £20 million, equivalent to 40 per cent of its annual budget at the time. Due to the magnitude of the loan (approximately £200 billion in 2019 currency), British taxpayers compensated enslavers and their descendants for 182 years, until 2015 (Manjapra, 2019).

Over centuries, the Trans-Atlantic Trade in Africans, followed by colonisation and neo-colonialism, has exploited Africa and compromised its capacity to deliver a just transition without external finance. As described previously, the Trans-Atlantic Trade in Africans robbed Africa of the chance to foster healthy societies and economies (Beckles and Shepherd, 2000). Colonialism halted Africa's economic growth and led to its economies being transformed into a network of extractive industries to benefit its colonisers (Fofack, 2019). Some of this harm continues today in the form of neo-colonialism, notably with regard to the imposition of French monetary policies in fourteen African countries (Taylor, n.d.). Thus, strong arguments can be made in favour of reparations which would attempt to restore Africa to the economic condition it would likely have been in without its former and ongoing oppression (Osabu-Kle, 2000).

The call for reparations is ambitious and yet firmly rooted in the principles of justice. By demanding reparations, African countries position themselves as survivors of heinous crimes with an ethical claim to adequate capital to finance their just transition. Whether or not reparatory justice is ever delivered, the demand for reparations is itself healing for Africans. It heals because it acknowledges enduring harms in the form of institutional white supremacy, plundered goods, assassination of freedom fighters, and more. In other words, reparations can 'provide psychological healing to victimised populations as collectives and individuals' (Moffett and Schwarz, 2018, p. 22).

4. Climate-compatible development through trade

This part will focus on the capacity of trade to facilitate climate-compatible leapfrogging, i.e., leaping over the carbon intensive steps toward development that were pursued by industrialised nations by charting a pathway to economic development that respects planetary boundaries (Goldemberg, 1998; Perkins, 2003). It serves to demonstrate two points: firstly, that a just transition can be delivered in part through trade and climate-compatible development; and secondly, that the AfCFTA is a suitable facilitator of climate-compatible trade.

As previously stated, data show that the industrial revolution relied on fossil fuels to generate economic growth (Mgbemene, Nnaji and Nwozor, 2016). High-income countries expanded their economies in a carbon-intensive manner, and at the expense of the environment. Our planet cannot afford for the African continent to do the same; therefore, Africa is faced with the complex challenge of attaining economic development through low-carbon means.

Much inter-disciplinary research has been published on the connections between trade and the environment (Antweiler, Copeland and Taylor, 2001; Cole, 2004; Ben Jebli, Ben Youssef and Ozturk, 2015; Vale, Perobelli and Chimeli, 2018). According to the World Trade Organization, 'although trade generates GHG emissions, trade and trade policies can foster the transition to a low-carbon economy' (World Trade Organization (WTO), n.d., p. 9). Moreover, according to the 2030 United Nations Agenda for Sustainable Development, "international trade is an engine for inclusive economic growth and poverty reduction, and contributes to the promotion of sustainable development" (United Nations, 2015b, para 68). Action that renders trade climate-compatible is necessary for the attainment of the objectives set out in the Paris Agreement. Trade and environment scholar Brandi studied all Intended Nationally Determined Contributions submitted in advance of COP21[8] and found that around 45 per cent contain action that is directly related to trade or trade measures (Brandi, 2017).

In this context, the AfCFTA is an appropriate mechanism by which to distribute potential reparations and facilitate a just transition in a way that enables a low-carbon developmental pathway. As noted earlier, the AfCFTA is born of the African Union's Agenda 2063, Africa's 'strategic framework that aims to deliver on its goal for inclusive and sustainable development' (African Union, n.d.a). Furthermore, the AfCFTA's general objectives include its intended aim to 'promote and attain sustainable and inclusive socio-economic development' (African Union, 2018, Article 3(e)). Thus, achieving sustainable development is amongst the objectives and aspirations of the AfCFTA. Indeed, through the AfCFTA's section on general exceptions, allowances are made for trade-restrictive climate-compatible measures if they are 'necessary to protect human, animal or plant life or health' (African Union, 2018, Article 26(b)) or 'relating to the conservation of exhaustible natural resources if such measures are made effective in conjunction with restriction on domestic production or consumption' (African Union, 2018, Article 26(g)).

Yet it must be acknowledged that policy measures designed to facilitate a just transition that also act as trade barriers could be construed as arbitrary or unjustifiable and thus struck down. Due to the nascency of the AfCFTA, no disagreements had been presented to its Disputes Settlement Body as at the date of writing, so there is no jurisprudence pertaining to green protectionism in the AfCFTA trading zone. As such, it is not possible to predict whether climate action would be protected under the General Exceptions clauses or if measures in question would be struck down in favour of trade liberalisation, and of course, such evaluations will depend on the facts surrounding any given policy measure.

For these reasons, it would be more strategic for AfCFTA State Parties to propose climate-compatible amendments to the AfCFTA itself rather than hoping for expansive interpretations of its general exceptions. Arguably there is room to do this pursuant to Article 8.3 of the AfCFTA, which stipulates that 'any additional instruments, within the scope of this Agreement, deemed necessary, shall be concluded in furtherance of the objectives of the AfCFTA and shall, upon adoption, form an integral part of this Agreement' (African Union, 2018, Article 8.3). In theory at least, adjustments to the AfCFTA could be made in one of two ways. First, State Parties could adopt a Protocol on the Environment and Sustainable Development that incorporates climate-compatible measures such as a carbon tax, limits on fossil fuel subsidies and non-discriminatory renewable energy subsidies, among others. There are precedents for the integration of such measures into analogous treaties, namely the 2018 Comprehensive and Progressive Agreement for Trans-Pacific Partnership and the 2014 Korea-Australia Free Trade Agreement (Economist Intelligence Unit, 2019). Secondly, a climate waiver could be integrated into the AfCFTA agreement. Such a provision was first recommended by trade lawyer James Bacchus in the context of the World Trade Organization (Bacchus, 2017). In his words, a climate waiver would apply to 'all trade-restrictive climate response measures that are based on the amount of carbon used or emitted in making a product, and that are taken in furtherance of and in compliance with the Paris Agreement and the UNFCCC' (Bacchus, 2017, p. 20). Whether either of these two approaches could work in practice is a topic that is ripe for empirical investigation.

5. Financing Africa's just transition through the AfCFTA

This part discusses the possibility of financing Africa's just transition with capital derived from reparations and distributed through the AfCFTA Secretariat. The AfCFTA is managed by a Secretariat that serves as a coordinating body and administrative organ. It is tasked with overseeing the implementation of the AfCFTA agreement, capacity building, advocacy, and dispute resolution (AU-AfCFTA, 2021). With the approval of member states, the AfCFTA Secretariat could receive financial reparations and distribute those resources across its various activities. This solution is pragmatic and realistic as it relies on institutions that are already in place, thereby limiting the need for superfluous administrative costs. Furthermore, the Secretariat is well placed to expand the climate compatibility of the AfCFTA agreement through either the inclusion of a climate waiver or of a Protocol on Sustainable Development. If adopted, these measures have the potential to chart the course for a just transition in Africa.

The first challenge with issuing financial reparations is answering the following question: Precisely who is entitled to reparations? Evidence shows that the Trans-Atlantic Trade in Africans, colonialism, and neo-colonialism did not affect the fifty-five African countries recognised by the African Union in the same way (African Union, n.d.b). Pan-Africanism offers an answer to this question as it advocates for unity between people of African descent. As discussed previously, it advocates for unity as a driver of economic, social, and political progress (Adi, 2018). Therefore, a Pan-African approach to the allocation of financial reparations would recognise the interwovenness of African history and advocate for an even distribution of monetary compensation across the African continent. It would acknowledge that in so doing, Africa's collective future, and that of its diaspora are interconnected and one part cannot flourish if another lags behind.

Related to the issue of entitlement, counterarguments may be raised regarding primacy and eligibility for reparations for the Trans-Atlantic Trade in Africans. One question is if it would be ethical to compensate Africans in Africa for the horrors of the Trans-Atlantic Trade before Africans in the diaspora are first compensated. This argument should be struck down on three grounds. Firstly, it falsely assumes that it would not be possible to deliver reparations to Africans in the diaspora and Africans in the continent simultaneously. Secondly, it fails to consider the harms suffered by Africans in the continent at the time of the Trans-Atlantic Trade in Africans in terms of damage to social ties and institutions (Nunn, 2008). Thirdly, it stokes division between Africans based on geographical lines which is detrimental to the current and future prosperity of people of African descent as their futures are interlinked.

The second question queries whether or not reparations should be reserved for the direct descendants of enslaved Africans or whether they should extend to Africans in the diaspora. This argument is based on the premise that only the direct descendants of enslaved Africans experienced harm, which, as discussed above, was not the case. It is, however, important to recognise that the harm suffered by the legacy of the Trans-Atlantic Trade in Africans is different. For example, the direct descendants of enslaved Africans living in the US experience institutional racism that harms their educational, professional, housing, and healthcare outcomes (Ray and Perry, 2020).

The second challenge when issuing financial reparations is determining how the transfer of capital should take place. Here the answer lies with both Pan-Africanism and Afrocentricity as they call for the execution of solutions generated by Africans and for the liberation of Africans. The starting point of the search for African solutions should be the African Union's Agenda 2063 as it lays out an internally driven articulation of Africa's aspirations. It is important to note that the AfCFTA is a flagship project of Agenda 2063 and it is a treaty that enjoys widespread support from African countries (AfCFTA, n.d.). For these reasons, the AfCFTA's viability as a mechanism through which 'the how' of reparations could be channelled merits further scholarly study. Notably, the international conference hosted by the African Union in November 2023 titled 'Building a united front to advance the cause of justice and reparations to Africans' took place in Accra, Ghana, and was attended by delegates from every region of Africa and the diaspora. Three outcomes of that conference are particularly relevant here. First, delegates called for a Committee of Experts on Reparations to be established by the African Union Commission in consultation with other AU organs (which includes the AfCFTA Secretariat). Secondly, delegates recommended a partnership framework between the African Union, Caribbean countries, and the African diaspora. Thirdly, delegates interwove climate considerations by noting the connections between the Trans-Atlantic Trade in Africans and climate justice. In their words:

> ... descendants of the victims of Trans-Atlantic enslavement and colonialism have also been exposed to the dangers of climate change, including the impact of environmental damage caused by the exploitative forces of colonialism and through the forced relocation of enslaved African labour to other regions. (Accra Proclamation on Reparations, 2023, para 12)

6. Conclusion

This chapter sought to answer how Africa's just transition could be facilitated through financial reparations for the Trans-Atlantic Trade in Africans, colonialism, and neocolonialism as distributed through the AfCFTA. To do so, it relied on Pan-Africanism and Afrocentricity as epistemic frameworks to situate Africans and their needs at the heart of the inquiry. The argument is that, if reparations come, they ought to be channelled throughout Africa via trade rather than merely taking the form of government aid. In so doing, such reparations delivered via the AfCFTA could further African efforts towards achieving a net zero transition that is just in Africa.

These findings are highly relevant to Africans in the continent and the diaspora as they illuminate another route towards sustainable economic development in Africa. As the future of Africans in Africa and in the diaspora is inextricably linked, winning the fight for reparations is one that would benefit all Africans irrespective of their geographic location.

Beyond Africa, this discussion is also of interest to other victims of present or historical injustices who seek to hold their oppressors to account and channel reparatory funds into their own sustainable development through regional trade agreements specifically or developmental organisations more broadly.

Any ambitious project faces practical limitations to its realisation. In this instance, notable difficulties of channelling reparations through the AfCFTA, as discussed, are determining primacy and eligibility of funds. Hopefully, as momentum grows in the call for reparations, further scholarship will become available on which projects the AfCFTA should prioritise to finance a just transition in a way that evenly benefits all Africans.

Notes

1. This chapter refers to the enslavement of Africans by Western nations during this period of history as the Trans-Atlantic Trade in Africans for two reasons. Firstly, this terminology encapsulates the human element of the trade as it was not of goods or services, but in enslaved African people. Secondly, it includes the vast distance that enslaved Africans were transported across, which is in contrast to some other forms of slavery in history.
2. According to the United Nations Environment Programme (UNEP), Africa as a whole will need an estimated US$50 billion by 2050 and US$350 billion by the 2070s if we reach 3.5–4°C of warming by 2100 (United Nations Environment Programme (UNEP), 2013).
3. Colonialism shaped African economies into extraction sites of natural resources, which is a phenomenon that hinders the continent's economic development ambitions (Fofack, 2019).
4. These countries are: Benin, Burkina Faso, Côte d'Ivoire, Guinea-Bissau, Mali, Niger, Senegal, Togo, Cameroon, Central African Republic, Chad, Republic of Congo, Equatorial Guinea, and Gabon (International Monetary Fund, n.d.).
5. Osabu-Kle writes '… super profits from the labor of African slaves made possible the investments that resulted in the industrial revolution that has so far benefited other human societies more than Africans' (Osabu-Kle, 2000, p. 333).
6. This database 'contains a comprehensive list of slave-ship manifests for the period from 1501 to 1875 with information about how many enslaved were shipped under what flag from what port of origin to what destination. It estimates that a total of about 12,521,337 enslaved individuals were shipped out of Africa of whom about 10,702,657 arrived in the New World, with 1,818,680 enslaved individuals (14.5%) dying on the transatlantic passage under direct European control' (Craemer, 2018, p. 10).
7. The Statutes Project 2020). NB: for the original text of the 1833 Act for the Abolition of Slavery throughout the British Colonies; for promoting the Industry of the manumitted Slaves; and for compensating the Persons hitherto entitled to the Services of such Slaves, refer to Abolition of Slavery Act (UK Parliament, n.d.).
8. COP21 was the 21st Conference of the Parties to the United Nations Framework Convention on Climate Change and led to the Paris Agreement.

References

Adi, H. (2018) *Pan Africanism: a history*. Bloomsbury Academic.

AfCFTA (n.d.). *Home*. Available at: https://au-afcfta.org/ (Accessed: 26 July 2023).

AfCFTA (2021) *The secretariat*, 2 November. Available at: https://au-afcfta.org/secretariat/ (Accessed: 18 January 2024).

African Development Bank Group (2022) 'Financing climate resilience and a just energy transition in Africa: new strategies and instruments', in *African Economic Outlook 2022*. African Development Bank. Available at: https://www.afdb.org/sites/default/files/2022/05/25/aeo22_chapter3_eng.pdf (Accessed: 16 January 2024).

African Development Bank Group (2023) *A just transition to address climate change in the African context*. African Development Bank Group. Available at: https://www.afdb.org/en/documents/just-transition-address-climate-change-african-context.

African Union (n.d.a) *Agenda 2063: the Africa we want*. Available at: https://au.int/en/agenda2063/overview (Accessed: 18 January 2024).

African Union (n.d.b) *Member states*. Available at: https://au.int/en/member_states/countryprofiles2 (Accessed: 18 January 2024).

African Union (2018) *Agreement establishing the African Continental Free Trade Area*. Available at: https://au.int/sites/default/files/treaties/36437-treaty-consolidated_text_on_cfta_-_en.pdf (Accessed: 26 May 2023).

African Union (2023) *Accra proclamation on reparations*, pp. 1–6. Available at: https://au.int/sites/default/files/decisions/43383-Declaration_-_CIDO_.pdf (Accessed: 8 July 2024).

Aniche, E.T., Mike Alumona, I. and H. Mlambo, V. (2022) 'Pan-Africanism and development in Africa: trajectories and prognoses', in Sooryamoorthy, R. and Khalema, N.E. (eds) *The Oxford handbook of the sociology of Africa*. Oxford University Press, pp. 285–304. Available at: https://doi.org/10.1093/oxfordhb/9780197608494.001.0001.

Antweiler, W., Copeland, B.R. and Taylor, M.S. (2001) 'Is free trade good for the environment?', *The American Economic Review*, 91(4), pp. 877–908. Available at: https://www.proquest.com/docview/233037704/abstract/4C115CFBE17F470FPQ/1 (Accessed: 17 January 2024).

Arblaster, J. *et al.* (2007) 'IPCC, 2007: summary for policymakers', in *Climate change 2007: the physical science basis. Contribution of Working Group I to the Fourth Assessment Report of the Intergovernmental Panel on Climate Change*, pp. 1–18. Available at: https://www.ipcc.ch/site/assets/uploads/2018/02/ar4-wg1-spm-1.pdf.

AU-AfCFTA (n.d.) *Purpose of the AfCFTA*. Available at: https://au-afcfta.org/purpose-the-afcfta/ (Accessed: 9 January 2024).

Bacchus, J. (2017) *The case for a WTO climate waiver*. Centre for International Governance Innovation. Available at: https://www.cigionline.org/sites/default/files/documents/NEWEST%20Climate%20Waiver%20-%20Bacchus.pdf (Accessed: 18 January 2024).

Bassiouni, M.C. (2000) 'The right to restitution, compensation and rehabilitation for victims of gross violations of human rights and fundamental freedoms: final report of the Special Rapporteur, M. Cherif Bassiouni, submitted in accordance with Commission resolution 1999/33 (E/CN.4/2000/62)'. Available at: https://digitallibrary.un.org/record/407931 (Accessed: 26 May 2023).

Beckles, H.M. and Shepherd, V.A. (2000) *Trading souls: Europe's transatlantic trade in Africans*. Ian Randle Publishers.

Ben Jebli, M., Ben Youssef, S. and Ozturk, I. (2015) 'The role of renewable energy consumption and trade: environmental Kuznets curve analysis for Sub-Saharan Africa countries', *African Development Review/Revue Africaine de Développement*, 27(3), pp. 288–300. Available at: https://doi.org/10.1111/1467-8268.12147.

Brandi, C. (2017) *Trade elements in countries' climate contributions under the Paris Agreement*. International Centre for Trade and Sustainable Development (ICTSD).

Burkett, M. (2009) 'Climate reparations', *Melbourne Journal of International Law*, 10(2), pp. 509–542. Available at: https://ssrn.com/abstract=1539726.

Burkett, M. (2015) 'Rehabilitation: a proposal for a climate compensation mechanism for small island states', *Santa Clara Journal of International Law*, 13(1), pp. 81–124.

Callendar, G.S. (1938) 'The artificial production of carbon dioxide and its influence on temperature', *Quarterly Journal of the Royal Meteorological Society*, 64(275), pp. 223–240. Available at: https://doi.org/10.1002/qj.49706427503.

Case, S.R. (2023) 'Looking to the horizon: the meanings of reparations for unbearable crises', *AJIL Unbound*, 117, pp. 49–54. Available at: https://doi.org/10.1017/aju.2023.4.

Case, S.R. and Dehm, J. (2020) 'Redressing historical responsibility for the unjust precarities of climate change in the present', in Mayer, B. and Zahar, A. (eds) *Debating climate law*. Available at: https://doi.org/10.2139/ssrn.3658437.

Climate Action Tracker (2022) *Temperatures: addressing global warming*. Available at: https://climateactiontracker.org/global/temperatures/ (Accessed: 25 July 2023).

Cole, M.A. (2004) 'Trade, the pollution haven hypothesis and the environmental Kuznets curve: examining the linkages', *Ecological Economics*, 48(1), pp. 71–81. Available at: https://doi.org/10.1016/j.ecolecon.2003.09.007.

Craemer, T. (2018) 'International reparations for slavery and the slave trade', *Journal of Black Studies*, 49(7), pp. 694–713. Available at: https://www.jstor.org/stable/26574589 (Accessed: 25 May 2023).

Economist Intelligence Unit (2019) *Climate change and trade agreements: friends or foes?* Economist Intelligence Unit. Available at: https://assets.ctfassets.net/bxxzjfpinfqw/2wknHxem99maM5ue4wzpAJ/6153c2e821869fc370e1960856496537/TradeandClimateChange2019.pdf (Accessed: 5 December 2025).

Fofack, H. (2019) 'Overcoming the colonial development model of resource extraction for sustainable development in Africa', *Brookings*, 31 January. Available at: https://www.brookings.edu/blog/africa-in-focus/2019/01/31/overcoming-the-colonial-development-model-of-resource-extraction-for-sustainable-development-in-africa/ (Accessed: 24 May 2023).

French Senate (2023) *La Zone franc: entre symboles et incompréhensions, la nécessité de clarifier et d'apaiser le débat* (2023) *Sénat*. Available at: https://www.senat.fr/rap/r19-729/r19-729.html (Accessed: 25 May 2023).

Goldemberg, J. (1998) 'Leapfrog energy technologies', *Energy Policy*, 26(10), pp. 729–741.

Hickel, J. and Kallis, G. (2020) 'Is green growth possible?', *New Political Economy*, 25(4), pp. 469–486. Available at: https://doi.org/10.1080/13563467.2019.1598964.

Hostettler, N. (2012) 'Introduction: Eurocentrism, capitalism and modernity', in *Eurocentrism: a Marxian critical realist critique*. Routledge, pp. 1–19. Available at: https://www.routledge.com/Eurocentrism-a-marxian-critical-realist-critique/Hostettler/p/book/9781138798496 (Accessed: 7 May 2024).

Howard-Hassmann, R.E. (2004) 'Reparations to Africa and the group of eminent persons', *Cahiers d'études africaines*, 44(173–174), pp. 81–97. Available at: https://doi.org/10.4000/etudesafricaines.4543.

Intergovernmental Panel on Climate Change (IPCC) Sixth Assessment Report (2022) *WGII summary for policymakers headline statements*, 28 February. Available at: https://www.ipcc.ch/report/ar6/wg2/resources/spm-headline-statements/ (Accessed: 29 May 2023).

Intergovernmental Panel on Climate Change (IPCC) (2023a) 'Chapter 09 – Africa', in *Climate change 2022 – impacts, adaptation and vulnerability*. 1st edn. Cambridge University Press. Available at: https://doi.org/10.1017/9781009325844.

Intergovernmental Panel on Climate Change (IPCC) (2023b) *IPCC, 2022: summary for policymakers*. 1st edn. Cambridge University Press. Available at: https://doi.org/10.1017/9781009325844.

International Trade Administration (n.d.) *Free trade agreement overview*. Available at: https://www.trade.gov/free-trade-agreement-overview (Accessed: 26 May 2023).

Johansson, V. (2023) 'Just transition as an evolving concept in international climate law', *Journal of Environmental Law*, 35(2), pp. 229–249. Available at: https://doi.org/10.1093/jel/eqad017.

DeGruy, J. (2005) *Post traumatic slave syndrome: America's legacy of enduring injury and healing*. Uptone Press.

Kete Asante, M. (2020) 'Afrocentricity', in Rabaka, R. (ed.) *Routledge handbook of Pan-Africanism*. Routledge. Available at: https://doi.org/10.4324/9780429020193.

Langan, M. (2020) 'Neo-colonialism, Nkrumah and Africa-Europe ties', in Rabaka, R. (ed.) *Routledge handbook of Pan-Africanism*. Routledge.

Manjapra, K. (2019) 'The scandal of the British Slavery Abolition Act loan', *Social and Economic Studies*, 68(3/4), pp. 165–184. Available at: https://www.jstor.org/stable/45299245 (Accessed: 25 May 2023).

Mazama, A. (ed.) (2003) 'The Afrocentric paradigm', in *The Afrocentric paradigm*. Africa World Press.

Mebratu, D. and Swilling, M. (eds) (2019) *Transformational infrastructure for development of a wellbeing economy in Africa*. 1st edn. African Sun Media. Available at: https://doi.org/10.18820/9781928480419.

Mgbemene, C.A., Nnaji, C.C. and Nwozor, C. (2016) 'Industrialization and its backlash: focus on climate change and its consequences', 9(4), pp. 301–316. Available at: https://doi.org/10.3923/jest.2016.301.316.

Mitchell, T. and Maxwell, S. (2010) *Defining climate compatible development*. Climate & Development Knowledge Network. Available at: https://cdkn.org/sites/default/files/files/CDKN-CCD-Planning_english.pdf (Accessed: 6 May 2024).

Moffett, L. and Schwarz, K. (2018) 'Reparations for the transatlantic slave trade and historical enslavement: linking past atrocities with contemporary victim populations', *Netherlands Quarterly of Human Rights*, 36(4), pp. 247–269. Available at: https://doi.org/10.1177/0924051918801612.

Mohammed, O. (2022) *AfDB head: to tackle climate, Africa needs 'finance and more finance*. African Development Bank Group. Available at: https://www.afdb.org/en/news-and-events/afdb-head-tackle-climate-africa-needs-finance-and-more-finance-55426 (Accessed: 25 May 2023).

Mushanga, M. (2011) *Slavery and colonialism: man's inhumanity to man for which Africans must demand reparations*. LawAfrica Publishing Limited.

Niang, I., Ruppel, O.C., Abdrabo, M.A., Essel, A., Lennard, C., Padgham, J. and Urquhart P. (n.d.) 'Chapter 22 – Africa', in *Climate change 2014: impacts, adaptation, and vulnerability*. Intergovernmental Panel on Climate Change.

Nkrumah, K. (1970) *Africa must unite*. International Publishers.

Nunn, N. (2008) 'The long-term effects of Africa's slave trades', *The Quarterly Journal of Economics*, 123(1), pp. 139–176. Available at: https://www.jstor.org/stable/25098896 (Accessed: 8 July 2024).

Ocheni, S. and Nwankwo, B. (2012) 'Analysis of colonialism and its impact in Africa', *Cross-Cultural Communication*, 8(3), pp. 46–54. Available at: https://doi.org/10.3968/j.ccc.1923670020120803.1189.

Omeje, K. (2021) 'The "French–Africa connection" and the refusal to decolonize', in Omeje, K. (ed.) *The failure and feasibility of capitalism in Africa*. Springer International Publishing (International Political Economy Series), pp. 67–84. Available at: https://doi.org/10.1007/978-3-030-75170-8_3.

Osabu-Kle, D.T. (2000) 'The African reparation cry: rationale, estimate, prospects, and strategies', *Journal of Black Studies*, 30(3), pp. 331–350. Available at: https://www.jstor.org/stable/2645941 (Accessed: 24 May 2023).

Owomoyela, O. (1994) 'With friends like these ... a critique of pervasive anti-Africanisms in current African Studies epistemology and methodology', *African Studies Review*, 37(3). Available at: https://doi.org/10.2307/524903.

Perkins, R. (2003) 'Environmental leapfrogging in developing countries: a critical assessment and reconstruction', *Natural Resources Forum*, 27(3), pp. 177–188. Available at: https://doi.org/10.1111/1477-8947.00053.

Ray, R. and Perry, A.M. (2020) *Why we need reparations for Black Americans*. The Brookings Institution. Available at: https://www.brookings.edu/wp-content/uploads/2020/04/BigIdeas_Ray_Perry_Reparations-1.pdf (Accessed: 5 December 2025).

Reuters (2019) 'France summons Italian envoy after Di Maio's comments on Africa', 21 January. Available at: https://www.reuters.com/article/us-france-italy-idUSKCN1PF1QE (Accessed: 25 May 2023).

Rodney, W. (2018) *How Europe underdeveloped Africa*. Verso US.

Roger Lokongo, A. (2012) 'African nations can no longer afford to be France's garden', *Global Times*, 22 October. Available at: https://www.globaltimes.cn/content/739771.shtml (Accessed: 25 May 2023).

Táíwò, O.O. (2022) *Reconsidering reparations*. Oxford University Press. Available at: https://doi.org/10.1093/oso/9780197508893.001.0001.

Taylor, I. (n.d.) 'France à fric: the CFA zone in Africa and neocolonialism', *Third World Quarterly*, 40(6), pp. 1064–1088. Available at: https://www.tandfonline.com/doi/abs/10.1080/01436597.2019.1585183?journalCode=ctwq20 (Accessed: 25 May 2023).

The Statutes Project (2020) *1833: 3 & 4 William 4 c.73: Abolition of Slavery Act*. 20 July. Available at: https://statutes.org.uk/site/the-statutes/nineteenth-century/1833-3-4-william-4-c-73-abolition-of-slavery-act/ (Accessed: 29 May 2023).

Trebilcock, M., Howse, R. and Eliason, A. (2012) 'Preferential trade agreements', *The regulation of international trade*. 4th edn. Routledge. Available at: https://doi.org/10.4324/9780203114650 (Accessed: 12 December 2025).

UK Parliament (n.d.) *Abolition of Slavery Act*. Available at: https://digitalarchive.parliament.uk/book/view?bookName=Abolition%20of%20Slavery%20Act&catRef=HL%2fPO%2fPU%2f1%2f1833%2f3%264W4n223&mfstId=1aa2b86c-59d5-4936-a597-f3c1d7508cfa#page/n1/mode/2up (Accessed: 29 May 2023).

UK Parliament (2024) *Parliament and the British slave trade: key dates*. Available at: https://www.parliament.uk/about/living-heritage/transformingsociety/tradeindustry/slavetrade/key-dates/ (Accessed: 24 May 2023).

United Nations (2015a) *Paris Agreement*. Available at: https://unfccc.int/sites/default/files/english_paris_agreement.pdf (Accessed: 25 July 2023).

United Nations (2015b) *United Nations General Assembly Resolution A/RES/70/1 – Transforming our world: the 2030 Agenda for Sustainable Development*. Available at: https://sdgs.un.org/2030agenda (Accessed: 8 July 2024).

United Nations Development Programme (UNDP) (2018) *Climate change adaptation in Africa*. United Nations Development Programme. Available at: https://www.undp.org/publications/climate-change-adaptation-africa (Accessed: 25 July 2023).

United Nations Economic Commission for Africa (UNECA) (2024) *Economic report on Africa 2024: Investing in a just and sustainable transition in Africa*. Available at: https://doi.org/10.18356/9789213589373.

United Nations Environment Programme (UNEP) (2013) *Africa's adaptation gap technical report: climate-change impacts, adaptation challenges and costs for Africa*. Available at: https://wedocs.unep.org/handle/20.500.11822/8376;jsessionid=A2FAB0F4073AAD225B0F6AE6D189BFB0 (Accessed: 17 January 2024).

Vale, V.A., Perobelli, F.S. and Chimeli, A.B. (2018) 'International trade, pollution, and economic structure: evidence on CO2 emissions for the North and the South', *Economic Systems Research*, 30(1), pp. 1–17. Available at: https://doi.org/10.1080/09535314.2017.1361907.

Williams, T. (2022) 'The many faces of Pan-Africanism', *African Studies Review*, 65(2), pp. 504–520. Available at: https://doi.org/10.1017/asr.2021.141.

World Bank Group (n.d.) *GDP (current US$), World Bank Open Data*. Available at: https://data.worldbank.org (Accessed: 18 January 2024).
World Bank Group (2020) *The African Continental Free Trade Area: economic and distributional effects*. Available at: https://openknowledge.worldbank.org/server/api/core/bitstreams/ef1aa41f-60de-5bd2-a63e-75f2c3ff0f43/content (Accessed: 24 May 2023).
World Trade Organization (WTO) (n.d.) *World trade report 2022: Climate change and international trade*. Available at: https://www.wto.org/english/res_e/publications_e/wtr22_e.htm (Accessed: 6 May 2024).

12 Damming the flow from fiction to praxis: coining a carbon currency

Jose Raisey-Skeats, Bronwen Morgan and Naga Aditya Koneru

1. Introduction

This chapter traces the arc of an idea as it journeys from disruptive imaginative vision to attempted real-world implementation. Kim Stanley Robinson's (2020) acclaimed science fiction novel, *The Ministry for the Future,* portrays a narrative where an idea for a 'carbon coin' is implemented by a coalition of central banks supported by the creative, interpretive capacities of key United Nations bureaucrats. The fictional carbon coin is inspired by a real policy, now known as the Global Carbon Reward (referred to in Robinson 2020, ch. 42, and discussed in outline in an earlier version called 4C: Chen, van der Beek and Cloud 2017).[1] The full proposal is still in development and unpublished at the time of writing; therefore, a direct evaluation of its theoretical foundations and economic efficacy is not appropriate. Instead, the chapter focuses on exploring the fictional depiction of the carbon coin in Robinson's novel by conducting a speculative exercise to examine its technical mechanics and reflecting on governance and political challenges inherent in its implementation.

From Robinson's authorial perspective, the carbon coin was portrayed as a form of Keynesian intervention that would tie the use of fiat currency (a currency not backed by any commodity such as gold) to decarbonizing economic activity (Hagens, 2023). The novel is representative of a broader global consciousness shift towards addressing concerns of material growth limits and infinitely expanding economies (see, e.g., Raworth, 2017; Rockström et al., 2023). Both the politics and the technical viability of the carbon coin in the novel, appropriate to the genre, are implicit and open-ended, embedded in a multifaceted plot that weaves together narrative arcs that range from incremental political reform to radical resistance. Where the carbon currency sits on this spectrum in its disruption of the existing financial system remains ambiguous, a positionality that sits comfortably within fiction but which this chapter seeks to flesh out in both technical and political directions. Overall, the tenor of this chapter aims to blend descriptive-analytical commentary regarding the technical operation of a carbon coin with critical-interpretive and speculative insights into its political dimensions, especially how governance might play out. This combination is necessitated by the carbon coin's origin as a science fiction thought experiment (Ali and Rehman, 2024). This speculative quality generates critical uncertainties in relation to political, legal, and economic aspects. It is these aspects that this chapter explores but does not seek to resolve.

Bridging questions of political and cultural feasibility through fiction, Robinson's novel narrates the dynamics of massive cultural macro shifts without excessive technical specificity. This is particularly evident in the description of major crises, such as the catastrophic heatwave in India that opens the novel itself, which creates what Peter Sloterdijk calls an 'atmosphere', or 'spaces of resonance in which the oxygen of certain kinds of thought and practice seems natural and desirable' (Amin and Thrift 2013, p. 5). While narrative arcs generate atmospheres that make otherwise unimaginable trajectories plausible, ideas such as the carbon coin in fictional form can imply the details of the path 'from here to there' in ways that maintain both legitimacy and legibility. Our exploration is distinct from a literary review of the novel (for examples, see Ali and Rehman, 2024; Haines, 2023; La Manna, 2024; Pratha, 2023; Rani et al., 2024; Tejero-Marín, 2023), focusing instead on the practical legal and governance challenges inherent in any form of radical intervention. As will become evident, we consider that there may be an inverse relationship between legibility and legitimacy in 'real life' policy, distinct from their open-textured and productive complementarity in fiction.

Section 2 contextualizes the concept of the carbon coin, exploring its potential to raise finance for addressing climate change. Section 3 reflects on the policy design and approach of another contemporary effort in this space, the Ecocore proposal, along with a discussion on what potential role current institutions may play, such as the International Monetary Fund (IMF). To aid turning an abstract concept concrete, section 4 extrapolates the carbon coin concept to a hypothetical nature-related river regeneration scenario to illustrate the practical challenges relating to both governance and compliance, focusing specifically on institutional design, technical expertise, and monitoring.

2. Charting the course: contextualizing the carbon currency

The Ministry for the Future is a seminal work within the genre of 'climate science fiction', exploring potential pathways for radical societal transformations in response to anthropogenic climate change. The novel's harrowing opening scene, a devastating heatwave, illustrates the harsh realities of climate change and serves as the catalyst for the formation of a new international body, the Ministry for the Future. This organization is bestowed with an ambitious mandate to safeguard the interests of future generations, both human and non-human. The plot follows the journey of this Ministry and its key players as they navigate the complexities of global politics, economic systems, and technological possibilities in an effort to mitigate the worst effects of climate change.

The concept of a carbon coin emerges as a primary mechanism to shift economic incentives following the devastating climate events depicted in the novel. Mary

Murphy, the head of the Ministry for the Future, becomes the central character advocating for the adoption of the carbon coin by global financial institutions. However, the implementation of the carbon coin is far from straightforward. Over the decades depicted in the novel, the carbon coin gradually gains traction and becomes a significant driver of change, incentivizing a wide range of carbon reduction and mitigation activities, from reforestation and regenerative agriculture to direct air capture technologies and the preservation of carbon sinks. Despite initial scepticism from financial institutions, the carbon coin plays a key role in the economic transition away from fossil fuel dependency. Depicted as a digital currency, the carbon coin incentivizes carbon sequestration and the transition to a decarbonized economy. The fundamental principle of the carbon coin is that it is issued for every ton of carbon dioxide (or equivalent greenhouse gas) that is either verifiably removed from the atmosphere, or not emitted by leaving fossil fuels in the ground. The carbon coin's integrity requires robust methods for verification and measurement, and its price stability necessitates backing from major central banks. The carbon coin functions alongside existing national currencies and does not act as a replacement.

Robinson's portrayal of the carbon coin offers a thought-provoking exploration of how monetary policy could be radically transformed to align economic activity with ecological imperatives. The novel directly challenges traditional market mechanisms that often fail to account for the ecological foundations of the economy. It steers us towards an economic model that advocates a more holistic balance between human well-being and planetary health (Patra, 2021; Robinson, 2020, chs. 16–17). This perspective aligns with the principles articulated in regenerative economic frameworks which emphasize the need for an economic system that operates within planetary boundaries (Raworth, 2017). Notably, the novel embeds this perspective in a multifaceted plot that combines diverse pathways towards change, from top-down strategies to grassroots technological solutions and back-to-nature projects (Monticelli and Frantzen, 2024). Despite this networked plurality, which lends the novel's utopian elements a sociological and critical flavour that is distinct from any technocratic 'blueprint', the carbon coin plays a critical role worthy of in-depth exploration. The novel's innovative and speculative solution may prove to be a fertile space for bridging fiction with praxis (La Manna, 2024). Within the framework of 'utopian realism' (Moylan, 2014), the novel's exploration of a carbon coin represents a significant departure from conventional economic thinking, offering potential pathways towards a more sustainable and equitable future.

In the novel, the carbon coin serves as the Ministry's primary tool to influence behaviour and drive decarbonization by making climate action economically attractive. The increasing value and stability of the carbon coin gradually encourages investment away from fossil fuels, but its implementation and management become the subject of geopolitical tensions. By examining the fictional coin and the broader narrative of *The Ministry for the Future*, this chapter seeks to bridge the gap between speculative fiction and the practical considerations involved in implementing novel financial instruments for climate action.

The following section delves deeper into the potential mechanisms and design considerations of a carbon coin, drawing inspiration from the novel's thought experiment while also considering real-world parallels that raise important questions for the legal and political dimensions that are crucial for its viability. Notably, this gap between fiction and praxis is an especially fertile space for reflecting on purpose and meaning, one of this volume's three core connecting threads. The novel's plot directly confronts the dominant logic of purely monetary-driven finance by proposing a system in which financial value is linked to a normative imperative, the urgent need for climate mitigation. The carbon coin redefines the discursive space and material purpose of finance, away from abstract (and extractive) monetary gains to tangible benefits for the planet, including a mandate to look beyond purely human interests. Connections can be made with other work in this volume that explores links between economic and financial frameworks on the one hand, and nature, environment, or climate on the other (Foerster, 2026, Sjåfjell and Mähönen, 2026). However, the novel's implications extend further by challenging entrenched legal and economic structural assumptions that treat the natural world as an externality rather than the foundation of all economic activity.

3. Converging currents: comparing alternative proposals

Armed with this broad outline of the key dimensions of Robinson's carbon coin, it is appropriate to position it within the broader landscape of alternative real-world financial proposals. The transition from fiction to praxis would likely blend a deep understanding of biophysical limits with a nuanced sensitivity to market frameworks and monetary theory, resonating with emerging debates in regenerative economics (Raworth, 2017; Rockström et al., 2023).

3.1 Carbon currency versus carbon pricing mechanisms

To understand a carbon currency, it is helpful to draw a distinction between more familiar carbon policies, such as carbon tax and cap-and-trade schemes,[2] and the concepts of Social Cost of Carbon and Risk Cost of Carbon (Chen, van der Beek and Cloud, 2017).

The Social Cost of Carbon measures the economic welfare loss incurred when one metric tonne of carbon dioxide (CO_2) equivalent is emitted into the atmosphere (Chen, van der Beek and Cloud 2017). A carbon tax is an example that accounts for negative externalities, market failure, and inefficient resource allocation by placing a monetary value on emissions through the 'Polluter Pays Principle' (Chen, van der Beek and Cloud 2017). However, this policy fails to consider positive externalities, where an economic transaction creates an indirect benefit or a public good is gained when carbon is voluntarily mitigated (Chen, van der Beek and Cloud, 2017).

In contrast, the Risk Cost of Carbon prices these positive externalities as the amount of currency per one metric tonne of CO_2 equivalent mitigated within a specified risk tolerance (for example, maintaining a <4 per cent change of complete failure of climate mitigation) (Chen, van der Beek and Cloud, 2017). A carbon-based currency is the policy tool designed to internalize the Risk Cost of Carbon, unlike the carbon tax, which only internalizes the Social Cost of Carbon. While a subsidy[3] also rewards mitigation, complementing instruments like carbon taxes by incentivizing positive changes, its design and pricing do not aim to internalize positive externalities as comprehensively as a carbon-based currency based on the Risk Cost of Carbon (Beeks and Lambert, 2018; Chen, Zappalà and van der Beek, 2018; Kaufman, 2018). Furthermore, a carbon-based currency would be priced in carbon units with an exchange rate to convert to fiat currency (Chen, van der Beek and Cloud 2017), whereas carbon taxes and subsidies are directly denominated in fiat currency. Measuring carbon in carbon units provides a direct accounting of actual mitigation, rather than an estimate of its fiat value.

Finally, a carbon currency differs from cap-and-trade schemes, which do not internalize the Risk Cost of Carbon (Chen, van der Beek and Cloud, 2017). While cap-and-trade schemes are measured in carbon units, they function as tradable permits to pollute rather than as rewards for mitigation. The aim of a carbon currency is to holistically capture positive externalities by internalizing the Risk Cost of Carbon, administering it as a reward policy that complements other policy mechanisms. Section 4 outlines a hypothetical river regeneration project that further illustrates these distinctions and aids in concretizing an abstract concept.

3.2 Economic implications

The introduction of a carbon coin, as explored in Robinson's *The Ministry of the Future*, raises significant economic questions, particularly concerning its financing mechanism and the potential for inflation. The novel mentions the concept of carbon quantitative easing (Robinson, 2020, ch. 42) as a central tool to fund initiatives aimed at mitigating climate change. This involves the creation and strategic injection of the carbon currency into the economy, serving as a means to direct investment towards decarbonization.

However, a key concern with such a mechanism is the potential for monetary inflation. Conventional quantitative easing expands overall money supply and involves central banks creating digital money to purchase government debt to spur economic activity. Similar to periods following significant economic disruptions, this approach carries the risk of 'diluting' the capital supply, potentially causing a deterioration in currency value and generating inflation if the injected capital does not increase demand and stimulate productive capacity (Chen, van der Beek and Cloud, 2017). Consequently, a carbon-focused quantitative easing, if implemented with fiscal responsibility, regulation, and constraints, may have the potential to stimulate demand for the jobs, services, and skilled labour necessary for greenhouse gas mitigation. It may also unlock economic multipliers as demand for the currency encourages investments to increase global productive capacity. This perspective aligns with the prevention principle in international environmental law (see Duvic-Paoli, 2018), which prioritizes avoiding or minimizing environmental damage before it occurs, rather than attempting to mitigate or repair harm after the fact.

From this viewpoint, the potential inflation is justified by the immense societal, economic, and environmental benefits of preventing severe climate impacts (Bryant and Webber, 2024). However, as a technocratic, top-down solution, it could be insulated from public scrutiny. Historically, quantitative easing, particularly in the aftermath of the 2008 global financial crisis, injected capital into financial markets, rather than directly boosting lending to the real economy, leading to wealth transfer and increased inequality (Matikainen, Campiglio and Zenghelis, 2017). While past contexts differ, this highlights the risks of quantitative easing and underscores the need for caution. The question remains the same: Do the means justify the ends, especially when balanced against the severe consequences of climate change and the dearth of alternative, less scalable solutions?

It is important to acknowledge that the arrangements for mobilizing green finance at scale are not inherently problematic. For example, the green bond market shares similar objectives with a carbon currency (see Liu, 2026). However, a carbon currency may encounter similar obstacles, such as scalability, addressing social issues, and ensuring investment aligns with climate goals (García-Lamarca and Ullström, 2020; OECD, 2017). This is not to say that a carbon currency will follow the same destiny, but it is important to proceed with caution and learn lessons from the past.

3.3 Real world parallels: ecocore and IMF/World Bank initiatives

To bridge the gap between fiction and praxis, two specific non-fictional proposals merit brief discussion. The first is a proposal from the London-based non-profit Ecocore, with significant input from heterodox economist Steve Keen. Ecocore proposes a personalized cap-and-trade framework, where a tokenized emissions allowance functions as a universal carbon currency. Under this system, a national carbon budget would allocate each citizen a quota of carbon tokens (Hardy and Keen, 2023).

When purchasing goods or services, individuals would pay a carbon price (in carbon tokens from their allowance) reflecting the CO_2 generated by those items, in addition to the financial cost. This would incentivize businesses to produce low-carbon products and services, driving innovations as manufacturers and other industries seek out or develop low-carbon technologies to reduce their own carbon costs. This approach emphasizes national priorities with decentralized and community-based actions (see also Robinson, 2020, ch. 42). The proposal acknowledges the importance of international coordination and highlights the pervasive need for any disruptive carbon currency proposal to link multiple governance levels. Any carbon currency proposal that seeks to significantly disrupt the current 'business-as-usual' model to respond to climate change will face design issues related to multi-level governance where the details regarding allocation of decision-making power will be critical to both feasibility and legitimacy.

Moreover, there appear to be inevitable trade-offs between global impact and bottom-up granularity. Arguably, a deep systemic shift to a more biophysical understanding of the global economy is more culturally feasible when grounded in small-scale group and individual choices at the level of everyday livelihoods, which Ecocore (Hardy and

Keen, 2023) puts at its centre. But pathways are likely to be more politically impactful and more responsive to the urgency of change when applied at the level of globally coordinated decision-making by central banks and transnational authorities, as described in Robinson's (2020) novel.

Given the importance of multiple levels of governance, global financial institutions and their leverage over monetary policy offer a speculative path for alternative potentials. Robinson's novel (2020, ch. 42) alludes to a 'path not taken' after the Second World War, when Keynes proposed the 'bancor' as a global currency (Robinson, 2020, ch. 42) but the United States (US) dollar ultimately prevailed, and the World Bank and IMF were not given monetary powers. In contemporary times, while neither institution has proposed an instrument directly similar to the carbon coin, the IMF and World Bank are exploring blockchain and quasi-cryptocurrencies, such as the 'Learning Coin', to understand emerging technologies (Wigglesworth, 2019). Moreover, the IMF is exploring a platform for central bank digital currencies to facilitate transactions between countries, with a strong emphasis on asset-based cryptocurrencies. This emphasis on the need for asset backing, which the IMF ties to its capacity to incentivize investment rather than fuel inflation (Eljechtimi, 2023), suggests the potential for a carbon-backed digital currency (see Robinson, 2020, ch. 42 for implicit references to blockchain backing in the fictional setting, and Lagarde 2017 for a speech presented by a former IMF Director regarding a tentative preliminary idea in the realm of praxis).

A global digital currency has multiple speculative dimensions. Lagarde (2017) has suggested it would behave similarly to Bitcoin through the Special Drawing Rights mechanism, potentially replacing existing reserve currencies. It is this trajectory visible in the grey literature that could provide the foundation for a hypothetical 'Climate Stablecoin' that an institution such as the IMF could develop to offer incentives to nations to decarbonize their economy (Van Gansbeke, 2022), providing mitigated carbon as the asset backing to the Stablecoin. This could also prevent volatility in the currency market due to trade imbalances, preventing countries from hoarding physical currency in international trade transactions through the IMF digitally adjusting the number of coins in circulation based on economic conditions to avoid economic contractions (Sharma, 2019).

However, there are likely powerful political obstacles to this, relating to tension between IMF members who may favour the proposal to diminish the US dollar's role as reserve currency, and resistance from the US (Sharma, 2019; Xu, 2022). Any IMF proposal carries political implications that directly link to this volume's theme on justice and responsibilities. The unevenly distributed responsibility for historical emissions, the enduring resistance of economically prosperous countries to adequately finance loss and damage and adaptation programmes in less prosperous countries, and their failure to meet their own national climate targets, underscore these challenges.

The introduction of a global carbon currency scheme would require careful consideration of the equitable distribution of benefits and burdens across countries as well as within them in the transition to a low-carbon economy. While the carbon currency 'carrot' incentives are less demanding to administer and enforce than punitive 'sticks', there is a risk of enabling bad actors to game the system and reinforce existing inequalities. Where a carbon coin becomes a viable and profitable mechanism, it may advantage already wealthy countries and fail to address historic asymmetries relating to countries that will likely be the most impacted by climate change and require more intervention. A carbon currency may also exacerbate the existing issue of wealthy countries controlling assets and distorting the autonomy of other nations. Given these issues, robust governance, encompassing both legal frameworks and inevitable political dynamics, will be crucial.

4. Navigating the rapids: governance and compliance challenges

To illustrate the potential governance and compliance challenges of implementing a carbon coin, we portray a hypothetical scenario involving the regeneration of a river system. This scenario draws inspiration from real-world initiatives, such as the Birrarung Yarra River project undertaken by the Yarra City Council in Melbourne, Australia, which aims to restore the ecological health of urban waterways (Regen Melbourne, 2025).

Consider a nation-state rich in biodiversity but also possessing significant fossil fuel resources. In the current economic paradigm, this state might be driven to extract and export those fossil fuels to generate revenue and improve its national balance of payments. While this provides immediate economic benefits, it exposes communities and ecosystems to long-term climate and sustainability risks. Furthermore, constructing climate-friendly, low-carbon infrastructure often entails high upfront costs. Fortunately, the Ministry for the Future could incentivize this nation-state to leave its fossil fuels in the ground and instead invest in decarbonizing activities and biodiversity restoration.

Let us say that the nation-state decides to participate in the carbon coin system to incentivize the regeneration of the rapidly degrading major river. The river's decline is characterized by a combination of factors, including industrial pollution, agricultural runoff, and deforestation in the surrounding areas, which have led to a decline in water quality, loss of biodiversity, and increased vulnerability to flooding. The government establishes a dedicated agency, the River Regeneration Agency, to collaborate with the Ministry for the Future, tasked with delivering the project and administering the carbon coin system.

The legal and political questions of how any carbon currency would be governed are central to its feasibility and legitimacy in any 'real-world' context. It is noteworthy that in both the emergent real-world projects discussed in the scenario and in Robinson's (2020) novel, governance dimensions are only implicitly or very lightly touched upon. To delve deeper into this, we offer a critical speculative discussion on three of the most important aspects of governance in this hypothetical scenario: institutional design, technical expertise, and compliance monitoring. For this illustrative discussion, we suggest the following fictitious mandate for the River Regeneration Agency:

- Define the eligible activities for carbon coin generation. It must include wider co-benefits beyond solely the cessation of greenhouse gas emissions and other pollution; for example, the measured reversal of damage, such as rubbish removal or wetland restoration.
- Establish rigorous standards for monitoring, reporting, and verification of carbon sequestration, avoidance, and removal.
- Issue carbon coin units proportional to verified carbon credits; for example, one unit per one litre of waste removed from the riverbed.
- Regulate the circulation and trade of the carbon coin within the national economy and international context, while maintaining an exchange rate for the carbon coin.
- Ensure compliance with environmental regulations and project goals.

Section 3 of this chapter has drawn distinctions between a carbon tax, a cap-and-trade scheme, and a carbon currency. In the river regeneration scenario, the carbon tax would apply as an extra fee for activities that pollute the river, such as fishing in the river and recreational or commercial boat riding, to offset negative externalities, such as harm to aquatic life. A cap-and-trade scheme, by contrast, would involve polluting allowances, in the form of litres of waste, within a time-bound permit for polluting activities. In all these cases, quantifying negative externalities, such as the health effects of pollution on humans and wildlife, is challenging due to their long-term and indirect nature.

The following sections explore the challenges of flexible governance frameworks that can enable the River Regeneration Agency to fulfil its fictional mandate. The difficulty stems from the balance between integrating bottom-up, grassroots initiatives with top-down, technocratic oversight across national, transnational, and international levels. This complex combination, particularly in how decisions are made and implemented across diverse stakeholders and governmental levels, gives rise to three key issues that are considered in the following sections: institutional design, technical expertise, and compliance monitoring.

Analogies with the river regeneration scenario are provided for clarity.

4.1 Institutional design

The institutional design of any international body that governs a carbon currency, such as the Ministry for the Future in Robinson's (2020) novel or a cognate specialized authority operating under the United Nations, is critical to the viability and trajectory of any pilot of this idea. Key challenges include clarifying its technical functions and designing its structure, staffing, and distribution of powers and resources. Robinson's novel, predating COP29, sketches a fictional pathway rooted in actual provisions of the 2015 Paris Agreement:

> the Parties to the Agreement created a new Subsidiary Body for Implementation of the Agreement, as authorised by Articles 16 and 18, to be funded using the funding protocols outlined in Article 8, which bound all Parties to the methods outlined in the Warsaw International Mechanism for Loss and Damage. The announcement said:
>
> 'Be it resolved that a Subsidiary Body authorised by this twenty-ninth Conference of the Parties serving as the meeting of the parties to the Paris Climate Agreement, is hereby established, to work with the Intergovernmental Panel on Climate Change, and all the agencies of the United Nations, and all the governments signatory to the Paris Agreement, to advocate for the world's future generations of citizens, whose rights, as defined in the Universal Declaration of Human Rights, are as valid as our own. This new Subsidiary Body is furthermore charged with defending all living creatures present and future who cannot speak for themselves, by promoting their legal standing and physical protection.' (Robinson, 2020, pp. 15–16)

From these clauses, infused with legal, human rights, and deep ecological language, Robinson spins a plot where the carbon coin serves as the central financial mechanism.

In order for the carbon coin to operate as a key tool to create a 'seat at the table' for the denizens of future generations, both technical and political institutional frameworks are required. The key technical challenge would be establishing a mechanism for converting carbon coin units into national currencies, and determining an appropriate conversion rate or price signal for incentivizing participation. A rate that is too low would be economically unattractive, while one that is too high could lead to inflation and other unintended economic distortions. The key political challenge would involve specifying how the international authority interacts with cognate national agencies, such as the River Regeneration Agency in our scenario above, ensuring the integrity and effectiveness of the carbon currency system through oversight and compliance, dispute resolution, and long-term vision. A particular role would certainly involve overseeing the application of measurement, reporting, and verification standards (MRV) that ensure compliance with legal agreements that link national and international commitments.

In our river regeneration scenario, an agency, such as the River Regeneration Agency, could issue tokens (analogous to the carbon coin) based on the amount of eligible activities (such as clearing up plastic waste) an individual or company has completed. For instance, clearing one litre of waste from the riverbed could lead to eligibility for one token. An overarching body would maintain the token's exchange rate to fiat currency (for example, the US dollar). Depending on the amount of plastic waste removed, the token price could be adjusted, by buying tokens in circulation or increasing supply. If the overarching body purchases the tokens in circulation, they become rarer and their price increases, incentivizing more participants to engage in eligible activities for profit. The mechanism is analogous to the 'carbon quantitative easing' developed in Robinson's plot, effectively maintaining an appropriate conversion rate to incentivize participation. The token price could then rise to encourage greater engagement in eligible activities.

A critical question is whether the River Regeneration Agency's institutional design could resemble the framework governing the IMF's Special Drawing Rights (SDRs). Created in 1969, SDRs are not a currency but are valued based on a basket of five major currencies: the US dollar, Euro, Chinese renminbi, Japanese yen, and British sterling pound. This allows countries to borrow against their official reserves to meet their balance of payments (Sharma, 2019). SDRs, created to address liquidity concerns within the framework of the 1944 Bretton Woods Agreement, were initially intended to supplement international reserves in a system of fixed exchange rates. However, with the collapse of that Agreement and subsequent move to a floating exchange rate mechanism, the role and prominence of such international reserve assets also changed. Nevertheless, a similar structure could still underpin an entity such as the Ministry for the Future or subsidiary agencies such as the River Regeneration Agency operating under its aegis.

A critical issue, if such a model were adopted, would be the question of whether relying on something similar to SDRs might institutionalize a bias towards the interests of OECD countries, a critique often leveled against structural adjustment policies and international finance in the 1990s (Babb, 2005). Concerns about the political and social justice implications of financialized responses to the challenge of climate change have persisted since then (Dehm, 2023). A common thread in elaborating such concerns is the challenge of moving away from abstract financialization, even when consciously integrating biophysical limits into economic frameworks. In this context, an essential factor would be the institutional design choices that, for example, specify which experts would govern assessments of the climate mitigation that occurs as a direct result of the carbon coin usage.

4.2 Technical expertise governing assessments of climate mitigation

This brings us to the central salience of measurement, reporting, and verification, or 'MRV', long critical to the efficacy of global climate regulation (Falconer et al., 2012; UN Climate Change Secretariat, 2014). Countries engage in MRV when they measure emissions, estimate the impact of mitigation actions, publish emissions inventories, issue reports on their climate change mitigation efforts, or attempt to verify the accuracy of data on emissions or policy performance (Falconer et al., 2012). While often conducted by inter-ministerial committees at the national level, the financial incentive structure of a currency backed by mitigated carbon treated as an asset differs significantly. This approach synthesizes existing climate response techniques, adding a novel contribution – it blends incentives from asset trading with direct support for specific emissions avoidance or mitigation projects (as opposed to legislating an overarching emissions cap). Connecting this to our analogy, the amount of pollution in the river represents an asset and the tokens issued serve as an incentive for the direct removal of debris from the riverbed. The fixed amount of pollution directly corresponds to a limited number of tokens, assuring investors and participants that the asset will not be oversupplied. Strict monitoring is essential to maintain this link between the eligible activity and token issuance.

This approach clearly demands careful monitoring and verification, certainly more than a carbon tax, which is not measured in carbon units, and potentially more so than cap-and-trade regimes, which are permits, not direct rewards tied to atmospheric carbon (Chen, van der Beek and Cloud, 2017). Historically, technical assessments for MRV in the climate regime, even under international oversight, have relied on fee-based professional services (Chung, Li and Loh, 2024; Bellassen et al., 2015). While transnational certification initiatives frequently use third-party auditors dominated by technocratic expertise in finance and energy (Chung, Li and Loh, 2024), a key question is whether the number of intermediaries and brokers can be reduced, especially compared to carbon offsets, where competition among intermediaries has raised concerns about efficacy and probity (Coggan et al., 2013). In terms of our river regeneration, would it be sufficient to measure the weight of rubbish cleared from the riverbanks, or would further scrutiny concerning the types of eligible waste be required? Periodic checks on remaining pollution levels based on water quality measurements may also be necessary to ensure correct token issuance. The question remains as to whether government bodies possess the required expertise or if consultant scientists would be needed.

Interestingly, Robinson's (2020) fictional scenario implies a much longer temporal commitment than most contemporary MRV design frameworks, as well as a concentration of supervisory power in the Ministry for the Future. This suggests that collaborative coherence, rather than quasi-market certification competition, defines Robinson's speculative institutional design. This also creates considerable opportunity for including broad participatory elements in designing an entity like the Ministry for the Future. Specifically, there is scope to invite diverse stakeholders to form groups that provide input on co-benefits. The governance, involving membership criteria and guidelines developed by the overarching regulatory authority, should be adapted to include co-benefits that consider the impacts on communities and ecosystems.

This participatory element can extend the effects of mitigation projects beyond emission control to shape outcomes such as creating local jobs, ensuring local determination and autonomy on decision-making, protecting ecosystems such as heritage sites, or granting natural entities the rights of legal corporeal entities. In the river regeneration scheme, planting trees around the riverbed could represent a co-benefit for local wildlife, warranting additional tokens. Wildlife activists, organizations, and local communities could participate as stakeholder groups to assess this benefit. Improved water quality naturally benefits aquatic ecosystems and engages marine life organizations. The project's scope thus expands. Local volunteers could engage in eligible activities to earn tokens, which could be converted and spent on local infrastructure improvements (such as a local park), raising funds for local councils. The focus on co-benefits counterbalances legitimacy critiques that arise from MRV that relies too heavily on expert review groups dominated by Global North actors, an issue that has historically been politically contentious (Breidenich and Bodansky, 2009).

A persistent challenge will be to balance the top-down technocratic planning, necessary for a smooth transition away from fossil fuels, with the bottom-up stakeholder input on co-benefits. The top-down governance layer would need to encompass issues such as stabilizing energy prices and prioritizing specific sectors for decarbonization based on supply chain considerations. This process would inevitably spark arguments over which nations benefit the most, making the bottom-up participatory layer critical, especially regarding appropriate compensation, through social and ecological co-benefits, to nations and industry sectors that lose out. Administrative systems for achieving co-benefit goals are perhaps more likely to emerge at national rather than international levels, but in either case, compared to top-down technocratic planning, they could accommodate a wider, more diverse, and decentralized array of stakeholder participation. Just as the allocation of internet domains by the Internet Corporation for Assigned Names and Numbers (ICANN) in the early days of the internet fostered global participation and representation (Klein, 2001), interested stakeholders could help evaluate low-carbon mitigation projects for their community and ecological co-benefits in specific locales.

Overall, at this level of governance, there will likely be an effort to blend transnational technical expertise with a mode of functional representation of different interests. This mix edges toward political modes of governance that can redistribute carbon currency rewards to account for both harms and co-benefits that may flow from large-scale ecological, social, and industrial mitigation outcomes under urgent conditions.

4.3 Compliance agreements

In Robinson's novel, the difficulty of ensuring compliance is illustrated at the international level when the Indian Government unilaterally engages in atmospheric intervention (Robinson, 2020, ch. 4), despite international agreements to the contrary, and the novel alludes to the weakness of international courts more broadly (Robinson, 2020, chs. 9, 56). Unsurprisingly, monitoring compliance at the granular local level with contractual arrangements necessary to implement mitigation projects, funded by the carbon currency, is a setting where existing political and legal structures, at national and local levels, are likely to become highly salient. Here, MRV's centrality to technical assessments, made under the framework of a global carbon currency, intersects with national and local political and legal authorities in order to secure compliance with the promised low-carbon project outcomes.

If a project, as a condition for attracting carbon coin investment for mitigation, is backed by a contractual agreement promising certain outcomes, what forms of monitoring will ensure that technical assessments of the outcomes rely on secure data, transparent records, and reliable methodologies? Would the availability of carbon coin investment fall foul of international and domestic trade rules prohibiting barriers to investment depending on the commercial structure of low carbon projects? Such questions highlight the potentially significant scope of these two compliance dimensions, policing across multiple levels of governance, and potentially major reforms to the key legal infrastructure of trade. This ambition is, however, appropriate for a mechanism intended to catalyze systemic disruptive change. This is especially true because, while MRV under the Paris Agreement is built around a range of intersecting reporting obligations,[4] a carbon coin governance framework could incorporate an economic penalty dimension, to be levied if and when projects fail to deliver on their contractual mitigation agreements.

In the river regeneration analogy, if tokens were offered without adherence to agreements on eligible activities, their price would decrease due to oversupply unless the pollution level was fixed and linked to a limited number of tokens. A failure to monitor token issuance would lead to inaccurate waste removal, requiring a higher number of tokens due to duplication. This mismatch between the risk of the river becoming unusable and the eligible activity cost would necessitate the overarching bodies to spend more to raise token prices (by buying them out of the market) to incentivize continued waste removal. To avoid this repercussion, compliance would need to be monitored, and if the waste removal did not occur as per the token issuance agreements, tokens should be revoked and penalties imposed as a disincentive to system manipulation. Strict monitoring would build investor trust in the tokens as a reputable asset, which could be bought and sold, reducing the pressure on the overarching bodies to maintain the asset's price.

The question of which legal-political institution would have the authority to police compliance, including the levying of penalties, is critical for governance legitimacy. Perhaps a potential real-world model for securing project-level compliance might be something akin to the monitoring of Social Value procurement in the UK. Social value requires 10 per cent of government contracts' value to implement social and environmental goals (Boeger, 2017; Craven, 2020; UK Government, 2020), a mechanism that can be used as a stepping stone to expand the carbon coin's impact. But notably, governments increasingly outsource the monitoring of this, moving from independent regulatory bodies such as audit commissions, to private third party experts in social auditing (Eckersley et al., 2023). This trend, common across various compliance contexts, suggests that the governance implications for securing compliance of a potential carbon coin framework may ultimately mirror those that shape the technical assessments within existing transnational and national/local dimensions. Overall, the design of decision-making power within any proposed regulatory authority for such a currency, and the precise functioning of multi-stakeholder participation, will be central to the political and legal legibility and legitimacy of this innovative mechanism.

5. Conclusion

Throughout this chapter, we have primarily engaged in a positive narration and description of the concept of a carbon currency animating Robinson's (2020) fictional carbon coin, supplemented by an interpretive commentary on legal-political governance issues. This approach is necessitated by the proposal's speculative nature; a practical pilot is required to test its hypotheses and theories to provide ground for evaluations of economic efficacy. This speculative quality generates uncertainty regarding key political aspects of a carbon currency.

Politically, the stance of this innovation is ambiguous. In the novel, this ambiguity may be deliberate and constructive for fostering broad consensus for a real-world pilot. Nonetheless, the often complex blend of market incentives and administrative design that characterizes the carbon coin reflects practical limitations that challenge most existing approaches to the wicked problem of climate change. While this may imply uncertainty relating to the legibility of a carbon currency, there are also uncertainties regarding the carbon coin's legitimacy. The novel's position in debates on economic growth – a key facet of systemic change discussions that often pit green growth against degrowth (Saito, 2023; Pollin, 2018) – remains unclear. On balance, the carbon coin in Robinson's novel appears to chart a careful middle path, although the emphasis of the policy design still largely focuses on market incentives harnessed for positive mitigation.

Against this, one might argue that 'balanced growth' as catalyzed by a carbon currency would be necessary to ensure consistency with the growth-agnostic development envisaged by planetary boundaries (Rockström et al., 2023) or doughnut economics scholarship (Raworth, 2017), which emphatically integrate biophysical limits into economies. If, as Robinson's carbon coin seems to do (though it is never explicitly clear), the design can avoid the issuance of interest-bearing debt, that too would temper the inherent bias towards continual growth embedded in the current financial system. From this perspective, even if planetary boundaries or doughnut economics frameworks are not currently viable within the current economic paradigm, mechanisms like the carbon coin in Robinson's novel could dramatically reorient current paradigms and open the opportunity for deeper, more systemic cultural shifts relating to the position of growth.

At present, a clear pathway from our current state to this future is not fully discernible. It may be achieved through the cumulative impact of local-level contractual frameworks incorporating sustainability thresholds, as suggested by doughnut economics. However, even this would likely require complementary support from strategies that can buttress the social facets of integrated market, monetary, and biophysical perspectives. Such strategies could include robust operationalization of social baselines via human rights or sensitivity to diverse and informal economies, such as household and commons strategies for securing economic security, human well-being, and ecological resilience. While attention to co-benefits can be included in the governance framework of a carbon coin, as well as through its capacity to adjust and weight the allocation of this currency, the politics of such a mechanism may inevitably tilt towards, firstly, a technocratic adjustment of global financial market design, and only secondarily towards structurally embedding social and political dimensions that foster deeper shifts in economic paradigms.

In our view, the carbon coin is a well-intentioned, commendable, and sophisticated concept worthy of further consideration. The significance of the political and economic questions explored in this chapter, alongside the potential legal and governance design details to be fleshed out down the line, will undoubtedly require real-world pilots to demonstrate the efficacy of a carbon currency in managing inevitable trade-offs. Strong compliance and enforcement mechanisms will also be crucial for its effectiveness (Boyce, 2018).

While the elision between fiction and policy with which we opened our discussion provides a stimulating foundation for literary persuasion on questions of political and cultural feasibility, the specific technical challenges of moving into praxis face distinct challenges. While the narrative arcs of Robinson's novel suture legitimacy and legibility together, a real-world application of this innovative idea, in spelling out the path 'from here to there' invites challenges to, and tensions between, legitimacy and legibility. Once the details of the path begin to be interrogated, as our chapter has done, the stakes become clearer, winners and losers emerge, politically powerful groups may resist, or technocratic paralysis or obscurity may set in as compromises dilute disrupted potential. As this process repeats, the imaginative power of the disruptive alternative can lose ground. This leads to our closing question for the challenging task of charting a pathway from imaginative fiction to usable praxis. Is the language and framing capacity of technical economic policy reform, even when disruptive, innovative, and focused on ecological purposes and goals, simply unable to accommodate the tension between expert presumptions based on the current system, and the system-changing pressures of both earth system shifts and human aspirations for a different path forward? How can innovative disruptive ideas in climate finance remain both widely legible and legitimate? We propose that in the transition from fiction to praxis, there may be an inverse relationship between legibility, the clarity of a detailed proposal, and legitimacy, its acceptance, and perceived fairness, a dynamic far more complex than the open-textured complementarity found in fiction.

Notes

1. Interested readers can engage with the ongoing development of the real-world proposal by exploring a range of publicly available materials on the internet, including the Global Carbon Reward project website: https://globalcarbonreward.org/.
2. Carbon tax and cap-and-trade schemes are regulatory approaches for reducing greenhouse gas emissions. Carbon taxes set a fixed price per unit of emissions, while cap-and-trade schemes establish a limit on total emissions and allow businesses to trade emission allowances (Haites, 2018).
3. A subsidy is a direct or indirect financial aid provided, typically by governments, to individuals, businesses, or projects. In this case, it could be used to reduce carbon emissions or adopt environmentally friendly practices.
4. Communication and reporting obligations flow from at least three facets of the Paris Agreement: the communication of Nationally Determined Contributions under Art 4, the Enhanced Transparency Framework of Art 13, and the Global Stocktake required by Art 14. See UN Climate Change Secretariat, 2021.

References

Ali, A. and Rehman, F. (2024) 'Economic inequality, climate change, and hope: a multidisciplinary reading of The Ministry for the Future', *Panacea Journal of Linguistics & Literature*, 3(2), pp. 29–40.

Amin, A. and Thrift, N. (2013) *Arts of the political: new openings for the left*. Duke University Press.

Babb, S. (2005) 'The social consequences of structural adjustment: recent evidence and current debates', *Annual Review of Sociology*, 31(1), pp. 199–222.

Beeks, J.C. and Lambert, T. (2018) 'Addressing externalities: an externality factor tax-subsidy proposal', *European Journal of Sustainable Development Research*, 2(2), article no. 19, pp. 1–19.

Bellassen, V., Stephan, N., Afriat, M., Alberola, E., Barker, A., Chang, J-P, Chiquet, C., Cochran, I., Deheza, M., Dimopoulos, C., Foucherot, C., Jacquier, G., Morel, R., Robinson, R. and Shishlov, I. (2015) 'Monitoring, reporting and verifying emissions in the climate economy', *Nature Climate Change*, 5(4), pp. 319–328.

Boeger, N. (2017) 'Reappraising the UK social value legislation', *Public Money and Management*, 37(2), pp. 113–120.

Boyce, J.K. (2018) *Carbon pricing: effectiveness and equity*. Political Economy Research Group, Working Paper Series Number 457, University of Massachusetts Amherst. Available at: https://scholarworks.umass.edu/entities/publication/a7321d33-425f-40fd-827d-edf665393acf (Accessed: 18 June 2025).

Breidenich, C. and Bodansky, D. (2009) *Measurement, reporting and verification in a post-2012 climate agreement*. Pew Center on Global Climate Change. Available at: https://transparency-partnership.net/sites/default/files/2009_pew_center_breidenich_mrv_in_a_post_2012_climate_agreement.pdf (Accessed: 18 June 2025).

Bryant, G. and Webber, S. (2024) *Climate finance: taking a position on climate futures*. Agenda Publishing.

Chen, D.B., van der Beek, J. and Cloud, J. (2017) 'Climate mitigation policy as a system solution: addressing the risk cost of carbon', *Journal of Sustainable Finance & Investment*, 7(3), pp. 233–274.

Chen, D.B., Zappalà, G. and van der Beek, J. (2018) *Carbon quantitative easing: scalable climate finance for managing systemic risk*. Global Carbon Reward. Available at: https://globalcarbonreward.org/wp-content/uploads/2021/05/CLIMATE-RISK_Chen-Zappala-Beek_Paper_V2.17.pdf (Accessed: 8 June 2025).

Chung, H.C., Li, W. and Loh, C. (2024) 'Professionalism: bridging the missing link between environmental MRV and carbon neutrality', *Data & Policy*, 6, article no. e40, pp. 1–8.

Coggan, A., Buitelaar, E., Whitten, S.M. and Bennett, J. (2013) 'Intermediaries in environmental offset markets: actions and incentives', *Land Use Policy*, 32, pp. 145–154.

Craven, R. (2020) 'The legal and social construction of value in government procurement markets', *Journal of Law and Society*, 47(1), pp. 29–59.

Dehm, J. (2023) 'Legally constituting the value of nature: the green economy and stranded assets', in Feichtner, I. and Gordon, G. (eds) *Constitutions of value*. Routledge, pp. 255–275.

Duvic-Paoli, L-A. (2018) *The prevention principle in international environmental law*. Cambridge University Press.

Eckersley, P., Flynn, A., Ferry, L. and Lakoma, K. (2023) 'Austerity, political control and supplier selection in English local government: implications for autonomy in multi-level systems', *Public Management Review*, 25(1), pp. 1–21.

Eljechtimi, A. (2023) 'IMF working on global central bank digital currency platform', *Reuters*, 19 June. Available at: https://www.reuters.com/markets/imf-working-global-central-bank-digital-currency-platform-2023-06-19/ (Accessed: 31 December 2023).

Falconer, A., Hogan, P., Micale, V., Vasa, A., Yu, Y., Zhang, X., Zhao, X. and Zuckerman, J. (2012) *Tracking emissions and mitigation actions: evaluation of MRV systems in China, Germany, Italy and the United States*. Climate Policy Initiative, CPI Working Paper, June. Available at: https://climatepolicyinitiative.org/wp-content/uploads/2012/05/Tracking-Emissions-and-Mitigation-Actions-Evaluation.pdf (Accessed: 19 January 2024).

Foerster, A. (2026) 'From climate risk to net-zero and beyond: is ecologically rational regulation emerging in the finance sector?', in Bowman, M. and Mai, L. (eds) *A research agenda for law, finance and the environment*. Edward Elgar Publishing, pp. 125–151.

García-Lamarca, M. and Ullström, S. (2020) '"Everyone wants this market to grow": the affective post-politics of municipal green bonds', *Environment and Planning E: Nature and Space*, 5(1), pp. 207–224.

Hagens, N. (2023) *Kim Stanley Robinson: climate, fiction and the future* [Podcast]. *The Great Simplification with Nate Hagens*. 12 April. Available at: https://podcasts.apple.com/us/podcast/kim-stanley-robinson-climate-fiction-and-the-future/id1604218333?i=1000608603928 (Accessed: 18 January 2024).

Haines, C.P. (2023) 'Planetary utopianism: geoengineering, speculative fiction, and the planetary turn', *Textual Practice*, 37(9), pp. 1343–1363.

Haites, E. (2018) 'Carbon taxes and greenhouse gas emissions trading systems: what have we learned?', *Climate Policy*, 18(8), pp. 955–966.

Hardy, A. and Keen, S. (2023) *Our proposal for a carbon currency based on carbon allowances*. Ecocore. Available at: https://ecocore.org/proposal/ (Accessed: 31 December 2023).

Kaufman, N. (2018) *The social cost of carbon in taxes and subsidies. Part 2: alternatives to the US Government SC-CO2 estimates*. Colombia University Center on Global Energy Policy, June. Available at: https://www.energypolicy.columbia.edu/publications/alternatives-social-cost-carbon-taxes-and-subsidies/ (Accessed: 21 June 2025).

Klein, H. (2001) 'The feasibility of global democracy: understanding ICANN's at-large election', *info*, 3(4), pp. 333–345.

La Manna, M. (2024) 'A close enough dystopia? International law and climate change in Kim Stanley Robinson's *The Ministry for the Future*', in Bruno, V.A., Campati, A., Carelli, P. and Sfardini, A. (eds) *Dystopian worlds beyond storytelling. Representations of dehumanized societies in literature, media, and political discourses: multidisciplinary perspectives*. ibidem-Verlag, pp. 435–448.

Lagarde, C. (2017) *Central banking and fintech – a brave new world* [Speech]. IMF Managing Director, Bank of England conference, London, UK. 29 September. Available at: https://www.imf.org/en/News/Articles/2017/09/28/sp092917-central-banking-and-fintech-a-brave-new-world (Accessed: 31 December 2023).

Liu, F.H.M. (2026) 'Governing finance and sustainability in Asia: actors, processes, and politics', in Bowman, M. and Mai, L. (eds) *A research agenda for law, finance and the environment*. Edward Elgar Publishing, pp. 13–34.

Matikainen, S., Campiglio, E. and Zenghelis, D. (2017) *The climate impact of quantitative easing*. Grantham Research Institute on Climate Change and the Environment, Centre for Climate Change Economics and Policy, Policy Brief, May. Available at: https://www.lse.ac.uk/granthaminstitute/wp-content/uploads/2017/05/ClimateImpactQuantEasing_Matikainen-et-al-1.pdf (Accessed 29 June 2025).

Monticelli, L. and Frantzen, M.K. (2024) 'Capitalist realism is dead. Long live utopian realism! A sociological exegesis of Kim Stanley Robinson's *The Ministry for the Future*', *The Sociological Review*, 73(3), pp. 583–606.

Moylan, T. (2014) *Demand the impossible: science fiction and the utopian imagination*. 2nd edn. Ralahine Utopian Studies, Peter Lang.

OECD (2017) *Mobilising bond markets for a low-carbon transition, green finance and investment*. OECD Publishing. Available at: http://dx.doi.org/10.1787/9789264272323-en (Accessed: 19 January 2024).

Patra, I. (2021) 'Mapping the contours of the future: an ecosophical explication of the elements of good and bad anthropocene in Kim Stanley Robinson's *The Ministry for the Future*', *Review of International Geographical Education*, 11(8), pp. 123–142.

Pollin, R. (2018) 'De-growth vs a green new deal', *New Left Review*, 112(Jul/Aug), pp. 5–25.

Pratha, R.J. (2023) 'Cli-Fi fiction and the catastrophic depiction by Margaret Atwood and Kim Stanley Robinson – a comparative study', in Dattagupta, M. and Das, A. (eds) *Posthumanism and the ecological crisis*. Brainware University, pp. 43–47.

Rani, M., Shaheen, S., Bilal, M. and Rafiq, M. (2024) 'Representing the anthropocene through climate fiction (Cli-Fi): analyzing environmental crises and resilience in *Ministry for the Future* by Kim Stanley Robinson', *Kashf Journal of Multidisciplinary Research*, 1(11), pp. 15–23.

Raworth, K. (2017) *Doughnut economics: seven ways to think like a 21st century economist*. Chelsea Green Publishing.

Regen Melbourne (2025) *Swimmable Birrarung*. Available at:https://www.regen.melbourne/swimmable-birrarung (Accessed: 19 June 2025).

Robinson, K.S. (2020) *The ministry for the future*. Orbit.

Rockström, J., Gupta, J., Qin, D., Lade, S.J., Abrams, J.F., Andersen, L.S., McKay, D.I.A., Bai, X., Bala, G., Bunn, S.E., Ciobanu, D., DeClerck, F., Ebi, K., Gifford, L., Gordon, C., Hasan, S., Kanie, N., Lenton, T.M., Loriani, S., Liverman, D.M., Mohamed, A., Nakicenovic, N., Obura, D., Ospina, D., Prodani, K., Rammelt, C., Sakschewski, B., Scholtens, J., Stewart-Koster, B., Tharammal, T., van Vuuren, D., Verburg, P.H., Winkelmann, R., Zimm, C., Bennett, E.M., Bringezu, S., Broadgate, W., Green, P.A., Huang, L., Jacobson, L., Ndehedehe, C., Pedde, S., Rocha, J., Scheffer, M., Schulte-Uebbing, L., de Vries, W., Xiao, C., Xu, C., Xu, X., Zafra-Calvo, N. and Zhang, X. (2023) 'Safe and just earth system boundaries', *Nature*, 619(7968), pp. 102–111.

Saito, K. (2023) *Marx in the anthropocene: towards the idea of degrowth communism*. Cambridge University Press.

Sharma, R. (2019) 'IMF chief suggests IMFCoin cryptocurrency as possibility', *Investopedia*, 25 June. Available at: https://www.investopedia.com/news/imf-chief-suggests-imfcoin-cryptocurrency-possibility/ (Accessed: 31 December 2023).

Sjåfjell, B. and Mähönen, J. (2026) 'Reimagining corporate purpose for a safe and just world' in Bowman, M. and Mai, L. (eds) *A research agenda for law, finance and the environment*. Edward Elgar Publishing, pp. 169–187.

Tejero-Marín, A. (2023) 'Projecting utopian thought: the conceptualization of the "good anthropocene" in Kim Stanley Robinson's *The ministry for the future*', *Ilha do Desterro*, 76(2), pp. 313–331.

UK Government (2020) *Procurement policy note 06/20 – taking account of social value in the award of central government contracts*. Cabinet Office, Department for Culture, Media and Sport, and Department for Digital, Culture, Media & Sport, 24 September. Available at: https://www.gov.uk/government/publications/procurement-policy-note-0620-taking-account-of-social-value-in-the-award-of-central-government-contracts (Accessed: 21 June 2025).

UN Climate Change Secretariat (2014) *Handbook on measurement, reporting and verification for developing country parties*. United Nation Framework Convention on Climate Change, December. Available at: https://unfccc.int/files/national_reports/annex_i_natcom_/application/pdf/non-annex_i_mrv_handbook.pdf (Accessed: 13 June 2024).

UN Climate Change Secretariat (2021) *Transparency under the Paris Agreement.* UNECE Expert Forum for Producers and Users of Climate Change-Related Statistics, 31 August. Available at: https://unece.org/sites/default/files/2021-09/S1-4_UNFCCC_Transparency_under_Paris%20Agreement.pdf (Accessed: 12 June 2024).

Van Gansbeke, F. (2022) 'The IMF climate coin revisited', *Forbes*, 14 September. Available at: https://www.forbes.com/sites/frankvangansbeke/2022/09/14/the-imf-climate-coin-revisited-33/?sh=260e64fb1ca1 (Accessed: 31 December 2023).

Wigglesworth, R. (2019) 'IMF and World Bank explore crypto merits with blockchain project', *Financial Times*, 12 April. Available at: https://www.ft.com/content/1cfb6d46-5d5a-11e9-939a-341f5ada9d40 (Accessed: 31 December 2023).

Xu, F. (2022) 'The feasibility study of issuing carbon coins from the perspective of currency attributes', in Li, C.G., Lin, J.J., Huang, T., Abedin, M.Z. and Ahmed, S. (eds) *Proceedings of the 2022 7th International Conference on Financial Innovation and Economic Development (ICFIED 2022)*, Harbin, China. Available at: https://www.atlantis-press.com/proceedings/icfied-22/125971553 (Accessed: 31 December 2023).

13 Tapping into public procurement to fund a transition to a circular construction economy in Europe: opportunities and challenges

Feja Lesniewska

1. Introduction

The current dominant global linear economic model is based on a take-make-waste paradigm, which must urgently be replaced if life on Earth is to remain viable for most species. Each year, more than one hundred billion tons of resources enter the global economy including metals, minerals, fossil fuels, and organic materials from plants and animals, an extraction rate equivalent to the consumption of 1.7 Earths (Conway, 2023). Between 1970 and 2017, global mineral extraction alone more than tripled, reaching 92 billion tons annually. If current trends continue, the global material demand is projected to reach 190 billion tons of materials per year by 2060 (UNECE, 2022).[1] Based on these global demand forecasts, it is anticipated that natural resources, particularly those necessary for the transition away from fossil fuels, such as rare earth elements and other critical minerals, will become increasingly scarce (UNEP, 2024). This scarcity is likely to drive up costs and create significant supply chain vulnerabilities for many countries and industries (Adams et al., 2017).

While the linear economic model continues to deplete the planet's natural resources, a circular economy offers an alternative approach designed to reduce overconsumption and eliminate waste. Unlike the traditional model, a circular economy seeks to 'design out' waste by rethinking the way products are made and used, with an emphasis on reusing, repairing, refurbishing, and recycling materials. Ideally, a circular economy will restore and regenerate ecosystems and natural capital by maintaining the value of resources for as long as possible through slowing, narrowing, and closing the materials loop (Al-Sinan and Bubshait, 2022). Incorporating circular economy principles into law and policy could therefore help to limit or optimize resource usage. The growing popularity of the circular economy concept suggests it could serve as a new economic paradigm needed to support a system-wide transformation toward sustainable resource use (Barrie et al., 2024).

A major part of any transformation to a circular economy is the role of the global financial sector. Significant financial investment is required to incentivize circular business models, scale innovations, and foster new markets to drive a transformation away from the linear economic system. This transformation needs to span multiple, often interconnected, industrial sectors, from textiles to chemicals to minerals (UNEP, 2020). Arguably, transitioning to a circular economy presents a systemic opportunity to realign the finance sector with the integrated UN Sustainable Development Goals, particularly Goal 12 on Responsible Production and Consumption (Schröder and Raes, 2021). A systemic approach to regulatory and legal reforms, including in the economic and financial sectors, must be strategically coordinated to successfully transform an economic system which is currently orientated towards unlimited consumption of resources (Lesniewska and Steenmans, 2023).

'Responsible investment' by governments and international organizations, such as the United Nations, has long been identified as a means to achieve specific social, economic, and environmental outcomes (Lingegård et al., 2021; Morlino, 2019). A key source of investment is public procurement funding. Public procurement is increasingly recognized for its potential to drive changes that can help meet social, economic, and environmental objectives (Grandia and Voncken, 2019; Alhola et al., 2019; Bosio et al., 2022). Since the 1990s, sustainable and green procurement have evolved, with governments, international organizations, businesses, and non-governmental organizations (NGOs) developing taxonomies and guiding frameworks (Rejeb et al., 2023). Circular economy advocates also see public procurement as a critical source of funding to stimulate change, arguing that strategic investment can enable a transition away from a linear take-make-waste economy (Witjes and Lozano, 2016; Siminică et al., 2020). Consequently, strategic use of procurement is frequently included in governments' circular economy roadmaps, policies, and related laws, as well as by international organizations including the United Nations Environment Programme (UNEP) and the World Bank (UNEP, 2018; World Bank, 2022).

One sector where procurement is identified as having significant potential to enable greater circularity is construction. Construction is not only one of the most resource and energy intensive sectors in the global economy, it also generates huge volumes of waste and greenhouse gas emissions (Huang et al., 2018). Public sector investment in construction, including infrastructure projects to transition to net zero, such as renewable energy, public and residential buildings, and transport infrastructure, is significant and growing globally (Akomea-Frimpong et al., 2022). Governments can use public procurement to embed regulatory and fiscal specifications to move away from the status quo, facilitating a more rapid transition to a net zero circular economy (Ahmed, Majava and Aaltonen, 2023). For instance, government specifications can require businesses submitting procurement tenders to demonstrate how they will meet circularity requirements, including in relation to design, material reuse and/or remanufacturing targets, recycled content, and repairability (Adams et al., 2017). However, realizing the potential to transform the construction industry into a circular economy will only succeed if complimentary laws and policies are adopted. These should include circular design, secondary materials use targets and standards, taxonomies, metrics, and indicators to monitor circular procurement strategies at local, national, and regional levels.

This chapter begins with a critical introduction to the concept of circular economy, highlighting both its potential and limitations in relation to attracting finance to transition away from a linear economic system. Section 3 explores why procurement is regarded as a key strategic tool for advancing the circular economy, particularly through increasing financial flows and creating market opportunities for innovative business models. Section 4 introduces the construction sector, outlining the necessity of transitioning to a circular economy and the role procurement can play in enabling this shift. Section 5 examines the measures implemented in the Netherlands to promote circular public procurement (CPP). Section 6 then situates these developments within the broader context of EU-level initiatives. The chapter concludes with recommendations for future research.

2. The circular economy: potential and limitations

As a concept, the circular economy emerged from various fields from the late 1960s onwards, including industrial ecology, systems thinking, and ecological economics (Lesniewska and Steenmans, 2023). It entails a 'system overhaul' that aims to reduce overconsumption of resources in traditional 'linear' economies, design out waste from production and consumption systems, and restore and regenerate ecosystems and natural capital (Stahel, 2019). It is suggested that a circular economy could slow, narrow, and close socio-economic material cycles by retaining value as long as possible (Haas et al., 2020). As such, moving towards a circular economy could reduce the use of primary materials, protect material resources, and lower the ecosystem footprint from production and consumption (Witjes and Lozano, 2016).

Interest in the circular economy concept has increased rapidly since 2015 (Clear Hill, 2023). There is no universal definition of the circular economy concept, and by 2023, approximately 221 different definitions had been identified (Kirchherr et al., 2023). The lack of a universal definition for a circular economy, or even a set of widely accepted guidelines, could be seen as problematic, as what constitutes circular activities in reality remains open to interpretation (Korhonen et al., 2018). However, Geissdoerfer et al. (2017) claim that, overall, there is a convergence around key objectives across all the definitions: a circular economy aims to narrow, slow, and close material loops by following the '3R' value retention options of reducing, reusing, and recycling.

Significant economic opportunities are predicted to arise from the transition to a circular sustainable growth-based economy. For example, in 2024, the Ellen MacArthur Foundation estimated that moving to a circular economy could unlock up to US$1.5 trillion in value in just three industrial sectors of the US economy alone (textiles, construction, and electronics) (Ellen MacArthur Foundation, 2024). However, in 2023 the global economy, excluding the informal economy, was only 9 per cent circular (Fraser, Haigh and Soria, 2023).[2] It is clear that any exponential growth of the circular economy will require substantial capital investment. The implementation of a circular economy requires new business models, value chains, and innovations in the allocation of producer and consumer responsibilities.

To realize the market potential of transitioning to a sustainable, net-zero circular economy, it is necessary to identify obstacles to sourcing large-scale finance. The main challenge for circular economy finance is how to translate the need for slowing and narrowing resource flows into viable business models that can be financed at scale. To provide a framework for investment, clearer laws and policies are needed to enable a transition to a circular economy. Policy and regulatory instruments need to be designed to de-risk and incentivize financial investments that target circular economic development (UNEP, 2020; Schröder and Raes, 2021). Currently, there is a lack of data on circular economy investment in terms of overall levels, composition, and trends. In light of the lack of a coherent definition, gathering such data is not straightforward as it is difficult to identify whether an area of spending is fully circular or not (Lawlor and Spratt, 2021). Regardless of these challenges, the need to finance a more circular economy remains. One way in which governments can provide support to realize ambitions for transitioning to a more circular economic system is through using public procurement funding.

3. Public procurement for a circular economy

Public procurement can direct crucial investment to facilitate the transition to a net-zero sustainable circular economy. Governments worldwide wield substantial influence over global markets due to their purchasing power, though this influence varies significantly among countries, particularly in least developed economies. Public procurement serves as a primary channel through which public funds flow into the private sector, accounting for about 13 per cent of global gross domestic product (GDP) – about US$11 trillion in 2018 (Bosio et al., 2022). The Organisation for Economic Co-Operation and Development (OECD) (2019) estimates that public procurement among its member states represents around 12 per cent of GDP. The percentage of GDP allocated to public procurement varies across countries and regions. For instance, in 2021 nearly 45 per cent of total government expenditure in the Netherlands was channelled through procurement, equating to about 20 per cent of the country's GDP. In contrast, China and India allocated an average of 35 per cent and 30 per cent of their GDP to public procurement respectively. Meanwhile, in Indonesia, public procurement accounted for a mere 7 per cent of the country's GDP (Morales et al., 2023). Strategic use of public procurement can stimulate demand for sustainable goods and services that might otherwise struggle to compete in the conventional linear market. Such an approach aligns with the United Nations 2030 Agenda for Sustainable Development, which under SDG 12.7, encourages states to 'promote public procurement practices that are sustainable, in line with national policies and priorities' (UN, 2015).

Edler and Georghiou (2007) observe that the public sector is not only a dominant buyer but can also influence demand-side innovations by being an early adopter of new technological solutions and offering fiscal support to start-ups. Cattolica (2018) argues that Sustainable Public Procurement (SPP) can be strategically utilized as part of a government's economic policy to support innovations aimed at achieving a wide array of social and environmental goals, including climate policy objectives such as rapid decarbonization. For example, the Dutch Ministry of Infrastructure and Water Management (Rijkswaterstaat), through its public procurement process for a new bridge, required modular design, the use of recycled materials, and consideration of lifecycle value. This approach stimulated innovation in circular construction and supported emerging technologies and start-ups, resulting in the Circular Viaduct at Kampen (Rijkswaterstaat, 2019).

The European Commission has highlighted 'the importance of demand-side approaches to innovation and, more concretely, in the use of public demand as an engine for innovation' at European Union level (EC, 2017). This combination of potential support for technical innovation and the pursuit of social and environmental goals within the market makes public procurement an ideal vehicle to channel funding through to enable a circular economy.

The EU has led the way globally in framing CPP as a 'process by which public authorities purchase works, goods, or services that seek to contribute to closed energy and material loops within supply chains, while minimising, and in the best case avoiding, negative environmental impacts and waste creation across their whole life-cycle' (EC, 2017). During the procurement process, technical aspects of products or services should be as circular as possible. CPP requires that calls for tenders promote product durability, resource efficiency, reuse, recyclability, and, for buildings, potential for refurbishment, retrofitting, and disassembly. The European Commission differentiates between system-level procurement (including, for instance, public-private partnerships), supplier-level procurement, and product-level procurement. Supplier-level CPP includes, for example, supplier take-back systems, design for disassembly practices, reparability of standard products, external reuse or sale of products, and internal reuse of products (Wurster et al., 2021). Public procurement methods should be based on defined criteria, checklists, and rankings of products for suppliers (Al-Sinan and Bubshait, 2022).

In practice, however, embedding circularity within public procurement faces major challenges. Making procurement projects more circular requires an approach that differs from that of traditional projects. To develop a comprehensive, structured framework for circular procurement, it is essential to understand the procurement ecosystem as a whole. While pilots provide examples, there is no unified, structured approach to CPP contracting or its implementation. Jones and Comfort (2018) propose that to achieve CPP, two new principles – collaboration and innovation – need to be added to the four existing principles within procurement law tendering procedure: non-discrimination, equal treatment, transparency, and proportionality. The innovation and collaboration principles are interconnected because increased stakeholder collaboration can lead to a more rapid development and deployment of innovative circular products and services at competitive rates (Al-Sinan and Bubshait, 2022). In particular, collaborative procurement methods facilitate the involvement of major stakeholders in planning, as well as in sharing risks and goals, resulting in more equitable distribution across the entire building life cycle (Ahmed, Majava and Aaltonen, 2023).

Suppliers and manufacturers will only embrace circularity once clients start demanding and are willing to pay for circular products and services. Although CPP can create demand, there needs to be a source of supply of materials and products that can meet the circularity specifications required in the procurement tender. The lack of standards for evaluating circularity, both at the supplier and product levels, poses a significant challenge for governments aiming to implement CPP. Al-Sinan and Bubshait (2022) argue that the adoption of international, regional, and national standards to assess and certify the circularity of products and services would significantly accelerate CPP. When such standards are recognized in law, they can unlock both private and public funding by reducing the perceived risks for investors to support circular businesses (Qazi and Appolloni, 2022). One sector where legally recognized standards are particularly critical for enabling a faster transition to a circular economy is construction.

4. Construction, the circular economy, and procurement: opportunities and challenges

The construction sector is a significant part of the global economy. In 2016, the sector accounted for 6.2 per cent of global GDP (Ruiz et al., 2020). However, it predominantly operates under a linear economic model (Tirado et al., 2022). The construction sector consumes more resources than any other industry, approximately 32 per cent of the world's natural resources, including minerals and forest products (Oluleye et al., 2022), and it emits over 40 per cent of the world's carbon emissions (Pomponi and Moncaster, 2017). Meanwhile, construction generates the largest volume of waste globally, sending on average 35 per cent of its waste to landfill, though figures vary significantly between countries, especially between developed and least developed nations (Ghaffar et al., 2020). This situation is expected to worsen, as the land area of the built environment is predicted to double globally by 2060 (Architecture 2030, 2022).

There is clear potential within the construction industry to implement circular economy strategies to reduce the use of primary raw materials and energy, its carbon footprint, and waste generation (Hjaltadóttir and Hild, 2021). Increasing recognition of the need to prioritize and accelerate the transition from a linear to a circular system in the construction sector is evident in policies, strategies, and plans within both the public and private sectors globally (World Green Building Council, 2023). However, the sector has yet to commit to ambitious circular strategies that reduce demolitions and solid waste generation once a building, infrastructure, or facility reaches the end of its life. Where action has been taken, the industry has mostly focused on recycling, primarily downcycling, where materials lose economic value. The global construction waste recycling market was valued at US$126 billion in 2019 and is expected to reach US$149 billion by 2027 (Rios and Grau, 2019). The predicted growth in the recycling market can act as a disincentive to invest in upstream circular manufacturing, including designs to extend the durability of products, repairability, as well as capacity for disassembly and reuse.

CPP in construction could require the industry to focus on material choices, design, the reuse and recyclability of materials, efficient use of space, energy demand, and strategic long-term planning of buildings and infrastructure. Multiple and fragmented supply chains, stakeholder relations, and lengthy project timelines add to this complexity (Oyegoke et al., 2009). For instance, traditional procurement methods can result in a lack of involvement of the main contractor in the project's early planning and design stages, which can undermine effective collaboration and communication (Elhag et al., 2020; Moradi and Kähkönen, 2022). This is compounded by problems of incomplete information, lack of management support, poor planning, changing requirements, rising costs, and ongoing delays in completion (Yu and Shen, 2013; Bao et al., 2019). As such, adopting CPP in the construction industry is procedurally more challenging than in other areas of procurement, such as, for instance, in hospitality (Jones and Comfort, 2018). This is particularly true for large-scale infrastructure construction projects, including airports and roads, where traditional procurement methods make addressing sustainability problems even more challenging (Ershadi et al., 2021).

Addressing the challenges of CPP in construction will require greater coordination and collaboration, with agreements on sharing information, skills, and resources made much earlier in the process. Accordingly, circular business models will require changes within the construction sector, shaping how it operates, especially in relation to small and medium-sized enterprises (Sajid et al., 2024). Circular revenue models are essential for the successful implementation of CPP and for displacing linear practices within the construction sector. To ensure that circular commitments made during the procurement process are delivered effectively, financial incentive mechanisms play a critical role. So-called 'servitization models', such as leasing, rental, or pay-per-use arrangements, shift the emphasis from product ownership to long-term service provision, thus aligning economic incentives with circular economy objectives. In essence, these models extend the supplier's responsibility for the product's performance over a longer timeframe, thereby encouraging durability, maintenance, and reuse (Khadim and van Marrewijk, 2025).

Circular revenue models are already being used in the construction industry, including the leasing of building fronts and pay-per-use arrangements for lighting and lifts. But a lack of a circular premium means that lenders struggle to ensure that financing adequately reflects the advantages of servitization contracts. A life-cycle approach to contracts, under which implementation is maintained through monitoring and maintenance of service agreements, could lay the foundation for a circular tender over the long term. Adopting a framework agreement with a contractor, where follow-up contracts will be offered if promises from previous projects are fulfilled, can provide monetary incentives for service providers. Such a framework agreement is likely to be most effective with repeatable design concepts such as social housing (Khadim and van Marrewijk, 2025). Integral to such incentive-based schemes for meeting circular targets under CPP is having clear contractual arrangements among all stakeholders. For CPP, tenderers should be required to submit measurable circular commitments, such as on the degree of reusability and/or repairability. These circular commitments could be included in the contract as key performance indicators, for which penalties or bonus arrangements could be agreed upon.

The success of incorporating specific requirements in CPP contracts for tenderers hinges upon the ability to assess outcomes. Achieving reductions in material flows and waste generation in the construction sector through CPP will require the gathering of data, monitoring, and building long-term relationships between stakeholders. Requiring tenderers to submit a digital material and product passport could help fill existing data gaps. A material or product passport documents the materials, components, and parts that make up a building. In addition to listing these elements it can include information about how materials and products are physically connected, thus supporting planned future disassembly. By making this data easily accessible, a digital passport provides a foundation for high-quality reuse of components, helping to extend their lifecycle and support circular construction practices (Al-Sinan and Bubshait, 2022).

5. Case study: CPP and construction in the Netherlands – from small steps to grand plans

Several countries in the EU, most notably Denmark[3] and Sweden,[4] have taken important steps in advancing CPP in the construction sector, including by adopting domestic plans and regulations. However, the Netherlands stands out as a European leader, having recognized CPP as a key tool for driving circularity across the construction industry. In the Netherlands, almost 45 per cent of total government expenditure is channelled through public procurement, amounting to nearly 20 per cent of the country's GDP (OECD, 2023). Building on existing sustainable development objectives and standards, the Dutch government has introduced a range of initiatives and collaborations to advance its circular economy goals. The Ministry of Infrastructure and Water Management aims to reduce primary resource usage and achieve a fully functioning circular economy by 2050. To support this ambition, a nationwide programme, the 'Netherlands Circular', was launched in 2016, and followed by a Raw Materials Agreement in 2017. By 2030, the government plans for all public procurement tenders to incorporate full circularity. In the construction sector, the Dutch government has set ambitious goals, including a 50 per cent reduction in the use of primary abiotic raw materials, including minerals, fossil fuels, and metals, by 2030.[5]

One of the earliest examples of CPP in Dutch construction was the 'Stadstuin Overtoom' project in Amsterdam in 2008.[6] The housing association Eigen Haard, one of the largest social landlords in the Netherlands with 60,000 properties, oversaw the demolition of 350 existing houses and the construction of approximately 480 new units. The goal was to minimize virgin material consumption using circular procurement methods. Rather than proceeding with a conventional demolition, the buildings were carefully dismantled in stages. Pre-demolition audits assessed the quality and value of the existing materials. Old bricks were reused or processed into new ones, and concrete was recycled for new builds. The project involved close collaboration across the supply chain, especially with small businesses, to ensure the quality of reused materials despite the absence of formal standards at the time. Around 30 per cent of the demolition materials were reused on-site, while the remainder were stored for future use in other social housing projects. The project not only lowered construction and emissions costs, but also supported long-term financial stability for participating businesses as many were offered ongoing maintenance contracts. The Stadstuin Overtoom project served as proof of concept, demonstrating that CPP requires a fundamentally different business model than traditional linear construction approaches. It became a benchmark for national policy development in the Netherlands and influenced approaches to CPP by the European Commission and in other EU member states.

Building on this early experience, the Dutch government launched a major initiative to embed CPP in the construction sector. In 2018, the Circular Construction Economy Transition Agenda was introduced by an interdisciplinary team of experts from government, academia, and industry. It defined circular construction as the 'means to develop, use, and reuse buildings, areas, and infrastructure without unnecessarily depleting natural resources, polluting the living environment, and damaging ecosystems. Building in a way that is economically sound and contributes to the well-being of people and animals alike. Here and there, now and later'.[7] This was followed in 2019 by the Circular Economy Implementation Program, which translated the construction transition agenda into concrete actions.[8] To help achieve these goals, the government promoted specific requirements in procurement processes, such as the Circular Building Index,[9] Building Information Modelling,[10] and a National Environmental Database.[11] Furthermore, in line with the objectives outlined in the Circular Construction Economy Transition Agenda,[12] the Platform Circular Construction 2023 has developed guidelines for the implementation of circular procurement and design for industry.[13] These guidelines provide practical steps for businesses to effectively incorporate circularity principles into tender bids for government public procurement construction projects.

6. CPP, construction, and a circular economy systems transition progress in the EU

Public procurement within the EU consistently accounts for between 14 to 19 per cent of GDP. Although public procurement is identified as an important tool to leverage a transition to a circular economy, it is not seen in isolation (European Commission, 2017). Iacovidou et al. (2021) argue that a systems approach is essential for transitioning to a circular economy. However, translating the technical systems approach into practice, particularly into law and policy, presents challenges. In legislative design, systems transformation is complex, as legal change does not occur in a vacuum (Lesniewska and Steenmans, 2023). Arguably, the EU offers a unique legal environment to undertake such a systems-wide transformation (de Waal, 2021). Circular economy policy, like all EU policy, is underpinned by treaty obligations. On environmental matters, key provisions include articles 191 to 193 of the Treaty on the Functioning of the European Union (TFEU). These provisions require member states to pursue sustainable development goals.

Moreover, the integration principle, as outlined in Article 11 of the TFEU, states that environmental protection must be considered in the creation and implementation of all EU policies and activities, particularly to promote sustainable development. This means that environmental concerns should not be treated separately or as an afterthought, but instead must be embedded into every policy area, including the internal market, which governs trade, competition, and economic activity across all EU member states. As Sjåfjell (2014) points out, the principle has direct implications for businesses, because they must operate in a regulatory environment where sustainability and environmental integration are increasingly required, not just in environmental sectors, but in all areas of economic activity. For example, the EU's Taxonomy for Sustainable Finance, established under the EU Taxonomy Regulation (Regulation (EU) 2020/852), defines what qualifies as an environmentally sustainable economic activity. This is part of the EU's broader effort to integrate sustainability into the financial system. The taxonomy guides investment decisions to try to promote that financial policies support the green transition, including a circular economy.

In 2020, all EU member states reaffirmed their commitment to advancing the circular economy through the second Circular Economy Action Plan (CEAP) as part of the European Green Deal.[14] The 2021 Circular Economy Action Plan (CEAP) recognizes that material flows and the life cycle of resources, and their management through laws, regulations, and standards across the EU, is fundamental to moving toward a more circular economy (European Commission, 2021). Indeed in the original communication on the European Green Deal, green public procurement and sustainable product policy were presented as complementary elements of a strategy to mobilize industry for a clean and circular economy. The European Commission's 2025 Clean Industrial Plan continues the same sentiment in its strategic vision for the internal market to boost EU competitiveness and accelerate the transition to a net zero circular economy.[15]

The interconnections between numerous pieces of EU legislation and CPP is typified in the construction sector. It has been the object of a number of sectoral legislative measures that regulate procurement, or at least are relevant to it, such as the Ecodesign Directive 2009/125/EC, the Construction Product Regulation (CPR) (EU) No 305/2011, and the recent the European Climate Act (Regulation (EU) 2021/1119).

As such, a revision to one piece of legislation will inevitably have an effect on others, either positive or negative. For example, the CPR (EU) No 305/2011 laid down harmonized conditions for the marketing of construction products. Meanwhile, amendments to the CPR in 2024 aimed to advance circularity in the sector by promoting the reuse, recycling, and repair of construction products and the monitoring of digital product passports through a harmonized approach.[16] The amendments to the CPR are part of EU initiatives to broaden the scope of sustainable product design in which circular design is embedded to minimize waste and increase the durability of the product lifecycle, as well as decarbonize the economy.

Innovation in product design to increase circularity is seen as key to CPP being possible. According to the European Commission, 80 per cent of the environmental impact of a product is determined during the design phase.[17] To drive innovation, the EU has replaced the Ecodesign Directive (2009/125/EC) with the Ecodesign for Sustainable Products Regulation (ESPR) (Regulation (EU) 2024/1781).[18] The ESPR sets ecological standards for the design of a range of product groups, including those used in the construction sector not covered by the CPR. Design decisions are to be driven by circular economy principles and environmental data. The gathering and use of data is becoming increasingly important for circular design to demonstrate how it meets evaluation criteria on durability, repairability, reusability, and end-of-life management. New requirements for material and product passports under the ESPR and revised CPR are aimed at closing the information gaps, as well as creating opportunities for new business models across the material use life cycle (Jensen et al., 2023). Such system-wide initiatives should de-risk investing in CPP for businesses and open up new frontiers for circular entrepreneurial innovation in construction. However, Fitch-Roy, Benson and Monciardini (2020) caution that the systems approach to legislative revisions adopted by the EU is conservative, top down and technical, leaving limited scope for more ambitious sustainable circular innovations by small and medium-sized enterprises.

7. Conclusion and further research

With trillions of US dollars channelled globally through public procurement each year, it is unsurprising that CPP is increasingly viewed as a means to achieve urgently needed environmental, social, and economic transformation. Circular economy policies and laws are emerging across sectors such as textiles, food, and construction. However, implementation has remained relatively limited. In practice, linear approaches still dominate, particularly in construction, one of the most materially and carbon-intensive sectors globally.

CPP relies on a belief in the market-shaping power of government spending to incentivize innovation and circular business models in the private sector. As discussed in this chapter, meaningful change in the construction sector requires more than procurement investments. It demands broader regulatory and policy alignment to encourage innovation and value retention throughout the product life cycle (Harland et al., 2021). This is especially the case with CPP for large-scale construction projects where economic value must be captured over long timeframes. Although strategic public procurement can deliver multiple environmental, social, and economic benefits, the intersection of CPP and construction remains under-researched (Ahmed, Majava and Aaltonen, 2023).

At the EU level, CPP is integral to the green economic agenda. Member states like the Netherlands, but also Denmark and Sweden, are piloting CPP innovations in construction, producing valuable insights for future developments including in understanding how to create successful investment and circular business models, particularly for small- and medium-scale enterprises. This chapter has argued that a systems-wide approach is necessary to capture interconnections across CPP-related legal and policy domains (see also Lesniewska, 2025). Tracking the impact of recent changes in EU law, including in relation to digital material and product passports and sustainability standards for circular product design, will be essential to understanding CPP's role in influencing the construction sector.

Further research is needed to explore the barriers that countries face when incorporating CPP into broader social, environmental, and circular economic reforms. Such reforms are often difficult to implement due to limited capacity and knowledge within governments and businesses along the supply chain. These challenges are more pronounced in developing countries where public procurement practices are frequently sites of contestation and corruption. Much of the current academic research, including this chapter, on CPP and construction focuses on developments in selected EU countries, where there are strong policy commitments to circular economy transitions. Without investment in knowledge-sharing and capacity-building, the impact of CPP on the construction sector will remain limited. A failure to address this gap will undermine efforts to establish circular finance and business models capable of driving a global transition to a circular economy.

Notes

1. There are significant disparities between the consumption of resources between elites and the poor (people and countries) globally: see Newell and Mulvaney (2013), Bennett et al. (2019).
2. The informal sector refers to economic units that produce goods or services for the market but are not formally recognized. Informal employment refers to activities for pay or profit that are not covered by formal arrangements, regardless of whether they take place in the informal sector or the formal sector. This represents nearly 2 billion people earning a living in the informal economy, according to International Labour Organization (ILO) estimates. This represents close to 60 per cent of the world's workers. This sector represents roughly 35 per cent of the GDP in low- and middle-income countries, while it accounts for 15 per cent in advanced economies: see ILO (2023) Women and men in the informal economy: a statistical update. Available at: https://www.ilo.org/sites/default/files/wcmsp5/groups/public/%40ed_protect/%40protrav/%40travail/documents/publication/wcms_869188.pdf

3. In 2006, Denmark established a Partnership for Green Public Procurement, a collaborative initiative between Danish regions, municipalities, and the Ministry of Environment and Food. The partnership integrates green goals into procurement policies across eleven specific product groups, including construction. Criteria for procurement include recyclability, product lifespan, and total cost of ownership. All of these elements are essential for the transition to a circular economy.
4. Sweden's National Strategy for a Circular Economy (2020) includes initiatives for the construction sector, such as product passports, climate declarations for new buildings, and public circular procurement. The goal is to reduce emissions in the building sector by 50 per cent by 2030 and achieve net-zero emissions by 2045.
5. See Netherlands National Agreement on Circular Economy 2017. Available at: https://www.government.nl/topics/circular-economy/documents/discussion-documents/2017/01/24/national-agreement-on-the-circular-economy.
6. For a detailed overview of the project see *Stadstuin Overtoom: climate and cost neutral demolition and development.* Available at: https://www.copper8.com/en/projects/stadstuin-overtoom-klimaat-en-kostenneutrale-sloop-en-nieuwbouw-voor-corporatie-eigen-haard%E2%80%A8/.
7. See Circular Construction Economy. Available at: https://circulairebouweconomie.nl/over-ons/.
8. See Circular Economy Implementation Programme 2019–2023. Available at: https://hollandcircularhotspot.nl/wp-content/uploads/2019/09/Circular-Economy-Implementation-Programme-2019-2023.pdf.
9. Circular Building Index (Platform CB'23) is a tool developed to evaluate buildings based on criteria such as material reuse, design for disassembly, and environmental impact. Available at: https://platformcb23.nl/english/
10. Building Information Modelling (BIM) involves creating a digital representation (a 3D model) of the physical and functional characteristics of a facility. But it's much more than just a 3D model – it's a shared information platform that enables collaboration between architects, engineers, contractors, clients, and facility managers. In the Netherlands, BIM is often used in combination with material passports and circular performance indicators (like the Circular Building Index) in public procurement projects to ensure transparency, traceability, and circular design integration from the outset.
11. Netherlands National Environmental Database (Nationale Milieudatabase, NMD). The database compiles data from Life Cycle Assessments (LCAs) to provide standardized environmental impact profiles for a wide array of construction materials. Available at: https://milieudatabase.nl/en/.
12. Circular Construction Economy Transition Agenda is a strategic framework developed by a coalition of government bodies, industry stakeholders, and academic experts. It outlines the pathway for achieving a fully circular construction sector by 2050, building upon the broader national initiative. See *Nederland Circulair in 2050.* Available at: https://circulairebouweconomie.nl/wp-content/uploads/2019/09/Circular-Construction-Economy-1.pdf.
13. See the Netherlands National Circular Economy Programme 2023–2030 for details. Available at: https://www.government.nl/documents/reports/2023/09/27/national-circular-economy-programme-2023-2030#:~:text=In%202016%2C%20the%20Netherlands%20was,which%20have%20already%20been%20laid.
14. The first EU Circular Economy Action Plan was adopted in 2015. See European Commission, *Closing the loop: an EU action plan for the circular economy.* COM(2015)

614. Available at: https://eur-lex.europa.eu/resource.html?uri=cellar:8a8ef5e8-99a0-11e5-b3b7-01aa75ed71a1.0012.02/DOC_1&format=PDF.

15. The 2025 Clean Industrial Deal from the EU Commission includes a proposal to draft a Circular Economy Act by 2026 which will provide further opportunity for a more integrated systemic approach to revising laws in a transition away from a linear economic model. See EU Commission, *A clean industrial deal for competitiveness and decarbonisation in the EU* [Press release]. 26 February 2025. Available at: https://ec.europa.eu/commission/presscorner/detail/en/ip_25_550.
16. See Construction Products Regulation (EU) 2024/3110 of the European Parliament and of the Council of 27 November 2024 laying down harmonized rules for the marketing of construction products and repealing Regulation (EU) No 305/2011. Available at: https://eur-lex.europa.eu/eli/reg/2024/3110/oj/eng.
17. See further European Commission, *Circular economy*. Available at: https://environment.ec.europa.eu/topics/circular-economy_en.
18. See Regulation (EU) 2024/1781 of the European Parliament and of the Council of 13 June 2024 establishing a framework for the setting of ecodesign requirements for sustainable products. Available at: https://eur-lex.europa.eu/eli/reg/2024/1781/oj/eng.

References

Adams, K.T., Osmani, M., Thorpe, T. and Thornback, J. (2017) 'Circular economy in construction: current awareness, challenges and enablers', *Proceedings of the Institution of Civil Engineers-Waste and Resource Management*, 170(1), pp. 15–24.

Ahmed, S., Majava, J. and Aaltonen, K. (2023) 'Implementation of circular economy in construction projects: a procurement strategy approach', *Construction Innovation*, 24(7), pp. 204–222.

Alhola, K., Ryding, S.O., Salmenperä, H. and Busch, N.J. (2019) 'Exploiting the potential of public procurement: opportunities for circular economy', *Journal of Industrial Ecology*, 23(1), pp. 96–109.

Akomea-Frimpong, I., Jin, X. and Osei-Kyei, R. (2022) 'Reaching net zero targets in the construction industry by 2050: critical review of the role of public-private partnerships', *45th AUBEA Conference, Sydney, Australia* 34, pp. 1–11.

Al-Sinan, M.A. and Bubshait, A.A. (2022) 'The procurement agenda for the transition to a circular economy', *Sustainability*, 14(18), pp. 11528–11549.

Architecture 2030. *Why the built environment?* Available at: https://www.architecture2030.org/why-the-built-environment/

Bao, Z., Lu, W., Chi, B., Yuan, H. and Hao, J. (2019) 'Procurement innovation for a circular economy of construction and demolition waste: lessons learnt from Suzhou, China', *Waste Management*, 99, pp. 12–21.

Barrie, J., Salminen. I., Schroder, P. and Stucki, J. (2024) *National circular economy roadmaps: a global stocktake for 2024*. UNIDO and Chatham House. Available at: https://www.unido.org/sites/default/files/unido-publications/2024-05/UNIDO_National%20circular%20economy%20roadmaps_v07.pdf

Bennett, N.J., Blythe, J., Cisneros-Montemayor, A.M., Singh, G.G. and Sumaila, U.R. (2019) 'Just transformations to sustainability', *Sustainability*, 11(14), pp. 3881–3899.

Bosio, E., Djankov, S., Glaeser, E. and Shleifer, A. (2022) 'Public procurement in law and practice', *American Economic Review*, 112(4), pp. 1091–1117.

Cattolica, D. (2018) *Advancing the circular economy: exploring landscape and developments for circular public procurement in Sweden and Scotland*. IIIEE Master Thesis. Available

at: https://lup.lub.lu.se/luur/download?func=downloadFile&recordOId=8962453&fileOId=8962455
Clear Hill, B. (2023) 'What does a circular economy look like… with multiple circles?', *ICMM*, 22 May. Available at: https://www.icmm.com/en-gb/stories/2023/just-transition-circular-economy
Conway, E. (2023) *Material world: a substantial story of our past and future*. Random House.
de Waal, I.M. (2021) 'Coherence in law: a way to stimulate the transition towards a circular economy? A critical analysis of the European Commission's aspiration to achieve full coherence between chemicals legislation and waste legislation – and product legislation', *Maastricht Journal of European and Comparative Law*, 28(6), pp. 760–783.
Edler, J. and Georghiou, L. (2007) 'Public procurement and innovation – resurrecting the demand side', *Research Policy*, 36(7), pp. 949–963.
Elhag, T., Eapen, S. and Ballal, T. (2020) 'Moderating claims and disputes through collaborative procurement', *Construction Innovation*, 20(1), pp. 79–95.
Ellen MacArthur Foundation (2024) An innovation pathway to decarbonization: circular economy solutions for policymakers and industry in the US. Available at: https://content.ellenmacarthurfoundation.org/m/63c61d3f0f4d234c/original/An-innovation-pathway-to-decarbonization.pdf
Ershadi, M., Jefferies, M., Davis, P. and Mojtahedi, M. (2021) 'Barriers to achieving sustainable construction project procurement in the private sector', *Cleaner Engineering and Technology*, 3, pp. 100125–100136.
European Commission (2015) *Closing the loop – an EU action plan for the Circular Economy*. Brussels, 2.12.2015 COM(2015) 614. Available at: https://eur-lex.europa.eu/resource.html?uri=cellar:8a8ef5e8-99a0-11e5-b3b7-01aa75ed71a1.0012.02/DOC_1&format=PDF
European Commission (2017) *Public procurement for a circular economy. Good practice and guidance*. Available at: https://ec.europa.eu/environment/gpp/pdf/Public_procurement_circular_economy_brochure.pdf.
European Commission (2021) *Why public procurement is important*. Available at: https://ec.europa.eu/growth/single-market/public-procurement_en (Accessed: 2 January 2022).
Fitch-Roy, O., Benson, D. and Monciardini, D. (2020) 'Going around in circles? Conceptual recycling, patching and policy layering in the EU circular economy package', *Environmental Politics*, 29(6), pp. 983–1003.
Fraser, M., Haigh, L. and Soria, A.C. (2023) *The circularity gap report 2023*. Available at: https://www.circularity-gap.world/2023
Geissdoerfer, M., Savaget, P., Bocken, N.M. and Hultink, E.J. (2017) 'The circular economy – a new sustainability paradigm?' *Journal of Cleaner Production*, 143, pp. 757–768.
Ghaffar, S.H., Burman, M. and Braimah, N. (2020) 'Pathways to circular construction: an integrated management of construction and demolition waste for resource recovery', *Journal of Cleaner Production*, 244, pp. 118710–118719.
Grandia, J. and Voncken, D. (2019) 'Sustainable public procurement: the impact of ability, motivation, and opportunity on the implementation of different types of sustainable public procurement', *Sustainability*, 11(19), pp. 5215–5232.
Haas, W., Krausmann, F., Wiedenhofer, D., Lauk, C. and Mayer, A. (2020) 'Spaceship earth's odyssey to a circular economy – a century long perspective', *Resources, Conservation and Recycling*, 163, pp. 105076–105086.
Harland, C.M., Eßig, M., Lynch, J. and Patrucco, A. (2021) 'Policy-led public procurement: does strategic procurement deliver?', *Journal of Public Procurement*, 21(3), pp. 221–228.
Hjaltadóttir, R.E. and Hild, P. (2021) 'Circular economy in the building industry: European policy and local practices', *European Planning Studies*, 29(12), pp. 2226–2251.
Huang, L., Krigsvoll, G., Johansen, F., Liu, Y. and Zhang, X. (2018) 'Carbon emission of global construction sector', *Renewable and Sustainable Energy Reviews*, 81, pp. 1906–1916.

Iacovidou, E., Hahladakis, J.N. and Purnell, P. (2021) 'A systems thinking approach to understanding the challenges of achieving the circular economy', *Environmental Science and Pollution Research*, 28, pp. 24785–24806.

Jensen, S.F., Kristensen, J.H., Adamsen, S., Christensen, A., and Waehrens, B.V. (2023) 'Digital product passports for a circular economy: data needs for product life cycle decision-making', *Sustainable Production and Consumption*, 37, pp. 242–255.

Jones, P. and Comfort, D. (2018) 'The construction industry and the circular economy', *International Journal of Management Cases*, 20(1), pp. 4–15.

Khadim, N. and van Marrewijk, A. (2025) 'Circles of profit: a conceptual framework for economic and financial aspects in circular construction', *Sustainable Production and Consumption*, 55, pp. 444–457.

Kirchherr, J., Yang, N.H.N., Schulze-Spüntrup, F., Heerink, M.J. and Hartley, K. (2023) 'Conceptualizing the circular economy (revisited): an analysis of 221 definitions', *Resources, Conservation and Recycling*, 194, pp. 107001–107033.

Korhonen, J., Honkasalo, A. and Seppälä, J. (2018) Circular economy: the concept and its limitations. *Ecological Economics*, 143, pp. 37–46.

Lawlor, L. and Spratt, S. (2021) *Circular investment: a review of global spending and barriers to increasing it*. Chatham House and Just Economics. Available at: https://static.resourcetrade.earth/JE-07-Circular-Economy-Report-vf.pdf

Lesniewska, F. (2025) 'Making a case for radical circular economy legal research', in van Zeben, J. and Hilson C. (eds), *A research agenda for environmental law*. Edward Elgar Publishing, pp. 219–232.

Lesniewska, F. and Steenmans, K. (2023) *Circular economy and the law: bringing justice into the frame*. Routledge, Taylor & Francis.

Lingegård, S., Olsson, J.A., Kadefors, A. and Uppenberg, S. (2021) 'Sustainable public procurement in large infrastructure projects – policy implementation for carbon emission reductions', *Sustainability*, 13(20), pp. 11182–11203.

Moradi, S. and Kähkönen, K. (2022) 'Success in collaborative construction through the lens of project delivery elements', *Built Environment Project and Asset Management*, 12(6), pp. 973–991.

Morales, E., Skinner, F., Hemmingway, P., Axelsson, L. and Piirsalu, E. (2023) *Unlocking the G20's green public procurement potential*. Stockholm Environment Institute, UNIDO. Available at: https://t20ind.org/research/unlocking-the-g20s-green-public-procurement-potential/

Morlino, E. (2019) *Procurement by international organizations: a global administrative law perspective*. Cambridge University Press.

Newell, P. and Mulvaney, D. (2013) 'The political economy of the "just transition"', *The Geographical Journal*, 179(2), pp. 132–140.

OECD (2019) *Reforming public procurement: progress in implementing the 2015 OECD recommendation*. OECD Public Governance Reviews, OECD Publishing. Available at: https://doi.org/10.1787/1de41738-en.

Oluleye, B.I., Chan, D.W., Saka, A.B. and Olawumi, T.O. (2022) 'Circular economy research on building construction and demolition waste: a review of current trends and future research directions', *Journal of Cleaner Production*, 357, pp. 131927–131945.

Oyegoke, A.S., Dickinson, M., Khalfan, M.M., McDermott, P. and Rowlinson, S. (2009) 'Construction project procurement routes: an in-depth critique', *International Journal of Managing Projects in Business*, 2(3), pp. 338–354.

Pomponi, F. and Moncaster, A. (2017) 'A theoretical framework for circular economy research in the built environment', *Building Information Modelling, Building Performance, Design and Smart Construction*, SEEDS 2016 (Sustainable, Ecological, Engineering and Design for Society) Leeds Beckett University on 14–15 September, Conference Papers, pp. 31–44.

Qazi, A.A. and Appolloni, A. (2022) 'A systematic review on barriers and enablers toward circular procurement management', *Sustainable Production and Consumption*, 33, pp. 343–359.

Rejeb, A., Rejeb, K., Appolloni, A., Kayikci, Y. and Iranmanesh, M. (2023) 'The landscape of public procurement research: a bibliometric analysis and topic modelling based on Scopus', *Journal of Public Procurement*, 23(2), pp. 145–178.

Rijkswaterstaat (2019) *The future starts now: annual report 2019 impulse programme for the circular economy.* Available at: https://circulareconomy.europa.eu/platform/sites/default/files/the_future_starts_now_annual_report_2019_impulse_programme_for_the_circular_economy.pdf.

Rios, F.C. and Grau, D. (2019) 'Circular economy in the built environment: designing, deconstructing, and leasing reusable products', *Encyclopaedia of Renewable Sustainable Materials*, 5, pp. 338–343.

Ruiz, L.A.L., Ramón, X.R. and Domingo, S.G. (2020) 'The circular economy in the construction and demolition waste sector – a review and an integrative model approach', *Journal of Cleaner Production*, 248, pp. 119238–119253.

Sajid, Z.W., Aftab, U. and Ullah, F. (2024) 'Barriers to adopting circular procurement in the construction industry: the way forward', *Sustainable Futures*, 8, pp. 100244–100267.

Schröder, P. and Raes, J. (2021) *Financing an inclusive circular economy. De-risking investments for circular business models and the SDGs.* Chatham House. Available at: https://www.chathamhouse.org/sites/default/files/2021-07/2021-07-16-inclusive-circular-economy-schroder-raes_0.pdf

Siminică, M., Avram, M., Roxana, L.P. and Avram, L. (2020) 'The adoption of national green procurement plans from the perspective of circular economy', *Amfiteatru Economic*, 22(53), pp. 15–27.

Sjåfjell, B. (2014) 'The legal significance of Article 11 TFEU for EU institutions and member states', in Sjåfjell, B. and Wiesbrock, A. (eds), *The greening of European business under EU law.* Routledge, (pp. 51–72).

Stahel, W.R. (2019) *The circular economy: a user's guide.* Routledge, Taylor & Francis.

Tirado, R., Aublet, A., Laurenceau, S. and Habert, G. (2022) 'Challenges and opportunities for circular economy promotion in the building sector', *Sustainability*, 14(3), pp. 1569–1586.

UNECE (2022) *COP27: UNECE presents UN-approved system for natural resources management to support low-carbon transition* [Press release]. 9 November. Available at: https://unece.org/climate-change/press/cop27-unece-presents-un-approved-system-natural-resources-management-support

United Nations (2015) *The UN Sustainable Development Goals.*

United Nations Environment Programme (UNEP) (2018) *Building circularity into our economies through sustainable procurement.* Available at: https://www.unep.org/resources/report/building-circularity-our-economies-through-sustainable-procurement#:~:text=Building%20circularity%20into%20our%20economies%20through%20sustainable%20procurement%20aims%20to,conducted%20by%20the%20United%20Nations

United Nations Environment Programme (UNEP) Finance Initiative (2020) *Financing circularity: demystifying finance for circular economies.* Available at: https://www.unepfi.org/publications/financing-circularity/

United Nations Environment Programme (UNEP) (2024) *Global resources outlook 2024: bend the trend – pathways to a liveable planet as resource use spikes.* International Resource Panel. Available at: https://www.resourcepanel.org/reports/global-resources-outlook-2024

Witjes, S. and Lozano, R. (2016) 'Towards a more circular economy: proposing a framework linking sustainable public procurement and sustainable business models', *Resources, Conservation and Recycling*, 112, pp. 37–44.

World Bank (2022) *Squaring the circle: policies from Europe's circular economy transition*. Available at: https://www.worldbank.org/en/region/eca/publication/squaring-circle-europe-circular-economy-transition

World Green Building Council (2023) *Circular built environment playbook*. Available at: https://worldgbc.org/article/circular-built-environment-playbook/

Wurster, S., Schulze, R., Simon, R.G. and Hoyer, S. (2021) 'A grounded theory on sustainable circular public procurement in Germany: specific product cases and strategies', *Sustainability*, 13(24), pp. 13525–13554.

Yu, A.T. and Shen, G.Q. (2013) 'Problems and solutions of requirements management for construction projects under the traditional procurement systems', *Facilities*, 31(5/6), pp. 223-237

Index